Napoleon's 1796
Italian Campaign

Napoleon's 1796 Italian Campaign

CARL VON CLAUSEWITZ

Translated and Edited by

NICHOLAS MURRAY
AND
CHRISTOPHER PRINGLE

Foreword by Dennis E. Showalter

 University Press of Kansas

Published by the University Press of Kansas (Lawrence, Kansas 66045), which was organized by the Kansas Board of Regents and is operated and funded by Emporia State University, Fort Hays State University, Kansas State University, Pittsburg State University, the University of Kansas, and Wichita State University

Library of Congress Cataloging-in-Publication Data

Names: Clausewitz, Carl von, 1780–1831, author. | Murray, Nicholas, 1966– editor, translator. | Pringle, Christopher, editor, translator. | Showalter, Dennis E., writer of foreword.
Title: Napoleon's 1796 Italian campaign / Carl von Clausewitz ; translated and edited by Nicholas Murray and Christopher Pringle ; foreword by Dennis E. Showalter.
Other titles: Feldzug von 1796 in Italien. English
Description: Lawrence, Kansas : University Press of Kansas, [2018] | In English translated from the original German. | Includes bibliographical references and index.
Identifiers: LCCN 2018021885
ISBN 978-0-7006-2675-5 (cloth)
ISBN 978-0-7006-2676-2 (paperback)
ISBN 978-0-7006-2677-9 (ebook)
Subjects: LCSH: First Coalition, War of the, 1792–1797—Campaigns—Italy. | Napoleon I, Emperor of the French, 1769–1821—Military leadership. | France—History—Revolution, 1789–1799.
Classification: LCC DC223.4 .C5513 2018 | DDC 940.2/740945—dc23.
LC record available at https://lccn.loc.gov/2018021885.

British Library Cataloguing-in-Publication Data is available.

10 9 8 7 6 5 4 3 2

Contents

Maps

Foreword
Dennis E. Showalter

The work of Carl von Clausewitz resembles the Bible in being more often cited than studied, and in too often acting as a source of support for preconceptions. That in turn reflects the fact that Clausewitz's writings are usually discussed in their theoretical contexts: recognition of his acknowledged position as Western culture's foremost philosopher of war. But Clausewitz himself considered his historical writing no less important than his analytical work. Beginning in the 1820s and continuing until his death, he completed a massive amount of writing on the wars of the Revolutionary/Napoleonic era—not separate from but in conjunction with his philosophically oriented studies.

Clausewitz saw military history as the basis of military theory. History, he asserted, "makes us see things as they are and as they function."[1] War's diversity was no less significant than its commonalities. But it could be a good deal more difficult to determine and present. That was especially true in the modern era, with its plethora of sources whose details and interactions, given war's nature as the province of confusion, could be mutually exclusive or simply contradictory. Theory provided matrices for structuring, analyzing, and defining facts.

This case study is particularly useful because it was largely written toward the end of Clausewitz's career and correspondingly addresses in practical contexts a broad spectrum of the ideas raised theoretically in *On War*. The Clausewitzian triad of people, army, and government contributes to shaping the work without dominating the presentation. The synergy of marginal operations and major actions provides an understanding of the campaign as an entity shaped and structured by particular decisions, but with its own objective dynamic. And Clausewitz's constant comparison of contemporary reports and narrations with subsequent glosses is a model of textual criticism—particularly when Napoleon's memoirs are involved. These emerge as not exactly mendacious but definitely tendentious: the life story of a military genius

---

1. Carl von Clausewitz, *Principles of War*, ed. Hans W. Gatzke (Mineola, NY: Dover, 2003), 54.

by one who knows. In that sense, they establish a pattern all too familiar to historians—one Clausewitz presents a model for addressing.

Napoleon's 1796 Italian Campaign is an exercise in the appropriate use of limited sources. Clausewitz is doing detailed operational analysis from what would be considered by contemporary standards a significantly restricted database. In particular, he had no access to Austrian archival material. But war is a dialectical process, not an experience conducted in a vacuum. Explaining the Austrian perspective is vital for understanding Napoleon's decisions and behaviors. Clausewitz's painstaking care in reconstructing events and motives, the attention he gives to distinguishing reasoned inference from specific documentation, is a model for any military historian constrained, as is often the case, by the destruction of source material, as occurred in Germany during World War II, or its inaccessibility for political reasons, as is still the case with the archives and libraries of the Democratic Republic of Vietnam.

The production of this work is outstanding. "To translate is to betray" may be a familiar metaphor, but in this case, it is completely inapplicable. The editors are faithful to the sense of the manuscript as well as the text—not always easily achieved in Clausewitz's work. Their reference apparatus matches the body of the work in quality. The content footnotes are extremely valuable in developing the kinds of casual references that would have been familiar to soldiers a century ago but might be obscure to even knowledgeable contemporary readers. They reflect a solid, comprehensive command of the operational, institutional, and political aspects of an often convoluted operation. The extensive reference quotations from Jean Colin's nineteenth-century translation are a welcome bonus, providing an alternative perspective from an author and a source now unfortunately obscure.

Academic presses and academic faculties can contribute significantly to the historical profession and the historian's craft, even in this electronic age, by supporting what might be described as "reference texts." These works are valuable in themselves and in their ramifications to scholars—and often general readers as well—but difficult to access and often swingeingly expensive. This volume qualifies as a reference text for its own qualities and because the campaign itself has been significantly and oddly neglected. To all involved, a heartfelt "well done!"

Preface

The writings of Carl von Clausewitz are among the most important works on war ever written. Much of the focus has understandably been on his great theoretical work *On War*, which has been translated and reprinted across the world. That work, however, formed only the first three of the ten volumes of his published writings. This is significant because despite the importance of *On War*, it can be difficult to understand and decipher. This is where his historical writing and analysis play an exceptionally important role. He made it clear that his foundational writing helped him think through and more clearly form his theoretical understanding of war and that the process of so doing was difficult.[1] Given that, our neglect of his historical analysis when attempting to understand *On War* impedes our understanding of his main theoretical writing. This is criminally negligent (as Clausewitz might have put it), since Clausewitz spent a great deal of time analyzing the conflicts he fought in and creating, in the process, the theoretical underpinnings of *On War*. Thus, by reading and analyzing his histories of the series of wars from 1789 to 1815, the reader can more fully understand *On War* itself.

What Clausewitz tells us about his historical writing is important, and he addresses this in several of his notes. In *To an Unpublished Manuscript on the Theory of War* (Howard and Paret list this as being written between 1816 and 1818) Clausewitz criticizes past military writers for their lack of effective analysis of the evidence—that is, surely, the history.[2] He goes further in *On the Genesis of His Early Manuscript on the Theory of War*, where he states:

> The manner in which Montesquieu dealt with his subject is vaguely in my mind.[3] I thought that such concise, aphoristic chapters, which at the outset

---

1. Jan Willem Honig, "Clausewitz and the Politics of Early Modern Warfare," in *Clausewitz the State and War*, ed. Andreas Herberg-Rothe, Jan Willem Honig, and Daniel Moran (Stuttgart: Franz Steiner Verlag, 2011), 29–48.

2. Carl von Clausewitz, *On War*, ed. and trans. Michael Howard and Peter Paret (Princeton, NJ: Princeton University Press, 1989), 61.

3. The structure of *On War* resembles that of Montesquieu's *De l'Esprit des Loix*. That is, the work is divided into multiple smaller books, with each book consisting of multiple chapters, all punctuated with analysis and historical examples.

I simply wanted to call kernels, would attract the intelligent reader by what they suggested as much as by what they expressed; in other words, I had an intelligent reader in mind, who was already familiar with the subject.... From the studies I wrote on various topics in order to gain a clear and complete understanding of them, I managed for a time to lift only the most important conclusions and thus concentrate their essence in smaller compass. But eventually my tendency completely ran away with me; I elaborated as much as I could, and of course now had in mind a reader who was not yet acquainted with the subject.[4]

In other words, his histories and other writings were fundamental to the development of his understanding of war, and it seems reasonable to assume that this would be the case for a reader unfamiliar with the topic too. In his *Note of 10 July 1827* (and an unfinished note possibly from 1830),[5] Clausewitz again drives home the point about the historical study underpinning his work: "If critics would go to the trouble of thinking about the subject for years on end and testing each conclusion against the actual history of war, as I have done, they would undoubtedly be more careful of what they said."[6] With this criticism ringing in our ears, perhaps it is time to introduce Clausewitz's histories to a broader audience so that they too might benefit from his historical analysis and the testing of his theoretical models against the campaigns themselves. Indeed, that was our primary motivation for translating this work.

With this, it is important to turn to the text we chose to use. We selected the original version of the text published in 1833: Carl von Clausewitz, *Der Feldzug von 1796 in Italien* (Berlin: Ferdinand Dümmler, 1833). We made this choice because it reduced the chance of encountering the changes and errors sometimes found in subsequent publications. It is also the version of the work sanctioned by Clausewitz's widow, Marie von Clausewitz. Although she did not edit the work herself, she did rely on a trusted family friend, Major Franz August O'Etzel,[7] who was familiar with Clausewitz's writings, to compile the fourth of the ten volumes planned for publication—the first three volumes being *On War* itself. Indeed, because of the publication schedule, the campaign history translated in this book appeared before volume 3 (books 7 and

4. Clausewitz, *On War*, 63. Howard and Paret date this note between 1816 and 1818.
5. Howard and Paret believe this note to be from 1830. Ibid., 70.
6. Ibid., 69–71.
7. See Marie von Clausewitz's preface, ibid., 65–67.

8 of *On War*). Major O'Etzel stringently denied editing the text, so if we take him at his word—and we have no reason not to—the text is largely as Clausewitz left it.[8] Thus it is ideal for our purpose of using it as a tool better to understand *On War*.

In the translators' note we describe how we approached the translation, and we followed much the same ethos when it came to editors' commentary and analysis. Our use of modern terms such as "combat power" is intended to make the text more accessible rather than to replicate Clausewitz's words exactly. We have provided cross-references to *On War*, as well as explanations of what Clausewitz means and how his theoretical ideas relate to the campaign history that is the focus of this work. As such, we hope to make *On War* itself more understandable and usable for students and scholars alike.

In addition to translating Clausewitz's campaign history into English, for the sake of completeness we have included the explanatory notes from Captain J. Colin's translation of the same campaign history. Captain Colin wrote extensively for the Historical Section of the French General Staff and translated Clausewitz's campaign history into French.[9] Colin is often critical of Clausewitz, and not always fairly, as he seems to be intent on defending Napoleon against even reasonable criticism. Thus it behooves the reader to keep an open mind when reading Colin's comments, as well as closely examining what Clausewitz actually wrote. That being said, we believe that Colin's commentary aids in understanding Clausewitz's history, in that it provokes the reader to reflect critically on Clausewitz's own critical remarks. Furthermore, many of Colin's notes are valuable because they provide historical details that either correct errors on Clausewitz's part or add information that enables a more complete account of a given action.

Our commentary is not limited to Clausewitz's theory. We also tried to make the campaign narrative clearer and, where possible, to fill in gaps in our knowledge of the history of the campaign. We referred to other published campaign histories to ensure that the narrative is as accurate as possible, and

8. Carl von Clausewitz, *Die Feldzüge von 1799 in Italien und der Schweiz*, 2 vols. (Berlin: Ferdinand Dümmler, 1833), 1:viii. See also Vanya Eftimova Bellinger, *Marie von Clausewitz: The Woman behind the Making of* On War (Oxford: Oxford University Press, 2016), 230; Marie von Clausewitz, "Vorrede zum Dritte Theil," in Carl von Clausewitz, *Vom Kriege*, 3 vols. (Berlin: Ferdinand Dümmler, 1832–1834), 3:v–vi.

9. The edition we used is Carl von Clausewitz, *La Campagne de 1796 en Italie*, trans. Captain J. Colin (Paris: Librairie Militaire de L. Baudoin, 1899).

we used and referenced Napoleon's memoirs and his correspondence to shed light on his thinking where Clausewitz did not do so or where he provides no clear reference. All this was done to enable the reader to better understand what Clausewitz was saying, both here and in *On War*. Ultimately, we hope to further discussion of this important historical work and provide a tool that allows more people to access his writing and understand his ideas.

Acknowledgments

It is an honor for us to recognize the assistance we received in the completion of this book. We would like to thank Professor Hew Strachan of the School of International Relations at the University of St. Andrews, who patiently answered questions and provided guidance for our work. Lieutenant Colonel Anders Palmgren of the Swedish army generously shared his research and writing on Clausewitz, which was particularly helpful with regard to some of the key terminology. Dr. Jan Willem Honig of King's College, London, kindly assisted, on short notice, in answering a couple of important questions about the chronology and purpose of Clausewitz's publications. In addition, Harmut Steffin gave greatly of his time and knowledge to help us with particularly tricky German idioms, and Dr. Mark Hull of the US Army Command and General Staff College was kind enough to read the first few chapters and offer suggestions as to language. Dr. Dennis Showalter of Colorado College provided much appreciated encouragement for this project, and Dr. Mark Gerges of the US Army Command and General Staff College provided some extremely helpful suggestions for edits and source material. Finally, Drs. Anand Toprani and Michael Dennis, both of the US Naval War College, contributed much needed intellectual rigor when thinking through and interpreting Clausewitz's ideas.

In spite of their help, it is likely we missed something. Thus, any flaws contained herein are our own.

Translators' Note

Any translation presents challenges, the most obvious being the tension between adhering to the literal meaning of the author's original words and capturing the spirit of what he is trying to convey. A direct word-for-word translation inevitably sounds cumbersome and clunky, especially if the same sentence structure is retained. Some degree of rephrasing is always necessary, as well as reorganizing sentences and even whole paragraphs to make the work read more fluently. The problem is that the freer the translation, the greater the risk that some important nuance or emphasis may be lost. We have attempted to strike a balance and hope that in doing so, we have made the work easy to read while still allowing Clausewitz to make his points as he intended to make them and to speak in his own distinctive voice.

In fact, Clausewitz speaks to us with three different voices. The first is for the bald description of events in chronological order: "A and B did X and Y. C moved to Z. On the nth, W happened." Clausewitz's language here is clear and simple. His sentences are brief. His descriptions are unornamented. That is not to say that this voice is dull. On the contrary, his narration marches briskly and gives us a clear picture of each battle. Furthermore, his selective use of the historic present tense makes certain passages especially vivid. In German as in English, the historic present serves to lend a sense of drama and urgency to descriptions of past events. The effect of this in section 9, the battle of Montenotte, when Bonaparte first goes on the offensive, is tremendously powerful. It strikingly conveys the energy and vigor of the youthful Bonaparte bursting onto the scene and emphasizes the contrast between him and his ponderous, elderly Austrian opponent.

Clausewitz's second voice is for expounding on strategic theory and its implications. Here, his prose is as verbose and florid as his first voice is terse and clipped, and he allows himself lengthy and laborious philosophical discursions. The German language is notorious for its long sentences with multiple nested clauses—the so-called *Bandwurmsatz*, or tapeworm sentence. Clausewitz seems especially fond of the humble tapeworm (though we often felt obliged to cut the creature up). This, together with a penchant for not using a simple word or phrase when a more complicated one will do, results in what our good friend Hartmut "Hardy" Steffin exasperatedly dubbed "Clausewitzification." Clausewitz is not averse to a rather English usage of the understated double negative that means "very." If at times the translation seems not inconsiderably long-winded, it is not necessarily our fault nor that of the German language; it is simply Clausewitz in pontificatory mode.

But it is worth putting up with Clausewitz's pontifications for the delight that is his third voice. This is when he wields his quill like a scalpel to dissect the actions of the French and Austrian commanders, viewing them through the prism of his strategic analysis and flaying them for their manifold failings. He frequently claims to be baffled by their decisions, and his evaluation is littered with phrases such as "it is incomprehensible," "there seems to be no good reason why," or "it makes no sense." His bafflement often provokes him to lapse from philosophical or scientific language into idiom and vernacular: generals are likened to "feeble-minded beetles," their plans are "egomaniacal," they are "clueless." The remorseless logic he deploys to crush the beetles is a pleasure to read, as he shows step by unarguable step exactly why they were wrong and what they should have done instead.

Identifying geographic locations was not always straightforward. He sometimes gives German names that are long obsolete, now that these places are in Italy or Slovenia. This would have been less of a problem if his spellings were not so idiosyncratic, and occasionally a misspelled Italian name directs us to a different part of the country entirely. Near-contemporary maps from the Austrian Second Military Survey of 1806–1869 were helpful and can be found online.[1]

The names of the commanders presented similar challenges. In section 16 a chap named "Gugeur" crops up. Later on, we meet a brigadier named "Guyeur." Could these two be one and the same? And if so, could he in turn be related to the French general Jean Joseph Guieu, also known as Guyeux? Then there is the Croat general in Austrian service whom Clausewitz identifies as Wukassowitsch but who, in his native Croatian, would be Vukasović and appears in other histories variously as Vukassovich, Wukassovich, Vukassevich, or Vukaszovich.

The convention we used for the names of both places and individuals is as follows: When they first appear, we give Clausewitz's spelling, followed by the modern name in brackets. Thereafter, we use the modern name. For places

---

1. "Franziszeische Landesaufnahme (1806–1869)," accessed 12 September 2017, http://mapire.eu/de/map/secondsurvey.

that have different names in different languages, we give both or all—for example, Botzen (Bozen/Bolzano)—and then use one of those names consistently thereafter.

When it comes to distances, Clausewitz uses miles, German miles, *toises*, *lieues*, and leagues. Given the inherent problems with this and the lack of standardization at the time, we have chosen to translate German miles at the rate of 4.5 to 1 modern standard mile; leagues and *lieues* at 3.5 to 1; and *toises* into miles at the rate of 1 *toise* equals 1.94 miles.

This translation owes a great deal to the linguistic talents of Hardy Steffin. As a native German speaker with an excellent command of English and an interest in translation and wordplay, Hardy was consulted whenever we encountered an obscure or archaic idiom or a particularly tangled passage of Clausewitzification. His generous help was invaluable in eliminating many misunderstandings and the occasional crass error and in tracking down or teasing out the meanings of phrases we could not find in the dictionary. Still, there were some sentences that even Hardy struggled to make sense of. This is perhaps because Clausewitz's writings are often technical and abrupt, as readers of *On War* can attest, and the original work was published after his death. Some of the denser Clausewitzifications and ambiguities are probably due to the fact that Clausewitz never finished editing his work. A number of obvious mistakes he made (such as referring to the wrong bank of a river) tend to confirm this.

No doubt this work still contains some errors or interpretations that some will find problematic. We request the reader's indulgence, as we were not privy to Clausewitz's thoughts, and the work of translation is as much art as science. If any reader discovers an error, we would welcome being apprised of the correction.

Any such imperfections notwithstanding, we trust that we have done Clausewitz justice and have prepared a translation that is as faithful and authentic as possible. We hope you enjoy reading this work as much as we enjoyed translating it.

A Note on Wargaming

Clausewitz's theoretical writings are just one symptom of the broader phenomenon of the increasingly systematic approach to war adopted by the Prussian military in the nineteenth century. Another aspect of this phenomenon was the development of wargaming as a tool for professional military education.[1]

Since then, wargaming has been widely used by militaries around the world. At the time of this writing, there is renewed professional interest in wargaming in the United States in particular,[2] a movement in which we are directly involved. Wargaming gives participants the opportunity to practice rapid decision making in conditions of uncertainty, under time pressure, and in a competitive environment, which can offer profound insights and teach enduring lessons. It is "learning by doing," and it can be tremendously powerful.

As far as the present work is concerned, we encourage readers to explore wargaming as a method to gain a deeper appreciation of how and why the campaigns and battles described and analyzed by Clausewitz took the course they did. For an understanding of the campaign as a whole, one of us (Nick Murray) has developed a game for his students, which is also used by the US Army and US Marine Corps for training and education. For the grand tactical level, many commercial games are available; we favor *Bloody Big Battles!* (BBB), which Nick has also used in class. Scenarios for the major battles of the 1796 campaign are available for free via the BBB Yahoo group at https://uk.groups.yahoo.com/neo/groups/BBB_wargames/info.

---

1. Philipp von Hilgers, *Kriegspiele eine Geschichte der Ausnahmezustände und Unberechenberkeiten* (Munich: Wilhelm Fink Verlag, 2008), 58–71.

2. Deputy Secretary of Defense Robert Work, memorandum for secretaries of the Military Departments, "Wargaming and Innovation," 9 February 2015.

1. The Context of the Campaign

The great events of the Italian campaign of 1796 demand that we understand the true shape of this campaign as a whole, and that we examine the causes of the momentous decisions reached during it; yet the urgency of this demand is matched only by the inadequacy of the history written about it, and by the grimness of the task of trying to give even a very general overview of it.

In the second edition of his history of the revolutionary wars, Jomini[1] has presented this campaign as well as the poverty of his sources allowed; but his account is poor, sketchy, obscure, contradictory, in short everything that a coherent presentation of events in their relation to one another should not be. Still, he does at least provide the essential numbers and the major movements from the French side. However, he offers little about Austrian positions, intentions, or movements—all of which can easily be discovered from Austrian military journals[2]—in short, Jomini's account is so ignorant and confused about the main events that it appears to be a mere collection of fragments.[3]

1. Lieutenant-Général Jomini, *Histoire Critique et Militaire des Guerres de la Révolution*, 15 vols. (Paris: Chez Anselin et Pochard, 1819–1824). Antoine-Henri Jomini was a Swiss who served in the French and Russian armies during the Napoleonic Wars. He was a prominent writer on military affairs and is perhaps best known for his *Précis de l'Art de la Guerre*. His works, including history and theory, have often been compared with Clausewitz's, and there was certainly a rivalry of sorts between the two while Clausewitz was still alive.

2. Captain J. Colin notes: "Österreichische Militärische Zeitschrift." This journal is still published and can be found online; accessed 7 October 2017, https://www.oemz-online.at/display/ZLIintranet/STARTSEITE. The original note is from Carl von Clausewitz, *La Campagne de 1796 en Italie*, trans. Captain J. Colin (Paris: Librairie Militaire de L. Baudoin, 1899), 1; hereafter cited as Colin.

3. Clausewitz's criticism of Jomini's account of the 1796 campaign, and of the latter's defense of Archduke Charles regarding the 1799–1800 campaigns, irritated Jomini for the rest of his life. However, this was not the only source of friction between them. See Peter Paret, *Clausewitz and the State* (New York: Oxford University Press, 1976), 71.

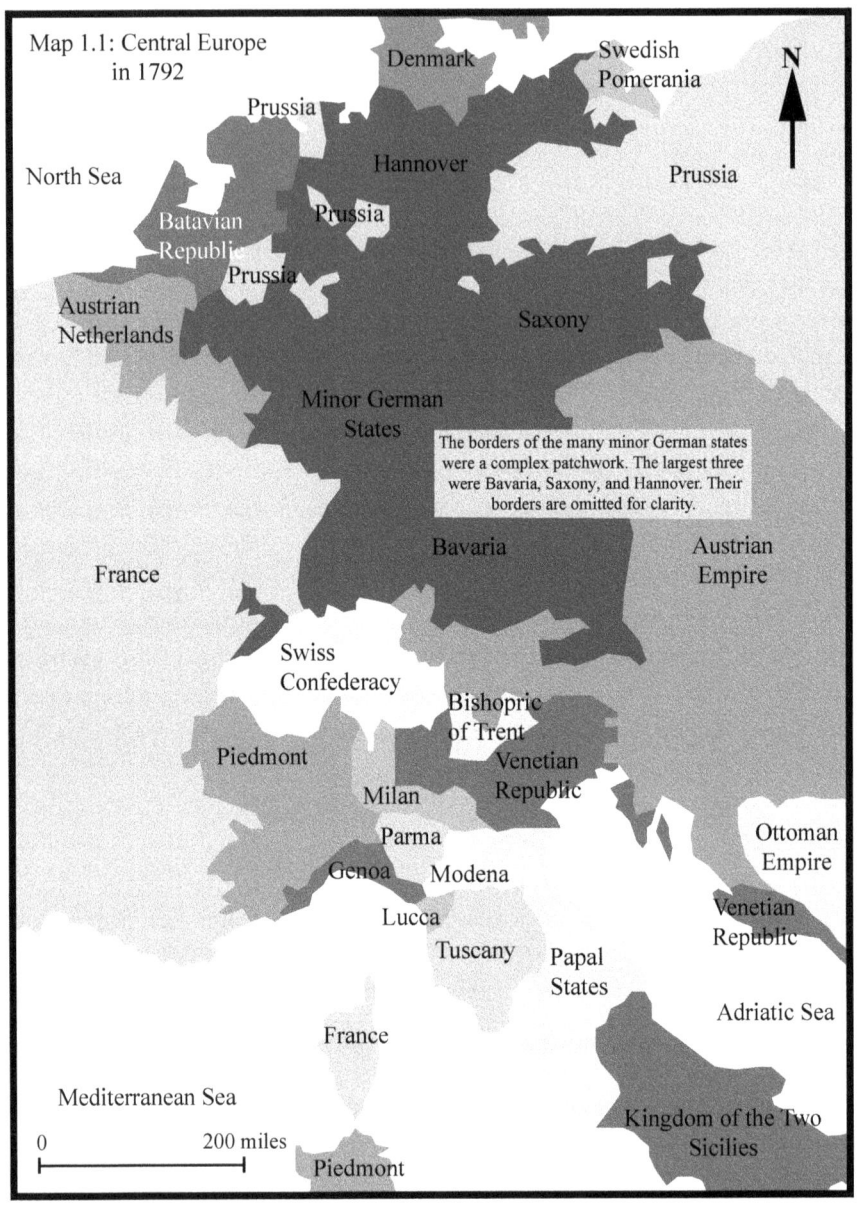

Map 1.1: Central Europe in 1792

Denmark

Swedish Pomerania

Prussia

North Sea

Hannover

Prussia

Prussia

Batavian Republic

Prussia

Austrian Netherlands

Saxony

Minor German States

The borders of the many minor German states were a complex patchwork. The largest three were Bavaria, Saxony, and Hannover. Their borders are omitted for clarity.

Bavaria

Austrian Empire

France

Swiss Confederacy

Bishopric of Trent

Piedmont

Venetian Republic

Milan

Parma

Ottoman Empire

Genoa

Modena

Lucca

Venetian Republic

Tuscany

Papal States

Adriatic Sea

France

Mediterranean Sea

Kingdom of the Two Sicilies

0   200 miles

Piedmont

N

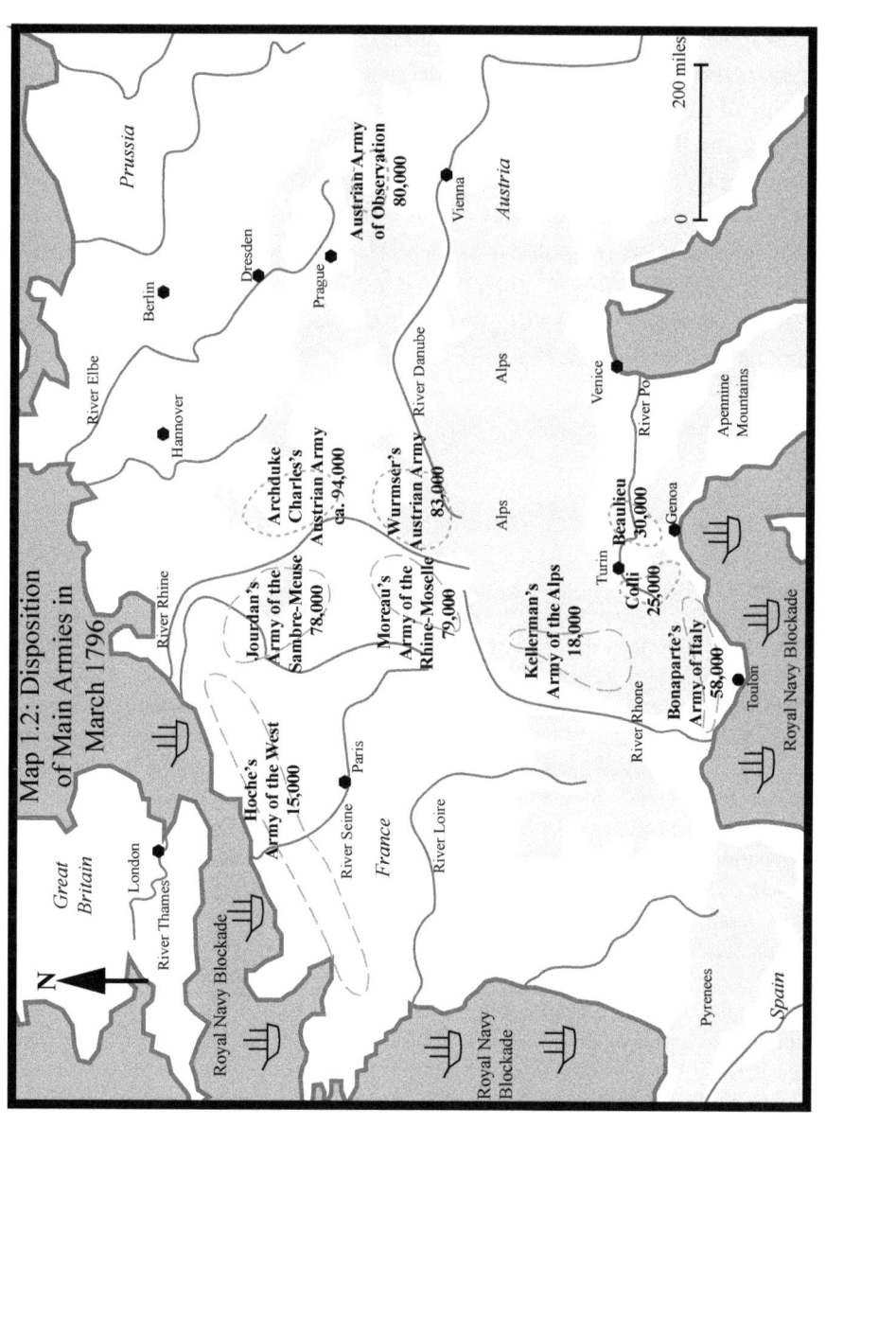

Map 1.2: Disposition of Main Armies in March 1796

Napoleon's *Memoirs*,[4] which should give us a ready source of great information about the whole campaign, deceive all our hopes in this respect. The events of earlier times pass by the prisoner of St. Helena like a vision in a dream, and the last thing one can hope to find in a dream is precision. This complete lack of interest in the truth also means his historical recollections are of no value as far as numbers are concerned. Even the motives and reflections that constitute the real content of these *Memoirs* are infected and corrupted by this spirit of deliberate untruth.[5] To grasp how little Bonaparte knew of actual tactical matters in this campaign, one has only to look at the reports contained in this volume that were sent to him by individual generals in reply

4. It is not clear to which edition of Napoleon's *Memoirs* Clausewitz is referring. However, in section 13 of chapter 2, Clausewitz provides a reference that matches the edition we have chosen to use here: Général Montholon, ed., *Mémoires pour servir à l'Histoire de France sous Napoléon*, 8 vols. (Paris: F. Didot, Père et Fils; Bossange, Frères, 1823–1825). Elsewhere, the citations do not consistently match up. It is worth noting that Montholon was a somewhat shady character (there were a number of incidents involving false claims about military service, corruption, and the like); thus, Napoleon's *Mémoires* need to be treated with extra caution, both for the reasons Clausewitz provides and because Montholon was described as a "poltroon and a liar" by Barry O'Meara, Napoleon's medical attendant (he had served in the British Royal Navy as a surgeon) on St. Helena. See William Forsyth, *History of the Captivity of Napoleon at St. Helena; from the Letters and Journals of the Late Lieut.-Gen. Sir Hudson Lowe*, 3 vols. (London: John Murray, 1853), 1:76–77, 184, 186.

5. Colin, 2, notes: "Bonaparte's reports to the Directory have been published in various places, notably in the *Campagne du général Buonaparte en Italie pendant les années IV et V, par un officier général*, which Clausewitz had; they are only unclear concerning the actions at Lonato, which could have been clarified in part by certain sections of the *Correspondance inédite*, and for the rest from the Austrian accounts. The *Mémoires de Napoléon* were only inaccurate as far as numbers of men were concerned, for which those Jomini supplies are close enough. If Clausewitz had taken the trouble to do so, he could have reconstructed this campaign quite adequately, and could have avoided some of the factual errors he commits." Colin's criticism of Clausewitz for these reasons is somewhat harsh, given the fact that Napoleon's *Memoirs* are not entirely reliable. Colin is referring to *Correspondance inédite, officielle et confidentielle, de Napoléon Bonaparte avec les cours étrangères, les princes, les ministres et les généraux français et étrangers en Italie, en Allemagne et en Égypte*, 14 vols. (Paris: C. L. F. Panckoucke, 1819–1820).

to his questions; the first question is to General Ménard,[6] asking of him, under whose orders he served at Montenotte,[7] and so it goes on.[8]

In the circumstances, in the following overview of this notable campaign, very often all that is possible is to talk in more general terms rather than with the great detail it demands, and to guess at the true historical motivations.[9]

1 FRENCH STRENGTHS AND DISPOSITIONS

The events of the 1795 campaign had left the French in possession of the Genoese Riviera, as well as of the crests of the Apennines [Ligurian Alps] that shape it.

At the end of March, the strengths and dispositions of the French forces in the field were:

6. Montholon, *Mémoires pour servir à l'Histoire de France sous Napoléon*, 4:372. This is General Philippe Ménard, who served as a brigade commander under (later) Marshal André Masséna (who went on to become one of Napoleon's best generals) at the battle of Montenotte in 1796. One would expect Napoleon to know this; hence Clausewitz's criticism. However, Napoleon had just taken over command of the French army in Italy, which was in a poorly organized state, and it is understandable that he might not know who was doing what, and at what time. Thus Clausewitz's comments are unduly harsh.

7. Colin, 2, notes: "These questions were not asked by Napoleon, but by Montholon himself, undoubtedly after his return from St. Helena. Their tone alone indicates that they do not come from a superior. How could Clausewitz have made this mistake?" Even if this is a mistake on Clausewitz's part, his position on the matter is reasonable, given the times, distances, and means of communications involved, as well as the other problems mentioned in note 6 above.

8. Clausewitz notes that there is another volume on this conflict, but he dismisses its value: "The most recent history of this campaign to appear, that by Major von Decker, is even more useless than all the others and deserves no serious mention." This is almost certainly Karl von Decker, *Der Feldzug in Italien in den Jahren 1796 und 1797* (Berlin: Ernst Siegfried Mittler, 1825). Decker was a prolific writer on a variety of military topics, from the technical to the historic. Clausewitz's comments are interesting, as Peter Paret points out that Clausewitz had previously respected Decker's work. Paret, *Clausewitz and the State*, 314.

9. It is important to go through the rather arcane recitation of armies, places, strengths, and so forth to better understand the analysis Clausewitz provides.

A. Army of Italy

This comprised these divisions:[10]

La Harpe	8,000 men
Masséna	9,000
Augereau	8,000
Sérurier	7,000
Macquard	3,700
Garnier	3,200
Cavalry	4,000

In total, 43,000 men with no more than 60 cannon.[11]

At the beginning of April the first three divisions were on the Riviera from Savona to Loano. La Harpe had pushed forward a brigade under General Cer-

---

10. It is worth noting the ages of the French commanders at the beginning of the campaign in 1796: Napoleon was 26; La Harpe, 41; Andre Masséna, 37; Augereau, 38; Sérurier, 53; Macquard, 57; and Garnier, 39. Division general Amédée La Harpe was accidentally killed by his own men in May 1796; Charles Pierre François Augereau went on to become a marshal of France, as did Jean-Mathieu-Philibert Sérurier; François Macquard and Pierre Philippe Garnier both went on to division command. There are two main sources for biographical data. For the Austrians, see Dr. Constant von Wurzbach, *Biographisches Lexikon des Kaiserthums Oesterreich*, 60 vols. (Vienna: Universitäts Buchruderei von L. E. Zamarski, 1856–1891), accessed 5 September 2017, http://www .literature.at/mdsearch.alo?orderby=author&sortorder=a&quicksearch=true&allfields =Biographisches+Lexikon+des+Kaisertums+%C3%96sterreich. For the French, see Georges Six, *Dictionnaire Biographique des Generaux & Amiraux de la Revolution et de L'Empire (1792–1814)*, 2 vols. (Paris: Librarie Historique et Nobiliaire, 1934), accessed 5 September 2017, http://gallica.bnf.fr/ark:/12148/bpt6k33369055/f11.image.

11. Colin, 3–4, notes: "On 10 April, the Army of Italy comprised: Advance guard under Masséna (divisions Laharpe and Meynier) 18,000 men; Division Augereau (less brigade Rusca, detached to division Sérurier) 7,300; Division Sérurier (including brigade Rusca) 12,000; 1st cavalry division (Loano) 3,000; Artillery, etc. 1,700; Division Macquard 3,700; Division Garnier 3,100; 2nd cavalry division (Oneille) 1,800. Total field army: 50,600. Coastal divisions 10,400. Grand total: 61,000 men." Colin's numbers are too high, as are Clausewitz's. Frederick Schneid gives the strength as 30,266, based on his research in the French archives. See Frederick C. Schneid, "The Campaign against Piedmont-Sardinia, April 1796," in *Napoleon and the Operational Art of War Essays in Honor of Donald D. Horward*, ed. Michael V. Leggiere (Leiden, Netherlands: Brill, 2016), 105 (n49).

voni[12] as far as Voltri, where its threatening proximity would support the Directory's[13] current request to the government of Genoa for supplies.[14] This brigade was therefore not part of the main French positions. Apart from this, these three divisions had occupied the crests of the Apennine mountains between the sources of the Bormida[15] with small outposts,[16] entrenched in places. One discovers this only through the course of events, so we remain ignorant of the nature of these outposts, their supports, etc., and therefore also of the significance that these mountain defensive positions might have had.[17]

Sérurier's division was by the sources of the Tanaro, i.e., in the upper end of its valley.

12. This is Jean-Baptise Cervoni, who went on to command a division. He was 30 at the beginning of the campaign.

13. The French government's ruling body.

14. Genoa was officially neutral but favored the allies, especially while the Royal Navy maintained a presence in the city. The French routinely requested supplies, cash, and other contributions (such as artwork) from states they could pressure.

15. The Bormida River has two main sources in the Apennine mountains. They lie to the northwest of the coastal road.

16. It is reasonable to assume that these outposts were in place to warn against any Piedmontese or Austrian movement to cut off the French from their line of supply along the coast from Savona to Loano. Even small posts in the mountains could have delayed even a serious move to cut off the French lines of communications along the coast. Given the Royal Navy's control of the sea off the French coast, it was vital to protect French land communications to Italy.

17. Colin, 4, notes: "It is hard to understand this remark of Clausewitz's when we know that he had in his hands the *Correspondance inédite de Napoléon Bonaparte*, which includes 12 letters from Masséna, 2 from Marmont, and 9 from Rusca and Sérurier relating to the outposts. In particular, Masséna's letter of 30 March (page 26) enumerates the positions held by his two divisions, and his other letters (pages 23, 26, 30, 31, 37, 38, 39, 40, 41, 50, 51) show how he was constantly busy with reconnaissances and improvements, as well as the changes made each day in response to enemy movements. Note that Bonaparte had not organised an outpost line in the true sense of the word: each of the posts held in the mountains (Stella, Monte-Legino, etc.) was held by several battalions (1,500 to 4,000 men), and there was only a third of the advance guard in the second line from Savona to Loano: Augereau had 7,000 men on the coast, but Rusca and Sérurier had their 12,000 men in the first line. The army was deployed, not concentrated behind an outpost line. Its front was 50 miles." See also *Correspondance inédite de Napoléon Bonaparte*, 1:23–51. In fairness, Colin's points are correct, in that a more detailed description of the outposts and their purpose is given in the letters identified by him. See in particular Marmont's letter of 30 March 1796, ibid., 23–25.

The cavalry were encamped on the Riviera in rear of the infantry.

Both Macquard's and Garnier's divisions were in the valleys running from the Col de Tende and the Col de Cerise; they were considered a detached corps, maintaining communications between the Army of Italy and the Army of the Alps.

The Army of the Alps under Kellermann[18] was some 20,000 strong and was holding the approaches to the Dauphiné and Savona.

Apart from these, the French had two reserve divisions, 20,000 strong, in the county of Nice and in Provence. They served as depots and as garrisons for the coastal cities threatened by the English, as well as maintaining internal security.

Bonaparte was put in charge of the Army of Italy, while Kellermann and the reserve divisions operated independently of him.[19]

The French army suffered from serious shortages of weapons and equipment. In the hands of a highly enterprising 28-year-old general,[20] however, this force was sufficient for the vigorous offensive with which the campaign began.

2 THE ALLIES

The Austrian main army under Beaulieu's[21] personal command: 32,000 men

---

18. Marshal François Kellermann led his army guarding the mountain passes during the campaign in Italy. Kellermann's forces were screened by the Duke of Aosta, who had between 10,000 and 20,000 men on the frontier. It is not exactly clear what these forces consisted of, but it seems reasonable to suggest that they consisted of garrison troops, militia, and possibly some regulars. Elijah Adlow describes the size and dispositions of the Piedmontese army but provides no references. Elijah Adlow, *Napoleon in Italy 1796–1797* (Boston: William J. Rochefort, 1948), 16.

19. Colin, 5, notes: "The coastal divisions, of which there were not two but three, had been reduced to 10,400 men by Bonaparte, including one demi-brigade (the 16th) en route to join the field army. These divisions were part of the Army of Italy and did not constitute an independent army like that in the Alps. The movement of troops from the rear to the front carried out between 4 and 10 April, under cover of confusion and by means of discreet operations, is one of the most remarkable aspects of the maneuver."

20. Clausewitz was incorrect about Napoleon's age. He was 26 at the time, having been born on 15 August 1769.

21. General Johann Beaulieu was in his 70s when he faced Napoleon in Italy. He was replaced after a string of failures in the spring of 1796.

In addition, there were Neapolitan cavalry: 1,500 men
The Austrian auxiliary[22] corps[23] under General Colli:[24] 5,000 men
Sardinian [Piedmont] troops likewise under Colli: 20,000 men
In total under Beaulieu's overall command: 57,000 men with 148 guns

The Austrian main army was divided into right and left wings.
The right wing under Argenteau[25] comprised these brigades:

Liptay:	4 battalions
Ruccavino:	4 battalions
Pittoni:	7 battalions
Sullich:	5 battalions and 2 squadrons
Total:	20 battalions, 2 squadrons

The left wing under Sebottendorf comprised these brigades:

Kerpen:	5 battalions
Nicoletti:	6 battalions
Rosselmino:	4 battalions
Schubirts:	18 squadrons
Neapolitans:	15 squadrons
Total:	15 battalions, 33 squadrons[26]

22. This *Hilfskorps* comprised Austrian troops operating under Sardinian command.

23. It should be noted that although these units are referred to as corps, the organizational structure is different from that of the organizations the French and later the Austrians created between 1803 and 1809. Here, it simply refers to a body of soldiers rather than a balanced combined-arms force.

24. General Michelangelo Colli-Marchi was the commander in chief of the Sardinian (Piedmont) army. Like many of the senior leaders on the Austrian side, he was in his 50s (or older) in 1796 and had a long record of service.

25. Generals Eugène-Guillaume Argenteau and Karl Philipp Sebottendorf were also in their 50s at the start of the 1796 campaign.

26. The ages of the Austrian commanders at the beginning of the campaign were as follows: Anton Liptay was 50; Ruccavino is almost certainly Mathias Rukavina von Boynograd, who was 59; Philipp Freiherr Pittoni von Dannenfeld was in his 70s; Wilhelm Lothar Maria Freiherr von Kerpen was 54; Gerhard Ritter von Rosselmino [Rosselmini] was in his 50s; and Anton Freiherr von Schubirts [Schubirtž] was 47. As for Sullich and Nicoletti, we were unable to establish with certainty who they were.

Since the combined total of 35 battalions and 35 squadrons is given as coming to 27,000 infantry and 5,000 cavalry, we may reckon a battalion to have 700–800 men, from which it follows that Argenteau had 15,000–16,000 men and Sebottendorf 16,000–17,000.

However, these were not their effective strengths, since at the end of March the Austrian army had about 7,000 sick, more than a fifth of the total, so we may reckon Colli's corps at no more than 20,000, the right wing of the Austrian main army at no more than 12,000, the left wing at no more than 14,000, and the entire allied force 46,000 at most.

In attempting to say anything clear and detailed about the Austrian positions, in respect of the tactical level we soon find ourselves at a loss, and even more so concerning their intentions and character. We are thus obliged to be satisfied with only the most general outlines.

At first, General Colli had served as a kind of advance guard[27] on the northern foothills of the Apennines, while the Austrian troops camped in their winter quarters along the Po River and up as far as the Adda River valley. This was still the situation at the end of March.

At the beginning of April, Argenteau, who was in the vicinity of Aqui [Ac-

---

However, the other officers provide a good baseline for establishing the age difference compared with the French. For a useful collection of information about the Napoleonic Wars, see "The Napoleon Series," accessed 28 August 2017, http://www .napoleon-series.org/. Also see Digby Smith, *The Greenhill Napoleonic Wars Data Book* (London: Greenhill Books, 1998). For the orders of battle for the campaign, see Hermann Joseph von Kuhl, *Bonapartes erster Feldzug 1796: der Ausgangspunkt moderner Kriegführung* (Berlin: R. Eisenschmidt, 1902). We have translated the main orders of battle and included them as an appendix.

27. Colin, 7, notes: "The Sardinian army was entirely distinct from and independent of the Austrian army; this organic division of the allied forces largely explains their commanders' conduct and Bonaparte's success. The Austro-Sardinian outposts did not form a continuous line, but more like two circles with their centres at Ceva and Acqui, and intersecting at a very acute angle at Dego. The Sardinian army could not be likened to an advance guard for the Austrian army; it had its own mission: to defend Piedmont inch by inch and to protect Turin right up to the day when it pleased the King to reach terms with France. The Austrian army, being unable either to provision itself or to receive reinforcements via Turin, had to protect its communications with Milan. It was therefore impossible to combine these two armies and for them to follow a single line of operations."

qui Terme] with two brigades, was pushed further forward into the mountain valleys, and Colli moved to his right to link up.

The latter took up position at Ceva with the core of his force, i.e., eight battalions, posted Provera with four battalions at Millesimo to maintain communications with Argenteau, two battalions at Murialto, outposts toward Geressio, and a couple of flank guards, one at Mondovi, the other on the left at Podagera.

Argenteau adopted a line about 10 leagues [35 miles][28] from Ovada in the Orba valley to Cairo [Cairo Montenotte], which, taking into account detours, could be considered 50 miles across. But at first he had fewer than half his troops, and by the start of the campaign, still not many more than half, just eleven battalions and two squadrons, the rest apparently remaining on the Po. Consequently, on the ground he had just a kind of chain of outposts, since when 6,000 or 7,000 men are deployed in mountainous terrain on a 50-mile front that cuts across all the valleys and ridges, and all these valleys and ridges need to be occupied with something, one can imagine how everything has to be split up into individual battalions and companies. Argenteau himself was at the main position at Sassello with three battalions.

From the Austrian left wing, which was drawn up around Pozzolo Formigaro, four battalions were pushed forward to the Bocchetta Pass and two to Campo Freddo. A large part of this wing was still on the march from its winter quarters around Milan.

In order to get a clear picture of the situation of the allied armies in the first eight days of April in relation to the ground, one must think of them in the following way.

During the winter, the French remained masters of the crests of the Apennines, which, in this harsh season, they occupied only with weak outposts, but enough that they could consider it theirs; without this crestline, they could not have remained in the narrow strip of land along the coast. The allies,

---

28. The Germans did not standardize distances until 1872, after German unification. Prior to that, each region had its own weights and measures. A league was typically between 2 and 3.5 miles long (in standardized miles), and a Prussian mile was 4.7 miles. For purposes of this book, and given the lack of clarity, we treat a league as being 3.5 miles, and 1 mile in the original as 4.5 miles here. All distances have been converted to modern miles for the reader's convenience, with some rounding where appropriate. For more on German historical measures, see "Projekt zur Erschliessung historisch wertvoller Altkartenbestände," accessed 2 February 2017, http://ikar.sbb.spk-berlin.de /werkzeugkasten/sonderregeln/4_3.htm.

for their part, recognized the very constricted French position as a significant advantage for their forthcoming offensive and therefore believed they needed to remain on the northern slopes of the mountains, so as to prevent the French from expanding the area they occupied, thereby increasing their means of support and facilitating their breakout into the Piedmontese plain. Thus, while they occupied winter quarters on the Lombard plains, they left Colli's corps in the mountains, with General Argenteau and half of his corps in support at Aqui. As spring approached, Beaulieu also pushed General Argenteau into the mountains to prepare for his forthcoming offensive and to serve as a reinforced outpost line to cover the rest of the army as it gathered around Aqui and Novi. Thus, one half of the allied army found itself in a very extended position right in front of the French, while the other half was still mustering several days' march to the rear.

Beaulieu himself arrived in Alessandria on 27 March to take over command, from which it may be assumed that this is when the muster [of the allied forces] was completed.

In these conditions, which, as we can see, arose quite naturally, there would have been no reason for any major misfortune if a position further back had been chosen for the concentration of the main body, and if the forward units had been allowed to fall back on this position in the event of a serious enemy attack.

Beaulieu's failure to prepare such a defensive position in case the enemy attacked him is, however, a serious error.

In fact, there was no mention of establishing an extended defensive position in the mountains. But this army, addicted to cordons, involuntarily crystallized in its provisional positions, with part of its force on every mountain and rise, to form a sort of cordon; as one can see, this tells its own story of how the importance of every topographical detail was grasped and taken into account by both the higher- and the lower-level general staff. In the absence of any other plan for the defense, everything seems to have been based on local defense and on the feeble and tardy assistance that each outpost could afford to its neighbor.

Both armies found themselves in this same situation, since, as we shall see, both sides intended to open the campaign with an offensive, and their opposing plans must be assessed in the light of this mutual position.

Because of the results of the previous year's campaign, the French found themselves in a difficult strategic position that they could not maintain for long.[29] In a theater of operations 12 to 15 miles wide, hemmed in by mountains and the sea, with their backs to a coast harassed by the Royal Navy, with a single line of communications on their extreme left flank, they had no hope of holding out for an entire campaign. Any successful attack on their left wing could lead to dangerous disaster.

The allies' situation had become dangerous through their own mistakes. Half the army in a 50- to 70-mile-long chain of outposts stretched right across the ridges and valleys of the Apennines, with very poor roads connecting them, could not be expected to successfully resist an energetic attack; rather, one could foresee the likely loss of many individual posts, adding up to entire battalions.

3 COMPARISON OF THE TWO ARMIES AND THEIR LEADERS

While the French army lacked a thousand necessities, the Austrians were richly provided for, and given their numerous artillery and the wealthy theater of operations with its administrative system, one may readily conclude that they lacked no essentials, even if some reports speak of all manner of shortages of materiel that supposedly delayed the start of the campaign. But this abundance, which the French writers attribute to the allies to emphasize the contrast with their own army's misery, should by no means be taken to have had an advantageous influence on the morale of the troops or the efficiency of the forces. On the allied side, at that time, it was still customary to keep their soldiers systemically starved of supplies in the manner peculiar to eighteenth-century armies. The abundance consisted of a thousand more or less dispensable items of baggage and provisions with which unimaginative force of habit encumbered the armies of the time but which had nothing to do with the soldiers' welfare. While on duty on the high ridges and in the harsh valleys of the Apennines, the soldiers suffered much more from privation, exhaustion, and resentment, as eyewitness reports show,[30] and this situation, to-

---

29. In November 1795 the French army had won a victory at Loano, which provided a foothold, albeit a vulnerable one, into the southern Ligurian Alps.

30. Based on his reading of *Briefe aus Italien, ein Beitrag zur Geschichte und Charakteristik der östreichischen Armee in Italien, in den Feldzügen von 1794, 95, 96 und 97*, Clausewitz noted: "While a general judgement cannot be made on the basis of the claims of such jeremiads as this book, written from a fairly junior point of view,

gether with the unfortunate defeats of the previous campaign, induced a quite miserable mood among the Austrian soldiery. The Sardinians were probably no better, since in their case, all manner of subversive political factors came into play as well.[31]

Thus, if one assesses the situation and the resulting morale and combat power[32] of both armies with common sense, it is clear that more might be expected from a hungry, ragged, passionately excited mob greedy for the flesh-pots of Italy—as one may characterize the French army—than from down-trodden, unthinking, unaware Austrian mercenaries with no interest in the past, present, or future. We say this not to express praise or blame, still less to impugn national character, but rather to seek the causes of events in the naked facts of the situation.[33]

As far as the leaders are concerned, the contrast was just as bad. Bonaparte was 25 years old, Beaulieu 72.[34] To the first, a great career had opened up in which with boldness and audacity there was everything to gain and nothing to lose; as for the latter, his career must soon come to a close. Bonaparte had a thorough classical education, and events of global importance had taken place before his very eyes; Beaulieu was the product of 60 years of unremark-

---

since they always over-value the individual case, they are nonetheless useful, since it is also necessary to look at the individual." This work was published in 1798, without an author's name; accessed 22 February 2017, https://books.google.com/books?id=5L pBAAAAcAAJ&printsec=frontcover&dq=Briefe+aus+Italien:+Ein+Beitrag+zur+G eschichte&hl=en&sa=X&ved=0ahUKEwjxjb-4i6TSAhWq54MKHWllCpYQ6AEIH zAA#v=onepage&q=Briefe%20aus%20Italien%3A%20Ein%20Beitrag%20zur%20 Geschichte&f=false.

31. Since the beginning of the French Revolution, French calls for liberty, fraternity, and equality had been used to persuade some people disaffected by monarchical systems to side with France or to undermine their monarchs.

32. Clausewitz uses the word *Brauchbarkeit* (usefulness), but the modern term "combat power" makes more sense in this context.

33. Colin, 12, notes: "This observation seems unfair. The Austrian troops constantly demonstrated irreproachable courage and energy." This comment misses the point, as Clausewitz does not question the courage or energy of the Austrian troops; he is getting at their motivation, or the lack thereof, which he weighs against that of the revolutionary French. His implication is that despite their poor training, more can be expected of the French because they are filled with revolutionary fervor. Furthermore, it is worth pointing out that Clausewitz focuses most of his ire on the Austrian generals.

34. As mentioned, Napoleon was 26 at the beginning of the campaign, and Beaulieu was 70. Although Clausewitz gets their ages wrong, his central point is still valid.

able, mind-numbing, dutiful box-ticking.[35] Bonaparte could regard the rulers of France as his equals, who had his sword to thank for their survival on 13 Vendemière [*sic*] (5 October 1795);[36] Beaulieu was the servant of an old imperial dynasty and the tool of a rigid and uncooperative court war council. Bonaparte knew the Apennines like the back of his hand, since during the 1794 campaign he had played a fairly important role there; for Beaulieu, the combination of mountains and the art of war was a completely new experience. All the same, Beaulieu was no ordinary man. He had fought in the Netherlands with distinction, thereby earning the honor of this command; nor did he lack energy, and he stood out as more than a mere career officer. But in such a comparison, that was far from sufficient. Indeed, from the very beginning, it was not enough to win Beaulieu the trust of his own army; on the contrary, his arrival seems to have awakened in the Austrian army a spirit of cabal and opposition. How very different—and this is the last contrast we have to offer—things were with Bonaparte. At his first parade he told his soldiers:

> Soldiers, you are naked and starving; the government owes you much, and can give you nothing. The patience and courage you show among these rocks are admirable; but they will win you no glory, no light shines on you. I will lead you into the most fertile plains in the world. Rich provinces and great cities will be in your power; there you will find honor, glory, and riches. Soldiers of Italy! Do you lack courage or steadfastness?[37]

Could such a speech to such soldiers possibly fail to have an effect? And that from the mouth of a talented, determined young man. How could he not awaken true enthusiasm and become the idol of his army?

Bonaparte never wrote nor spoke better words than these.

---

35. Although this criticism is harsh, it is not altogether unwarranted: Beaulieu had largely distinguished himself through his personal bravery and for commanding small forces.

36. This was the "Whiff of Grapeshot" made famous in Thomas Carlyle, *The French Revolution: A History in Three Volumes* (London: Chapman and Hall, 1896), 3:320.

37. "*Soldats, vous êtes nus, mal nourris; le gouvernement vous doit beaucoup, il ne peut rien vous donner. Votre patience, le courage que vous montriez au milieu de ces roches sont admirables; mais ils ne vous procurent aucune gloire, aucun éclat ne rejaillit sur vous. Je veux vous conduire dans les plus fertiles plaines du monde. Des riches provinces, de grandes villes seront en votre pouvoir; vous y trouverez honneur, gloire et richesses. Soldats d'Italie!* [sic] *manqueriez vous de courage ou de constance?*" Montholon, *Mémoires pour servir à l'Histoire de France sous Napoléon*, 3:146.

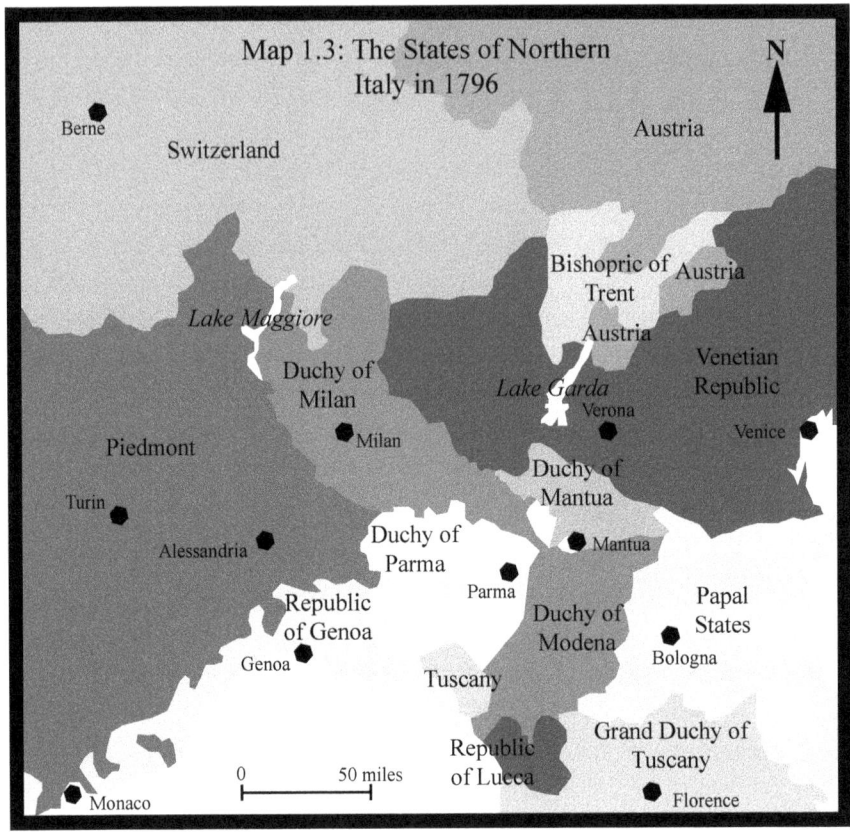

4 THE ITALIAN STATES

Although Genoa was in the theater of operations, the city itself was still in a kind of state of neutrality, which kept its fortifications out of the contest.

Although the governments of the other northern Italian states—Parma, Modena, Tuscany, Lucca, and Venice—favored the Austrians, they were afraid to join in the war and thought they could remain neutral, even though it was predictable that the French would not respect their neutrality.

Of the southern Italian states, the Papacy was still at peace with France, albeit there was considerable tension between them, but the king of Naples had a contingent of 1,500 cavalry with Beaulieu's army.

2. The Opening of the Campaign to the Battle of Dego

5 THE OPERATIONAL PLANS

Both commanders were under instructions to attack, but of course, with very different intentions.

Beaulieu's offensive was designed merely to drive the French out of the Riviera, to seize the Maritime Alps, to shorten the defensive line, to reach the sea, and to establish close communications with the English [operating in the Mediterranean]. Having achieved this, he might hope to regain control of the region[1] by means of a war of mountain outposts, perhaps even occasionally harassing the French in Provence.

Under normal circumstances, and against an ordinary general, this plan would not have been inappropriate, and the previous year, roughly the same plan had been executed by General de Vins.[2] This plan had the same character as a thousand other campaign plans used in indecisive wars. But when faced with Bonaparte as we have come to know him since then, of course, nothing was more natural than that such a feeble attack against this powerful enemy should collapse and lead to the most ruinous consequences. But at the time, Bonaparte was still unknown, and the new era of French arms had not yet begun. The campaigns of 1793, '94, and '95 in the Alps were conducted with fluctuating fortunes; the defeat at the battle of Loano in November 1795 could be considered another event of this kind. While the French had enjoyed unusual success in Holland and the Low Countries, the Austrian cabinet knew very well that political factors had played a large part; by contrast, in the campaign of 1795 on the Rhine, Austrian arms had been reasonably successful. Taking all

1. Control over the area had effectively been lost after the French victory at the battle of Loano on 23–34 November 1795.

2. Joseph de Vins had been in command of Austrian and Sardinian forces in the region until just before their defeat by France at Loano. He was in his mid-60s at the time of his command.

these circumstances into consideration, it is not surprising that the Austrian government did not seek to strike such decisive blows in the Apennines as those they received, but instead felt justified in expecting mediocre efforts to yield mediocre results.[3]

Bonaparte was likewise ordered by the Directory to go over to the offensive, and even if he had not been, he would have ordered himself to do it. His rallying cry to his soldiers tells us all we need to know. He needed money, clothing, horses, and provisions, all of which were to be found on the plains of Lombardy. Even if the enemy army was a third stronger than his own, as he may well have believed, it could not fight united against a sudden attack. There was a chance to destroy the Austrian and Piedmontese army in detail, and any attempt it made to resist in place in the mountains would offer the attacker the method to do so; it was an allied army with two diverging lines of retreat, so it could be hoped that one early success might break this alliance, and further successes could be built on that.

To a commander like Bonaparte, these considerations were too obvious to need any orders from above. All the same, it is an essential part of the history of this campaign that the instructions Bonaparte received from the Directory entailed primarily this very thing. To prise Sardinia loose from its alliance with the Austrians and expand it, at Milan's expense, in order to establish a defensive alliance with it was the intrinsic aim. But the shortest route to that was to encounter the Austrians first, as the major power, and to drive them off [and away from Piedmont]. Thus the French blows should be directed mainly at the Austrians, while demonstrating just enough against the Sardinians at Ceva to keep that flank reasonably secure; then the Austrians were to be driven across the Po and the province of Milan conquered. These were the main ideas

---

3. This is important, as Clausewitz spends time examining this very problem in *On War*. The most popular translation in English is Carl von Clausewitz, *On War*, ed. and trans. Michael Howard and Peter Paret (Princeton, NJ: Princeton University Press, 1989); page citations are to this edition unless otherwise noted. For Clausewitz's thoughts on this, see, for example, The Maximum Exertion of Strength (book 1, chap. 1, p. 77) and Scale of the Military Objective and of the Effort to Be Made (book 8, chap. 4, p. 585). Clausewitz is clearly pointing out the problem of not thinking through what one wants to achieve from the conflict and of expecting "mediocre" efforts to produce the desired results. Although Austrian thinking might have been effective in the eighteenth century, Napoleon and the French Revolution caused things to change—as Austria and Sardinia were about to find out.

in the somewhat confused instructions drafted (not without disagreement) by the Directory on 6 March, which naturally must be attributed to Carnot[4] alone.

The central idea of preferring to strike at the Austrians as the main enemy is indisputably highly commendable and emerges reasonably well from the confused ideas of the earlier strategy; but it is still far from being a matter of simple sequence and clarity, and even the sheer scale of what was to be done and what was to be achieved remains hidden behind the rough outlines that the campaign itself reveals.

We are obliged to dwell a moment longer on this principal idea, since it contains one of the most important strategic questions, namely, that of the enemy forces' *Schwerpunkt*.[5]

4. Lazare Carnot was a member of France's Directory and a successful military commander. He is often credited with being the creator of the mass mobilization that did so much to aid France's success during the revolutionary period.

5. Clausewitz's term *Schwerpunkt* is often rendered as "center of gravity." See Clausewitz, *On War*, 595–596; F. G. Zimmerman, *Military Vocabulary German-English and English German* (London: Hugh Rees, 1915). Some dispute this, arguing that it really means "weight (or focus) of effort." See Milan Vego, "Clausewitz's Schwerpunkt: Mistranslated from German, Misunderstood in English," *Military Review* 87, 1 (January–February 2007): 101–109. In the context of this work, center of gravity is the better definition. *Schwerpunkt* is a German word used in early-nineteenth-century physics to describe a center of gravity, and Clausewitz often used scientific analogies in *On War* to illustrate his thinking. For example, see book 1, chap. 1, pt. 28, for his analogy of the use of magnets and his "paradoxical [wondrous, fickle, whimsical, or strange] trinity" (89), and book 4, chap. 11, for comments on the effects of concentrated sun rays (258). In the original German (book 1, chap. 1, sec. 8), this is "*Die Aufgabe ist also, daß sich die Theorie zwischen diesen drei Tendenzen, wie zwischen drei Anziehungspunkten Schwebend erhalte.*" Carl von Clausewitz, *Vom Kriege*, 3 vols. (Berlin: Ferdinand Dümmler, 1832–1834) 1:31–32. Although it is possible to translate *zwischen drei Anziehungspunkten Schwebend erhalte* as "suspended between three points of attraction," the magnet analogy also makes sense. This view is reinforced by Clausewitz's own experience observing the classes of German physicist Paul Erman and his interaction with Erman's son, Adolph, who was studying magnetism. See Paret, *Clausewitz and the State*, 310–311, 310n. Therefore, it seems reasonable that Clausewitz is using the word *Schwerpunkt* as it might be understood by scientists. But in *On War* he also uses it differently, depending on which level of war he is discussing. See Christopher Bassford, "Clausewitz and his Works," accessed 23 February 2017, http://www.clausewitz.com/readings/Bassford/Cworks/Works.htm. For purposes of this translation, we have chosen the word or phrase that makes most sense in the context.

At first glance, at least, it seems obvious that the Austrians constituted the major power and therefore contained the center of gravity of the combined force. But how far does this extend? In the Directory's view, it had no limits; it expected that an emphatic victory over the might of Austria would paralyze the Sardinians and force them to sue for peace. The instruction seems to permit the commander to deliver only a small, brief strike against the Sardinians. Bonaparte, who printed this instruction in his *Memoirs*, along with a few brief but very rude annotations, treated this idea as being completely inept. This stark disagreement demands, all the more, that we discuss this subject according to our principles, since even if we have long abandoned any fashionable view of General Carnot as a strategist par excellence, we must still beware of making a misjudgment simply because of the disdain of a great commander. Our purpose here is to reveal the underlying relationship between these conditions, and we must not let the authority of a name deter us.

If the French had been sufficiently superior to be totally certain of driving the Austrians not only out of Lombardy but also out of Friuli and over the Carinthian Alps and marching on Vienna, then it is surely beyond doubt that the court of Turin would have been forced to submit to France *eo ipso*, without any further action against it being necessary. As things stood in 1796, no reasonable person could think otherwise.

In this situation, could one have left the Sardinians alone entirely and consequently focused the whole of one's undivided strength against the Austrians?

At best, this might have been possible in a different geographical situation, for example, if the kingdom of Sardinia had been closer to Austria itself or, at least, not next to the French base of operations. But Sardinia lay right beside the French line of communications, entirely in the rear of the French army, separating it completely from France, and was in a position to close the narrow gorge of the Riviera, through which the French line of communications ran, virtually with the pressure of a single finger. In an extended campaign, with all the effort, casualties, and consequences that would entail, if the main enemy were attacked, there would be nothing to fear from the weaker state, and in that case, one could safely disregard it; but of course, if simple passivity with just a few patrols would suffice to do us serious harm, then some division of forces is unavoidable, so that an albeit weaker but still not inconsiderable force could bring enough effort to bear against the foe according to the conditions of the moment, as well as whatever other eventualities might arise.

Thus, if success could come only from striking an emphatic blow against the Austrians, at the same time, it could not happen without leaving a secondary force to face the Sardinians.

But if the French force was not superior enough to guarantee that success with complete certainty, then failure was possible, and if that possibility came into play, the Sardinian forces would become much more important. If the French force was no longer in a procession to untrammelled victory, its communications with France became much more important and demanded much more consideration; if the French army were beaten and needed to quit Italy, the Sardinians could bring about its downfall.

In this case, too, the Austrians might still initially be considered the main force containing the common center of gravity, whose movements up to a point determined those of the Sardinians. But on this point rests the further consequence that the effectiveness of a blow against the common center of gravity would be weaker, less certain, inadequate, and thus the Sardinian force must be considered an independent one that could not be hit just by striking the Austrians.

Let us summarize the consequences.

So long as the two armies operated close together in the same theater of operations under unified command, the Austrians were undoubtedly the part of the enemy force that contained the center of gravity. This would have remained the case for the whole campaign, even if they had been driven out of Italy entirely, if the Sardinians could have been completely isolated. But as soon as the French managed to drive them as far as the Mincio or the Adige, with the separation of the Austrians from the Sardinians, it would cease to apply; the Sardinians would effectively become independent and, by virtue of their position, would become more important than the Austrians.[6]

Now in this campaign, the French obviously did not have the superiority

---

6. This is where the translation of *Schwerpunkt* as center of effort or focus of effort makes as much sense as center of gravity. In this case, the center of effort would shift from Austria to Sardinia. Whereas, theoretically, repeated blows against a center of gravity should bring down the enemy, it is clear that either the center of gravity has moved or the focus of effort has to change, based on the changing context of the campaign. Indeed, it is possible that some combination of this is also true. Thus, it is easy to see how this phrase is the subject of so much discussion and confusion. This also relates to Clausewitz's idea that continually applied pressure (the principle of continuity) increases the intensity of the action and thereby enhances the results. Furthermore, if continuity is applied against the enemy's center of gravity, the results are likely

to satisfy the first prerequisite, but it could be assumed that a fortunate success could force the Austrians out of the province of Milan. Whether such a success would have enough repercussions in the Sardinian court to persuade them to inaction and peace is a highly doubtful question, and not one to which the French commander could afford to entrust the safety of his army. With such a question mark over the political behavior of the court of Turin, if he did succeed in driving the Austrians back beyond the Po, he could not leave 10,000 of his 40,000 men facing Colli and cross the Po with 30,000, drive the Austrians out of the province of Milan, then cross the Mincio, besiege Mantua, and move up to the Adige—not while leaving 30,000–40,000 Sardinians in his rear with a mass of fortified locations that were closed against him, standing like a gatekeeper on his exceptionally poor line of communications. This is what Bonaparte labels nonsense, and in this he is completely justified, and everything the instructions from the Directory said about not wasting his strength against the Sardinians but saving it all for the Austrians is just muddled thinking, lacking precision or clarity.

If a victory were achieved over the Austrians, the pursuit could continue to the Po, but it would then be necessary to achieve another victory against the Sardinians, and this one must lead to peace or armistice.

Just as a subordinate state requires little attention if it can be overcome by defeating the major power, so it is advisable, when this is not the case, to turn one's main force on it as soon as possible, because it will be the quickest to yield and make peace.

We believe the question of where to direct the main force must be answered in this manner, insofar as it helps us determine the location of the enemy's center of gravity. But the location of the enemy's center of gravity is not decided in isolation; there is a second consideration, concerning the immediate successes that are offered [by the chosen direction]. As a rule, of course, these will be greatest if the main force is used continuously in a single direction,[7] but this is not of exclusive importance; rather, chance circumstances may mean that one can expect much greater rewards from

---

to be significantly enhanced and more favorable in terms of achieving the goals of the conflict. See Clausewitz, *On War*, 82–83 (book 1, chap. 1, secs. 12–14).

7. This again relates to Clausewitz's principle of continuity. This is a complex issue, and it is worth reading the explanation in Michael Handel, *Masters of War: Classical Strategic Thought*, 3rd ed. (London: Frank Cass, 2001), 170–179.

victory in the subordinate direction. This particular immediate advantage may outweigh the more distant general one. And this second point was, of course, another reason for turning on the Sardinians at a certain point. The Austrians might evade, and their troops were better and more reliable than the Sardinians', so in terms of trophies and the destruction of enemy armed forces, one could not expect to get the same results against the Austrians as against the Sardinians, who could be driven back to their capital and then, if they did not quickly sue for peace, could easily face disaster because of the popular mood in the country.

Thus, in our opinion, we believe Bonaparte's view was completely justified.

6 OPENING OF THE CAMPAIGN

Bonaparte arrived in Nice on 27 March; after spending just a few days on various important orders concerning administration, he placed himself at the head of the entire headquarters column—which had virtually sat rusting in Nice for two years—and led it along the route of the so-called Corniche, under the guns of the Royal Navy, to give it a taste of the future character of the war.

On 9 April he entered Savona and decided to open his offensive immediately.

He decided to cross the mountains between the sources of the Bormida with the three divisions that were between Savona and Loano. This is the junction of the Apennines with the Alps and is a saddle in the mountains, from which the Alps rise more steeply to the west and the Apennines to the east. With these three divisions—25,000 men combined, apart from the sick[8]—he meant to attack the Austrian center,[9] striking at the corps facing him there and

8. Clausewitz notes: "Here we abstract the sick of both sides and keep to the original numbers, because the numbers of sick on both sides were probably not in very different proportions (or at least, we do not know anything to the contrary), and so in each instance this gives us the relative strengths."

9. Colin, 22, notes: "Bonaparte does not attack the Austrian center; he moves into the gap left between the Sardinians and the Imperials. He does not divide Beaulieu's two wings, but overwhelms and crushes his advanced right wing at Montenotte, taking it in the flank." Note that Clausewitz did not claim Napoleon attacked the Austrian center; he said Napoleon "meant to attack the Austrian center," which is not the same thing.

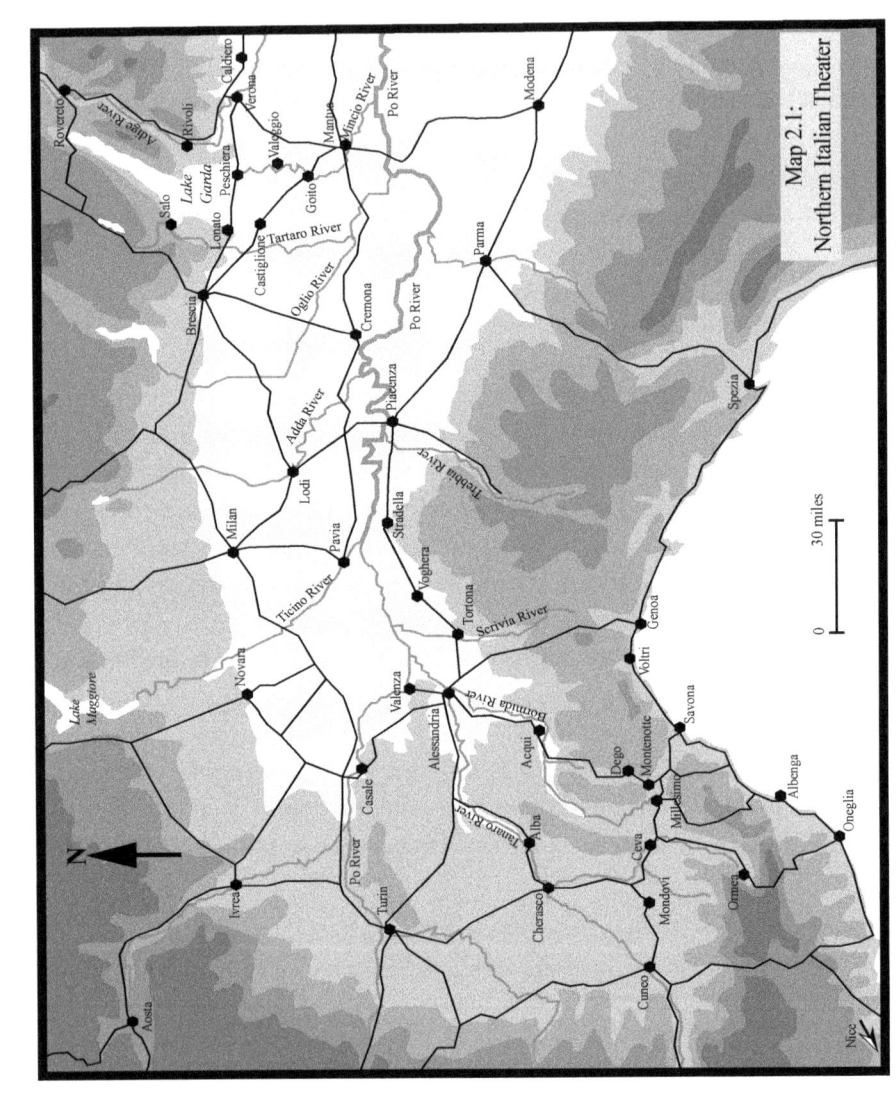

Map 2.1:
Northern Italian Theater

0   30 miles

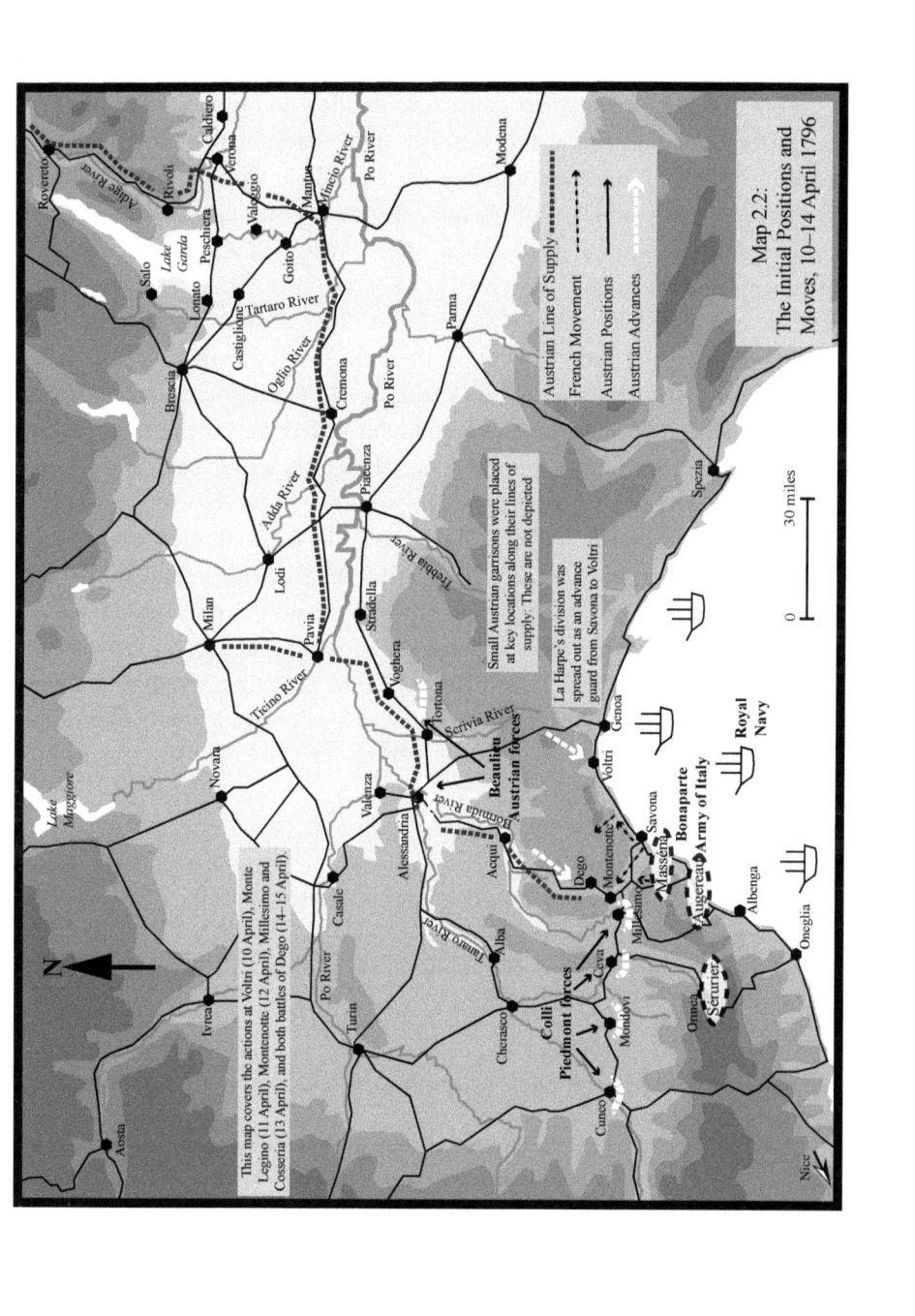

Map 2.2:
The Initial Positions and
Moves, 10–14 April 1796

Austrian Line of Supply
French Movement
Austrian Positions
Austrian Advances

Small Austrian garrisons were placed at key locations along their lines of supply. These are not depicted

La Harpe's division was spread out as an advance guard from Savona to Voltri

Royal
Navy

0   30 miles

This map covers the actions at Voltri (10 April), Monte Legino (11 April), Montenotte (12 April), Millesimo and Cosseria (13 April), and both battles of Dego (14–15 April).

N

thus separating the two wings, while Sérurier advanced up the Tanaro valley through Garessio against Ceva to pin Colli.[10] What he did after that would depend on the situation.[11]

At the same moment when Bonaparte decided on his attack and ordered the movements outlined above, Beaulieu unleashed his own offensive, even before bringing all his army together. General Colli, who had been fighting in this region for several years already, proposed to Beaulieu that with their combined forces—about 38,000 men, after leaving out a few significant detachments and the cavalry, which was of no use in the high mountains—they should march in two columns from Cairo and Ceva on the center of the French position at Loano and cut off the French right wing. This was indisputably the best plan for a serious attack. It had the best chance of success, would produce the most decisive result, and risked the least in the event of failure. Since Beaulieu had the whole of Italy for his supply base, and since it was impossible for the French right wing to threaten this base in any serious way from such a narrow valley as the Riviera, the concentration of the main force in the center gave no cause for concern. When one is united, in the best case, there is everything to hope for, and in the worst, there is nothing to fear.

Beaulieu rejected this plan. He wanted a more limited operation initially directed at just the French right flank, which he probably perceived as being extended and somewhat exposed because Cervoni's brigade was at Voltri. He hoped thereby:

10. Colin, 22, notes: "Sérurier does not pin Colli by descending on Ceva. On the contrary, what immobilizes the Sardinian army is the presence of the French between Garessio and Ormea, from where they can descend upon Mondovi and cut the Piedmontese line of communication if the latter move east from Ceva. Colli remains concentrated between Ceva and Mondovi, and only leaves the latter town on the day that Sérurier declares his attack on Ceva." Again, Clausewitz did not say what Colin claims. Rather than pick apart each of Colin's criticisms of Clausewitz, we advise the reader to treat his comments with caution. However, we will continue to comment when appropriate.

11. Colin, 23, notes: "On the contrary, Bonaparte has already decided what should be done next. He has one fixed aim before he acts: he wants to separate the Sardinians from the Imperials and to force them to make peace. His plan has been finalized two years earlier: to defeat the Austrians in the Montenotte-Sassello-Dego area, then to turn against the Piedmontese, to capture their camp at Ceva, and to march on Turin. He is not going on an adventure, and he is not making plans day by day."

1. To cut off French communications with Genoa,[12] whose weakness made him apprehensive;
2. To establish immediate communications with Admiral Jervis's fleet patrolling the coast;
3. To avoid combat with the enemy's main force and consequently risk less by operating only against a subordinate formation.

The first two of these aims were obviously very much secondary considerations, while the last was risk free only if the decisive action Beaulieu wanted to avoid was not desired by his opponent either.

The most remarkable thing is that Beaulieu set off on his attack before he had all his army with him, since his first clash was on 10 April, and apparently troops were still arriving in Aqui from Lombardy on 15 and 16 April.

The reason for this excessive haste was, in the first place, his anxiety about Genoa, which might have been able to defend itself tolerably well except that, owing to timidity, it had not taken any appropriate measures to do so; thus he felt far more threatened by Cervoni's brigade than was in fact warranted. Second, when engaged in such limited operations as this, the Austrians had long been in the habit of expecting only limited success on one side or the other and thus saw no cause for concern in embarking on this operation before their whole force was available.[13]

Thus we find both commanders about to go over to the offensive. Beaulieu began two days before his opponent, and from 10 to 15 April a series of actions

---

12. Genoa was nominally neutral, but it was clear that it could not be relied on to act as a neutral power. The communications of Commodore Horatio Nelson demonstrate that the problem was not unique to Austria. Nelson clearly indicated, in a 10 March 1796 dispatch, that he did not know whether the Genoese would act with neutrality, and he was worried about Genoa's possible lack of preparations and the consequent risks for the campaign. See Commodore Horatio Nelson to Sir John Jervis K. B., 10 March 1796, and memorandum to Mr. Brame, British Consul in Genoa, 15 May 1796, in *The Letters and Dispatches of Vice Admiral Lord Nelson*, ed. Nicholas Harris Nicolas, 7 vols. (New York: Cambridge University Press, 2011), 2:134, 2:170.

13. Colin, 24, notes: "It is important to note that Beaulieu was attempting to *dislodge* Masséna's two divisions in mountainous terrain with a more or less equal force. This disposes of the need to seek any further reason for his failure." Taking Colin at his word would prevent the reader from fully examining what happened and learning lessons from it.

ensued that are known collectively as the battles of Montenotte and Millesimo and, in the comprehensiveness of their success, are comparable with the most decisive victories.

7 THE ACTION AT VOLTRI ON 10 APRIL

On 10 April Beaulieu advanced against the French right wing with ten battalions and four squadrons in two columns, with the intention of attacking it on two sides, hurling it back with casualties, and (to use the popular term) rolling it up. He wanted then to continue this rolling up as far as was possible with the 8,000 men he committed to the operation.

The left-wing column of five battalions and four squadrons under General Pittoni[14] marched by the highway[15] through the Bocchetta Pass to Cornigliano[16] and then turned toward Voltri. This attack was deferred until the next day.

The other column comprised six battalions under General Sebottendorf, accompanied by Beaulieu himself. It marched via Campo Freddo and over the mountains into General Cervoni's left flank. This column's advance guard, a battalion under Colonel Wukassowitsch,[17] attacked the outposts covering the French left flank, drove them back, and, as dusk fell, attacked Voltri itself. General Cervoni managed to withdraw under cover of darkness, leaving behind 10 officers and 170 men (probably wounded) in Voltri. And that was the sum total result of this attack.

On the 11th General Cervoni continued his withdrawal to the Savona re-

14. Clausewitz refers to this general as Pettony, but it should be General Pittoni, mentioned earlier. This seems to be a simple error of transcription.

15. Clausewitz uses the word *Chaussee,* which often referred to metalled highways. Metalled highways were becoming more common and consisted of a densely packed gravel or cinder surface over a roadbed set up for drainage. As such, they were much more useful for all-weather travel.

16. In the original, Clausewitz names the town of Conegliano, which is near Venice. Cornigliano bisects the junction of the main road along the coast and one of the main roads south from Bochetta Pass. To arrive at Voltri, General Pittoni would have had to turn right. It is clear that Cornigliano is the correct location and that Clausewitz, or his publisher, made an error of transcription.

17. This is Joseph Philipp von Wukassovitch (or Vukassovich). At 41, he was one of the younger Austrian leaders and was later promoted to high rank.

gion, specifically, to Madonna di Savona, where he joined La Harpe's division.

How far Beaulieu's men pursued along the coast road cannot be found in any account. Beaulieu was in Voltri to confer with Nelson.[18]

8 THE ACTION AT MONTE LEGINO ON 11 APRIL

On 9 April Argenteau received Beaulieu's order to advance on Montenotte the next day and drive the French off the heights there, which were only weakly held. Through possession of these heights, Beaulieu intended to establish close communications between his left wing and his center and then decide what to do next according to the situation.

Argenteau believed that, with so many outposts to man, he could use no more than six battalions[19] for this local attack, and he had another couple of battalions move from Sassello to cover his right flank, indicating that these two were intended to be left there. Both those battalions stayed out of the fight, and the six with which he advanced must have had 3,000–4,000 men.

He set off on the march to Montenotte at 3:00 a.m. on 11 April, probably because he had used 10 April to organize his troops.

On the high ridges, Argenteau encountered only weak French outposts, which gave way without serious resistance and withdrew to Monte Legino [Monte Negino], atop which were some unarmed redoubts on its narrowest point.[20] At this moment, Colonel Rampon[21] took charge; he had been sent to support the outposts with two battalions from one of La Harpe's brigades. Rampon threw his 1,200 men into the redoubts and, under enemy fire, made

18. Colin, 27, notes: "Sebottendorf's troops halted at Voltri on the evening of the 10th. They stayed there pointlessly until the 16th, on which day the moves to concentrate at Acqui began."

19. Although he had access to more troops, Argenteau was unable to concentrate them in the time available because they were spread out over the mountains in many outposts. Thus he could not use all the troops at his disposal for the attack. See Martin Boycott-Brown, *The Road to Rivoli: Napoleon's First Campaign* (London: Cassell, 2001), 195.

20. Clausewitz says they were unarmed, by which he almost certainly meant there were no cannon. The redoubts were situated on one of the high ridges running from the Montenotte area toward Savona and dominated the route through the mountains.

21. He was a French officer who had been tasked with securing this important position. Boycott-Brown, *Road to Rivoli*, 207–208.

them swear an oath to die rather than leave their post.[22] At this point, the Austrians were perhaps just 2,000–3,000 strong, and every effort they made to carry the redoubts was in vain. Night fell, and they had to withdraw to the heights behind them.

9 THE BATTLE OF MONTENOTTE ON 12 APRIL

On 11 April, when Bonaparte saw that Beaulieu had advanced into the Genoese Riviera and Argenteau had made himself master of the point of Montenotte,[23] he immediately decided to go on the attack with La Harpe's, Masséna's, and Augereau's three divisions against Argenteau, intending to smash the latter by means of superior numbers and, if possible, an enveloping attack.[24]

Bonaparte's three divisions are set in motion on the night of 11–12 April. La Harpe climbs to the top of Monte Legino, positions himself behind the redoubts, and then attacks Argenteau frontally at dawn. Masséna's two columns, accompanied by Bonaparte himself, cross the mountains somewhat further to the left, via Altare, and immediately outflank the Austrian right. Augereau, who has already reached the heights of San Giacomo, bears still further left toward Cairo, to bypass the Austrians more widely and then turn right to reach out his hand toward Masséna.[25] At dawn La Harpe strikes the Austrian front. The fog favors Masséna's outflanking maneuver; he finds just one battalion positioned at Ferreiro [Ferrania][26] to protect the Austrian right flank, quickly

22. Rampon's call to arms is often disputed. Boycott-Brown examines the claim and presents evidence that this incident may have actually occurred. Ibid., 211–212.

23. Clausewitz uses the word *Punktes*. This point is south of the town on the modern road Via Cimavalle, although its exact location cannot be determined with certainty. Any position along this stretch of road would be vulnerable to a French move from Altare.

24. It is worth noting that in the next paragraph Clausewitz switches to the historical present tense, which might have been done for dramatic effect, as it emphasizes the urgency of the moment. This happens periodically throughout the work.

25. Colin, 30, notes: "Augereau does not attack. With his 6,000 men, the 5,000 under Joubert and Dommartin, 1,500 gunners and 500 cavalry, he moves to occupy the central position between the Sardinians and the Austrians at Carcare and Cairo. It is not intended at the outset that he should carry out a great turning maneuver around these places. Once Cairo is occupied, he is to act according to the situation."

26. Colin, 31, notes: "Clausewitz undoubtedly means Ca di Ferro; but Masséna

routs it, and moves right around the right flank, almost into Argenteau's rear, while the latter is busy vigorously defending himself to his front. As soon as Argenteau realizes this, he leaves a couple of battalions to face La Harpe so that he can use the rest to clear his rear, but it is too late; he has to flee in disorder into the Erro valley and escapes to Ponte Ivrea with just 700 men. According to the Austrians' accounts, they lost fewer than 300 dead or wounded and 400 missing, but since their own report states that two battalions were lost entirely and that of the three others, only 700 men returned, their total losses can be assumed to be between 2,000 and 3,000, even if some stragglers may have found their way back later and rejoined the colors.

Incomprehensibly, Argenteau did not lead his remnants toward the four battalions at Sassello, nor toward the three and a half battalions at Dego, but right between the two along the road to Aqui as far as Paretto [Pareto] in the region of Spingo [Spigno Monferrato].

Augereau's division took no part in this battle.

The result of these strategic combinations thus had been that Masséna and La Harpe—effectively, perhaps 14,000–15,000 men—had fought against 3,000–4,000 Austrians.[27]

On 11 April, as soon as Beaulieu sees Argenteau heavily engaged, he sends Colonel Wukassowitsch with three battalions to Monte Pajole,[28] where he arrives on the 12th. Since he finds no enemy here, he continues his march to Sassello, where there are therefore now seven battalions combined. But he subsequently marches to Dego with just five battalions, and it remains undetermined whether he really left two battalions behind in Sassello or there was a mistake in the previous numbers in the Austrian account.[29]

Beaulieu himself hurried to Aqui, his army's muster point.

----

actually attacked at the Bric Castlas." This highlights the problem of identifying times and places in historical campaigns when there are many names for the same places.

27. Schneid gives the figures of 16,500 for the French and 4,000 for the Austrians and Piedmontese. Schneid, "Campaign against Piedmont-Sardinia, April 1796," 106.

28. It is not clear exactly where this is, although it would have to be between Voltri and Sassello. Boycott-Brown comments that it was typical for tracks to follow the ridge, and they were often more usable than roads during times of heavy rain. Boycott-Brown, *Road to Rivoli*, 203. For obvious reasons, this makes identifying the exact routes almost impossible.

29. The most recent account sheds no further light on this. Boycott-Brown, *Road to Rivoli*, 213.

If we cast an eye over the distribution of the Austrian main army on 13 April, from the Austrian account we discover that there were fifteen battalions in total:

7 battalions in Sassello,
4 battalions at Dego (including 2 shattered at Montenotte),
2 battalions at Mioglia,
1 battalion at Paretto,
1 battalion at Molvizino.

Of these fifteen, three belonged to the left wing, and two, it seems, belonged to Colli's corps.

As for the remaining seven battalions of the left wing, we can assume they were either still on the Riviera or already retreating to Aqui.

We further discover that three battalions were on their way to Spigno, to come to Dego's aid.

This comes to twenty-five battalions in all, leaving another ten battalions that had either gathered at Aqui by now or perhaps had not yet arrived there.

Bonaparte probably did not know the Austrian dispositions at that moment. He only suspected there were significant detachments at Sassello and Dego because previously the Austrians had always treated these two places as central locations for their advance posts in the mountains and had heavily fortified Dego. This is where the dispositions for his continued advance were aimed.

La Harpe was ordered to pursue the enemy toward Sassello to attract the attention of the enemy forces there, but then turn into the Bormida valley to cooperate against Dego. Masséna followed with nine battalions toward Dego, which he was to attack in combination with La Harpe on the 13th. Bonaparte himself took some of Masséna's and Augereau's troops as far as Carcare.

On 12 April the French forces stood thus:

La Harpe facing Sassello.
Masséna with nine battalions before Cairo.
Bonaparte with some of Masséna's and Augereau's troops at Carcare.
Part of Augereau's division at Cossario[30] [Cosseria] facing Millesimo.
Sérurier in the Tanaro valley at Garessio.

---

30. This seems to be a typographical error, as after this, the spelling is Cosseria.

10 THE BATTLE OF MILLESIMO ON 13 APRIL

General Colli had taken no part in the battles of 11 and 12 April. The general order he received was to occupy the enemy by mounting a feint attack. Beyond that, it was left up to him. We cannot relate in detail what measures the general took, since the Austrian account is such a tangle of incomplete reports on the distribution of individual battalions that one cannot bring it to an acceptable level of coherence.[31] We must therefore satisfy ourselves with the main result, which was that on 12 April, after detaching a few companies from his four battalions at Salicetto, General Provera moved toward Cosseria, an old castle near Millesimo on the ridge separating the two arms of the Bormida. He took position there on 13 April with 1,800 men.[32]

Bonaparte intended that on the 13th Masséna and La Harpe should attack Dego, while he would turn against Millesimo.

During the night Masséna received the order to attack; but since Bonaparte had kept back one of his brigades at Cairo, and La Harpe could not arrive before midday, Masséna felt he was too weak to launch the attack on Dego that morning. He only moved off around midday and limited himself to a reconnaissance, while taking up position at La Rocchetta, half an hour from Dego.

However, Bonaparte turned on General Provera with two brigades. At dawn Augereau had seized the locality of Millesimo, while at the same time Bonaparte advanced. Provera saw he was facing an enveloping attack by a greatly superior

---

31. Colin, 34, notes: "Colli's movements are very simple and essentially he does almost nothing. Unable to leave Mondovi without leaving the Piedmont plain and the road to Turin open to Sérurier and Macquart, he only moved a few elite battalions towards Millesimo to receive the outposts, and he avoided becoming engaged. Without Provera's resistance in the exceptional Cosseria position, Augereau would not have had any real fighting before reaching Ceva." Despite Colin's implicit criticism of Clausewitz here, he provides little additional detail.

32. Schneid gives the figures of 2,100 for the Austrians and Piedmontese and 11,000 for the French, based on archival sources. Schneid, "Campaign against Piedmont-Sardinia, April 1796," 106. The discrepancy in numbers is interesting, but it might simply be that Clausewitz excluded the detached parts (which he mentions) of the Austrian-Piedmontese force. Furthermore, the fact that a number is stated in the archives does not mean it exactly matches the number of troops on a given battlefield at a particular moment. Given that Schneid had access to more detailed information, it seems reasonable that his numbers are more accurate overall, but it is also reasonable to suggest that this might not be true for the figures in any particular action.

enemy, leaving him no path of retreat, so he had to seek refuge with his 1,500 men (per Austrian reports, 1,000) in the old castle of Cosseria on its high knoll. Although it was a ruin, it still offered a position that could not easily be carried by storm. While Bonaparte with one brigade was occupied at Censio, repelling the attacks of some troops sent by Colli to Provera's aid, Augereau attempted several bloody and futile assaults on Cosseria. Night fell, and at this point, Colli's left wing had been ejected from its positions, and Provera, with what was left of the core of it, was formally besieged in the Cosseria castle.[33]

11 THE FIRST BATTLE OF DEGO ON 14 APRIL

As we have already related, on 12 April Argenteau retreated to Pareto after leaving two battalions in Mioglia, which probably had only a few hundred men. In Pareto on the afternoon of the 12th he received an urgent request from General Roccavino, who lay wounded in Dego, to rush help there, as it was under serious threat.

Argenteau reported this to Aqui, where Beaulieu had already arrived, and stated he could do nothing useful for Dego with the few exhausted rabble he had retreated with. But on 13 April he received orders from Beaulieu to do everything possible to hold Dego for a few days longer and to cover the roads leading to Aqui. At the same time, Beaulieu informed him that three battalions were marching on Spigno to reinforce Dego.

Beaulieu urged General Colli to strike the left flank of the enemy operating against Dego.

Accordingly, on the night of 13–14 April, Argenteau sent an order to Colonel Wukassowitsch at Sassello to march to the aid of the Dego position with five battalions and attack the enemy's flank. The three battalions marching through Spigno should arrive [according to the plan] at just the right time on 14 April to join the battle.

This was the Dego position's situation on 14 April, when Bonaparte himself turned on it.

He had left Augereau to face Provera. After the former had deflected one more attempt by Colli to render aid to the besieged Provera via Censio, the latter, being out of food and water, was obliged to surrender. So ended the battle

---

33. The castle is just to the west of Cosseria, on a small hill above the town.

of Millesimo, which had probably cost the Austrians 2,000–3,000 men dead, wounded, or prisoners. Here, 3,000–4,000 allies must have fought against 8,000–10,000 French.

Bonaparte had turned on Dego with the troops belonging to his center. Here, led by Bonaparte in person, and under the encouraging influence of the news of Provera's surrender, on 14 April there ensued a very heavy attack on the seven battalions and eighteen guns holding the earthworks, again in the form of an envelopment. We cannot claim with any confidence that the three battalions sent from Spigno as reinforcements were there right from the start. Since the Austrian account states that they broke camp at 3:00 a.m., one would think they should have been, but from all the various accounts, one gets the impression that by the time they reached the battlefield, there was nothing more they could do.

On 14 April Argenteau received a false report that on the 13th Masséna's division had retreated, which caused him to remain in place. When he heard gunfire at 2:00 p.m., he set off with the two battalions from Pareto and Malvicino and sent orders to those left in Mioglia to march on Dego as well.

Naturally, he himself arrived only in time to witness the defeat of his force at Dego, while the battalions from Mioglia arrived later still.

Thus, the force at Dego was almost wiped out. By the Austrians' own account, the seven battalions were almost all captured, and eighteen cannon lost.

Argenteau retreated through Spigno to Aqui with such forces as he could salvage, as well as the three battalions Beaulieu had sent to his aid on the 15th via Spigno.

12 THE SECOND BATTLE OF DEGO ON 15 APRIL

The order sent by Argenteau to Wukassowitsch on the night of 13–14 April read: "Since Dego is threatened by the enemy, the Colonel shall make a diversionary attack toward Dego tomorrow morning." The expression "tomorrow morning" was used by mistake, since the dispatch was dated 1:00 a.m. on 14 April. Since Colonel Wukassowitsch received it at 6:00 a.m., and since the Austrian account claims he had to march for eight hours (which is hard to understand, given the distance of 7 miles,[34] as the crow flies), he was

---

34. Clausewitz's *anderthalb Meilen* in the original translates as "almost 7 miles."

convinced it meant the morning of the 15th. Consequently, he did not move on the 14th until after he heard the cannonade from Dego at midday and received a second order from Argenteau. At that point, he set off with five battalions, 3,000 men strong. The Austrian report says he marched all night, and early on the 15th Wukassowitsch arrived an hour away from Dego. The report's author may be responsible for this, rather than the geography, but let us accept it as a fact.

During his night march, Wukassowitsch learned of the Austrian defeat at Dego; then at Mioglia he captured a French officer and 30 men, who told him there were 20,000 French at Dego.[35] His line of retreat to Sassello was still open, but a strong sense of duty compelled him onward into danger; he at least wanted to make sure for himself that the intelligence he had received was true. He continued his march and seems to have chosen his route so as to arrive at the road to Spigno north of Dego, where he hit the right flank of the French advance guard moving along it. This he attacked. Amazed at seeing a significant enemy force appear from the direction of Sassello, and perhaps thinking that this was the whole of Beaulieu's force at their throat, the French advance guard offered only feeble resistance. Wukassowitsch, fired up by this fortunate success and drawn on by the enemy's cries, pressed on unstoppably to the redoubts, which his own impetuous troops desired to storm. As the account goes, he found himself in the rear of the redoubts; if not for the fact that these works were partly enclosed,[36] any defense of them by the French would have been unthinkable.

As soon as victory was attained at Dego, Napoleon ordered La Harpe's division and Victor's reserve brigade[37] (this being the first mention of the latter) to move left through Saliceto against Ceva, where Colli's troops had been driven back by Augereau after Provera's surrender. Bonaparte felt he had done enough to Beaulieu for the time being and had won enough room for maneu-

---

That closely approximates the straight-line distance on a modern map between Sassello and Dego, so it is reasonable to suppose that this is the measure Clausewitz was using.

35. Schneid gives the figure of 13,000–16,000 for the French. Schneid, "Campaign against Piedmont-Sardinia, April 1796," 106.

36. An enclosed redoubt had only a small protected gorge (entrance) rather than an open rear, making it, for all intents and purposes, a fully walled fort.

37. Colin, 39, notes: "Victor's brigade was part of Augereau's division. It found itself acting as the general reserve on the 15th and for the next few days."

ver to turn on Colli at Ceva, inflict a defeat on him there, and thus make his left flank more secure.

Therefore, at the moment Wukassowitsch ventured his bold operation, there were not really 20,000 men at Dego. There was only Masséna's division, whose strength after deducting significant detachments and earlier losses could not have been more than 6,000 men.

Wukassowitsch did not hesitate to exploit his success, the enemy's panic, and the enthusiasm of his own troops for finishing the work they had begun. To transform Austrian defeat into victory, he stormed and carried the redoubts and their nineteen guns.

Masséna collected as many of his routed men as he could rally and quickly led them against the Austrian position again, but in vain; his shaken troops could do nothing.

Bonaparte himself was spending the night in Carcare. When he learned of the attack on Masséna, he too believed the whole of Beaulieu's army must be there, so he ordered La Harpe's division and Victor's reserve brigade to return as soon as possible. He himself went to find Masséna, whom he met at around 1:00 a.m. On the spot he ordered a new assault on the redoubts. The Austrians fought with exceptional courage, but Wukassowitsch had sent for help in vain, and not a single Austrian battalion was within six hours' march. Thus, he had to give way before a superior force, relinquish all the captured guns, and retreat to Spigno and Aqui after losing about half his men.

The result of the strategic combinations for the battles at Dego was that on both the 14th and the 15th, 15,000–20,000 Frenchmen fought 3,000–4,000 Austrians.[38]

After striking this latest blow against the Austrians, Bonaparte believed he had nothing to fear from Beaulieu and turned away from him and against Colli.

13 RESULT OF THESE FIRST BATTLES

The Austrians reckon their losses in these six battles at around 6,000 men, but that does not include the four Sardinian battalions that were almost totally de-

---

38. Schneid gives the figures of 13,000 and 16,000 for the French at Dego on 14 and 15 April, respectively. For the Austrian-Piedmontese forces, he gives 5,400 and 4,000, respectively. Schneid, "Campaign against Piedmont-Sardinia, April 1796," 106.

stroyed at Dego. We may probably assume, as Jomini does, that 10,000 would not be a great overestimate of their total losses. Jomini adds 40 cannon to this; this is harder to see, since apart from the 18 guns taken at Dego, nowhere in the French reports is there any mention of many guns being taken, but given his impartiality in reporting numbers, we have no reason to raise any serious doubts about this. Of course, for a force of 30,000 men, such a loss would be very considerable, representing about a third of its artillery, and in that respect, it is comparable to the effect of a complete defeat.[39]

In terms of morale, the effect was quite different. The Austrian troops felt that everywhere they had faced an enemy two or three times stronger than them; they probably attributed this to the French having overall numerical superiority, which they largely imagined, as always happens. If they could have perceived that their own forces were very fragmented, then their defeat would have been attributed to chance circumstances or even to the mistakes of their own high command, thus to things that could have been avoided and factors that would not have been present if they had given battle with their forces united.[40] Since the Austrian storming of Dego had now inserted itself as a fine feat of arms into this succession of little defeats, there was still scarcely an Austrian soldier who did not believe they could easily knock the French over if they met in the open, as opposed to the dense terrain of the mountains.[41] If instead both armies had indeed met in the open, and if the Austrians had been soundly beaten by a noticeably weaker enemy, then the effect on the relative morale of the two would have been much more decisive, and all illu-

39. This number seems high, given the circumstances, the forces involved, and the equipment of the armies. That being said, the number of weapons might include artillery captured at Montenotte and elsewhere. Other sources cite different numbers, and it is unlikely that the exact number of artillery can be ascertained. Boycott-Brown cites Félix Bouvier for his claim of at least sixteen artillery pieces and twenty-four ammunition caissons. However, an examination of Bouvier's footnotes provides two other estimates (thirteen cannon and five caissons, and eighteen cannon and twenty caissons). See Boycott-Brown, *Road to Rivoli*, 248; Félix Bouvier, *Bonaparte en Italie 1796* (Paris: Librairie Léopold Cerf., 1899), 299, 299n.

40. Clausewitz talks about this (in book 8, chap. 9) as being one of his "two basic principles that underlie all strategic planning. . . . Act with the utmost concentration." Clausewitz, *On War*, 617.

41. Colin, 42, notes: "It is difficult to reconcile this high opinion of the Austrian army's morale with that which he has expressed in chapter III [section 3]." See chapter 1, note 33, of this volume.

sions would have fallen away. But the troops who inflicted the loss of 10,000 men and 40 cannon on Beaulieu's army were basically just Masséna's and La Harpe's divisions, Victor's brigade, and a few cavalry—perhaps 20,000 men at most.

The point of this summary is that one big victory is always more valuable than a series of smaller actions, even if they inflict the same losses on the defeated army.[42]

If the moral force of this defeat was really smaller than if it had been suffered in a single battle, we must also say that, for the French, their victory was achieved much more easily and, by its nature, with much more certainty than if it had been accomplished in a single battle. In fact, as it turned out, in no single place was a cheap victory for the Austrians even possible, whereas if their 30,000 men and 140 cannon had stood united against 20,000 French with fewer than 30 guns, the latter would have had very little chance of winning.

This overall success rested mainly on the very successful French strategic combinations, which set up all the individual decisions so advantageously that they could not fail. Consequently, one may say that here, strategy was very strongly dominant to a degree rarely seen elsewhere, and indeed, this factor was decisive almost on its own. But of course, one must seek it not so much in the very skillfully constructed French combinations but rather in the very defective Austrian ones. Bonaparte followed very simple plans, and where great decisions are concerned, such plans are *eo ipso* always the best. We must also especially applaud the great energy,[43] the hunger for victory, with which

---

42. Clausewitz argues this point in *On War* (book 6, chap. 28, p. 489): "Even if a battle were not the primary, the most common, the most effective means of reaching a decision (as we think we have already shown more than once), the mere fact that it is one of the means of obtaining a decision should be enough to call for the utmost possible concentration of strength permissible under the circumstances. A major battle in a theater of operations is a collision between two centers of gravity; the more forces we can concentrate in our center of gravity, the more certain and massive the effect will be."

43. This is where the age gap between the leaders is worth mentioning again. Broadly speaking, the Austrians and Sardinians were significantly older than their French counterparts. Of course, one cannot know for certain what role age played in the campaign, but it is reasonable to assume that age contributed positively to the more energetic and dynamic French leadership, their ability to better withstand the rigors of campaigning, and their openness to new ideas about war fighting. As such, the age gap has, perhaps, some explanatory power.

he progressed from one operation to the next. But a much more important factor seems to be that the Austrians followed no plan at all, or at least none that suited the circumstances, and they fragmented their forces in an unprecedented manner, the causes of which can be neither discovered nor guessed at. In fact, one has scarcely ever seen a similar instance of an army deployed in a standing cordon without any interconnection.[44]

Of the 32,000 men constituting Beaulieu's main army, he led 7,000–8,000 men in a limited attack on the French left wing; 3,000–4,000 men were deployed against the center, merely in a supporting role; 5,000–6,000 men were left in individual posts on the slopes of the Apennines; and 14,000–15,000 men were still mustering at Aqui.

Such a large-scale division of forces was always very risky and could be done without disadvantage only if the enemy remained completely passive; but if the latter reacted forcefully, or even went over to the strategic offensive, this presented the most serious danger, and there would be no choice but to give up the risky endeavor of a limited offensive and, to forestall a possible or indeed probable reverse, to concentrate in a position to the rear, for which purpose the situation would seem to dictate Aqui.[45]

Now on 11 April, when Beaulieu was sufficiently impressed by the resistance met on Monte Legino—of which he only heard the heavy cannonade—that he gave up his offensive and personally hurried to Aqui, he really should have gone to Sassello or Dego as a center from which to organize his retreat.[46]

On the 11th it was already too late to prevent the loss suffered at Montenotte on 12 April. The enemy had countered Beaulieu's weak and halfhearted

---

44. This is important, as Clausewitz points out in *On War* (book 6, chap. 1, pp. 357–359): the "defensive form of warfare is intrinsically stronger than the offensive." His argument makes it clear that the defender must be poised to seize the initiative and attack in order to defeat the enemy. Thus, the defense serves to parry a blow and provides an opportunity to resume or begin the offensive at an advantage. On the role of the defense in war, it is worth reading book 6 of *On War* in its entirety (357–519). The concept of the use of a defensive cordon is examined in Nicholas Murray, *The Rocky Road to the Great War: The Evolution of Trench Warfare to 1914* (Washington, DC: Potomac Books, 2013), 1–44.

45. This ties in with the concept of a base of operations. See Murray, *Rocky Road to the Great War*, 33–39.

46. From this comment, Clausewitz is saying, in essence, that Beaulieu was giving up the opportunity to concentrate and launch a counteroffensive.

decision with a strong one, and for that, a price had to be paid, but the additional losses could have been avoided.

In Dego on 12 April, General Beaulieu would have very soon got a thorough overview of his situation and could have sent orders on the same day to Generals Colli and Provera to unite at Ceva and evade any major blows, while retreating on Mondovì, etc. Meanwhile, Beaulieu could have sent his own numerous detachments on their retreat to Aqui, where they would have met up on the 13th. The French probably would not have appeared before Aqui until the 14th or 15th, and there would have been no fear of a significant battle there before the 15th or 16th; but by then, Colli and his men should have been reasonably near. Even allowing for a couple of thousand men lost at Montenotte and another couple of thousand absent, and taking into account some significant detachments, Beaulieu probably could have gathered 20,000 men at Aqui by this time. With this force in such a good position, as Aqui seems to have been, for the time being, he would have had nothing to fear.

Most likely Bonaparte would have turned on Colli with the larger part of his army and sent just a single division toward Beaulieu, which would have offered the immediate opportunity to inflict loss through an aggressive response. If this did not improve matters, then at least enough time would have been gained for the main army to muster and to coordinate further operations with Colli.

Instead of this simple course of action, on 10 [this should be 11] April Beaulieu immediately hurries to Aqui; remains there, unsure of what is going on; and leaves his commanders in ignorance of his intentions. Consequently, all his dispositions are made too late. As well as dividing his forces at the higher level, he lets Argenteau's division remain split up into small detachments, and then, despite the great difficulty of communications, he expects the resistance of these weak posts and their combined attacks, mutual support, and diversions to be successful enough to hold up the enemy for three or four days. In general, such measures are effective only against a very cautious enemy, and above all, they require sufficient time to prepare.[47] But this was no cautious

---

47. In such a situation, eighteenth-century European armies would typically be expected to fortify their positions, which required equipment and time. Time is important here, as it is needed both for construction and to move the requisite engineers and their equipment to the location that needed to be fortified, given that picks and shovels were not routinely carried by troops until very late in the nineteenth century.

opponent Beaulieu was dealing with, and as far as time is concerned, the most cursory overview shows that none of the intended effects came about. Let us consider the strategic results for the position at Dego. Four battalions are attacked there on the 14th, and three more hurry to their aid from Spigno but arrive too late to make full use of their force; Argenteau and his two battalions from Pareto arrive only after the battle is decided, two more turn up from Mioglia even later, and the three Beaulieu sends from Aqui on the 14th meet the rest only as they are retreating through Montalto. Finally, Wukassowitsch and his five battalions arrive an entire day too late. Thus, while there were in fact nineteen battalions in action for this position, on the 14th only four had to try to withstand the actual French attack, and on the 15th, just five.[48]

Yet Beaulieu was so blind to what might really help that on 15 April, in response to Wukassowitsch's report of his success, he still ordered Colli and Provera (he knew nothing of the latter's surrender twenty-four hours earlier) to support Wukassowitsch as strongly as possible, adding: "I myself hasten to Dego, and the success of the campaign will depend on this moment." This is a drowning man clutching at a straw.

If an army is caught in the act of preparing for an attack and is itself attacked by the enemy while it is not yet united, only two courses of action remain open to it. Either it goes ahead with its own attack, based on the conviction that success there will gain as much as it loses elsewhere, or it tries to evade any decisive blows and to concentrate by retreating. It may attempt the first if it is sure of striking the enemy's center of gravity with superior force,[49] but if the enemy has this prospect, it must choose the other course. Neither advancing decisively nor retreating decisively, but ordering new combinations leading here to attack and there to defend and, in a sense, making do with discordant improvisation: this is truly a half-measure, the most culpable and pernicious a commander can commit even in normal terrain, and doubly foolish in the mountains. But this appears to have been the Austrian method.[50]

48. This brings us back to the earlier discussion of Clausewitz's call for concentration of effort.

49. Again, the term center of gravity makes more sense here. A blow against a center of gravity has the potential to decide the campaign, whereas a blow struck against the main effort, however successful, is likely to derail it at best and has little chance of deciding the campaign.

50. Clausewitz notes: "Bonaparte is also of the opinion that Beaulieu should not have sought to concentrate at Dego but further to his rear, at Aqui. He says in his

There is obviously so much here that is unexplained and incomprehensible that it would be most interesting and instructive to look up the relevant reports from this period in the Austrian military archives, which should fill in the main gaps. One would certainly find that it was not such a senseless business as it appears, and for this reason, it would not be against the interests of Austrian military honor to allow these things to be known.[51]

Memoirs, vol. 4, p. 251, '*Lorsque vous* êtes chassé d'une première position, il faut rallier vos colonnes assez en arrière pour que l'ennemi ne puisse les prevenir; car ce qui peut vous arriver le plus facheux, c'est que vos colonnes soient attaquées isolement avant leur reunion.' [As soon as you are driven out of your first position, you must rally your columns sufficiently far to the rear that the enemy cannot prevent them; for the most unfortunate thing that can happen to you is that your columns should be attacked in isolation before they can reunite.] As far as what Beaulieu should have done is concerned, the result of this criticism is the same, except that Bonaparte does the same as most historical critics: he takes matters en bloc and does not go into a meticulous elaboration of the specific relationships and considerations, but this is absolutely essential if, through this criticism, a theoretical proposition is to be related to a historical fact. In this instance it is not a question of Beaulieu having lost an initial position, since he was advancing and did not have a position to lose; neither is it the case that Beaulieu wanted to concentrate at Dego, it appears much more as though he wanted to do so at Aqui and Novi; but he still believed that he could hold on to such an intrinsically strong position as Dego with a detached corps; and he thought that the enemy who penetrated that far, whom he assumed to be only a single enemy column, could be driven back by a single combination like that of Argenteau and Wukassowitsch upon Dego. The reader may decide which kind of representation—Bonaparte's, or ours in the text above—corresponds more precisely to the present case, and which of the two theorems relates to it more closely." Clausewitz's reference relates to Montholon, *Mémoires pour servir à l'Histoire de France sous Napoléon*, 4:251.

51. Clausewitz notes: "After all, one can say in general that whenever unfortunate military operations result from a succession of mistakes, in their internal interactions these are never constituted in quite the way the public thinks. The men responsible, even if they were among the worst of field commanders, were not without sound common sense and would never perpetrate such outright absurdities as the public and critical historians impute to them. Most of these latter would be astonished if they only knew the specific reasons for these actions, and most probably would be just as easily misguided by these as was the commander who until then looked like a half-wit to them. Of course there will always be mistakes, but these usually only lie deeper, in errors of judgement or weakness of character, which do not appear as such at first glance, but which one only discovers and recognizes clearly if one compares the outcome with all the reasons which influenced the actions of the defeated party. Such historical hindsight is permissible in criticism and should not be accused of being mockery, as this is

14 REFLECTIONS ON BONAPARTE'S TURNING AGAINST COLLI

We have already pronounced sufficiently in section 5 on the direction the French commander must follow in the event of a decisive victory. This victory was attained and would have carried the French commander straight to the Po if he had wished it. We believe this barrier was the natural turning point for the direction of the French main body.[52] The French commander saw it differently. He changes direction much sooner, allows Beaulieu to rally his shattered forces at Aqui, and turns from Dego against Colli at Ceva.

The question of whether Bonaparte made an error here is important to us, not so much because of the case before us, since the outcome probably would not have been very different, but because of the theoretical importance of this frequently recurring and usually crucial question.

It is obviously the same as that which occupied us earlier (section 5), except that here it relates to narrower boundaries, smaller areas, and lesser results.

If the allies' common center of gravity lay in the Austrian army, then if Bonaparte continued to rain blows upon it,[53] its retreat to the Po must also

---

its essential concern, though of course it is far easier than doing the right thing at the time the action was taken. In fact it is therefore folly, when we see almost every army abiding by the principle of revealing as little as possible about their military disasters; such affairs always look better if they are understood in detail than in superficial over-view." It is worth looking at Clausewitz's views on this topic in *On War*, book 2, chaps. 5 and 6, pp. 156–176.

52. Here, Clausewitz uses the word *Hauptmacht*. Again, the use of a specific word to describe the main body of an army indicates that *Schwerpunkt* is better translated as center of gravity rather than center of effort or main effort, given Clausewitz's use of the term elsewhere.

53. Clausewitz's principle of continuity was previously discussed in section 5. His logic is that if the center of gravity is correctly identified, then continued successful blows against it will force the enemy to conform to one's will, and this is thus the best place to pressure. Of course, this also depends upon whether the magnitude and dura-tion of the effort required to attack the center of gravity will be sufficient to defeat the enemy, or to sufficiently weaken them, so that the cost for them to obtain their goals, or simply to deny the aggressor theirs, is sufficient to force them to negotiate or sur-render. The same calculation must, logically, be completed by the aggressor. However, as Clausewitz makes clear in *On War* in book 1 chap. 1, the play of chance and passion must also be taken into account as they play an important role. For a more in-depth discussion of Clausewitz's trinity, see chapter 3, note 23, of this volume.

cause Colli to retreat. By contrast, it could not be assumed that a blow against Colli that forced him to give way would be reason enough for the Austrians to fall back across the Po; one must assume that it is much more likely that Beaulieu would take advantage of the absence of the French main army to make good the damage his army had suffered, and in that case, he would support his subordinate. One cannot claim that the losses already inflicted on him would have put him out of action; although these were unquestionably large enough to prevent him from putting up serious resistance against the French main force if it continued to press him, it would be another matter altogether if the French turned against Colli. If Beaulieu did nothing of the kind, it could only be ascribed to the unnecessary and egregious dispersal of his forces and to his indecision; but neither of these could be relied on to this degree.

Bonaparte did not fear such an intervention by Beaulieu, and it must, of course, be acknowledged that he judged his opponent accurately.

On the contrary, Bonaparte was motivated to turn toward Colli by the danger the latter posed to his flank. We have already stated our conviction that Beaulieu's retreat across the Po would have led to Colli's as well; one may convince oneself of this simply by imagining the danger that now threatened Colli—of being entirely cut off from Turin. We do not wish to dwell on this any longer, but nobody can persuade us that, in the few days the French army would have needed to drive Beaulieu across the Po, Colli would have been in a position to do any serious damage against their flank. Thus, in this case, we find it impossible to recognize Bonaparte's reasoning as correct.[54]

Thus, if Bonaparte had sought out the Austrian commander at Aqui on the 16th and driven the scattered flock of his army beyond the Po, his operation against Colli would have been safe from any attack by Beaulieu, and if Colli

---

54. That being said, it is important to remember the precarious nature of the supply line to the French forces on the Genoese Riviera, and correct or not, this must have weighed on Napoleon's mind. Colin, 49, notes: "It is difficult to let such a criticism pass without discussion. If Bonaparte had first pursued Beaulieu with Masséna and Augereau, he would have had either to leave Sérurier at Carcare and Millesimo to contain Colli, or else to overwhelm the Austrians with his whole force. In the first case, he would have been fighting each of his adversaries with inferior forces; in the second, he would have abandoned his line of communication with Savona to the Piedmontese, and the French army would only have had enough ammunition for one action against Beaulieu."

did not retreat immediately, this would have offered an opportunity to entangle Colli in a serious catastrophe.

But there is no doubt that this general would have given way, and perhaps therein lies the reason why the victory- and trophy-hungry Bonaparte turned on him at this time. He could not effect any more major victories over Beaulieu, who would probably just fall back behind the Po; but if he turned on Colli straight after the deeds at Dego, before Colli learned the full extent of Beaulieu's misfortunes, he could expect results similar to those at Montenotte, Dego, etc.[55]

If this was the decisive reason, the operation is not to be deprecated, since in this early turn against Colli, there lay an enhancement of success. All the same, it cannot be seen as more prudent but rather as more risky; but to take a risk in order to gain a greater success should never be considered an error.

The fact that the operations against Colli in and of themselves did not immediately yield the results Bonaparte had flattered himself they would, even if they did lead to an armistice, cannot change this verdict, for tactics do not always deliver what strategy expects.

55. It is reasonable to surmise that even small victories would buy Napoleon time with the Directory in Paris. This is important because it indicates that even minor tactical successes can further a war's political objective if those tactical successes support political goals, thus allowing more time to accomplish strategic ones.

3. The Defeat of Piedmont

15 THE BATTLE OF CEVA ON 19 APRIL

Now the operations against Colli begin, which Bonaparte conducted with Sérurier's, Augereau's, and Masséna's three divisions, while La Harpe took position to observe the Austrians.

The so-called battle of Mondovi, in which the principal decision is constituted, is itself no more than a fighting withdrawal, and we must really apply the name of this battle collectively to the three actions against Colli that took place on 19, 20, and 22 April.

As soon as Provera surrendered, Augereau had headed for Monte Zemoto [Montezemolo] and driven Colli's troops back upon Ceva, arriving before that place on the 16th.

Sérurier had pressed down the valley of the Tanaro and now met up with Augereau before Ceva. Colli had chosen a position with about 15,000 men of his corps (Austrian reports say 13,000, but these are probably calculated from daily returns, thus allowing for men sick or on detached duties, etc.). He himself with 8,000 men stood behind Ceva, 4,000 more were 4.5 miles to the north at Pedagiera,[1] and he had 3,000 in reserve at Mondovi. His remaining troops were probably detached in the mountains further west toward Col de Tende, etc.

What Bonaparte does on the 16th and 17th with the two divisions of his right wing is not told anywhere,[2] but on the 18th we find both Masséna and

---

1. This is possibly the modern hamlet of Torelli or one of the small farms or hamlets nearby. Pedagiera is listed as being 1.25 miles (the unit of miles is unknown) northwest of Montezemolo in G. A. von Erdmannsdorf, *Der Feldzug von 1796 in Italien* (Magdeburg: Verlag von Fabricus und Schaefer, 1847), 63.

2. Colin, 51, notes: "On the 16th, Bonaparte feared an attack by Beaulieu, and had him observed by Laharpe and Masséna, whom he had left at Sassello and Dego to probe the roads to Acqui. That evening, upon learning that the Austrians are retreating upon Acqui at every point, and that Augereau is stalled in front of Ceva, he calls Laharpe back to Dego and posts Masséna at Mombarcaro to outflank Colli's left and divide him from Beaulieu. On the 17th, he moves to attack the fortified camp at Ceva,

La Harpe in the valley of the Bello [it should be Belbo], the former at Barcaro [Mombarcaro] on the march against Colli, the other at Benedetto [San Benedetto Belbo] observing Beaulieu.[3] Bonaparte's headquarters was at Salicetto on the Bormida. Victor's reserve brigade stood at Cairo covering the rear. All these places are only about 10–15 miles from Dego. Probably both days were spent partly in pursuit of the Austrians, partly resting, which of course, after such great exertions in marching and fighting, must have been very much needed.

Bonaparte now decides that Augereau should attack Colli frontally both at Ceva and at Pedagiera, while Sérurier outflanks his right via Montbasilico [Mombasiglio] and Masséna bypasses his left, to cross the Tanaro at Castellino [Castellino Tanaro].[4]

In the course of this attack, the Sardinians in their redoubts at Ceva fought against Sérurier to good effect, but as soon as Colli became aware of the outflanking maneuvers sweeping round him, in good time he ordered the retreat to a position he had chosen behind the Cursaglia.

We are not certain in claiming that the action at Ceva occurred on the 19th,[5] we only conclude this from the fact that Jomini says Bonaparte's headquarters relocated to Salicetto on the 18th.

On the 20th we find Colli in a very strong position on the very high and steep slope of the valley of the Cursaglia, with his right wing at Notredame de Vico [Vicoforte],[6] his center at St. Michel [San Michele Mondovi], and his left toward Lesegno.[7]

---

but finds it evacuated and occupies it without a fight. On the 18th, he moves against Colli with Augereau and Sérurier. The battle of the Cursaglia takes place on the 19th."

3. Mombarcaro is about 22.5 miles from Dego, and San Benedetto Belbo is a little further. Both are well within the distance of a few miles from Dego. Colin, 52, notes: "Mombarcaro and San Benedetto are two neighboring villages and in military terms they are the same position. Only Masséna is there; Laharpe remains at Dego."

4. Colin, 52, notes: "Masséna only got as far as Mombarcaro, and this maneuver sufficed to make Colli fear his flank was being turned."

5. Colin, 52, notes: "It was on the 16th that Augereau failed at Ceva."

6. This likely refers to the large church near Vicoforte: Santuario della Natività di Maria-Regina Montis Regalis.

7. Colin, 52, notes: "It was on the 17th that Colli established his position on the Cursaglia."

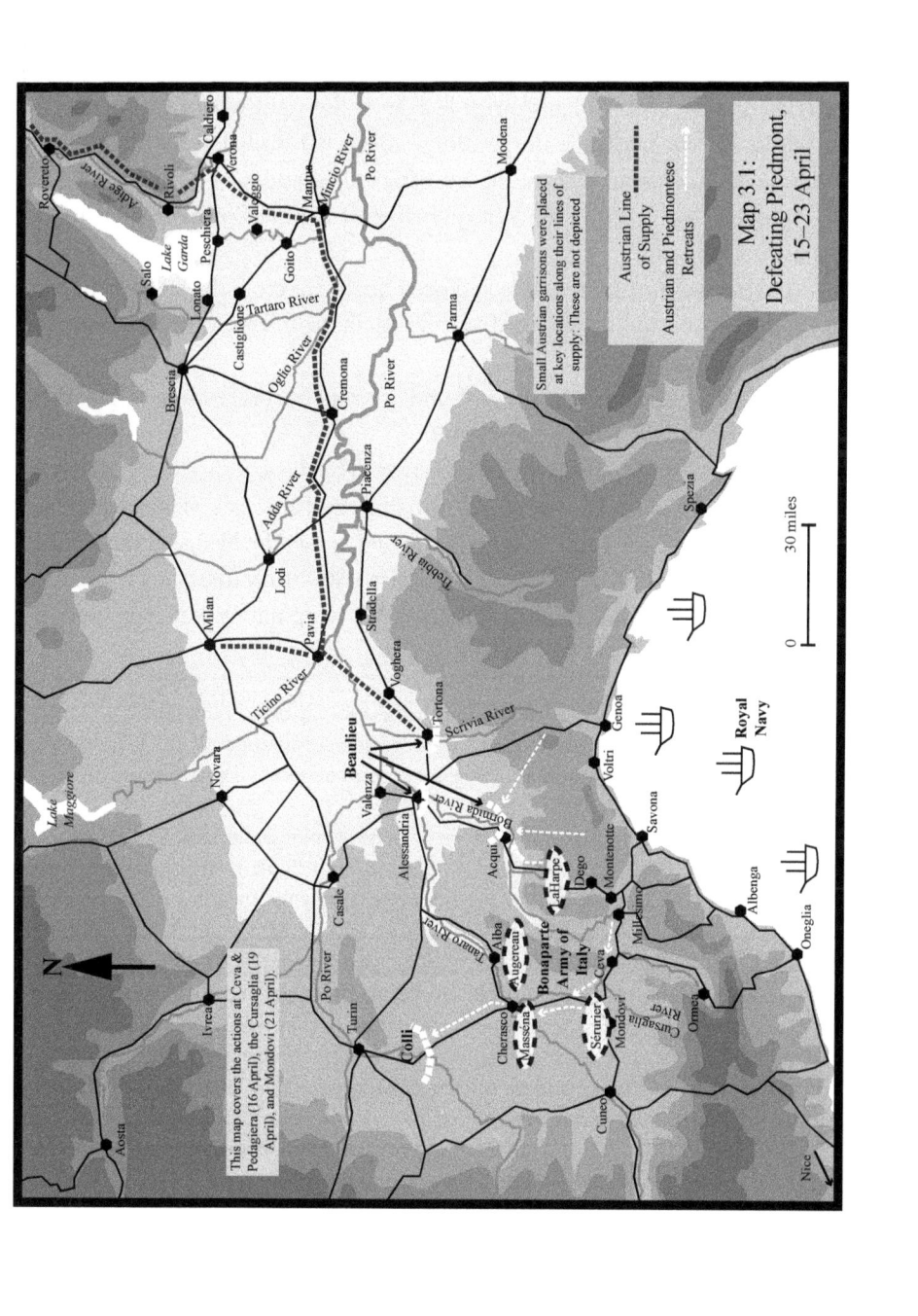

Map 3.1:
Defeating Piedmont,
15–23 April

Austrian Line
of Supply
Austrian and Piedmontese
Retreats

Small Austrian garrisons were placed
at key locations along their lines of
supply. These are not depicted

N

0   30 miles

This map covers the actions at Ceva &
Pedaggera (16 April), the Cursaglia (19
April), and Mondovi (21 April).

Royal
Navy

Bonaparte
Army of
Italy

Beaulieu

Adige River
Rovereto
Caldiero
Verona
Rivoli
Mincio River
Po River
Valeggio
Mantua
Peschiera
Goito
Lake
Garda
Salo
Lonato
Castiglione
Tartaro River
Modena
Brescia
Oglio River
Cremona
Parma
Adda River
Piacenza
Po River
Milan
Lodi
Trebbia River
Pavia
Ticino River
Stradella
Voghera
Novara
Tortona
Lake
Maggiore
Scrivia River
Valenza
Alessandria
Bormida River
Acqui
Genoa
Spezia
Casale
Po River
Tanaro River
Alba
Cherasco
Augereau
Massena
Laharpe
Dego
Montenotte
Voltri
Savona
Albenga
Oneglia
Cuneo
Serurier
Mondovi
Millesimo
Ceva
Colli
Cursaglia River
Ormea
Turin
Aosta
Ivrea
Nice

16 THE BATTLE OF THE CURSAGLIA ON 20 APRIL[8]

Bonaparte ordered that the position be attacked without delay. Sérurier was to attack frontally, with Guieu's[9] brigade against the right wing over the bridge at Torre, Fiorella's brigade in the center across the bridge at St. Michel, and Dommertin's brigade[10] against the left wing at Lesegno.

Augereau was to cross the Tanaro below where the Cursaglia joins it and bypass the left wing.

Masséna was not present. He had been unable to cross the swollen Tanaro at Castellino and so had returned to Ceva again, from where he did not arrive until the next day.[11]

This attack, ordered on the spot and without accurate knowledge of the situation, produced no favorable result.

At Lesegno, Dommertin found a destroyed bridge and no means of crossing. Augereau had as little success in crossing the Tanaro as Masséna had had the day before. In the center, Sérurier charged across the bridge at the head of Fiorella's brigade but was driven back again, with heavy losses, by Colli, who rushed there with some reserves. Only the left wing under Guieu crossed the

---

8. Colin, 53, notes: "The battle of the Cursaglia took place on the 19th."

9. This is John Joseph Guieu. He was a brigade commander at the beginning of the campaign and was promoted to division command by the Directory in Paris on 6 December 1796.

10. Clausewitz notes: "This brigade seems to have belonged originally to Masséna's division. But for this part of the campaign one must not think in terms of a fixed order of battle, partly because no author provides one, partly because Bonaparte seems to have been constantly tearing his divisions apart and in fact treated his brigades like divisions, i.e., as higher-level formations. Our ignorance must be seen as forgivable, since in the fourth volume of Napoleon's *Memoirs* we see Generals Ménard, Rampon, etc., answering a mass of questions submitted to them by Bonaparte himself, all resembling the first one in which Bonaparte asks General Ménard whether or not he was under Masséna's command on the day of Montenotte." Clausewitz is referring to Montholon, *Mémoires pour servir à l'Histoire de France sous Napoléon*, 4:372–376. Nor is the situation made clear in Napoleon's correspondence at the time. See Napoléon I, *Correspondance de Napoléon Ier*, 32 vols. (Paris: Henri Plon and J. Dumaine, 1858), 1:128–136.

11. Colin, 53, notes: "Masséna never arrived at Castellino, and never made the futile countermarch that Clausewitz imputes to him. Only Augereau was present at the Tanaro on the 19th, downstream from Lesegno."

Cursaglia above Torre [Torre Mondovi] and drove back the Austrian right wing [Sardinians and Italian allies]. However, this seems to have had no immediate impact on Colli's situation.

Thus, on 20 April Colli had won a victory of sorts. Five days had elapsed since the last action at Dego, so one could soon expect Beaulieu to advance and intervene without delay; Baron Latour, who liaised with Beaulieu in the name of the court of Turin, promised his imminent cooperation. The French troops were somewhat discouraged after the action of the 20th and were fairly exhausted by their continuous exertions; the French commander must be expecting Beaulieu to appear on his flank or rear at any moment. In short, a kind of crisis had arisen in which matters seemed to be in limbo, a calm before the storm.[12]

17 THE BATTLE OF MONDOVI ON 22 APRIL[13]

In these circumstances, on 21 April Bonaparte called a council of war in Lesegno, where he spelled out the crisis of the moment and the French generals themselves decided that their cause was lost unless they launched a new attack immediately, despite the fatigue and demoralization of their men, and forced a result before the situation got even worse.[14]

---

12. Colin, 54, notes: "Colli had 20,000 men, of whom 15,000 were available, and had suffered serious losses; he had just detached 4,000 men to guard the line of the Tanaro from Lesegno to Cherasco. He had scarcely 9,000 men left at St.-Michel, and this is what encouraged the attack on him by Sérurier's lone division. Furthermore, the Imperials had only begun their concentration at Acqui two days before; they could not complete it until the 20th, and would not become a threat until the 24th or 25th. Bonaparte therefore had 40,000 men against 9,000 Piedmontese, and his situation was not critical in any way. There may have been a certain degree of emotion at his headquarters because, for the second time, disorder and pillaging had put his troops at the mercy of an enemy counterattack, and he may have felt it necessary to reestablish discipline by whatever means."

13. Colin, 55, notes: "The battle of Mondovi took place on 21 April."

14. Colin, 55, notes: "If there was a council of war at Lesegno, after the failure at St.-Michel, this was only to explain to the divisional commanders the maneuvers they were to carry out on the 20th in preparation for the attack on the 21st. The line of communication ran via Ormea; it would have been pointless to protect the road to Savona."

Following this decision, the forces for the attack of the 22nd were organized as follows:

Sérurier was to cross at Torre and advance against the right wing with the
three brigades that had been distributed along the whole front on the 20th.

A new division under General Mennier, provisionally formed from Miolis's
and Pulletier's brigades, was to advance in the center via St. Michel; Masséna,
who had moved forward from Ceva to Lesegno, was reinforced again with
Joubert's[15] brigade and was to attack Colli's left wing; Augereau was to try
again to reach the enemy's line of communications via Castellino.

In his position behind the Cursaglia, General Colli had perhaps 10,000–
12,000 men. He probably believed he was dealing with an enemy twice or three
times as strong, and indeed, one can assume the four divisions facing him
probably had 20,000 men, including the cavalry. He could not hope for a repeat of his initial success of the 20th, and he could not accept a decisive battle
in this position, so if the French were intent on fighting one, he must fall back.
If matters were to improve, this could happen only through concerted action
with Beaulieu, so everything rested on gaining time until he arrived. General
Colli therefore decided not to wait for the attack on him planned for the 22nd
but to abandon his position overnight, this time to occupy another one just 4.5
miles from Mondovi, which he thought was strong enough to stay in for a few
days while evacuating Mondovi and awaiting Beaulieu's approach.

When the French advanced at dawn, they found to their great delight that
the position they were preparing (not without trepidation) to attack for a second time had been abandoned. Bonaparte immediately ordered his army to
descend to the plain of the Ellero, pursue the enemy, and attack him wherever
he might be found.

Colli's troops had been somewhat tardy in withdrawing. Sérurier quickly
caught up with them near Vico; the battalions that Colli hastily threw against
him did not do their duty, and before Colli could gain enough time to establish himself in his intended position, he found himself set upon by Sérurier and
Mennier just behind Vico and hurled back in disorder into the new position.
This was also attacked immediately. At first, Dommertin's brigade was success-

---

Laharpe therefore moved from Dego to San Benedetto to relieve Masséna, who moved
down to Lesegno to reinforce Sérurier."

15. Barthélemy Joubert was 26 at the start of the campaign and went on to command
a division by December 1796. He was killed at the battle of Novi on 15 August 1799.

fully resisted in the center at the so-called Briquet,[16] but Generals Guieu and Mennier outflanked the position, and the center was finally broken through as well. Colli found himself obliged to withdraw through Mondovi, with the loss of eight guns and 1,000 men, and continue his retreat to Fossano. An overly rash advance by the French cavalry under General Stengel was driven back by the enemy cavalry with significant losses, including the death of Stengel himself.

18 ARMISTICE WITH THE SARDINIANS

On hearing of the defeat at Mondovi, and probably how little support could be expected from Beaulieu, the court of Turin decided to propose an armistice and sue for peace.

Already on the 23rd Bonaparte had received a request for an armistice from General Colli, with a note that the king of Sardinia had sent a representative to Genoa to have the French agents there convey his peace proposals to the French government.

It was obviously in Bonaparte's interest to break off his operations against Piedmont as soon as possible so that he could turn against Beaulieu; furthermore, it could be anticipated that an armistice would lead to a separate peace, which was the intention of the French government and to its advantage.[17] It just depended on whether Bonaparte could secure a guarantee through the advantages he had gained over the Sardinians and make this a condition of the armistice. This guarantee was in the form of two Piedmontese fortresses that could serve as a base for continuing French operations on this side of the Alps and Apennines. Bonaparte replied to General Colli on the 24th that he had

16. It is not clear exactly what this was, but most sources agree that it was a defensible terrain feature that had been fortified, as had other parts of Colli's position. Boycott-Brown, *Road to Rivoli*, 260–263. See also Jomini, *Histoire Critique et Militaire des Guerres de la Révolution*, 8:94–95.

17. This is important, as it is reasonable to suppose that Napoleon turned on Colli to knock Sardinia out of the war, given that this action would suit his campaign objectives and the demands of the Directory in Paris. Judging that Beaulieu would remain inactive while he did so was a risk, but a reasoned one, given his age and lack of dynamism in the campaign up to this point. As such, Clausewitz's earlier criticism of Napoleon, based on what was known at the time, was unfair. Furthermore, Napoleon was sensibly splitting an enemy alliance and isolating his main enemy. This would be a pattern of his campaigns for the next quarter century.

faith in the prospect of peace between the two powers, but there was too much uncertainty for him to interrupt his victorious progress; the Sardinian government should therefore hand over to him two fortresses of its choice from the three at Alessandria, Tortona, and Coni [Cuneo].[18] When one considers that a republican party was stirring in Turin, that the loyalty of the army itself was suspect, and that the French army was just a couple days' march from Turin, such conditions seem very reasonable indeed.

Since Bonaparte saw the opportunity to take all of Lombardy from the Austrians, provided he did not give them a chance to gather their wits, and since there was no time to lose because Beaulieu was beginning to stir again, this reasonableness must be considered exceedingly wise. This would be less surprising if one were not so used to the constant and extremely arrogant ruthlessness of the French revolutionary generals of the time.

But to ensure there would be no lack of such arrogance, to these conditions the French commander added the unprecedented demand that the Imperial [Austrian] Auxiliary Corps serving in Colli's army should also be surrendered to him as a guarantee.

One can probably see this as just a crude attempt to dupe the Sardinian government, since the French commander did not insist on it any further.[19]

19 MOVEMENTS UNTIL CONCLUSION OF THE ARMISTICE

Bonaparte's army crossed the Ellero on the 23rd. Masséna moved to Caru [Carrù] on the 24th, Sérurier to La Trinité [Trinità] before Fossano, and Augereau was at Cherasco.

18. These three positions protected the main routes into and through Sardinia and thus gave France effective control over Piedmont and Liguria.

19. The demand to hand over Austrian troops seems reasonable in the circumstances. If they had remained in position, they would have posed a threat to the French rear or left flank had Napoleon wanted to move on Beaulieu immediately; thus they needed to be dealt with. By placing pressure on the Sardinians, Napoleon indirectly forced the Auxiliary Corps to take a circuitous route back to the Po valley. This kept the corps out of the way for the time being and prevented it from posing a threat to the next stage of his plan. Last, it seems reasonable that the demand relating to the Austrian forces in Sardinian territory was a perfectly sensible bargaining chip to extract the best deal possible from the Sardinians.

La Harpe remained at Benedetto.

On this day, the 24th, Beaulieu finally moved from Aqui to Nizza de la Paglia [Nizza Monferrato] with sixteen battalions and twenty-four squadrons, but left seven battalions and six squadrons in Aqui to protect his flank. When one considers that the dispositions for this march would have been given on the 23rd, we can probably assume it was undertaken as a consequence of the retreat that Colli decided upon on the 21st and carried out on the 22nd, and that the intention was to unite the two armies on the Tanaro, perhaps at Alba. The episode at Mondovi and the Sardinians' truce overtures quickly snipped the slender thread of this newly woven solidarity.

On the 25th Sérurier moved forward to Fossano and bombarded Colli, who retreated and continued overnight on the Turin road, reaching the vicinity of Carmagnola on the 26th.

On the 25th Fossano was occupied by Sérurier, Cherasco by Masséna, and Alba by Augereau.

On the 26th all three divisions were united at Alba,[20] whereby Bonaparte placed himself between Colli and Beaulieu. One brigade was detached to join Generals Macquard and Garnier in besieging Cuneo, and General Vaubois, commanding the right wing of the Army of the Alps, was urged by Bonaparte to move forward to Saluzzo.

20 TERMS OF THE ARMISTICE

On the 26th General Colli's reply arrived, saying that the king of Sardinia agreed to hand over Cuneo and Tortona, and the armistice was signed on the 28th.

Its main terms were these:

1. The surrender of Cuneo[21] and Tortona, and of Alessandria until Tortona could be surrendered;
2. The surrender of the citadel at Ceva;

20. Colin, 60, notes: "They remained at Fossano, Cherasco and Alba until the 29th. One brigade of Sérurier's division was sent towards the Col de Tende to maintain communications with Macquart and to join him as soon as possible. There was no point in besieging Cuneo, whose surrender was already no longer in doubt."

21. This was particularly important, as the seizure of this fortress opened up a supply route from France into Italy that could not be intercepted by the Royal Navy. It

3. A demarcation line along the Stura, then along the Tanaro to Asti, from there through Nizza to the Bormida, which it then followed to the Tanaro and the Po;

4. The French to be permitted to cross the Po at Valenza (which lies above the demarcation line).

Three weeks later, on 15 May, the peace treaty between Sardinia and France was concluded in Paris.

For the court of Turin to drop out of its alliance after an unsuccessful campaign is hardly an unusual event in the history of alliances, but it is doubly explicable when one considers the mood of the people and of the army.

21 SITUATION AFTER THE ARMISTICE

After Sardinia's force of some 40,000 men quit the campaign in this way, the military balance was so unfavorable to the Austrians that one could foresee them losing Lombardy as far as the Mincio or the Adige. The army that Bonaparte could deploy against them was admittedly only 30,000 strong, but Kellermann also had 20,000 men, and even if some stayed behind to man the border, 15,000 of them could join the Army of Italy, which could then continue its operations against Beaulieu with 45,000 men. The latter had received some reinforcements, increasing his force to thirty-six battalions and forty-four squadrons comprising some 26,000 men; but to these one must add 4,000–5,000 men who had been serving as auxiliaries alongside the Sardinians, whom he was summoning to him and apparently were not included in the numbers above.

There was therefore a very decided disparity in the numbers available.[22] Undoubtedly the preponderance of French morale must be estimated to be

---

also meant there were now two main routes into Italy, providing Napoleon with even greater flexibility.

22. This ties in closely with what Clausewitz argues are the four key factors in victory in battle: the tactical pattern, the terrain, the composition of forces, and the relative strength of the opposing armies. It is also worth pointing out that when Clausewitz discusses battle, he uses the term in a far broader sense than usual. For example, in terms of this history, it is clear that he means the physical struggle between competing parties in a series of engagements. Furthermore, he argues that the best way for a com-

at least as great. But now another major weight in the balance comes into consideration: the political situation in Italy. The governments of the Italian states were indeed pro-Austrian, but these weak regimes could not give any real support. Here and there, where the influence of the clergy was strong enough, the people could be incited to fanatical rage against the French, as later events showed, but this was usually successful only if they had already learned of French abuses. Through all this, there wove a powerful party that sympathized with French republicanism and attached hopes for Italy's magnificent renewal to it. To this party, the French commander was a Messiah, and they allowed themselves to believe that his proclamations would light a great fire in the whole of Italy, and all its regimes would be threatened with a devastating earthquake.[23]

---

mander to exercise control (that is, to impose his own will) is through a great battle. Clausewitz, *On War*, 258–262.

23. This section is interesting because it discusses the elements of Clausewitz's "paradoxical trinity." This is an important discussion, and it is worth quoting Clausewitz at length from different translators as well as the original German: "War is more than a true chameleon that slightly adapts characteristics to the given case. As a total phenomenon its dominant tendencies always make war a paradoxical trinity—composed of primordial violence, hatred, and enmity, which are to be regarded as blind natural force; of the play of chance and probability within which the creative spirit is free to roam; and of its element of subordination, as an instrument of policy, which makes it subject to reason alone." Clausewitz, *On War*, 89. It is important to note that the word "alone" was deliberately added by the translators of that particular version and does not appear in the original. Comparing this with another translation gives the reader a broader understanding of the original language and the variations in translation: "War is therefore, not only a veritable chameleon, because in each concrete case it changes somewhat its character, but it is also, when regarded as a whole, in relation to the tendencies predominating in it, a strange trinity, composed of the original violence of its essence, the hate and enmity which are to be regarded as a blind, natural impulse, of the play of probabilities and chance, which make it a free activity of the emotions, and of the subordinate character of a political tool, through which it belongs to the province of pure intelligence." Carl von Clausewitz, *On War*, trans. O. J. Matthijs Jolles (New York: Modern Library, 2000), 282. In the original German, it reads: "*Der Krieg ist also nicht nur ein wahres Chamäleon, weil er in jedem konkreten Falle seine Natur etwas ändert, sondern er ist auch seinen Gesamterscheinungen nach, in Beziehung auf die in ihm herrschenden Tendenzen, eine wunderliche Dreifaltigkeit, zusammengesetzt aus der ursprünglichen Gewaltsamkeit seines Elementes, dem Haß und der Feindschaft, die wie ein* blinder Naturtrieb *anzusehen sind, aus dem Spiel der Wahrscheinlichkeiten und des Zufalls, die ihn zu einer* freien Seelentätigkeit *machen, und aus der untergeord-*

In these circumstances, and in view of the general situation, it certainly would have been in the Austrians' best interest to hold their ground on the upper Po or the Sesia or the Tessino and thereby protect lower Italy indirectly; but obviously the physical and moral balance of forces was too unfavorable for that, and the popular mood made the task even more difficult because places in their rear, such as Milan, had to be more strongly occupied.

On the other hand, if the Austrians withdrew behind the Mincio or the Adige, abandoning military and political operations in lower Italy, the balance of forces facing the Austrians would be much better, at least for the moment. Because the Italian governments had contributed nothing to the war beyond the insignificant support of the 2,000 Neapolitan cavalry with Beaulieu's army, the Austrians would not lose any substantial combat power; conversely,

---

neten Natur eines politischen Werkzeuges, wodurch er dem bloßen Verstande *anheim-fällt."* Clausewitz, *Vom Kriege,* 1:31. The word *wunderliche* is more closely related to "wondrous" or "whimsical" or "strange" than it is to "paradoxical." Although some combination of these terms might provide the best meaning for the purpose of understanding Clausewitz's concept, that would be too clumsy and impractical. Furthermore, the word "paradox" is often associated with something contradictory or absurd, but we do not think Clausewitz's concept is contradictory. Neither do the words "strange" and "wondrous," in and of themselves, capture the whole meaning in its context. Anders Palmgren recently argued that "fickle trinity" best conveys Clausewitz's meaning, and his version certainly captures the randomness and arbitrariness of war, albeit without some of the magical connotation of "wondrous." In this work, we have chosen to use the phrase "wondrous or fickle trinity," as these adjectives together best capture Clausewitz's original meaning, especially if one considers the changeable and unpredictable nature of war itself; when we use the word "trinity," we are referring specifically to his wondrous or fickle trinity. Some of Clausewitz's analysis of the political problems in Italy is influenced by his trinity concept. In addition, Clausewitz seems to be poking fun at the Italians for their faith (later to be sadly disappointed) in Napoleon and the promises of the revolution. With these thoughts in mind, it is necessary to provide some clarity: Clausewitz's trinity comprises three parts; these parts are closely related and cannot be separated, hence the trinitarian nature of the concept: that is, they are three in one. For a helpful analysis of Clausewitz's trinity, see Christopher Bassford, "Tip-Toe through the Trinity: The Strange Persistence of Trinitarian Warfare," updated 5 January 2017, accessed 14 August 2017, https://www.clausewitz.com/mobile/trinity8.htm. See also Hew Strachan and Andreas Herberg-Rothe, eds., *Clausewitz in the Twenty-First Century* (Oxford: Oxford University Press, 2007); Hew Strachan, *Clausewitz's On War: A Biography* (New York: Atlantic Monthly Press, 2007), 176–190; Anders Palmgren, "Visions of Strategy: Following Clausewitz's Train of Thought" (doctoral diss., National Defence University, Helsinki, 2014), 352–353.

it could be foreseen that the French would initially be weakened rather than strengthened, because they would have to send troops to support their military and political operations in lower Italy.[24]

Taking all these circumstances into consideration, one is convinced that it would have been much better for the Austrian government to order General Beaulieu to evacuate Lombardy as far as the Mincio and establish himself behind it. There was no doubt that they were going to lose, and even the Austrians' most courageous resistance against the enemy to make him pay as dearly as possible for the ground would have brought only more defeats, more mistakes, and more evidence of incompetence and would have greatly increased the French morale advantage while further damaging the honor of Austrian arms. In a war that is bound up with an ideological struggle, both these things are doubly important.[25]

In addition to these general reasons, there is a specific one, concerning the Austrian strategic base. This base lay between the Tyrol and the Adriatic. It corresponded with a front running from Genoa to the foot of the Swiss Alps. As soon as the Austrians were driven from the left bank of the Po, their left flank would be under constant strategic threat because the base is very narrow and the balance of forces, as well as the other circumstances, would not permit any retaliation to this threat. This would necessarily put the Austrian commander in an impossible situation, as it indeed turned out.

24. Having to garrison key points in the Po valley would presumably further weaken the French striking power.

25. Given the ideological nature of the war, Clausewitz's trinity is all the more useful as a tool for understanding the nature of the conflict.

4. Bonaparte Crosses the Po

Bonaparte recognized all the advantages of his situation and let himself get carried away, beyond the mere conquest of Lombardy, giving free rein to his fantasies, as he did so often subsequently.

On 28 April he wrote the following to the Directory:

> If you cannot reach an accord with the King of Sardinia, I will march on Turin, … meanwhile I march tomorrow against Beaulieu, I will force him to retreat across the Po, I will cross it immediately behind him, I will seize all of Lombardy and within a month I hope to be in the mountains of the Tyrol, to meet the army of the Rhine, and together to carry the war into Bavaria. Order 15,000 men of the army of the Alps to join me; then I will have an army of 45,000 men and it is possible that I will send some of them against Rome.[1]

1. "*Si vous ne vous accordez pas avec le roi de Sardaigne, je marcherai sur Turin, . . . en attendant je marche demain sur Beaulieu, je l'oblige de repasser le Po, je le passe immediatement après lui, je m'empare de toute la Lombardie et avant un moi j'espère être sur les montagnes du Tyrol, trouver l'armée du Rhin, et porter de concert la guerre dans la Bavière. Ordonnez que 15,000 hommes de l'armée des Alpes viennent me rejoindre; j'aurai alors une armée de 45,000 hommes et il est possible que j'en envoye une parte sur Rome.*" What is interesting is that this quotation does not exactly match either Napoleon's *Memoirs* or the relevant letter contained in his correspondence. The gist is the same, but Clausewitz has omitted a piece or failed to add an ellipsis. The full opening is: "*Si vous ne vous accordez pas avec le roi de Sardaigne, je garderai ces places et je marcherai sur Turin.*" This is translated: "If you cannot reach an accord with the king of Sardinia, I will keep these fortresses [Cuneo and Alessandria] and I will march on Turin." We are not sure why Clausewitz omitted this piece, and his comments later in this section indicate he is aware that Napoleon thought about his lines of communication. Thus it appears to be a simple oversight on Clausewitz's part. For a transcription of the original letter, see Montholon, *Mémoires pour servir à l'Histoire de France sous Napoléon,* 4:352–363; Napoléon I, *Correspondance de Napoléon Ier,* 1:201–202.

Bonaparte forgets that relations with Naples were hostile, those with Rome were very tense, those with the other states were dubious; that if these various relations were to be so transformed as to allow the French army's rear[2] to be tolerably secure, that would take time and would need part of the army for that time to demonstrate in support of the negotiations; that several small fortresses in Lombardy would need to be besieged, such as Pizzighetone [Pizzighettone], the citadel of Milan, Brescia, etc.; that Mantua, a very important fortress probably furnished with a strong garrison, could not be left in his rear without a considerable force to besiege it;[3] and that Venice and the highway from Villach in Austria could not be left unguarded if he wanted to invade Tyrol via the Adige valley.[4]

In light of all these factors, when and with what force might Bonaparte have been able to appear in Tyrol, and in what dangerous strategic situation would this advance vanguard have found itself!

Not only did the Directory reject this extravagant idea, but as we shall see, he himself thought no more about it.[5]

2. Colin, 66, notes: "In [sections] 31 and 32, Clausewitz maintains on the contrary that it would be pointless to act against central Italy to guarantee the army's [rear] security. We may therefore refute this argument by invoking the author himself. It seems as though Bonaparte never regarded the Italian powers as dangerous, and his expeditions to Livorno, Bologna, Tolentino, etc., had as their primary aim to provide for his army's needs. The matter is proven at least insofar as the expedition to Tolentino is concerned. In any case, at least until August, Bonaparte planned to combine with Moreau, and the central Italian states did not seem sufficiently formidable to divert him from this path."

3. Colin, 67, notes: "A regular siege of Mantua would have required 12,000 men, but the blockading corps was at times as few as 6,000 or even 4,000 men."

4. Colin, 67, notes: "It was the fear of being attacked along the road from Friuli that delayed Bonaparte's march on Innsbruck after Wurmser moved part of his force to the Brenta; but after the battle of Castiglione, he had nothing to fear from this direction, because the Austrians had no forces available there. Clausewitz should have remembered this argument at the point where he mentions Bonaparte's idea of an offensive against Trieste."

5. Colin, 67, notes: "Bonaparte reiterates his intention of crossing the Tyrol and combining with Moreau in such terms that today it is impossible to doubt that that was the essential aim of his operations up until Wurmser's offensive. It took the arrival of Wurmser's 60,000 men, and above all the dispatch of an Austrian army corps to the Brenta, to reverse his project."

23 BEAULIEU CROSSES THE PO

On the 27th, probably after receiving the news that armistice negotiations had begun, Beaulieu had moved his army toward Alessandria. He had his main force there, another corps at Aqui, and a third at Pozzolo Formigaro.

Upon the news of the armistice, Beaulieu had resolved on the audacious decision to use his cavalry to seize the three citadels of Alessandria, Tortona, and Valenza by coup de main. He succeeded at Valenza, but the other two operations failed.

Perhaps Beaulieu had hoped to be able to stay awhile on the right bank of the Po in the triangle formed by these three places. Indeed, this triangle looks very like a strategic bastion, which would be well suited to command the enemy's respect and thereby to cover the line of the Lesia [Sesia] as well as the lower Po. Of course, so it would have proved, if Beaulieu had been a Turenne and Bonaparte a Montecuculi [*sic*].[6] But against a Bonaparte at the head of a revolutionary army, this artificial strategic construct was not a practical measure; he would probably quickly have torn the web apart and inflicted a disaster upon Beaulieu.

In any case, since the attempts on Alessandria and Tortona misfired and Valenza was no use on its own, on 2 May Beaulieu crossed the Po at Valenza, relinquished the citadel, and destroyed the bridge. He occupied a position with his main army behind the Cogna [Agogna] at Valeggio and at Lomello, with the intention of defending the line of the Agogna rather than the Po in this area. His left wing under General Rosselmini was at Sommo on the road from Voghera to Pavia, between the Po and the Ticino. The outposts of his right wing were on the Lesia, those of his left on the Po, with a flank detachment observing toward Olona [close to Corteolona e Genzone].

This position was clearly not fit for any of the purposes the Austrian commander intended it to serve.

Its front faced the west, which was not where the enemy was coming from.

---

6. The Vicomte de Turenne and Raimondo Montecúccoli were both great seventeenth-century generals famed for their expertise in positional or siege warfare. What Clausewitz is saying is that if Beaulieu were Turenne, he would have dug in and awaited siege, and in that case, if Napoleon were Montecúccoli, he would have accepted the offer. Clausewitz's larger point is that Napoleon and the French Revolution had fundamentally changed the way wars were fought.

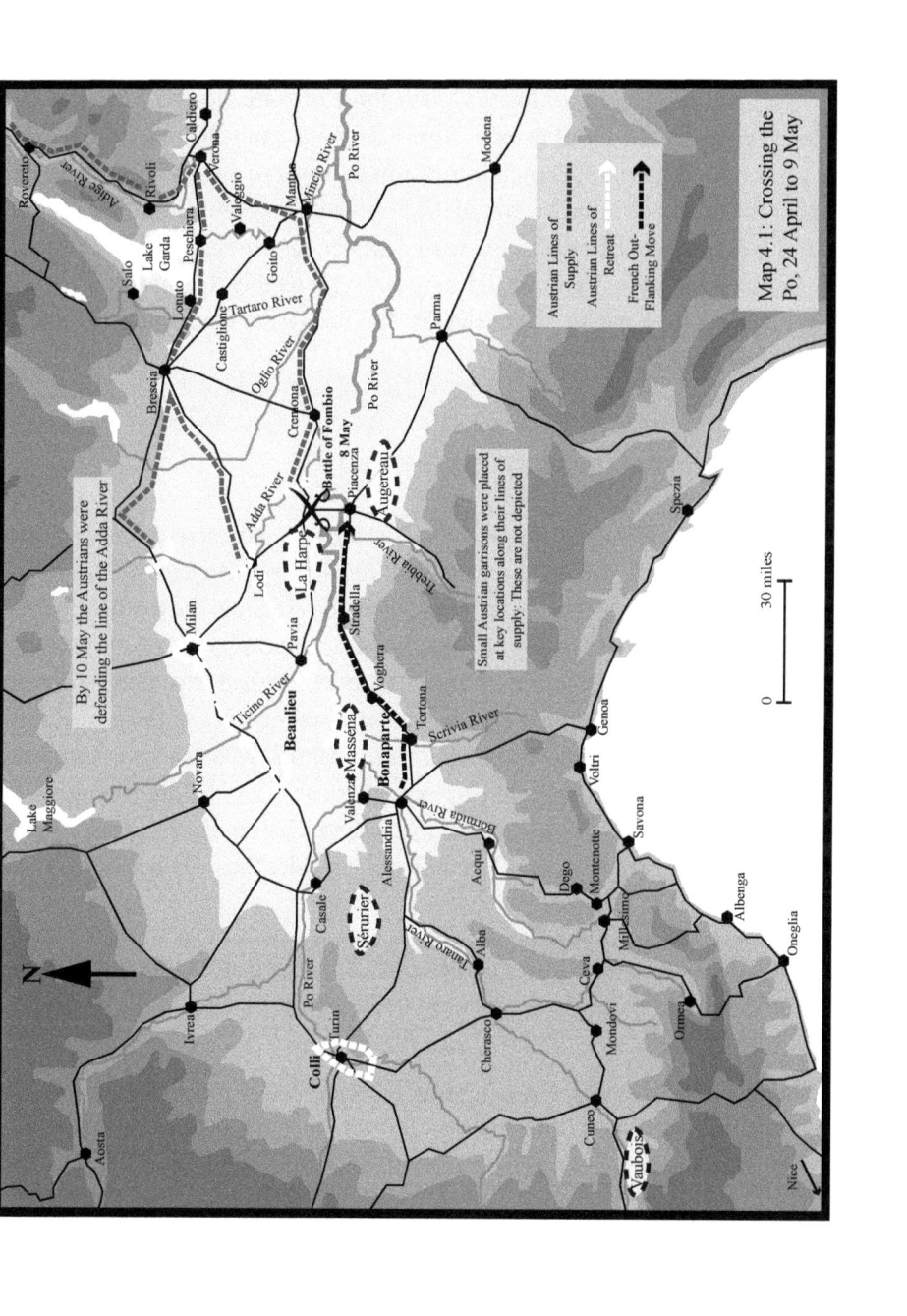

N

By 10 May the Austrians were
defending the line of the Adda River

Small Austrian garrisons were placed
at key locations along their lines of
supply. These are not depicted

Austrian Lines of
Supply
Austrian Lines of
Retreat
French Out-
Flanking Move

Map 4.1: Crossing the
Po, 24 April to 9 May

0   30 miles

Aosta

Ivrea

Lake
Maggiore

Novara

Milan

Lodi

Adda River

Brescia

Salo

Lake
Garda

Lonato

Peschiera

Castiglione

Goito

Valeggio

Verona

Rovereto

Adige River

Rivoli

Caldiero

Mincio River

Mantua

Po River

Tartaro River

Oglio River

Cremona

Battle of Fombio
8 May

Piacenza

Augereau

Parma

Modena

Po River

Po River

Turin

Colli

Casale

Séruier

Po River

Tanaro River

Alessandria

Valenza

Pavia

Ticino River

La Harpe

Beaulieu

Massena

Bonaparte

Voghera

Stradella

Trebbia River

Spezia

Cherasco

Alba

Acqui

Bormida River

Tortona

Scrivia River

Genoa

Voltri

Cuneo

Mondovi

Ceva

Montenotte

Dego

Millesimo

Savona

Ormea

Albenga

Oneglia

Nice

Vaubois

It entrusted its flanks and rear to a neutral zone, which the French would not respect. It was obviously primarily founded on the expectation, induced by Bonaparte himself, that he would cross at Valenza.[7]

Meanwhile, since the Austrian main force of some 20,000 men was deployed on a front of about 18 miles from Sommo to Lomello, and until 6 April the position of the main French formations between Alessandria and Voghera primarily threatened that section of the Po above the confluence of the Ticino, admittedly we cannot call the Austrian deployment utterly defective. Perhaps a central position at Pavia would have been preferable, because that would have covered a longer stretch of the Po, and the Ticino could have been used instead of the Agogna.

24 BONAPARTE'S CROSSING OF THE PO

The clause in the armistice agreement with Sardinia that allowed the French to cross the Po at Valenza was inserted by Bonaparte only to deceive Beaulieu.[8] It was obvious: the further east he undertook the crossing, the further back he obliged the enemy to relocate the theater of operations, and the more of the rivers running down from the Alps he avoided. He had this ability because he was the stronger, the victor, who could dictate the rules of the game to his opponent. However, this outflanking had its limits. He could not march to the Adriatic and cross there, to displace the Austrians to behind the Adige at a single stroke. Since he would have to come to a halt in the vicinity of Mantua, this close to the Austrians he could not consider the province of Milan as

---

7. For this purpose, Beaulieu's dispositions made sense, as they would allow him to cover the Po River crossings. That being said, they relied on a number of assumptions about the behavior of neutral Italian states that had already proved false, as evidenced by Beaulieu's own distrust of Genoese actions. As such, Clausewitz's criticism is reasonable and fair.

8. This is not certain. It is reasonable to think that Napoleon was keen to keep his options open for crossing the Po River. Furthermore, given that the Austrians controlled the crossing and could destroy any bridge at any time, it seems unlikely they planned solely for that one French course of action. Indeed, Beaulieu's dispositions would allow the Austrians to threaten Alessandria and any direct French eastward move south of the Po. Thus, while Clausewitz may be correct that Napoleon deliberately inserted the clause, there is no direct link between Napoleon's action and its effect on Austrian deployments.

being truly conquered. If he could have driven the Austrians straight over the mountains, the province of Milan would have fallen automatically, but not in this situation; rather, the French army must advance into it properly, drive out the Austrian garrisons and military administrations that could still be dotted around here and there, besiege the citadel of Milan and the fortress of Pizzighettone, and establish the theater of war there in the province of Milan by its advance. If the French did not clear a path while conducting their advance through the province, they would have to leave a special detachment of troops to secure their communications, which would be an evil.[9] This, therefore, limited the extent to which the French could outflank the theater of operations on the Austrian left [i.e., south of the Po].[10]

Another consideration limited it still more. The Po is a sizable water obstacle, and although the French army nominally had the personnel of a bridging train, it had no pontoons and consequently no means of crossing other than what could be found in the area; therefore, much depended on seizing a crossing uncontested, at a point where there was no significant enemy force. To make sure of finding such a situation, rather than marching his whole army to the right down the Po, Bonaparte felt it was better to pin the enemy army by demonstrating in the area where they expected him to advance and had already prepared to defend, and to seize a crossing downstream using a detached corps initially but then following it rapidly with the main army. This restricted the strategic outflanking maneuver much more, because the further the crossing place was from the two armies, the less the chance of achieving surprise.

Because of this latter consideration, Bonaparte felt he could not go downstream as far as Cremona, which would have had the advantage of bypassing

---

9. This would both reduce the size of the force available to Napoleon and violate Clausewitz's rules regarding the concentration of force. Hence Clausewitz's description of this as "an evil."

10. This brings us back to the earlier point about Beaulieu's dispositions. Given that they covered the Austrian possessions around Milan, it seems reasonable that Beaulieu wanted to keep these under Austrian rule and that he recognized the problems Napoleon would face if he marched straight to the east, south of the Po. Thus, Clausewitz's earlier criticism is, perhaps, somewhat harsh, as it is not clear exactly what Beaulieu's alternatives were, short of a withdrawal behind the Quadrilateral fortresses (securing the eastern end of the Po valley). Such a move would have surrendered much of the exceedingly fertile and wealthy Po valley to Napoleon without a fight.

the Adda and cutting the highway to Mantua at Cremona itself. Instead, he chose to cross at Piacenza, on the basis of the local conditions, which in such situations are always the decisive factor.

Thus the French commander planned his crossing according to the simplest and most sweeping strategic principles, and there is certainly no doubt that these were in his mind, even if not in this exact form. Many readers may also imagine that he must have been thinking of how an entire march to his right would put the French line of communication in danger if Beaulieu were to operate against it from Pavia. It is not impossible that this notion also influenced the French commander's decision, but we must declare it invalid. In the Austrians' situation, their own line of communication was just as threatened as the French, but as we have already said, the French army was physically and morally superior and had the initiative, so the fact that the opposing lines of communication were offset only presented an opportunity to the French.[11] Where would reasoning end if we always let ourselves return to giving each individual circumstance equal weight, without asking which is ultimately decisive?[12]

Soon after the armistice, in the first days of May, Bonaparte had set his army in motion from the region of Alessandria and Tortona. Without knowing any more precise details, on 4 May we find his forces in the following positions:

Sérurier: Alessandria and Valenza
Masséna: Tortona and Salé
Augereau: Castellanio [Castellania]
La Harpe: Voghera, with an advance guard in Casteggio

11. An Austrian move across the Po would have been a huge risk, given the disparity in forces. Napoleon could have delayed any Austrian crossing and still had sufficient force to threaten the Austrian lines of communication back to Milan and beyond.

12. Colin, 72, notes: "Clausewitz has explained perfectly the choice of Piacenza for the crossing of the Po, in saying that a more extended maneuver would not have allowed Bonaparte to surprise the enemy. This point having been made, there is no need to discuss any further the possibility of choosing Cremona, nor to consider the details of the local terrain." Again, Colin is somewhat harsh, as Clausewitz's analysis gives the reader a better idea of how the decision was made, which in turn enables the reader to gain a deeper understanding of why the decision was made and how it worked out. Thus, the extra analysis aids our understanding of the campaign more broadly. Of course, Colin's criticism might simply be attributable to a belief that he owed his readers value for their time—an accusation that might reasonably be thrown at us.

This position obviously threatened a crossing of the Po around Valenza. Only La Harpe's division with its advance guard seemed poised to pounce, but in fact, it actually threatened the area below Pavia.

On 6 May the pounce came. At the head of 3,000 grenadiers and 1,500 cavalry, Bonaparte force-marched to Piacenza, reaching it on the 7th, and crossed using craft collected from along the right bank of the Po. On the opposite bank the Austrians had two squadrons of cavalry that were soon driven off.

The rest of the army quickly followed this advance guard, part of it also reaching the crossing on the 7th, but because of the limited number of boats available, it spent the 7th, 8th, and 9th completing the crossing.

25 THE BATTLE OF FOMBIO ON 8 MAY

The French move to Voghera on 4 May had already alerted Beaulieu to the danger to his left flank. For his part, he now initiated a succession of movements and detachments that must be considered his true defense of the Po, whose crisis was resolved by the battle of Fombio on 7 and 8 May and resulted in the loss of the line of the Po.

It is best if we present this entirely in chronological order.

On 4 May, upon the news of the movement of the French lead elements to the right at Casteggio, Beaulieu dispatches General Liptay with eight battalions and eight squadrons to Belgioioso; he arrives there on the 5th and occupies the line of the Po as far as the Lombro [Lambro River].[13]

On the 6th Liptay moves to Porto Morena [Pieve Porto Morone], quite close to the Po, about halfway between the Lambro and Olona Rivers.

Beaulieu moves to Grupello [Gropello Cairoli] with the intention of retreating behind the Ticino. He sends Colli with four battalions and two squadrons to Buffalora.

Wukassowitsch moves to Valeggio.

The detachment to Buffalora is for no good reason other than a vague aim of covering Milan. Now Beaulieu's army is spread across 54 miles.[14]

---

13. Again, it is worth noting that Clausewitz has switched to present tense.

14. This is 54 miles if the Buffalora mentioned above is the one next to Brescia. There is also a small hamlet called Buffalora southeast of Voghera, but it is unlikely Clausewitz meant this location. In either case, the decision does not make sense.

On the 7th Beaulieu moves to Pavia, stays there a few hours, and then moves with seven battalions and twelve squadrons to Belgioioso, a march of 25 miles. He therefore must already have known that not just the French advance guard but also the whole of La Harpe's division had marched to Piacenza.

Sebottendorf remains in Pavia with six battalions and six squadrons to try to salvage the magazine, which, however, he fails to do.

Wukassowitsch follows the main army to behind the Terdopio [Terdoppio].

Liptay gets pushed across in between the Lambro and the Adda.

Beaulieu sends Colonel Wetzel to Corteolona in support of Liptay.

On this day, then, even leaving aside the detachment at Buffalora, the Austrian army is still strung out on a 36-mile front from the area of Fombio (where Liptay is headed) to the Terdoppio, and it is dispersed in five detachments—Wukassowitsch, Sebottendorf, Beaulieu, Wetzel, and Liptay—even though the hour of decision is at hand.[15]

As we have seen, on 7 May Bonaparte crossed with the advance guard at Piacenza, followed by La Harpe. The two squadrons he encountered were Liptay's lead element. On the 7th, while on the march to the Lambro, Liptay and his 8,000 men[16] received word of the initial crossing. He quickened his pace, and at Guardo Miglio, about 7 miles from the crossing point in the direction of Castel Pusterlengo [Casalpusterlengo], he first encountered the leading French units. In a protracted action lasting into the night, he drove these back quite close to the river. General Liptay was worried about running into too many enemy troops, so during the night he withdrew as far as Fombio.

15. This is significant because, as Clausewitz argues, concentration in the face of the enemy is critical to success. Beaulieu failed in this regard. His forces could not cover the whole front, and he would have done better to concentrate his main force (probably starting in Belgioioso) and leave very small forces to cover the likely crossing sites. From there, he could have marched east to cover Piacenza or west to cover Milan, depending on where the enemy crossed the Po. His dispositions meant that he could never effectively cover any French crossing, and he risked losing many of his men west of the likely enemy crossing point. When looking at the valley, Piacenza and Cremona were the most likely crossing points, which meant that his dispositions were too spread out and too far west to guarantee a safe retreat to Mantua and the Adige valley back to Austria, should that have been necessary.

16. Clausewitz notes: "As the Austrian account specifically states, though it is hard to grasp how eight battalions and eight squadrons could still have had this effective strength."

If General Liptay really had 8,000 men when he set off, as the Austrian account claims, then it is doubtful that a significantly larger French force was on the left bank of the Po by then. But as the saying goes, *tel maître, tel valet* [like master, like servant]: most likely Liptay had also detached many men—men he could not do without if he wanted to launch a really decisive attack on the French when they were fighting for their lives and destroy them.

At 1:00 on 8 May,[17] Bonaparte moves against Liptay in three columns, one of which is to cut him off from Beaulieu and Casalpusterlengo, the second from Codogno and Pizzighettone, while the third attacks his front. The French may have had 10,000–12,000 men. After a lively action in which Liptay loses 600 men, and fearing in particular that his line of retreat to Pizzighettone will be cut off, Liptay begins his retreat through Codogno, already having to force a path through enemy detachments for some of the way.

La Harpe pursues to Codogno, Dallemagne with the grenadiers as far as Pizzighettone, and Bonaparte goes back to Piacenza.

Liptay's corps has now virtually disintegrated. During the battle, three battalions have become so cut off that they have to retreat to Lodi; in accordance with his previous orders, he sends three battalions and five squadrons ahead to Casal Maggiore, where the highway from Mantua to Parma crosses the Po; he keeps two battalions and three squadrons at Pizzighettone.

On this day Beaulieu intended to shift another 6 or 7 miles leftward from Belgioioso to Santa Christina [Santa Cristina e Bessone], enabling him to support Sebottendorf on the right and Liptay on the left from this central position. He had planned to set off after his men cooked a meal. However, during the morning he learns of the action of the 7th, so he sets off with nine battalions and twelve squadrons toward Ospedaletto [Ospedaletto Lodigiano]. This place is some 18 miles from Belgioioso on the Cremona highway, and Casalpusterlengo is just another 4.5 miles beyond it. Thus he set off at about the same time as General Liptay was being attacked and beaten 29 miles away, in what may be considered the decisive action.

General Beaulieu seems to think it is not yet time to summon Generals Sebottendorf and Colli to him, as he still fears that part of the French army will cross the Ticino to threaten Milan, and he feels that his and Liptay's 13,000–

17. It is not clear whether this is morning or afternoon. However, as Napoleon's forces were already on the move by daybreak on 8 May, it is reasonable to assume Clausewitz means 1:00 a.m.

14,000 men combined will be enough to throw whatever French force crosses at Piacenza back across the river.

On the march to Ospedaletto, Beaulieu splits up his force in the following way, sending:

1 battalion to Senne [Senna Lodigiana],
1 battalion to Somaglia,
2 battalions to Fombio,
2 battalions and 4 squadrons to Codogno.

Just 3 battalions and 8 squadrons remain with him in Ospedaletto.

The purpose of this astonishing dispersion is explained in the Austrian account in these words: "to secure the right flank toward the Po and to prepare for a general attack. These battalions should support and reinforce General Liptay's forces wherever they should find them."

That evening in Ospedaletto, Beaulieu received a delayed message from Liptay saying that he was still holding Fombio and had repelled the enemy's attack. Later in the evening, however, patrols reported that Liptay had been beaten and the enemy had occupied Codogno. General Beaulieu thereupon resolved to fight his way through to Liptay at dawn on the 9th.

Meanwhile, General Schubirts—who commanded the two battalions detached to Codogno and was near that place with these battalions plus four squadrons, so may be considered Beaulieu's advance guard—had attempted a night attack on La Harpe's division. This raid was successful but apparently encountered only La Harpe's pickets. The Austrians claim to have taken six cannon, but the French make no mention of this. The Austrians were unable to maintain their position in Codogno, and on the morning of the 9th, General Schubirts was obliged to withdraw to Casalpusterlengo. During the night action, General La Harpe was accidentally shot dead by his own men.

The news of General Schubirts's successful raid confirmed General Beaulieu in his intention to attack. He sent orders to Liptay, Schubirts, and Pittoni that at 3:00 a.m. they should attack the enemy at Codogno and Fombio from all sides. However, General Beaulieu soon became convinced that none of his couriers could get through to Liptay, and this induced him to give up any idea of further resistance and to think only of his army's retreat across the Adda. He sent orders to Colli to move via Milan, leave a garrison in the citadel, and cross the Adda at Cassano; Sebottendorf and Wukassowitsch were to march as soon as possible and join him at Lodi, which he himself set off for early on the 9th.

Bonaparte let his army rest on the 9th. He still had no bridge over the Po, this not being completed until the 10th, so he was still busy getting his cavalry and artillery across the river.

This pause allowed Beaulieu's detachments (for that is how we must describe his constantly divided main body) to reach Lodi without further loss. Sebottendorf and Wukassowitsch were also able to cross the Adda there and join him.

Bonaparte used the 9th to impose a treaty on the Duke of Parma, levying a contribution of 2 million [livres][18] from him, even though Parma was not at war with France.

26 THE BATTLE OF LODI ON 10 MAY

On the 10th Napoleon marched on Lodi at the head of his grenadiers, followed by Masséna's division. Augereau followed somewhat later.

La Harpe's division, now under temporary command of General Ménard, remained facing Pizzighettone; Sérurier's division marched on Pavia, to secure that place and then march on Milan.

Beaulieu had so little intention of making a stand behind the Adda that on the evening of the 10th he had already set off to Crema with six battalions and ten squadrons, leaving General Schubirts in Lodi with four battalions and four squadrons to await Sebottendorf before following on to Crema.

At 11:00 [a.m.][19] on the 10th, the last of Sebottendorf's troops arrived, and

18. According to the terms of the treaty Napoleon imposed on Parma, he received "two millions of livres, French money . . . twelve hundred draught horses, with their harnesses; four hundred dragoon horses with their harnesses, and 100 saddle horses for the superior officers of the army . . . twenty paintings to be chosen by the General-in-Chief . . . ten thousand quintals of wheat and five thousand of oats . . . [and] two thousand oxen." François René Jean Pommereul, *Campaign of General Buonaparte in Italy, in 1796–7*, trans. T. E. Ritchie (Edinburgh: G. Houston, 1799), 30–31n. This is important, as it is a clear example of how the French army used coercion to resupply its forces and enrich itself. The French army routinely subsidized its war effort by imposing the costs on the peoples and states where it waged war.

19. Sebottendorf's troops were marching in that direction at 9:00 a.m., so it is reasonable to assume that Clausewitz means 11:00 a.m., given the events of the day.

after Schubirts marched off, the Lodi position consisted of twelve battalions and sixteen squadrons, 12,600 strong.[20]

The distribution of the Austrian forces on the 10th is thus:

12 battalions and 16 squadrons at Lodi;
10 battalions and 14 squadrons at Crema;
2 battalions and 3 squadrons at Pizzighettone;
3 battalions and 5 squadrons at Casalmaggiore;
4 battalions and 2 squadrons at Cassano.
A sum total of 31 battalions and 40 squadrons.

Since the Austrian army comprised 35 battalions and 44 squadrons, there are 4 battalions and 4 squadrons unaccounted for, whose assignment cannot be ascertained from the Austrian account.

Sebottendorf was supposed to hold the line of the Adda for about twenty-four hours only, providing security for at least a day so the troops could recover from their forced march. He entrusted the defense of the bridge over the Adda to three battalions of Croats[21] and deployed fourteen guns with them. Five battalions and the cavalry were in reserve somewhat to the rear.

20. Clausewitz notes: "This figure given in the Austrian account is also strange, since the same account gives the total strength of the Austrian army for May as being 35 battalions and 44 squadrons with just 26,000 men. There is obviously a contradiction here, which is especially remarkable as this account is taken from the Austrian military archives." Figures in the various accounts are all over the place, and we are unable to provide an exact number or force breakdown.

21. The Croats from Austria's military border (*Grenze*) with the Ottoman Empire were used as light infantry in *Grenz* regiments. These played an important role in the Austrian army, given its lack of regular light infantry capable of skirmishing on the battlefield. The new tactics inspired by the French Revolution gave rise to hordes of light infantry skirmishers who operated as individuals or in small groups, taking cover and harassing formed bodies of soldiers. These tactics often befuddled more traditional armies, and it took other armies a long time to adapt to the French style. Hence Clausewitz's earlier comments about the huge changes in warfare. In Austria's case, the change did not come until after the defeats of 1809. It took time because in a rigidly controlled, centrally directed army, the organizational culture did not allow large numbers of men freedom of action on the battlefield, and men out of sight of their officers often chose to desert. Only when armies were made up of citizens, or men with more rights, did it become possible to emulate the French, and only at enormous risk to societal cohesion. See Murray, *Rocky Road to the Great War*, 22–25.

Three battalions were detached to Credo, 3.5 miles[22] below Lodi, where there was also a crossing (probably a ferry or ford).

One battalion and two squadrons remained on the far side of the bridge in Lodi to receive Wukassowitsch.

With these dispositions, who could have believed that the honor of Austrian arms was to suffer a blow the likes of which had never been seen before? Seven thousand men and fourteen cannon, deployed to defend a single bridge 300 paces long, across an unfordable river! Who would not have declared such a position to be impregnable?

It is a crying shame for military history that we know next to nothing about the specific circumstances of this battle or the details of the terrain in this almost unprecedented event. But it is in the terrain and in the precise details of the defensive arrangements that we must seek the key, and then, presumably, the outcome will seem less amazing.[23]

Wukassowitsch and his rear guard appear to have reached the bridge at Lodi and crossed it without mishap, although they were hard pressed.[24] The battalion and the two squadrons that had remained on the right bank also withdrew, without the enemy following so closely as to be able to force his way across right behind them. The Austrian artillery still obliged the French to show due respect. But of course, in this situation, no part of the bridge had yet been destroyed, as it seemed neither necessary nor feasible.

During the action Bonaparte fought against the battalion deployed at the entrance to the town, he had concluded from its presence that the bridge could not have been destroyed. He therefore hurried in person to the bridge's entrance and, under intense enemy canister fire, immediately had two guns from his advance guard brought up and deployed right by the bridge (probably behind some kind of cover) to prevent it from being destroyed.

Formidable batteries were installed on those sections of Lodi's city wall facing the bridge. Now they opened up a ferocious fire on the Austrian batteries,

---

22. Given that a league was between 2 and 4 miles, this could be near modern-day Casaletto, Ceredano, or Credera. However, the exact location is not clear.

23. Boycott-Brown's history of the campaign provides seventeen pages on the battle, but even this does little to provide genuine clarity. Boycott-Brown, *Road to Rivoli,* 309–328.

24. Clausewitz notes: "*Briefe aus Italien,* 172." For the full reference, see chapter 1, note 30.

which, having no cover, suffered severely and were obliged to withdraw their guns some distance to escape from effective canister range.

This state of affairs continued for several hours, until 5:00 p.m. to be precise (according to Bonaparte's *Memoirs*),[25] while the two sides bombarded each other. Now Bonaparte decided to take the bridge by storm. The only support to this assault was to be rendered by General Beaumont by crossing a ford at Mozzanica,[26] half an hour upstream from Lodi, with part of the cavalry and opening fire on the Austrian right wing with his artillery. But this crossing encountered more difficulty than Bonaparte had expected, so General Beaumont was unable to cooperate effectively. However, it may be supposed that news of his attempt sowed some uncertainty among the Austrian troops.

Bonaparte had the 3,500 grenadiers form up in a dense column hidden behind the Lodi city wall, where they were very close to the bridge and also (so Bonaparte claims) closer to the Austrian guns than the Austrian troops themselves were. As soon as he detected the fire of these guns slackening somewhat, he let the column burst forth and hurl itself rapidly at the bridge.

At first the column faltered, but several generals placed themselves at its head, inspiring the troops' enthusiasm, and it advanced on the bridge on the double. But halfway across, another pause seemed to develop as a swarm of skirmishers climbed down from the bridge into the river, for they had noticed that beyond that point the river was very shallow. These troops quickly spread out and helped the column get across.[27]

25. Montholon, *Mémoires pour servir à l'Histoire de France sous Napoléon*, 3:176.

26. This location cannot be identified with any certainty. However, Clausewitz could be referring to the Muzzetta, which is now a nature reserve upstream from Lodi on the Adda River. It appears to have a ford across the river and would have been about the right distance from town.

27. Clausewitz notes: "The account in Jomini's *Campagne du Gl. Bonaparte en Italie pendant les années 4 et 5, par un officier général* is actually Bonaparte's own report to the Directory and reads as follows (p. 125, Pt. 8): 'This redoubtable mass of Grenadiers, with the 2nd Carabinier Battalion at its head, launched itself at the entrance to the bridge; the hail of fire that 20 cannon belched into their ranks caused a moment of hesitation, and as their funneling onto the bridge could have changed this hesitation to disorder, the generals placed themselves at the head of the troops and filled them with renewed enthusiasm. Arriving at the middle of the riverbed, the French soldiers noticed that the further half of the river, far from being as deep as the first half, could be crossed almost without getting a foot wet. Immediately a cloud of skirmishers slipped down around the foot of the bridge, and threw themselves upon the enemy with such

This description taken from Bonaparte's report of the battle is cryptic and not without its inconsistencies. We are not in a position to establish the facts now—more precise reports from the locality will be able to do that in the future[28]—but it seems probable that some features of the terrain made the operation somewhat easier. But in any case, it is beyond question that the Austrian infantry and artillery, being in a sadly reduced state both morally and physically after their long sequence of defeats, and shocked by the unprecedented audacity of the operation, failed to do their duty here.

The grenadier column was followed by Masséna's division, and in turn by Augereau's division that had just arrived; the Austrian battalions were easily driven off, and the enemy guns were taken.

Sebottendorf collected his infantry at Fontana [a small village just east of Lodi], screened by about twenty cavalry squadrons, and retreated in reasonable order to Benzona [a small hamlet on the road to Crema], halfway to Crema, and then overnight to Crema, having lost fifteen cannon and 2,000 men.

The French divisions did not harass his retreat to the degree that should have been expected, partly for lack of cavalry, of which they had very little present, and partly because of the troops' fatigue. However, this last is hard to

---

courage and intelligence as to facilitate the column's advance. With this help, the column redoubled its ardor and confidence, charged onto the bridge, crossed it at a run, collided with and overthrew Sebottendorf's first line, seized his guns and scattered his battalions etc.'" [*Cette redoutable masse de Grenadiers, ayant le 2me Bataillon de Carabiniers en tête, s'élança au debouché du pont; la mitraille que 20 pièces vomissoient dans ses rangs, y causa un moment d'incertitude, et le rétrécissement du defilé pouvant changer cette incertitude en désordre, les généraux se mirent à la tête des troupes et les enlevèrent avec enthousiasme. Parvenus au milieu du lit, les soldats françois apperçoivent que le côté opposé, loin d'offrir autant de profondeur que l'autre, pouvait presque se passer à pied sec. Aussitôt une nuée de tirailleurs se glisse au bas du pont, et avec autant d'intelligence que de courage se jette sur l'ennemi pour faciliter la marche de la colonne. Ainsi favorisée celle-ci redouble d'ardeur et de confiance, se précipite au pas de charge sur le pont, le franchit à la course, aborde et culbute dans un instant la première ligne de Sebottendorf, enleve ses pièces et disperse ses Bataillons etc.*] Here, Clausewitz's criticism of Jomini is reasonable. In Jomini's account of the campaign, referenced by Clausewitz, Jomini has closely paraphrased Napoleon's 11 May 1796 report to the Directory without clearly attributing it. See Napoléon I, *Correspondance de Napoléon Ier*, 1:260–262; Jomini, *Histoire Critique et Militaire des Guerres de la Révolution*, 8:124–126.

28. As mentioned above, the events of this battle are not entirely clear and possibly never will be.

understand, given that it is only 25 miles from Piacenza to Lodi, and most of them had already crossed the Po on 7 and 8 May.

27 OBSERVATIONS: BEAULIEU

With this so-called battle of Lodi, Bonaparte's operations against the Austrian army were finished for the time being, since, as we shall see below, he did not pursue it but turned his attention to other matters.

We wish to offer some observations on the events that had occurred since the armistice.

We have already said in section 21 that it would have been better for the Austrian army to retreat behind the Mincio straightaway. It is quite understandable that this did not happen, for no such order could have been expected to come from Vienna, and it would have been difficult for a mere general in Beaulieu's situation to take responsibility for a voluntary evacuation of the duchy of Milan.[29] But Beaulieu's position behind the Agogna at Valeggio cannot be excused in any way. The main considerations for his deployment had to be covering Milan for as long he could, but also protecting his line of retreat to the Mincio along the highway to Mantua as much as possible. He could not possibly believe that Parma's territory would protect his left flank, but the road to Mantua was almost on his left flank and lay very close to the Po. Thus he had to consider the line of the Po from the confluence of the Ticino onward as his main line of defense; conversely, the stretch of the Po above the Ticino was less important, as it was less threatened by the enemy and posed less danger to him. Since, above the confluence of the Agogna, he seems to have chosen not the Po itself but the Agogna for his main line of defense, he obviously would have done better to choose the Ticino, that is, to deploy his main force at Pavia. Then, if the French had turned north toward Milan, he would have had the shorter road there and could have interposed himself, if that seemed advisable; if the French had turned east to head down the Po, then, with the Mantua highway running parallel to the river at 700–800 paces

---

29. This had been an Austrian possession since the Treaty of Baden of 1714 ratified the previous Treaty of Utrecht of 1713. The duchy's significance lay as much in its geographic position in the west-central Po valley as in its relative wealth. Any decision to evacuate the region would have had enormous political and military consequences in Austria.

wide, and given the French lack of bridging equipment, he might have reasonably hoped to hold the line of the Po.

We say reasonably because we must imagine ourselves exactly in Beaulieu's position. He had 26,000 men and must have estimated the enemy's strength at 40,000, for even if no reinforcements from the Army of the Alps could have reached the Army of Italy yet, the proximity of this army allowed the enemy to cooperate closely with its forces. But if the Austrian side had estimated the combined strength of the French in the Alps and Apennines at 80,000—and not entirely without reason, as we have seen in section 1—then it would not be excessive to believe that Bonaparte might be able to cross the Po with 40,000 men at the beginning of May. But a 40 percent estimated numerical superiority (compared with Beaulieu's 26,000) would indeed put him in a position to make a crossing much easier by means of effective demonstrations.

The French troops were enjoying a succession of victories and good fortune; they were led by an impetuous, talented young general, and he could be expected to act with great boldness and energy. In these circumstances, part of the value of the Po as a line of defense entirely disappeared—the part that constitutes perhaps the greatest effectiveness of river lines in general: namely, the enemy's fear of getting into too dangerous a situation, which, given the caution of normal commanders, usually keeps them in check [in original, *en echec*] and prevents them from taking decisive action.

Thus, if we see Beaulieu behind a river like the Po, we must not assume that just because Catinat and Vendome could have defended it successfully against Eugene, Beaulieu could have done the same against Bonaparte.

Finally, although the Austrian army had not been beaten in any actual major battle, it had indisputably been very demoralized by the succession of reverses it suffered, and in particular, it had lost all confidence in its generals.

Taking all these factors into consideration, we must regard the position Beaulieu adopted to defend the line of the Po as highly questionable, for if things were to go badly for him there, he ran the risk of getting into very serious complications.[30]

---

30. If one looks at a map, one can clearly see the problem. Being too far west placed Beaulieu's force in an exposed position should Napoleon march east toward Piacenza. Given the demoralized state of the Austrian army, it seems reasonable to conclude that a relatively small French force could have prevented an Austrian countermove across the Po. Any aggressive French move east toward Pavia or Piacenza would have placed

If the defense of the Po was already a dangerous undertaking, and if the position at Valeggio was, by its nature, not the best deployment, then the manner in which Beaulieu tried to effect its defense—namely, his series of movements from the 4th onward—was even less suited to producing a successful outcome.

Here we wish to permit ourselves a couple of general observations on the defense of a major river.[31]

The direct defense of a significant water obstacle, such as those constituted by European rivers of the first order in the last third of their course, is not so unfeasible as is often claimed.[32] By direct defense, we mean that the enemy army is prevented from bringing its entire force across by being attacked before it can do so and before it can construct a bridge (or sufficient bridging). Naturally, then, we do not mean a defense of the riverbank itself, which can occur in particular places according to the locality but cannot characterize the whole defensive scheme. A direct defense of a river line, as we have defined it, occurs when the enemy attempts a crossing and always leads to a battle or at least a serious action between a significant part of both armies, a battle in which the river is simply the dominant factor.[33] The whole setup of the defense must be geared toward this battle, and since, as we shall see, this is not an uncommon aim at major rivers, the fear of this worst-case scenario is

the Austrians in grave danger of being cut off from the Quadrilateral fortresses further east and thus from their main line of supplies.

31. The tension between the need to spread out to cover an area and the need to concentrate forces in the face of an enemy is a common problem to this day. Does a commander concentrate his force so that it is not easily defeated, thereby potentially surrendering the river crossing to the enemy that chooses to cross elsewhere, or does he spread out (risking easy defeat) in the hope that any attempt to cross the obstacle can be identified, contained, and then repulsed? Think of the debate between Hitler and Rommel over the defense of the French coast in 1944.

32. Clausewitz argues in *On War* (book 6, chaps. 18–19) that the defense of a river falls into three main types: "1. Direct defense intended to prevent a crossing. 2. A more indirect form, in which the river and its valley serve only as components for a more favorable tactical development. 3. An absolutely direct defense, which consists of holding an unassailable position on the enemy side of the river." He then goes on to explain how these types of defense work. Clausewitz, *On War,* 434.

33. The successful Austrian defense of the Danube at Aspern-Essling on 21–22 May 1809 provides a famous example. The French got across the river, but an effective response and the nature of the terrain meant that they were unable to develop their initial bridgehead sufficiently to exploit the river crossing. After some very heavy fighting, they were forced to withdraw back across the Danube.

the very thing that deters the enemy from attempting a crossing and thus, in most cases, is what makes a river-line defense so effective. If it seems as though military history provides us with very few examples of a successful river-line defense, that is because of the omission of these silent successes.

We say: the conditions a decisive river-defense battle offers to the defender can easily be so advantageous that this type of decision is preferable to any in the open field, provided all the relevant factors are in the necessary proportions. These factors include the size of the defender's army, the length of the river line to be defended, the width of the river, and the means of crossing available. If one can arrive at any point with 20,000 men before the enemy can get more than 10,000 across, then without question the problem is solved.[34]

It seems to us that when trying to get as close as possible to this aim, people usually go about it the wrong way.

Armies position their main forces 13 to 18 miles back from the river, while it is our conviction that they should be as close to it as possible; they dissipate their strength into lots of small detachments, while we believe they must remain concentrated in as large a corps as the result of the calculation allows. Both of these cost time, and here, everything depends on gaining time.

The attacker will always choose his crossing point so that his first advance guard can be transported across without too much difficulty; the defender should therefore not attach too much weight to this moment of the whole act. But, this being the case, we assert that it is quite obvious that, while the attacker's action in crossing takes us by surprise and so initially gains time over us, his advantage is greatest at that first instant; but this advantage diminishes from the point we learn of his crossing until his bridge is completed, so that with each passing moment, we strike him on better terms. It is therefore not at all in the defender's interest to have troops on the spot immediately or even as soon as possible, but rather to have as many there as possible in the very last part of the crisis in which the attacker finds himself. This should dispel any notion of deploying one's troops scattered along the river, since anyone familiar with war knows what collecting together scattered groups means in terms of loss of time and how little can be expected in terms of cooperation between combat forces deployed in different places. If 20,000 men dedicated to the defense of a stretch of river are collected at a single point, then, in the

---

34. Clausewitz's argument and examples here closely match those in *On War*, 434–446.

event of a crossing at, say, 13 miles from their position, one knows that they are guaranteed to arrive there within six to eight hours and that they will enter battle effectively, united, and without any major misunderstandings. Thus, nothing should be detached from the force that is to deliver the decision beyond an observation cordon of cavalry pickets so few in number that they will not be missed at all in the battle.

Deployment of this force very close to the river has these advantages: shorter distances to march, namely, the cathetus [short side of a triangle] rather than the hypotenuse; the roads alongside a river are usually better than those running transverse to it; and the river is much better observed, mainly because the commander in chief is on the spot in person and sees with his own eyes what is happening at the river. In this situation, an advanced cordon of outposts is unnecessary because the river provides security.

To determine what are the largest forces—or, to put it another way, the smallest number of corps—into which the army must be divided, one must ask how much time the attacker needs to complete his bridge and what forces his means of crossing will allow him to bring over during that time.

The time it will take the attacker to build his bridge determines how far apart the corps may be deployed; dividing this into the length of the whole river defense gives the number and strength of the corps, and comparing this corps strength with the quantity of troops the enemy can transport across by other means while the bridge is being built gives the actual result that can be expected from the river defense.

Considering that the time it takes to build a bridge is at least thirty-six hours[35] (and there are very few major rivers where it could be built faster than that), each corps defending the river could look after a stretch of 27 to 36 miles and be deployed that far apart from each other. If each is in the middle of its stretch, they would have to march 13 to 18 miles left or right, which they could cover in eight to ten hours; allowing six to eight hours' loss of time that could be caused by darkness, and the same again for communications, the corps could arrive in twenty-four hours, twelve hours before the bridge

35. The amount of time required for a bridge to be constructed is not easily defined, as each case is different. However, it was one of the most difficult engineering tasks an army could undertake. For a detailed analysis of the crossing of the Danube in 1809 by Napoleon, see Major-General Sir Howard Douglas, *An Essay on the Principles and Construction of Military Bridges, and the Passage of Rivers in Military Operations* (London: Thomas and William Boone, 1832), 184–198.

is completed. If the stretch of river to be defended were some 90 miles long, this would require three corps; so if the army had 50,000 men, after allowing for observation detachments, each corps would be 16,000 strong. But if the means of crossing the river had been partly removed or destroyed in advance, it would certainly be possible only in very few cases to ship across an equivalent number of troops, and these would have to be without their cavalry or artillery. The most likely outcome would be that the defender would encounter 10,000–12,000 enemy infantry, with very few cavalry or artillery and no bridge.

Of course, we have made no allowance here for feint attacks. But in the first place, at major rivers where means of crossing are lacking, feint attacks are intrinsically very difficult and not very effective; and in the second place, in this setup, each corps is responsible for a section of river, so there is less to fear from a feint because, even if one corps commits itself against the feint attack, its neighbor will find the real one.

If, under normal conditions, 50,000 men are able to defend a 90-mile stretch of river, then this is certainly a not unremarkable result of strategy.

If we apply this to General Beaulieu, it follows quite simply that if, from the moment the French army began its move to the right, he had stayed at Pavia with half his army to keep an eye on the Ticino—where there was actually little to worry about—and had sent General Liptay to Porte Morena with not just a detachment but the other half of the army, then on the evening of the 7th, Liptay would have had 12,000 men to do battle with the French who had crossed the river, and Beaulieu himself could have done so with his entire force on the morning of the 9th. At that time, the French still did not have a bridge, nor had they finished ferrying their force across. A desperate attack here could have led to glittering successes that would have turned the whole campaign around.[36]

If this result is better than we wished to concede above in our general observations on Beaulieu's position, this is because Bonaparte really had only 30,000 men, not 40,000. Beaulieu's main mistake was the unprecedented fragmentation of his forces from Buffalora to Casal Maggiore. In doing so, he did what so often happens: he took the defense of the Po and the Ticino to be the aim, when in fact it should have been merely the means of delivering a battle or major action in advantageous circumstances. If the French had really had

---

36. Here again, Clausewitz is indicating the critical dynamic differences between the two sides.

any thought of extending themselves to one of these flanking positions, then for that purpose, Beaulieu would have been that much better off in a central position.

In his *Memoirs*, Bonaparte says that Beaulieu should have deployed at Stradella, somewhat below Pavia, astride the river—that is, constructing two bridges with strongly occupied bridgeheads.[37] Bonaparte is thinking as if he himself were in Beaulieu's situation, retaining all of his own completely superior characteristics. If he were in Beaulieu's position, and if his opponent in these circumstances had wanted to move on Piacenza, Bonaparte would have marched around behind him, as he did in the Brenta valley.[38] Bonaparte says that in this situation, he would not have risked crossing the river below Stradella because he would have feared an attack on his rear. Yet it seems to us that Bonaparte took quite a few other risks during his life. Beaulieu, who could no longer bring himself to face his foe in the open field, must have had justified misgivings about getting himself into such an indirectly contrived defense of the Po, where he could be pinned by Bonaparte and entirely cut off from his line of retreat. Besides, there was very little to be gained by possibly hindering Bonaparte from crossing below Stradella, since crossing above Pavia would now be that much easier, and at the point Beaulieu would have had to commit to a plan to oppose a crossing—which otherwise would not be ready in time—he could not possibly know exactly which crossing place the French commander had his eye on.

The so-called battle of Lodi and Beaulieu's measures on the far side of the Adda seem to us to provide no reason to blame him. The shame of Lodi belongs entirely to his troops and perhaps to General Sebottendorf's particular arrangements. If General Jomini regards the deployment of a battalion and two squadrons on the left bank [Clausewitz means the right bank of the Adda as it flows] as such a defective arrangement, this seems to us to be a curious confusion of two quite different cases. If a general chooses a position on the enemy side for the absolute defense of a point on a river, that can indeed be justified only from a single standpoint: that he wants to create a bridgehead from which his army can advance later. But even in this case it is a dangerous

37. Montholon, *Mémoires pour servir à l'Histoire de France sous Napoléon*, 4:251–252.

38. Later in the same year, in September 1796, Napoleon marched his troops through the Brenta valley in pursuit of the Austrians.

measure, and if time permits, it is certainly better just to construct a couple of strong redoubts that can be occupied by a couple of battalions. In any other case, a deployment on the enemy side is such a stupid measure that it would seem unbelievable anyone would think of doing such a thing, if military history did not provide us with so many examples (e.g., Montereau 1814).[39] But the arrangement at Lodi should not be confused with such a case. It is incomprehensible that anyone who understands war should be disconcerted by it or even consider it an error. If one wants to bring in one's rear guard, one must keep the bridge standing; and if one must keep the bridge standing, there is no objection to leaving some force on the far side to receive the rear guard, since it is a well-known fact that when troops are retreating in difficult positions such as a defile, it is far better to cover their retreat with other troops than for them to do it themselves. The troops posted there for this purpose have no more difficulty crossing the river than the new arrivals do, and if there is a danger that the enemy might press across right behind them, he must be countered in some other way. It has never been done differently anywhere in the world.

28 OBSERVATIONS: BONAPARTE

With regard to the French commander, there are three major concerns that may occupy us.

The first is the crossing point. In section 24 we already said what might have deterred Bonaparte from crossing the Po further down, but back there, we did not wish to digress too far from the actual events, so we return to the subject here.

Anyone who thinks that simply crossing at Cremona would have immedi-

---

39. This is where a sizable allied bridgehead over the Seine was smashed by the French. With Clausewitz's ideas in mind, this should have been defended by a small force manning field fortifications to enhance their combat power. As such, had the French attacked, the small force would have been relatively disposable, and it likely would have inflicted losses of material and time on the French out of proportion to its size. Of course, this relates to Clausewitz's concept of the value of the object one wishes to attain and the need to use only the force required to achieve that end. See Clausewitz, *On War*, The Maximum Exertion of Strength (book 1, chap. 1), 77; Scale of the Military Objective and of the Effort to Be Made (book 8, chap. 4), 585.

ately got him onto the highway to Mantua, that the Austrians thereby would have been entirely cut off from that fortress, and that the place would have been left without the appropriate means of defense and must fall swiftly, in which case the dashing undertaking against the bridge at Lodi would have been unnecessary, will probably not be satisfied with what we said in section 24. We must therefore show that there are some errors in these assumptions.

If Bonaparte had arrived in Cremona before the Austrians, then of course they would have been cut off from the direct route to Mantua. But to cut an opponent off from a fortress of such significant extent as Mantua, one must be able to formally invest it by thoroughly entrenching on each side of it.

The furthest detour via Brescia would have added only a couple of days to the Austrians' march, and a couple of days could not possibly give the French enough time to cross the Po, the Oglio, and the Mincio and effect that investment. Thus, they could not count on truly isolating Mantua. Besides, Bonaparte had probably expected to cross the lower Adda without too much difficulty, and so he thought Piacenza was as good a place as Cremona to get on the road to Mantua.

We have already mentioned that Piacenza was one hard march closer to his army (18 miles). But it lies on the right bank, while Cremona is on the left, and Piacenza also offered additional means of crossing.[40] Furthermore, Piacenza lies on the outside of a bend in the river,[41] which provides [flank] protection to the divisions that have crossed; and [from Piacenza], Cremona could eventually be occupied [by the French], or nearby Pizzighettone could be made into an obstacle [to the Austrians].

It seems to us that all these are sufficient reasons for the French commander's choice, and one would seriously misunderstand the storming of Lodi if one were to consider it as just filling a gap in the list above.

The second question is whether it should have been possible to cross the lower Adda and thereby not only cut off the Austrians' direct route to Mantua but also threaten their road to Brescia.

Bonaparte may have thought beforehand that this would not be too difficult. However, one appreciates the difficulty when one considers that there

---

40. There were islands in the Po River that would have offered an easier means of crossing via either boat or bridge construction, and Clausewitz implies that the enormous quantity of materials required was also available there.

41. As well as being close to the confluence of the Trebbia and Po Rivers.

was a serious lack of means for a rapid crossing at Piacenza; that the one bridging company Bonaparte's army possessed was badly needed there; that apart from the bridge at Pizzighettone, which was not available for the French commander to use, there was none below Lodi; and that the Adda is not the kind of river that can be crossed with a simple trestle bridge or clumsily knocked-together rafts.[42]

Besides, Bonaparte's main aim—or, rather, his greatest desire—was to strike at the Austrians. On the 8th they moved against him in considerable force via Casal, so nothing could have been more natural than to meet them on the road to Lodi and pursue them there when they retreated.

While he did not do this straightaway on the 9th, we must point out that not all his troops were across yet, and the bridge was not yet finished. In this situation, gaining time mattered more to him than forcing a decision.

Finally, the storming of the bridge at Lodi is an operation that, on the one hand, deviates so far from all conventional practice and, on the other, seems to have so little reason that we must ask ourselves whether it was justified. If it had been repulsed with a bloody nose, then it certainly would have been unanimously condemned as an utter blunder. But its very success warns us not to agree so readily; it indicates that there is food for thought here. But it is all the more important not to neglect this point, for here we find, virtually isolated, an element of war and especially of strategy to which we attach the greatest value throughout our thinking: we mean the moral effect of victory, as it exerts its influence on both sides in opposite directions.

Bonaparte is drunk on victory; he finds himself in that state of heightened optimism, courage, and confidence whereby the soul elevates itself above the usual calculations of the mind—he sees his opponent fleeing before him in dismay and confusion—and to him, at this moment, nothing seems impossible! This is not reprehensible arrogance nor rashness nor carelessness; rather, it is a feeling that arises from the nourishment and satisfaction of the spirit that his own actions and deeds have granted him. When a man observes that

---

42. Presumably, this is because it has a higher flow rate than most other nearby rivers, and in the spring it receives a great deal of snowmelt via Lake Como. C. Marchina, G. Bianchini, C. Natali, et al., "The Po River Water from the Alps to the Adriatic Sea (Italy): New Insights from Geochemical and Isotopic (δ18O-δD) Data," *Environmental Science and Pollution Research* 22, 7 (April 2015): 5184–5203, accessed 18 September 2017, http://link.springer.com/article/10.1007%2Fs11356-014-3750-6. See also Douglas, *Essay on the Principles and Construction of Military Bridges*, 260–263.

his method is suitably effective and that his ideas are unexpectedly, objectively true, there arises in him a natural enthusiasm for his work and for his occupation. Just as the writer and the artist are enthused by the success of their own works, so too is the general. And the less this is exposed as self-deception, the stronger and more powerfully this enthusiasm affects him.

This enthusiasm generally elevates courage and emotions above calculation. But one does not conduct a war with intellect alone, and the business of war is not simple arithmetic. War is fought by the whole human being, so he belongs as such in theory and in criticism.[43]

If we think of Bonaparte arriving at the bridge at Lodi in this state, we will no longer be surprised when this man who has had so much success against the Austrians, together with a couple of thousand brave Frenchmen fired up by wine and his words, tries to charge across the bridge, shock the enemy with his peerless audacity, and, under the aegis of that shock, seize laurels such as no other commander and no other army can boast. And if this unprecedented feat of arms succeeds, what does it say to an astonished Europe about this triumphant commander and his army, as well as about his defeated opponent, so devoid of courage or spirit! And what is the price if it fails? The loss of 300–400 men, the critical muttering of a few subordinates, and an embarrassment that will pass in a few days.[44]

Bonaparte's bold endeavor was completely successful, and its consequences were exactly those we have just described. Without question, no feat of arms has excited such amazement across Europe as this crossing of the Adda. It ignited huge enthusiasm in all the friends of France and of its commander. But we must judge its moral effect not by the place it holds in subsequent criticism but by its effects at that moment.

If one now says that there was no strategic reason for storming the bridge at Lodi, that Bonaparte could have had the bridge the next day for free, then one is only thinking of the spatial dimensions of strategy. But is that moral weight not also an object of strategy? He who can doubt this has not yet succeeded in understanding war in its entirety, in its living being.

In his report, Bonaparte deliberately christens this fight for a single bridge,

43. It is worth pointing out the similarity to Clausewitz's trinity. See Clausewitz, *On War* (book 1, chap. 1, pt. 28), 89.

44. It also fits with Clausewitz's principle of continuity; see chapter 2, section 14, of this translation.

this charge by a single column, as the battle of Lodi, adorned with the trophies of twenty guns and several thousand prisoners. In this form it infused all of Europe, here with happiness and rejoicing, there with fear and shame, elsewhere evoking anxiety and caution.

The proof that Bonaparte esteemed the storming of the bridge at Lodi so highly is the fact that after conquering this place, he did not pursue the Austrians but remained near Lodi for four days, because he felt that for the time being, there was nothing more he could achieve against Beaulieu, and he turned his gaze elsewhere.[45]

45. Colin, 96, notes: "Clausewitz highlights perfectly the character of the action at Lodi, its violence, and its deliberate intention of exerting a decisive morale effect on Beaulieu. But he justifies it by a metaphysical explanation whose very strangeness leads us to seek something more positive. If he could have read all the correspondence between Bonaparte and the Directory, he would have found a natural explanation for the problems presented here: he would have seen how possible a crisis with Piedmont still was, how much this preoccupied Bonaparte, and how he wanted to stay in range to swoop down on Turin without having Beaulieu at his heels. This situation obliged him to inflict a serious defeat on the Austrians, to be sure that they would retreat behind the Mincio, and then to return to the province of Milan. On 10 May, Bonaparte beat the Imperials; on the 11th, he believed they were in retreat and he did not move; on the 12th he learned that they were making a pretense of halting near Cremona; he pursues them beyond there, makes them flee behind the Mincio, and this time returns to Milan. Should we suppose that he halted in Milan to rest and reorganize his army, and to use the province's resources? These are clearly important matters but not of an urgent character, which he could conveniently have dealt with a few days sooner or later without inconvenience. The four more days' march it would take to chase Beaulieu out of Italy and invest Mantua were of no great importance if he was only bothered with exploiting Milan; but they were very important if he wanted to stay close to Piedmont."

5. Bonaparte Tightens His Grip

Of the French divisions, Augereau followed the Austrians through Crema, Masséna marched along the left bank of the Adda to Pizzighettone, while Sérurier had to give up his move on Pavia in order to complete the investment of Pizzighettone on the right bank. What becomes of La Harpe's former division is unclear:[1] its troops were probably shared out among Augereau, Masséna, and Sérurier, since from this point on, the Army of Italy comprises these three divisions.

Beaulieu continued his retreat through Pizzighettone and Cremona to the Oglio, which he crossed on the 14th, leaving it held by a rear guard while he himself moved through Mantua behind the Mincio.

Pizzighettone was held by only a couple of hundred men and surrendered as soon as Beaulieu had gone. As for the French, Masséna now took the direct route to Milan, Augereau detoured via Pavia, and Sérurier remained in Cremona to observe the Austrians. Bonaparte saw no point in pursuing the Austrians to the Mincio immediately, since he felt it was too dangerous to cross straightaway. First he wanted to tighten his grip on the province of Milan, and he felt a show of force in Pavia and Milan was advisable, the former being the home of a famous university and having a great influence on popular opinion, the latter being the capital. The correctness of this view expressed by Bonaparte himself may well be doubted. A continuous pursuit of the Austrians to the Mincio and beyond would have given them no chance to pause, and that would have had an important effect on the state of Mantua. While they could not have been prevented from reinforcing its garrison, everything would have been done in haste, and the fourteen days which were granted to this fortress probably made a very big difference to it being supplied with rations and other stores.

By contrast, turning back into the province of Milan was obviously not really necessary. The unrest that arose would perhaps have been much less if these divisions had not been given this chance to plunder from the inhabi-

---

1. La Harpe was killed on 8 May 1796. Napoléon I, *Correspondance de Napoléon Ier*, 1:257–258.

tants, but especially if this halt and this retrograde movement had not in itself encouraged rumors that Austrian reinforcements were approaching.

But of course we must say that here our criticism stands upon Bonaparte's own shoulders. The rapid pursuit we are demanding of him here is something we have only learned to do from Bonaparte himself, and perhaps in his first campaign it was still something new even for him.

Augereau had to take the road via Pavia, where he left a garrison of 300 men in the castle. On the 14th he joined Masséna at Milan, where Bonaparte made his ceremonial entrance on the 15th.

General Colli had put 1,800 men in the citadel; Bonaparte entrusted its siege to General Despinois.

While Bonaparte attended to the most important matters of civil and military administration and concluded a treaty with the Duke of Modena, his troops were in cantonments in the province of Milan for about eight days and enjoyed their first respite since the beginning of the campaign.[2]

On 23 May they mustered again on the Adda,[3] and Bonaparte himself had just arrived in Lodi on the 24th when he received news of the disturbances breaking out in the province of Milan.

The robbery, abuses, looting, and atrocities that were endemic to the French army of the time,[4] the forced levying of huge amounts of money and

2. Colin, 98, notes: "Bonaparte already totally understood the importance of unrelenting pursuit; as early as 1795 he wrote, 'Prompt pursuit after a victory is a sure guarantee of success.' If he did not pursue his beaten opponent all the way to Verona, that was because he had decisive reasons for not crossing the Adda." This ties in with Clausewitz's principle of continuity, discussed in chapter 2, note 6.

3. Colin, 99, notes: "On the 21st Bonaparte learned that the peace treaty with Sardinia had been signed. He set his troops in motion on the 22nd."

4. Clausewitz notes: "On 9 May General Dallemagne, [formerly] of La Harpe's division before Pizzighettone, wrote to Bonaparte: 'So far, General, I have tried in vain to stop the pillaging. The guards I have posted do no good, the disorder is at its height. It is necessary to make some grim examples, but I do not know if I have the power to make such examples. An honest and sensitive man suffers and is dishonored by marching at the head of a corps in which bad characters are so numerous. If I were not in the most advanced position, I would warn you to replace me with a man whose health and talents could bring greater success; but I must forget about myself, since this concerns our work for the glory of my country.'" [*J'ai fait, Général, de vains efforts jusqu'à ce jour pour arrêter le pillage. Les gardes que j'ai établies ne remédient à rien, le désordre est á son comble. Il faudrait des exemples terribles, mais ces exemples, je n'ignore*

provisions, and the revolutionary tendency that threatened all of the established order had engendered a fairly general hatred against them among nobles and peasants alike. Their party was severely weakened or cowed.

The clergy may have been willing in large degree to inflame that hatred into action. The spread of false rumors did the rest, such as of Condé invading from Switzerland or of Beaulieu having been reinforced with 60,000 men or of the English landing at Nice, so that in many places, the alarm bells were rung and the rear of the French army was threatened with a general uprising.

Milan itself manifested some unrest, but first and foremost it was Pavia that broke out in outright rebellion. Several thousand armed peasants entered its walls; the French garrison was forced to surrender the castle and was disarmed.

Bonaparte returned to Milan right away, arriving on the evening of the 24th with one battalion of infantry, 300 cavalry, and a horse artillery battery of six guns. Here, calm was soon restored and reinforced by the usual means of firing squads, floggings, and holding the civic bodies responsible.

Then he headed for Pavia with 1,800 men, dispersing 700–800 armed peasants at Binasco and arriving before the city gates on the 26th. After his ultimatum was rejected, he tried to blast the gates open with cannon. This did not succeed. However, by using canister he was able to drive off the peasants posted on the walls next to the gates, whereupon a column approached the gate and smashed it open with axes. Then the column pressed in and seized the houses nearby. Behind this cover the cavalry likewise moved in, hunted through the streets, and dispersed the armed peasants. Before long the city authorities, the clergy, etc. appeared and offered the city's surrender.

Bonaparte had every tenth man of the garrison shot; court-martialed the commandant, who was sentenced to death as well; plundered the city for several hours; and in some places burned it down.[5]

After this act of great decisiveness and harshness, Bonaparte returned to

---

si j'ai le pouvoir de les donner. L'homme honnête et sensible souffre et se déshonore en marchant à la tête d'un corps, où les mauvais sujets sont si nombreux. Si je n'étoit pas au poste le plus avancé, je vous préviendrais de me faire remplacer par un homme dont la santé et les talents puissent obtenir de plus grand succès; mais je dois m'oublier dès qu'il s'agit de travailler pour la gloire de mon pays.] This was brigade general Claude Dallemagne, whom Napoleon had placed in charge of the advance guard of the army on 8 May 1796. La Harpe's division was to follow the advance guard. See Napoléon I, *Correspondance de Napoléon Ier*, 1:246.

5. Napoleon devotes an entire chapter to the episode: Montholon, *Mémoires pour*

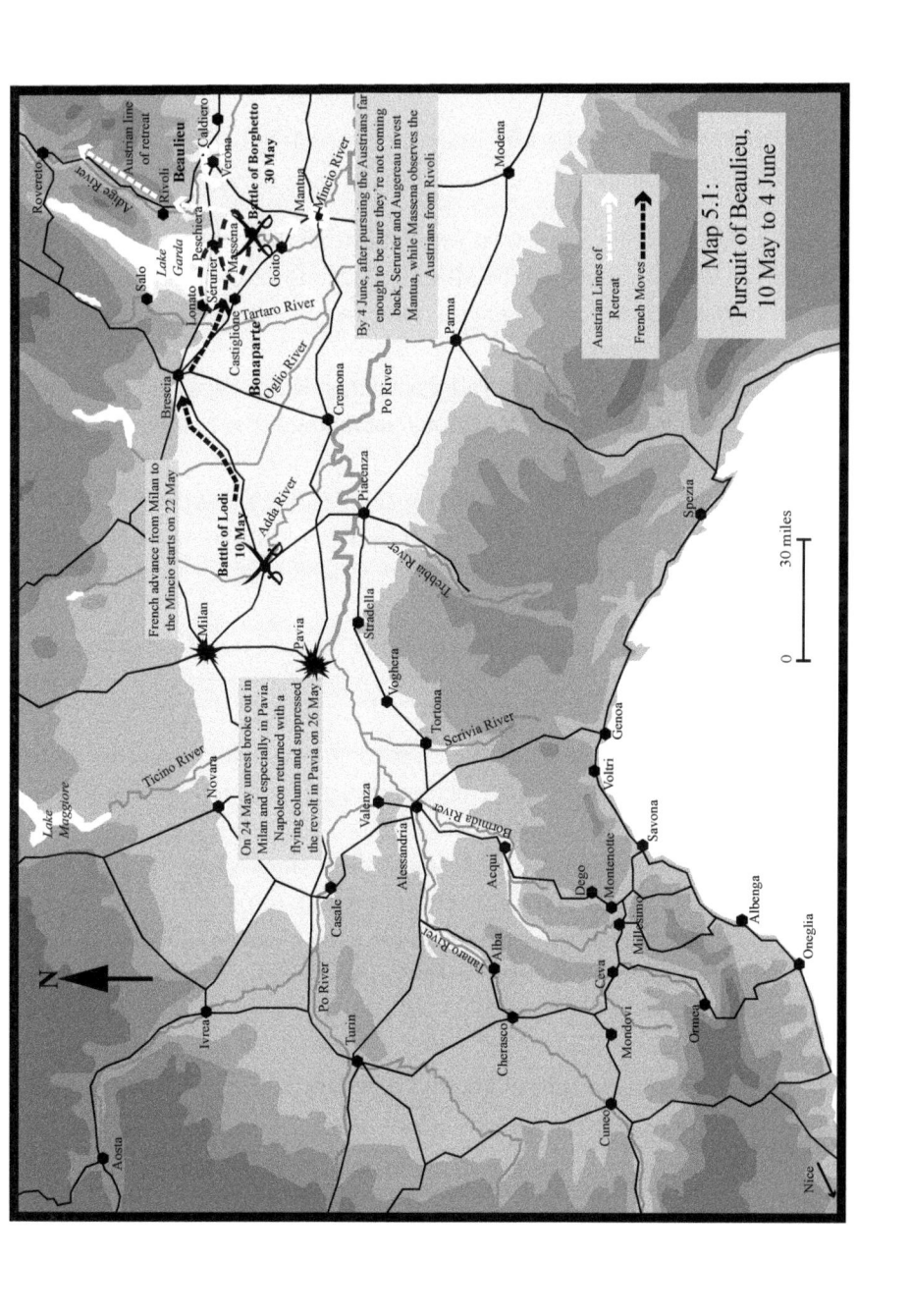

Map 5.1:
Pursuit of Beaulieu,
10 May to 4 June

Austrian Lines of
Retreat

French Moves

By 4 June, after pursuing the Austrians far
enough to be sure they're not coming
back, Serurier and Augereau invest
Mantua, while Massena observes the
Austrians from Rivoli

Austrian line
of retreat

Battle of Borghetto
30 May

French advance from Milan to
the Mincio starts on 22 May

Battle of Lodi
10 May

On 24 May unrest broke out in
Milan and especially in Pavia.
Napoleon returned with a
flying column and suppressed
the revolt in Pavia on 26 May

0   30 miles

N

Lodi and caught up with his army on its march to Brescia, entering the city with it on 28 May.

30 BONAPARTE CROSSES THE MINCIO: BATTLE OF BORGHETTO ON 30 MAY

Beaulieu had continued his retreat without further delay through Rivalta [sul Mincio] to Roverbella behind the Mincio. He reinforced Mantua with twenty of his best battalions, increasing the garrison to 13,000 men. He decided to try to defend the line of the Mincio.

His army had received some reinforcements, which increased it to forty-two battalions and forty-one squadrons, including those holding Mantua, a total of 31,000 men.

A few thousand of these were at the northern end of Lake Garda at Riva [del Garda], and even at the source of the Adige in the Münster valley at Taufers, where General Laudon kept an unnecessary watch on Graubünden [the Swiss canton of Grisons].

At the end of May the Austrian deployment behind the Mincio was essentially as follows:

General Liptay commanded the right wing, occupying Peschiera, which he had seized by surprising the Venetian garrison, and maintained outposts on the Chiese: 4,500 men
Melas[6] at Olioso [Oliosi] was effectively the reserve: 4,500
Sebottendorf at Valeggio constituted the center: 6,000
Colli formed the left wing at Goito with 4,500 men from the Mantua garrison and some of the army cavalry: 5,000
Total: 20,000

This left 8,000–9,000 men in Mantua, of whom 4,000–5,000 were detached toward the lower Chiese and the Po. Sebottendorf and Colli also still had their

servir à l'Histoire de France sous Napoléon, 3:231–252. See also *Correspondance de Napoléon Ier*, 1:341–343.

6. General Michael Melas was 66 at the beginning of the campaign but continued to serve in the Austrian army until well after his defeat by Napoleon at Marengo on 14 June 1800.

outposts on the right bank of the Mincio. Beaulieu's headquarters was at St. Georgio,[7] just below Borghetto on the Mincio.

There were four bridges across the Mincio at Peschiera, Borghetto, Goito, and Rivalta, none of which was destroyed. That at Peschiera was enclosed within the town; that at Rivalta was too close to Mantua for the French to use it. There are no fords across the Mincio, but of course many islands that make bridge-building easier, and also at that time, being the dry season, the river was low. Therefore, there was a place just below Borghetto where it could be waded if necessary, which the Austrians also occupied with two companies from Borghetto.

The situation was that the French had no pontoon bridges, and the only stretch of the Mincio that was threatened, that from Peschiera to Rivalta, is no more than 13 miles long, not counting the river's meandering, which would matter only for a riverbank defense. Additionally, it was the end of May, so the nights were very short. As such, suitable arrangements for the defense of the Mincio certainly still could have yielded a tolerable result. Even if Mantua were considered to need 8,000–9,000 men, initially to observe the lower Chiese and the Po, and later to defend the Mincio below Mantua if the enemy should advance in this area; even so, 20,000 men was still a very considerable combat strength for this short stretch of 13 miles. If we deduct a couple of thousand men for Peschiera and a couple of thousand to observe the river, that still leaves 16,000 with which, if he kept them together, Beaulieu could have reached any point where the French tried to cross within five or six hours.

There was just one factor that very much altered this result and so weakened the defense of the Mincio that it could not be expected to succeed completely, and instead should really be considered just a respectable rearguard action. This factor was the skewed position of the line of retreat. In the event

---

7. It is not clear where this is. There are two places named San Giorgio in the area that might be the location Clausewitz mentions: San Giorgio di Mantova is to the east of the city itself, along with an outwork of the fortress on the left riverbank called Lunetta di San Giorgio, and San Giorgio in Salici is to the east of Peschiera. The former seems more likely, as the location matches Clausewitz's description, but the latter would support Beaulieu's attempts to maintain his lines of communication up the Adige valley. However, the latter is not "just below Borghetto," whereas the former is. Of course, this could also refer to a church or monastery that no longer exists. That being said, Clausewitz could be referring to either town, as both were in locations where fighting occurred over the next several days.

of a further retreat, Beaulieu needed to move not toward Friuli but toward the Tyrol, thus into the valley of the Adige, which is the most direct route there; but the shortest route from the Mincio to the valley of the Adige is the one through Castelnuovo [del Garda]. It was therefore important that General Beaulieu should never let himself be driven away from there. But this is not right behind the position and does not run perpendicular to its front; instead, it lies on its extreme right wing, almost extending it. This put pressure on General Beaulieu to position himself with his main force between Valeggio and Peschiera, which is what he indeed did. Now, if he had really considered the Mincio below Valeggio as merely secondary, and if, in the event of the French army crossing there, he had sought advantage in confronting them and obliging them to adopt a position with their backs to Mantua, then it follows from this method that he must either dispense with posting the 4,000–5,000-man corps from Mantua at Goito or else use it for completely detached activity, in which case it could never be expected to operate at full effect. Given the way Beaulieu composed his forces, he would not have been able to oppose a French crossing with more than 10,000–12,000 men, and if the enemy crossed at or above Valeggio, he could hardly expect the troops posted at Goito to play any part in the decisive battle.

Nonetheless it was probably fair enough that Beaulieu attempted a defense of the Mincio, partly because it very easily could have produced a successful battle, partly because one can never know how much respect the enemy will give to an organized river defense or whether he might not expect it to cause him more difficulty than it actually presents. There was just one condition to add: that Beaulieu should make his plans in such a way that he would not incur heavy losses if his defense failed. This requirement concurred with that of a good defense, namely, to keep his forces concentrated.

At a major river, where one can hope to attack the enemy before he completes his bridge or collects sufficient craft for crossing, one may deploy close to the riverbank, relying on its great body of water; but at a river such as the Mincio, this is no longer the case. The defending army had to choose a position on the heights 3.5 or more miles behind the river, and it could expect to find the enemy's bridge already completed by the time it arrived at the crossing point. No advantage remained except to attack the enemy close to the river before he had time to get properly organized, and with a single point of retreat in his rear. This is the result generally obtained by the defense of smaller rivers. What matters is not so much actually preventing the enemy from crossing in his entirety but exploiting his restricted situation just after he crosses. An essential advantage of the defender lies in having many lines of retreat, while the attacker can only climb back into the egg from which he just hatched. But on this precise point, as we have seen,[8] Beaulieu was not in possession of his natural advantage.[9]

If, in the defense of medium-sized rivers like the Mincio, there is less reason for dividing and spreading out one's forces than at major rivers, one may say that in this case, where the line to defend was so short, there was no reason at all. With the exception of the garrison of Peschiera and an outpost line, the army should have been deployed at a single point, and the most suitable point would have been Oliosi, where Melas was posted with the reserve. Thus, we would describe the measures taken for the defense of the Mincio as suitable if:

1. All outposts were withdrawn from the right bank,
2. All bridges were destroyed,
3. Peschiera was garrisoned by a couple of thousand men,
4. A couple of thousand men formed an outpost line along the Mincio,
5. The area of Goito was occupied by 4,000–5,000 men from the Mantua garrison,
6. And Oliosi was chosen as the position for the 10,000–12,000-man main body.

We will now see the very different measures that Beaulieu took, how successful these were, and how successful he might have been if he had adopted those offered here.

As we have said, at the end of May Bonaparte advanced through Brescia against the Mincio with his three divisions under Masséna, Augereau, and Sérurier and the reserve under Kilmaine.[10] On 29 May Kilmaine was at Castiglione [delle Stiviere], Augereau at Desenzano [del Garda], Masséna at Montechiaro [Montichiari], and Sérurier at Monza.[11]

8. See the previous discussion of river crossings and the defense against them in chapter 4, section 27. Again, see Clausewitz, *On War*, 433–446.

9. Colin, 104, notes: "On the other hand, the fortress of Peschiera was a serious guarantee for his right wing and for his line of retreat."

10. Charles Kilmaine was an Irishman who served as a brigade and division commander in the French army.

11. It is not clear where Clausewitz means. Monza is just north of Milan, so it is

After Bonaparte had threatened Salò with a small detachment as though he were going to send a force through Riva toward the Tyrol, to draw off Austrian forces in that direction (which had little effect), at 2:00 a.m. on 30 May he set his troops in motion against the Mincio. Kilmaine, Sérurier, and Masséna moved against Borghetto; Augereau on Monzambano and Peschiera. The first three were to force a crossing at Borghetto, and Augereau was to try to cross further up, either to actually cut off the line of retreat to Castelnuovo or to threaten to do so.[12]

At this time the Austrian commander, Beaulieu, was at his headquarters in St. Georgio and was very unwell. There seems to have been a great lack of unity, indeed, a kind of confusion reigning in the Austrian army command. According to the Austrian account, it is because of this that, upon the news of the French advance, the Austrians went over from the already far too divided deployment of their combat forces already described to a formal riverbank defense. To that end, on the evening of the 29th Melas's reserve and Sebottendorf's center forces were distributed as follows:

1. At Salione [Salionze]: 2⅔ battalions
2. Facing Monzambano: 3 battalions
3. Oliosi: 1 battalion
4. Casa Borosina: 1 battalion
5. Valeggio: 1 battalion and 10 squadrons providing the outposts
6. Borghetto: 1 battalion
7. Campagnola, below Borghetto: 2 battalions and 7 squadrons
8. Pozzolo: 1 battalion
   Total: 13 battalions and 17 squadrons

These units themselves seem to have been very scattered in turn and to have held the river with detached companies and individual pickets, just as the artillery was spread out along the river as individual guns. The bridges at Borghetto and Goito were prepared for demolition but were not destroyed because the whole outpost line was still on the far side.

---

unlikely Sérurier's division was there at the time. Napoleon's correspondence places Sérurier at Calcinato on 29 May, and this is far more likely. Napoléon I, *Correspondance de Napoléon Ier*, 1:333.

12. Kilmaine was also to coordinate his actions with Augereau. Ibid., 1:336.

In the circumstances, it is no surprise that the key point—namely, the bridge at Borghetto, where the French actually broke through—was held by only one battalion with a single gun. Furthermore, a portion of this battalion was deployed in that part of the town on the far side of the Mincio to support the outposts, and first one, then two companies were sent to the place where the Mincio was wadeable.

At 7:00 a.m. on 30 May the three Austrian squadrons on outpost duty in front of Borghetto, supported by a few more troops of cavalry that had just been sent from the left bank, were violently driven back upon Borghetto by General Kilmaine, who captured a gun from them. The Austrians still had time to jettison the planks from the bridge and thereby prevented the French from pursuing. However, this does not seem to have gone off without some confusion, as part of the cavalry was forced to find its way across through the water at the shallow spot, for whose defense one company was deployed. Naturally, the French followed, and since they could not go over the bridge, Colonel Gardanne plunged into the river at the head of some of his grenadiers, and they crossed it holding their weapons high above their heads, with the water coming up to their armpits. The Austrians had immediately sent a second company there, but these two companies apparently did not offer the strongest resistance. At the bridge itself, the solitary cannon was naturally soon silenced, so it is no surprise that the town of Borghetto was also soon cleared, and the French were not hindered further in repairing the bridge. These Austrian troops withdrew to Monte Bianco and from there to Valeggio, where the French vanguard engaged the retreating Austrians in a serious melee. But the Austrian cavalry bought some breathing space with a few fine charges.

At this time, Bonaparte did not press too hard. Partly, he still had only a few troops across and was busy mending the bridge; partly, he was not entirely unhappy if the Austrian center lingered here because, while it did so, Augereau perhaps gained time to break through upriver and reach the Castelnuovo road first.[13]

---

13. Colin, 107, notes: "On the 30th, Augereau was to move towards Peschiera; to attract the enemy's attention on this flank, he was to advance as far as a small lake 3 km from the town; once there, he was to turn swiftly to the right towards Castellaro, and to cross to the left bank of the Mincio following Kilmaine. This order was carried out punctually. On the 31st, Augereau was charged with going back up from Valeggio to Peschiera and with taking the town. Kilmaine was to pursue the enemy on the Castelnuovo road, and Masséna was to move further east. Kilmaine was advised to cover

While the Austrians posted at Borghetto, Valeggio and Oliosi joined up under the orders of General Count Hohenzollern[14] and presented their vanguard as a rear guard against the French, Melas, acting on Beaulieu's order, pulled in those posted at Salionze and opposite Monzambano and began to retreat to Castelnuovo, sending an order to Count Hohenzollern to follow him.

Already that morning, Liptay had received Beaulieu's order to retreat and was getting ready to do so that afternoon when Augereau advanced against him. Liptay charged with some cavalry against the French vanguard and drove it back, bringing Augereau to a halt and winning enough time to withdraw to Castelnuovo, where he arrived at nightfall at the same time as Count Hohenzollern. They both continued to retreat during the night, following General Melas, and crossed the Adige on a bridge of boats at Bussolengo, heading for Dolce [Dolcè].

It is remarkable that during the attack on Borghetto, General Beaulieu was almost captured by the French in that same St. Georgio[15] where the French commander, likewise unwell, was in similar danger a few hours later.

Bonaparte was with Sérurier's division following his advance guard under Kilmaine on the road to Castelnuovo. When he saw that the Austrians were not going to make a stand anywhere, he turned back toward Masséna's division at St. Georgio, near Borghetto, to take a footbath to dispel a very serious headache.

The Austrian left wing under Sebottendorf and Colli had received no com-

---

Augereau against any counterattack by Beaulieu. Augereau was behind Kilmaine, not in front of him. In short, Bonaparte did not want to cut Beaulieu off from the Tyrol, but to drive him back there. Wishing to move via Innsbruck to meet up with Moreau, he did not want to leave any enemy in Venetia. The sluggish pursuit on the 30th can naturally be explained by the fact that the French had carried out a long night march before the battle, and could not manage to do another 18–21 miles that day. Clausewitz forgets that on the evening of the 29th, Augereau and Masséna were on the Chiese."

14. This is almost certainly Friedrich, Prince of Hohenzollern-Hechingen, then a general in the Austrian army in Italy.

15. Again, it is not clear where this is. Whereas the position on the left bank of the Mincio (San Giorgio di Mantova) made more sense previously, San Giorgio in Salici makes the most sense in this context, given its proximity to the river crossing detailed above. Based on Napoleon's correspondence, both places would have been important. The area to the east of Peschiera was significant because of the links to the Adige valley, and that to the east of Mantua because its control would help isolate Austrian forces in Mantua itself. See Napoléon I, *Correspondance de Napoléon Ier*, 1:336–350.

munications at all throughout the morning. When Sebottendorf observed that the firing was slackening at Borghetto, at midday he took a squadron to reconnoiter toward St. Georgio, where he so surprised Bonaparte that his guards had just enough time to bar the front door while Bonaparte, with one boot on and one bare foot, escaped out the back.[16]

Sebottendorf mustered his three battalions and seven squadrons as quickly as possible, and at first he thought he ought to make another attempt to attack Valeggio, with the intention of coming to Beaulieu's aid. But he was soon convinced there could be no more thought of doing that, and in the evening he began his retreat to Villa Franca [Villafranca], continuing it overnight via Sonna [Sona] to Bussolengo, where he ferried his infantry across the Adige after sending his cavalry to Castelnuovo.

Colli naturally came to understand the situation later than Sebottendorf did. At first, he likewise tried to move on Valeggio with his whole force, but when he realized that Beaulieu had retreated, he sent his infantry back to Mantua and took his cavalry through Villafranca to Castelnuovo, which he reached during the night and joined up with Count Hohenzollern and Liptay there.

The Austrian account gives their losses as four guns and 600 men.

The causes of this poor outcome are too obvious to need explaining again. Defending the bank of a river is generally feasible only under particularly favorable circumstances and in individual places, never along the whole extent of a line of defense, and to do so on the Mincio, which, given its width, can only be considered a river of the third order, is inexcusable. When it leads to a key point being defended by a single battalion with one gun, as Borghetto was here, we can probably say with good reason that the ABC of the conduct of war has been forgotten, since this certainly includes the knowledge that a single cannon, when used against a main enemy column, will be overwhelmed by the sheer weight of superior firepower and counts for nothing. Whether Beaulieu's illness had any significant impact on these arrangements is doubtful, since they were entirely in the spirit of his methods hitherto.

On the other hand, one may feel inclined to blame the French command-

---

16. Clausewitz notes: "After this Bonaparte established the *Compagnie des Guides*, charged with his personal protection, and under the command of Bessières." Napoleon describes this moment in his memoirs: "The danger which Napoleon had endured made him feel the necessity of having an elite guard of men selected for this service, and charged with his safety." Montholon, *Mémoires pour servir à l'Histoire de France sous Napoléon*, 3:202.

er's illness for the fact that he did not take better advantage of this penetration of the Austrian defensive line to cut off their left wing, except, of course, we would then have expected him to say something about this himself in his *Memoirs*.[17] Be that as it may, it cannot be denied that on this day we note the absence of Bonaparte's active exploitation of the advantages he had obtained—that exploitation which, in a certain sense, he may be considered virtually to have invented.

On 3 June Bonaparte had Masséna's division move to Verona, while he moved to Mantua with Sérurier's and Augereau's divisions, seizing the fort of St. George[18] on the 4th and sealing off all five approaches to the fortress.

Masséna followed Beaulieu into the valley of the Adige as far as Rivoli, whereupon the Austrian commander retreated to Caliano [Calliano], between Rovereto and Trient [Trento].

Even now, the Austrians still would not desist from dispersing themselves among myriad positions, which stretched from Graubünden on their right to the valley of the Brenta on their left.

31 LOWER ITALY

For the time being, the destiny of upper Italy had been decided militarily, and now the question for the French was what consideration they should give to lower Italy. They were entirely at peace with Tuscany, since the grand duke had recognized the French Republic. However, the French found it uncomfortable and worrisome that the English [the Royal Navy] were allowed into the harbor of Livorno.

The Republic was not actually at war with Rome, but relations were hostile. This was because the French envoy Basseville [*sic*] had been murdered there in January 1793, and until now, the French had not been able to obtain suitable reparation.[19] On the contrary, the pope's position had taken on a truly hostile

17. Montholon, *Mémoires pour servir à l'Histoire de France sous Napoléon*, 3:198–205.

18. This was the Lunetta di San Giorgio mentioned above.

19. Hugou de Bassville, a French diplomatic envoy to Rome, was murdered by a mob in Rome on 13 January 1793. The French claimed it was on the orders of the pope. As part of the Treaty of Tolentino of 19 February 1797, signed by representatives of Pope Pius VI and Napoleon Bonaparte, the French received financial

character with his repeated protests against everything that had happened in France concerning ecclesiastical affairs.

The Republic was in a state of open war with Naples, because a Neapolitan cavalry corps was serving in Beaulieu's army.

In this situation, and at a time when there was nothing to do in Lombardy that required all the forces available, it was indeed a very natural idea to use part of these forces to establish better relations with the states of lower Italy, whether by forcing their governments to sue for peace or by overthrowing them and making the country a republic. Evidently, it is too often claimed that this was absolutely necessary, whereas we would only go so far as to say it was desirable. For even with these dubious relations with lower Italy, the French army could have continued the war in upper Italy and indeed would have done so if, for instance, at that point the Austrians had appeared with a new army on the Adige. The resources of the governments of Rome and Naples were too weak to be a danger to the French army in upper Italy, and if this army had continued on its triumphant way, neither government would have stirred.

The Directory had discussed the question of lower Italy earlier, and Bonaparte had already received a letter about it at Lodi on 14 May, containing a plan for the future conduct of the war in Italy (albeit, of course, more hinted at than explicit, let alone ordered). This plan consisted of dividing the Franco-Italian combat forces, which were estimated at 40,000 men. One half under Bonaparte's command was to march against lower Italy, and apparently (at least from what Bonaparte says in his *Memoirs*), the intention was to bring the revolution to these regions. Meanwhile, the other half of the army, placed under Kellermann's command, was to besiege Mantua and hold the line of the Adige.

To compensate somewhat for the fact that this would completely abolish any unity of command, new powers would expressly be given to one of the existing institutions of the armies of the Republic: namely, to the government commissars, who exercised a kind of political supervision over the commanding generals they were attached to and could be considered representatives of

---

compensation and artwork—again, another means of paying for war. See Frédéric Masson, *Les Diplomates de la Révolution: Hugou de Bassville a Rome, Bernadotte a Vienne* (Paris: Charavay Fréres Editeurs, 1882), 88–91, accessed 17 August 2017, https:// books.google.com/books?id=2y0xAQAAIAAJ&printsec=frontcover&dq=Fr%C3%A 9d%C3%A9ric+Masson,+Les+Diplomates+de+la+R%C3%A9volution:&hl=en&sa= X&ved=0ahUKEwjeldqdr97VAhWI4iYKHTYPAUYQ6AEIKDAA#v=onepage&q&f= false.

the government in matters requiring an immediate decision. They were now given the authority to require troops from a neighboring army to support them. Thus, the government commissar of the Army of Lower Italy would have been in a position to shunt some of its troops across to the Army of Upper Italy, if his colleague so demanded.

What is notable in the Directory's letter of 7 May is the extremely timid and diffident manner with which it imparts these intentions and decisions to the triumphant general. It betrays the fear that he would find it highly displeasing and insulting and might either resign on the spot or offer open resistance, both of which would be equally dangerous to a weak regime.

Some have found this plan of the French government's completely incomprehensible and believe that it was intended to break the power of a commander who was becoming dangerous to the regime.[20] We believe this assumption is partly improbable, partly pointless.

When the Directory conceived this plan, it had heard only the news of the successful actions in the Apennines and the armistice with the Sardinians. Why should it so quickly become jealous of a commander who had always behaved with moderation and deference? Basically, the Directory wants exactly the same thing Bonaparte himself wants some weeks later: that is, as soon as the Austrians have been driven from the plains of Lombardy, to use the surplus troops to conduct an operation against Livorno, Rome, and Naples to drive out the English and impose peace on Rome and Naples. How far it would lead, how much time it would take, and what other troops might eventually be required could not be foreseen with any certainty by either Bonaparte or the Directory. The Directory wanted to push most of the Army of the Alps across to join the Italian army and then use half of the combined army. Bonaparte thought it could be done with a few divisions in echelon—the difference is not great. But whereas the Directory wanted to establish each army as an independent command, Bonaparte wanted to keep it all, and so he conceived the expedition to lower Italy as a subsidiary operation that must remain subordinate to the command of the Army of Italy.

20. With his success in Italy, Napoleon distinguished himself from the less successful generals fighting in Germany. In turn, Napoleon's success provided him with political capital to use with the Directory in Paris. This, along with his luck, lines up with Clausewitz's concept of the trinity, in that the combination of all three plays a key role in the type and nature of conflict.

Leaving aside his own personal interest, in this matter Bonaparte was absolutely right, since the two theaters of war are so dependent on each other that unity of command is indispensable, and it would be absurd to try to direct them both from Paris. But such absurdities often arise, and in this, the Directory is surpassed by a hundred other governments. The Directory thought that a march on Naples might be necessary; Naples is 360 miles from Mantua. If one overlooks the fact that both armies shared a narrow base between Piedmont and the sea, the distance between them could well lead to the idea of making the two commanders independent of each other.

The fact that the operations against lower Italy were assigned to General Bonaparte may be because the Directory had rejected (in that same letter of 7 May) his plans for an immediate invasion of Germany. Perhaps Carnot also feared that if Bonaparte kept the command in upper Italy, he would not let himself be deterred from a rash advance into the Alps.

As we see from his *Memoirs*, Bonaparte was incensed by the Directory's ingratitude. However, in the reply he wrote on 14 May, he settled for showing a little touchiness and averring the impracticality of a divided command. Upon receiving this letter, the Directory relented with obvious and almost comical embarrassment. In its letter of 28 May it wrote: "You appear, Citizen General, to wish to continue to conduct the rest of the military operations of the current campaign in Italy. The Directory has carefully considered this proposal, and the confidence it has in your talents and your Republican zeal have decided this issue in favour of the affirmative. Général en Chef Kellermann will remain at Chamberry [Chambéry] etc."[21]

32 REFLECTIONS

The question of whether the operation against lower Italy was advisable, and to what degree, is of too much strategic importance and too insufficiently resolved by events for us not to dwell on it. In war, such questions are infinitely

---

21. Clausewitz cites "*Memoirs*. Pt. 3, p 185." [*Vous paraissez desirer, citoyen general, de continuer à conduire toute la suite des operations militaires de la campagne actuelle en Italie. Le Directoire a mûrement réfléchi sur cette proposition et la confiance qu'il a dans vos talens et votre zèle republicain, ont decide cette question en faveur de l'affirmative. Le Général en Chef Kellermann restera à Chamberry etc.*] See Montholon, *Mémoires pour servir à l'Histoire de France sous Napoléon*, 4:417.

more decisive than any positioning of individual corps at times other than when the decision is actually delivered; they are much more far-reaching and comprehensive in their effects, and so it is in them that by far the most important part of strategy is to be found.[22]

When the French Directory decided on the operation against lower Italy, the armies were still on the upper Po; it expressly states in all its letters to Bonaparte (on 7, 15, again on 15, and 28 May) that there can be no question of beginning the operation until Beaulieu has been completely smashed and scattered by unrelenting pursuit. By that, it probably meant until he had been driven into the Tyrolese Alps; that is indeed perfectly sensible, but at that time, how could the Directory have known what reinforcements the Austrians might withdraw from Germany to send to Italy? Might the Sardinians dropping out of the war not have prompted the Austrian government to decide to reinforce its Italian army from the Rhine? Then these reinforcements would have arrived, conveniently, at the end of June, at the very time half the French army could have been 225, 270, or 360 miles away from the Po. The other half would not have been in a position to resist on the Mincio, as the events of August had shown [given the fresh Austrian army of 25,000 men that was sent into the Po valley]. Or did the French Directory think that as soon as it got news that reinforcements were on the way, it would call its army back from lower Italy as fast as possible? Politically, that would have made matters far worse, and besides, the army probably would have arrived too late. Even though Wurmser arrived quite late, an army that had advanced as far as Naples never would have been able to return in time. It therefore seems to us that there never should have been any consideration of an operation against Naples, and that in Paris at the start of May, it was impossible to know whether one would be in a position to act against Livorno and Rome.

There is therefore great uncertainty in the Directory's plans, which degenerates into confusion when both of the last two letters cited refer, on the one hand, to General Kellermann invading the Tyrol and threatening Germany and then state, on the other hand, that the Austrians are probably

22. These ideas tie in with his thoughts on what is war and how military objectives should be decided. See Clausewitz, *On War*, book 1, chap. 1, book 8, chaps. 3–6. For a useful explanation of some of the connections, see Antulio J. Echevarria II, "War, Politics, and RMA: The Legacy of Clausewitz." *Joint Forces Quarterly* 9 (Winter 1995–1996): 76–80.

right now (the end of May) transferring reinforcements from Germany to Italy, so the Directory will seize the moment to terminate the current truce on the Rhine; yet they observe that it will be necessary to wait until the harvest because the supply depots are empty! What use was such a mishmash of plans and ideas to the commander? In the higher-level direction of military affairs, such seesawing is disastrous. This direction should do no more than guide the commander's operations in line with the major political alignments the government has adopted, and it can and should do so with great clarity and precision.

When Bonaparte steered part of his force toward Tuscany and the Roman provinces after crossing the Mincio,[23] he had a much better overview of his situation. Beaulieu had been driven into the Alps; Bonaparte knew that 30,000 men from the Austrian army on the Rhine were supposed to join him, but they had not yet set off, and he could calculate they would not reach Beaulieu for six weeks.[24] Preparations needed to be made for the siege of Mantua, so he could use those six weeks to advance one division of his army into the Roman Legations and send another (Vaubois, who was joining him from the Army of the Alps) to Livorno. These two measures would probably be sufficient for their purposes concerning Livorno and for establishing peace with Rome and would have nothing like the consequences of a march on Rome itself, let alone one on Naples. These operations would take the French combat forces no more than 90 miles from Mantua.

If we see both the Directory's very vague original plan and Bonaparte's own plan as limiting themselves to an entirely subordinate operation, properly adapted to actual conditions, we can raise no objection to them; rather, we must praise their prudent economy of force. But if a plan to disappear off into the blue against lower Italy had been adopted on the grounds that it would protect the flanks and rear, then we could not accept it because the

23. The Roman provinces or Roman Legations refer to the northern regions of the Papal States.

24. General Dagobert Wurmser (another Austrian general in his 70s) was slated to replace Beaulieu, but this would not be clear to Napoleon until later in the summer. The point is that when the Directory sends its messages at the end of May, it does not know what reinforcements the Austrians will send, but by the time Napoleon is across the Mincio, he does know and can calculate that he has six weeks to act before the enemy reinforcements arrive.

flanks and rear were not threatened in any way, and because this flank protection would have abandoned the front to certain defeat.[25]

25. Colin, 117, notes: "The essential difference between the Directory's project and Bonaparte's is not in their military dispositions but in their aim: the Directory wanted a total reorganization of the Italian peninsula, which would have completely absorbed and detained the forces committed to it. Bonaparte simply goes to occupy the Romagna, which is indispensable for the security of his operations because it is adjacent to Mantua and divides Austria from the Pope, and secondly, he goes to levy contributions to sustain the war and to prepare his offensive against the Tyrol, which he has finally persuaded the Directory to agree to. The troops charged with this expedition can be recalled at a moment's notice, which would not have been the case if they had been charged with creating a revolution in Rome." Napoleon's idea would bring about the defeat of Austria, which would allow France to dominate the Italian peninsula. Simply subjugating Italy would not prevent future Austrian interference. As such, Napoleon's vision was more prescient than the Directory's.

6. The First Campaign for Mantua

33 EXECUTION

Bonaparte reinforced Masséna's division to some 12,000 men, with which he was to remain in the valley of the Adige to observe Beaulieu. Sérurier and his 10,000 men were to continue the blockade of Mantua on both sides of the Mincio, and Augereau with as many again started his march on Bologna, crossing the Po on 14 June at Borgoforte.

On 5 June, before Bonaparte had even begun this move, the Duke of Belmondo visited him in Brescia to propose a truce in the name of the king of Naples. From this it is clear how the impact of the preceding victories had reverberated in lower Italy, how these states could be completely prevailed upon in upper Italy, and how little fear there was of them attacking the French rear. Bonaparte granted this truce with alacrity, since it stipulated that the Neapolitan cavalry serving with Beaulieu's army were to be quartered around Brescia, so they would be left in French hands as a kind of bargaining chip [Clausewitz says "a whip"]. Now there was all the more reason to expect the operation against the Roman Legations to be a complete success.

Bonaparte took himself to Milan to oversee the commencement of the saps[1] before the citadel,[2] then went to Tortona on the 17th. Meanwhile, a flying column of 1,200 men under Colonel Lannes[3] moved to Arquata [Scrivia], where serious disturbances had broken out in the imperial fiefdoms, interrupting the French line of communications and even disarming some French detachments. This unrest was brought under control by means of fire, sword, and floggings, and any repeat episode was deterred by a stern dispatch to the

---

1. Trenches designed to approach a fortified enemy position. The citadel was on the site of modern-day Cittadella, across the river to the north, guarding the main northern entrance to the city.

2. This concerned Napoleon because of the drain on his forces by the siege of the Milan garrison. See Napoléon I, *Correspondance de Napoléon Ier*, 1:373–374.

3. This is Jean Lannes, who went on to become one of France's best marshals. He was mortally wounded at the battle of Aspern-Essling on 22 May 1809.

Senate of Genoa. Bonaparte then went via Modena to Bologna, which Augereau's division had entered on the 19th.

On the 23rd a papal plenipotentiary arrived to conclude an armistice. According to its terms, a peace treaty was to be negotiated in Paris. The French would remain in possession of Bologna, Ferrara, and Ancona until the treaty was signed, and the pope was to give a contribution of 21 million francs, deliver horses and other military supplies, and hand over 100 works of art.[4]

Bonaparte left Bologna on the 26th and joined Vaubois's division at Pistoia, which took Livorno on the 29th.

After seizing the English merchandise in Livorno and thereby earning 12 million for the Directory, General Vaubois stayed behind with a garrison of 2,000 men; the rest of his troops went back over the Apennines and the Po to rejoin the army on the Adige. Augereau's division did likewise, after sending seventy cannon taken in Urbino and Ferrara to the artillery park at Borgoforte for the siege of Mantua.

Apart from just one battalion in the citadel at Ferrara, Augereau left no troops on the right bank of the Po because, in all the big cities, the mood was so favorable toward the French that the national guards they established were sufficient to secure the occupation.

Augereau's division rejoined the army at the end of June.

Milan's citadel fell on 27 June.

34 BEGINNING OF THE SIEGE OF MANTUA

In Mantua the Austrians had a garrison of 13,000 men, 316 guns, and four months' supplies. In General Canto d'Yrles, an officer of great distinction, the garrison had a capable commandant. Being so well armed and so difficult to approach, the fortress could be expected to resist for a long time. However, the garrison suffered from an unusually high sickness rate, with Bonaparte alleging that the number of sick was as high as 4,000.[5]

4. In his correspondence, Napoleon details a number of instances in which cash and matériel were extracted from defeated or threatened opponents. See Napoléon I, *Correspondance de Napoléon Ier*, 1:398–450.

5. Given that the large lakes surrounding Mantua were a breeding ground for malarial mosquitoes, this is possible, especially as these lakes had been filled with water from the Mincio River beginning on 14 May. Phillip Cuccia's book on the sieges of

For the whole of June, Sérurier had invested Mantua with his division alone. Now that Augereau had arrived, the besiegers were reinforced and pushed forward the siege works more vigorously. Bonaparte knew that Wurmser had arrived in the Tyrol and that the storm would soon break from the mountains of this province. He was therefore uncertain whether to commence the siege before this campaign was concluded. General Chasseloup assured him that he would take the fortress within fourteen days, and this decided him. Still, the parallels could not be begun before 18 July. This was done at 300 paces' distance, and in a short time, the siege works made such significant progress that on 29 July, as Wurmser advanced to relieve it, the fall of the fortress already seemed nigh.

The French army that had crossed the Mincio 27,000 strong had gradually been reinforced, and with the return of the troops from the Apennines, it now numbered 44,000. Of these, 15,000–16,000 were between Verona and Rivoli under Masséna, whose headquarters was in Bussolengo, occupying the key points in this stretch of the valley of the Adige. They constituted the center of the army of observation. Augereau had 5,000–6,000 men at Legnago watching the Adige above and below that place, forming the right wing.[6]

Sauret[7] was on the western shore of Lake Garda with 4,000–5,000 men at Salò and in the valley of the Chiese, forming the left wing.

Despinois had some 5,000 men partly in reserve at Peschiera, partly observing the Adige below Verona at Zevio.

The reserve cavalry under Kilmaine, some 1,500–1,600 horses, was between Legnago and Verona at Valeze [Vallese].[8]

Thus, the whole army of observation comprised 33,000–34,000 men deployed in such a way that within two days they could concentrate either between the Adige and the Mincio or between the Mincio and the Chiese.

Sérurier's 10,000–11,000 men were the besieging force.

Mantua tells us that a thousand members of the garrison were sick by the end of May 1796. Phillip Cuccia, *Napoleon in Italy: The Sieges of Mantua 1796–1799* (Norman: University of Oklahoma Press, 2014), 17.

6. On 22 July Napoleon wrote to the Directory that he had more than 5,000 sick and reported that the "heat is excessive." Napoléon I, *Correspondance de Napoléon Ier*, 1:491–493.

7. Pierre François Sauret was a 52-year-old French officer who had risen from the rank of private soldier to general officer.

8. Napoleon gave Kilmaine permission to move to a less unhealthy location if he needed to. Later he ordered him to Castelnuovo. Napoléon I, *Correspondance de Napoléon Ier*, 1:469–501 (letters 745, 752, 757, 798).

35 WURMSER ADVANCES TO RELIEVE MANTUA

In June General Beaulieu relinquished command of the Austrian army, handing it over ad interim to General Melas, and he left at the end of the month.

As is well known, Jourdan had terminated the armistice on the Rhine at the end of May and advanced to the river Lahn, where he was repulsed by Archduke Charles and was obliged to withdraw behind the Rhine again.[9] Three weeks later, on 23 June, Moreau crossed the upper Rhine at Strasbourg with the Armies of the Rhine and of the Moselle.

While Archduke Charles was engaged with Jourdan, and before the truce on the upper Rhine had been broken, the Austrian government assigned General Wurmser to march to Italy with reinforcements and take over command there, handing over command on the upper Rhine to Archduke Charles.

Consequently, in mid-June Wurmser set off toward the Tyrol with 25,000 men from the Army of the Upper Rhine.[10] In addition, considerable reinforcements were sent from the interior, so the total force available for Italy reached 60,000, of which, however, 10,000 were left in the interior (probably in the Tyrol and Carinthia). Wurmser arrived in Trient [Trento] in mid-July, four weeks later. Since the distance to Trient from Offenburg in the Black Forest is about 270 miles, it was not unusual to take this long, and besides, great haste mattered less for success than otherwise being well prepared.

Wurmser decided to follow the plan of attack prepared by his chief of staff, Colonel Weirotter, which was to debouch from the mountains in two columns on either side of Lake Garda. The main column, 32,000 strong and under Wurmser's personal command, was to advance down the Adige valley, while the supporting column of 18,000 under Quosdanovich[11] moved along the western shore of Lake Garda via Riva and Salò.

The reasons for this division, which we will examine more closely in the next section, were indisputable:

9. The campaign in Germany began in June and saw two French armies under Generals Jean Baptiste Jourdan and Jean Victor Moreau penetrate deep into southern Germany before being repulsed by the end of October 1796.

10. Boycott-Brown places Wurmser as being in the Tyrol on 30 June. Boycott-Brown, *Road to Rivoli*, 372.

11. Peter Quosdanovich was in his mid-50s and had already had a long career in the Austrian army.

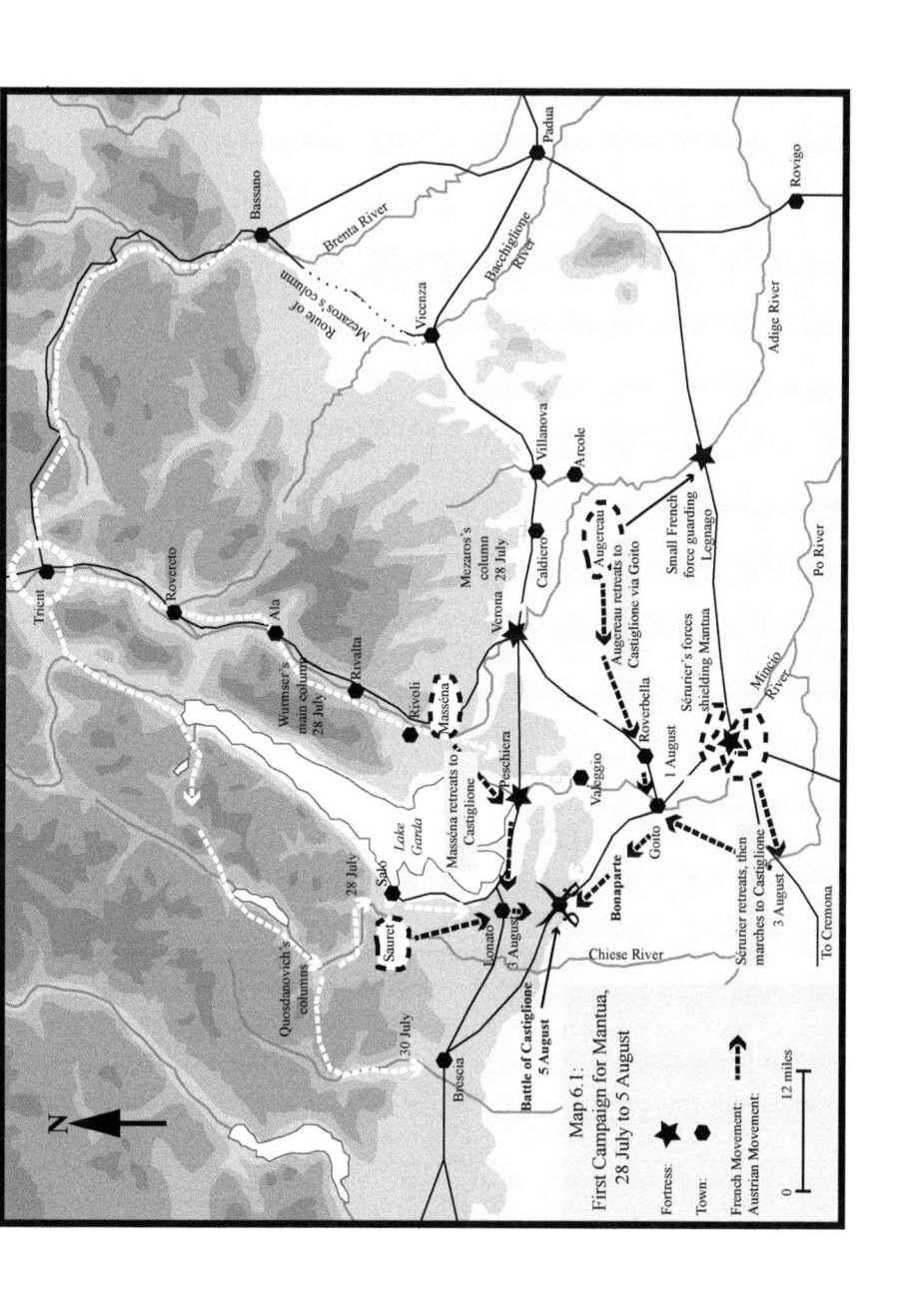

N

Map 6.1:
First Campaign for Mantua,
28 July to 5 August

Fortress: ★
Town: ⬡

French Movement: ◄╍╍╍
Austrian Movement:

0   12 miles

Battle of Castiglione
5 August

Bonaparte

Chiese River

Sérurier retreats, then
marches to Castiglione
3 August

To Cremona

Mincio River

Po River

Adige River

Rovigo

Small French
force guarding
Legnago

Sérurier's forces
shielding Mantua

1 August

Roverbella

Augereau retreats to
Castiglione via Goito

Augereau

Goito

Valeggio

Arcole

Caldiero

Villanova

Verona 28 July

Mezaros's
column

Bacchiglione River

Vicenza

Route of
Mezaros's column

Brenta River

Bassano

Padua

Masséna retreats to
Castiglione

Peschiera

Masséna

Rivoli

Rivalta

Ala

Wurmser's
main column
28 July

Rovereto

Trient

Lake
Garda

Salò

28 July

Sauret

Lonato
3 August

Quosdanovich's
columns

30 July

Brescia

1. To avoid restricting such a considerable force to just one road, and thereby to establish a broader base;[12]
2. To induce the French to divide their forces as well;
3. To threaten their rear and thereby to relieve Mantua simply by maneuver;
4. In the event this did not prove effective, to make the expected victory in battle more decisive.

The execution of this plan led to a series of eight major actions lasting from 29 July to 5 August, which are usually collectively called the battle of Castiglione. We will present them in chronological order.

36 THE ACTIONS AT RIVOLI AND SALÒ ON 29 JULY

Masséna and his 15,000 men had occupied the valley of the Adige from Verona to Rivoli. He had two main positions, one at Verona and that at Rivoli. This was a very strong position where the Adige valley widens on a plateau protected by an isolated mountain ridge, encompassing the minor road running down the valley on the right bank of the Adige. The main road was on the left bank, and 4.5 miles beyond the position at Rivoli it ran into the Chiuse, a narrow gorge barred by a small fort [the Forte di Chiusa, south of Ceraino]. But of course, there were some back roads that were perfectly usable by infantry at least. Three or four ran over Monte Baldo, which is the major mountain ridge between the Adige and Lake Garda, cradling the Rivoli plateau. But several more ran over the ridges that branched out from Monte Molare on the left bank of the Adige, straight to Verona.[13]

These actually quite numerous approaches, some of which had to be held, but others of which could be merely observed; plus the extent of the Rivoli plateau, whose front was 10 to 15 miles across; as well as the height that overlooks the fort in the Chiuse gorge make a defense of this mountain valley against a considerably more numerous enemy basically unfeasible, since the defending force is always in danger of losing its line of retreat if it holds for too long.

12. The same narrow mountain roads also caused problems for the Austrian advance in the Adige valley in January 1797.

13. These roads and the security of the position would play a key role in the battle of Rivoli, 14–15 January 1797. But as Clausewitz points out, the position itself does not fully control movement along the valley.

Although Bonaparte was relying on stout resistance in the Adige valley to buy him enough time to use the rest of his troops the way he wanted, an absolute defense of the valley was not his intention, or at least not an important element of his plan. Augereau was at Legnago, charged with observing the road from Brenta; Sauret was at Salò, watching the road from Riva down the western shore of Lake Garda; and Masséna was observing and covering the highway through Rivoli. Bonaparte's main aim was for these corps to resist just long enough for him to concentrate his forces at a suitable point, where giving battle to the enemy would be most advantageous. Naturally, the Rivoli road was the most important, so Masséna's force was the strongest; furthermore, his position there was so strong that it indeed offered the opportunity of giving battle in favorable conditions, if he could be supported in time.

Masséna's headquarters was in Bussolengo. Nothing is known of the specific distribution of his troops, other than that the Rivoli position's outposts were at Brentino on the so-called Corona, where several paths leading to the Rivoli plateau scale the foot of Monte Baldo, which is known as Monte Magnone. The defense of this point was to be the first line of resistance. The Rivoli plateau was fortified.

After sending another small detachment from his main army into the Brenta valley to distract the enemy's attention, Wurmser advanced down the Adige valley in two main columns and several small supporting ones.

Davidowitsch with the left wing was to move along the highway on the left bank of the Adige to Dolce, where he was to construct a bridge so as to attack the right of the Rivoli position. He was to detach General Mezaros to head straight for Verona across the Molare mountains, and General Mitrowski to move from Dolce upon the Chiuse.

The second main column, under Wurmser's personal command, moved over Monte Magnone directly against the front of Rivoli, with a flanking column under Melas on its right, which was to move via Lumini on Monte Baldo proper and penetrate between the Rivoli position and Lake Garda.

Thus, Wurmser's main army was dispersed in five columns on a 13- to 18-mile front. If it had had to contend here with the French main force, that deployment alone would have been enough to cause the Austrians to be beaten. But since Wurmser had about 30,000 men and was facing only Masséna's division of perhaps 8,000–10,000, we can probably say that the two main columns in the center would have fallen on the French with a two-to-one advantage [and beaten them] if the latter had put up stubborn resistance in their main position.

But when his outposts were attacked at 3:00 a.m. on 29 July, Masséna resisted only as long as was necessary to bring in the outposts, then retreated—apparently not without significant losses in dead, wounded, prisoners, and guns—to Piovetano [Piovezzano] between Rivoli and Castelnuovo, where he arrived shortly before evening.

While the main army was thus engaged on the 29th, Quosdanovich likewise advanced to Salò. In a fairly lively action, General Sauret was defeated, and General Guieu with an isolated battalion was forced to seek refuge in a large villa outside Salò. Quosdanovich advanced to Gavardo and sent General Klenau to Brescia, where he surprised the garrison and captured four companies, one squadron, and several generals.

Sauret retreated to Desenzano.

37 BONAPARTE TURNS ON QUOSDANOVICH

Bonaparte's headquarters was at Castelnuovo. There is some uncertainty about the decisions and movements of the 29th.[14] Kilmaine's and Despinois's divisions are supposed to have concentrated at Castelnuovo, and Augereau to have been ordered initially to march up the Adige against the enemy's left flank. There is no sign of this order having been carried out, so it must have been amended almost straightaway, but if indeed it was issued, it would prove that Bonaparte initially thought he could make a stand up in the mountains. Also, regarding the concentration of Kilmaine and Despinois, it is odd that on the next day they are at Villafranca, whereas it would have been more natural to let them wait for Masséna in Castelnuovo, if they really were already there on the 29th.

What is certain is that—after learning from Masséna's detailed reports that his division had been fairly roughly handled on the 29th, discovering in what strength Wurmser was advancing (probably with some exaggeration),

14. Napoleon certainly issued a flurry of orders on 29 July 1796. On that day his correspondence shows ten letters going to his commanders, whereas on a typical day, there would be two to four letters. On 20 July he had issued twelve letters, but these were largely correspondence with the Directory in Paris or other governmental business. Napoléon I, *Correspondance de Napoléon Ier*, 1:481–507.

and receiving word of an almost equally strong column advancing via Salò and Gavardo that had beaten General Sauret and whose cavalry were already roaming along the Milan road—Bonaparte realized the need for a concerted reaction.

If we were just to go by the course of events, we would say: On the 30th Bonaparte decided not only to raise the siege of Mantua but also not even to spend the time to recover his siege train; and instead, to abandon 120 guns (albeit ones he had taken from foreign arsenals), concentrate his army, and lead it against one of the enemy contingents separated by Lake Garda.[15] He chose Quosdanovich's,[16] first because this was the weaker column, and second because it was advancing into the rear of the French deployment, so in the event his attack went badly, at least his retreat would not be endangered.[17]

15. It is worth noting that Clausewitz discusses this moment in book 2, chap. 5 of *On War*, 161–162.

16. Napoleon explained his logic to the Directory in a letter of 6 August 1796. Boycott-Brown quotes this letter in part (*Road to Rivoli*, 384) but does not include the section before or after the portion he quotes. This omission is problematic, as this is where Napoleon lays out his logic for doing something so risky and on such a grand scale. It is also worth pointing out that despite the scale and the risk, he did much the same against Piedmont and Austria at the opening of the campaign in the spring. As such, it is worth quoting more fully: "The division of General Sauret, which should have covered Brescia, was retreating on Desenzano. In this difficult circumstance, threatened by a more numerous enemy army emboldened by their advantages, I felt that it was necessary to adopt a comprehensive plan. The enemy descending from the Tyrol via Brescia and the Adige [valley], put me in the middle [of the two approaching enemy columns]; if my army was too weak to face the two columns of the enemy [should they be combined], it could beat each of them separately, and by my position I was between them. It was therefore possible for me, with rapid marching, to envelop the enemy division at Brescia, to capture it or to defeat it completely, and then to return to the Mincio to attack Wurmser, and oblige him to retreat to the Tyrol. But in order to carry out this project, it was necessary, within twenty-four hours, to raise the siege of Mantua, which was about to be taken, and abandon the forty pieces of cannon which were in battery, for there was no means to delay even for six hours; it was [therefore] necessary for the execution of this project, to regain the Mincio immediately, and not give time to the two enemy columns to come nearer. Fortune smiled on us, and the fight of Desenzano, the two battles of Salo, the battle of Lonato, and that of Castiglione, were the result." Napoléon I, *Correspondance de Napoléon Ier*, 1:520–521 (letter 842).

17. Colin, 128, notes: "On the 29th Bonaparte was at Brescia; it was there that he first learned of Wurmser's arrival at Rivoli and ordered Masséna, Despinois and Kil-

Against this simple depiction, there is the fact that later, because of the constant dissension between Bonaparte and Augereau, the latter was moved to state that, in a council of war called in Roverbello on 30 July 1796, it was he who had been foremost in urging an attack on the enemy, whereas Bonaparte at first was completely despondent and thought only of retreating behind the Po.

Bonaparte's supporters dismiss this as a false portrayal; they do not deny there was a kind of council of war in Roverbello on the evening of the 30th, but they claim Bonaparte just wanted to canvass the views of his generals.

In fact, it is highly unlikely that Bonaparte, who never lost his head easily, would have lost it over an event whose development he had anticipated for several weeks and for which he was entirely prepared.[18] Besides, as a commander in chief who had just recently taken over command at the age of 27 and emerged from obscurity only a year earlier, he did not have the kind of relationship with his division commanders he would later have as emperor, and it is quite understandable that he should feel the need to be reasonably united with them at such a critical moment. Indeed, something similar had taken place at the Cursaglia. If this makes Bonaparte's decision seem less swift and clear than people like to think, still we must not let it mislead us into giving credence to a smear on his conduct. War is generally not as theatrical as people often imagine.

On 30 July we find the French combat forces assembled as follows: Masséna at Castelnuovo. Augereau and one of Sérurier's brigades at Roverbello. Despinois and Kilmaine at Villafranca. Sérurier and his two other brigades are occupied with lifting the siege and stand ready to retreat to Borgoforte and Marcaria, to cover the Cremona road. On the 30th Sauret is at Desenzano.

---

maine to concentrate at Castelnuovo, with Augereau following on behind them at Villafranca. After subsequently learning of the actions at Salo and Gavardo, he issues a counter-order and calls Despinois to Desenzano to support Sauret. On the 30th he moves to Desenzano and orders Sauret and Despinois to retake Salo the next day, then to continue towards Castelnuovo. Not being strong enough to give battle to Wurmser with just Masséna's and Augereau's divisions, he moves closer to Mantua to use Sérurier's division. He is already planning to keep the two enemy armies apart, since he constantly keeps his left resting on Lake Garda at Peschiera. His center is at Roverbella; his right at Castellaro." Colin is largely echoing Napoleon's own correspondence.

18. Despite its volume, the correspondence referenced in notes 14 and 16 does not indicate someone who was panicking, even if the reader allows for some revision after the fact.

The Austrians under Quosdanovich advance to Ponte di Marco and Montechiaro on the Chiese, while his left wing in Salò is busy attacking Guieu, who, as stated above, had holed up in a big villa with an isolated battalion on the 29th.

What the Austrian main army does on this day is not recorded. It is certainly advancing on Mantua, but since it does not get there until 1 August, and it was only two days' march away, its activity for these three days is not thoroughly proved.

The French Crossing of the Mincio on the Night of 30–31 July

On the night of 30–31 July, Masséna's division crosses the Mincio at Peschiera, Augereau's at Borghetto. Masséna leaves General Pigeon on the Mincio with a few thousand men; Augereau leaves General La Valette.[19]

The Second Battle of Salò on 31 July

Masséna marches on Lonato, Augereau on Montechiaro. Bonaparte hastens to Desenzano. He orders General Sauret to return to the Salò position and rescue General Guieu, who, despite running out of supplies, held off repeated Austrian attacks on the 29th and 30th with great fortitude. Sauret marches off; falls upon the left flank of the Austrians, who are not expecting an attack; defeats them; rescues Guieu; and then, on 1 August, returns to the position between Salò and Desenzano.[20]

19. Colin, 129, notes: "Masséna's division reaches the Mincio alone, on the night of 30–31 July. It is then that Bonaparte learns of the arrival of an enemy division at Brescia, seriously threatening his line of retreat, and which it is urgent to defeat first; it is during the day on the 31st that Kilmaine and Augereau are recalled from Roverbella and Castellaro towards Montechiaro, and that Sérurier receives the order to raise the siege and destroy the siege train. They march on the 31st and through the night of 31 July and 1 August, and arrive exhausted at Brescia and Marcaria during the day on the 1st. General La Valette belonged to Masséna's division."

20. Colin, 130, notes: "On 31 July, Sauret and Despinois move from Desenzano to Salò to rescue Guieu. They have 7,000 to 8,000 men, Arriving at Lonato, they detect an enemy brigade debouching from Ponte-San-Marco; Despinois attacks it while Sauret

The First Battle of Lonato on 31 July

General Despinois is the first to arrive at Lonato, but he is obliged to give way before the advancing superior numbers of General Ocskay, by whom he is roughly handled; but as soon as d'Allemagne's and Rampon's brigades of Masséna's division arrive, led by Bonaparte, the French superiority becomes decisive, and Ocskay is forced to retreat with the loss of 500–600 men.

Seeing his two columns beaten at Salò and Lonato, Quosdanovich recognizes that he is facing the French main body; he therefore does not wait for Augereau at Montechiaro but retreats to Gavardo.

Throughout the night of 31 July to 1 August, Bonaparte marches with Augereau's and Despinois's divisions to Brescia, arriving there at 8:00 a.m. and again driving off the Austrians without difficulty.

There is something wonderfully eccentric about this maneuver. Bonaparte probably expected to meet a considerable Austrian corps there, attack it, and cut it off from the Chiese. But when he found himself punching air, on 2 August he left Despinois's division there and turned back toward Montechiaro with Augereau. Masséna was still at Lonato, and Sauret was north of Desenzano.[21]

38 WURMSER CROSSES THE MINCIO

On 1 August, while Bonaparte is marching on Brescia and Quosdanovich is concentrating at Gavardo and Salò, Wurmser advances to the Mincio and enters newly relieved Mantua. He deploys part of his force along the river, and

continues his march on Salò, frees Guieu and returns to Desenzano, fearing becoming encircled himself. The action at Lonato is fought by Despinois with the 5th and 32nd [Demi-brigades] (Generals Bertin and Dallemagne). Bonaparte did not assist there; he was at Roverbella at the time."

21. Colin, 131, notes: "Bonaparte's priority task was to reestablish his line of communication with his supply depots. Only his advance guard reached Brescia. The rest of the column slept in place, exhausted, along the length of the road from Montechiaro to Brescia. Besides, Quosdanovich was at Brescia in significant force; but he vanished when Bonaparte approached. If [Bonaparte] had turned [Quosdanovich's] left by moving to Gavardo first, [Quosdanovich] would have rejoined Wurmser via Marcaria and crushed Sérurier's division. On 2 August, Bonaparte concentrates on the Chiese between Desenzano, Castiglione and Mezzane, ready to face either north or east. He cannot get involved in pursuing Quosdanovich into the mountains without danger."

his advance guard under Liptay moves forward to Goito, while part of the Mantua garrison pursues Sérurier's two brigades along the roads to Borgo-forte and Macario.

Wurmser probably thought the French army was in full retreat. He found the siege apparently abandoned in the greatest haste and confusion, the whole siege park and all its associated equipment left behind,[22] and General Sérurier withdrawing. It was like finding a room with everything left just as it was when its occupants suddenly fled. The Austrians were overcome with joy and amazement. Wurmser believed this was the result of his superior numbers, his enveloping attack, and his successful actions of the 29th at Rivoli and Salò; thus he believed he had obtained a complete victory and achieved his aim. Therefore, on the 2nd he rested in Mantua, just letting General Liptay advance from Goito to Castiglione in continued pursuit of the defeated enemy. It was not until the evening of the 2nd that he learned to his astonishment that Quosdanovich had been attacked on all sides and thrown back on Gavardo with considerable loss. The enemy's position be-tween him and Quosdanovich is sufficient explanation of this delay in re-porting.

39 THE BATTLE OF LONATO ON 3 AUGUST

Bonaparte had indeed driven back General Quosdanovich but had not yet had a decisive encounter with him; still less had he inflicted such a defeat on him as to be decisive overall. The advantage obtained could not compare with the loss of the entire siege train. The matter could not be left like this.[23] There had

22. See note 16.

23. Again, this clearly indicates the limitations of tactical military success and the requirement to connect one's actions and decisions to a broader military and politi-cal goal. It is important to remember, however, that multiple small successes can ac-cumulate into a larger whole. That being said, where there is no clear and obvious connection between small victories and a larger whole, it would be hard to show how small victories contributed to the political goals of a campaign. As such, Napoleon's and Clausewitz's seeming emphasis on larger successful actions is perhaps both un-derstandable and justified, given that a large victory is easy to show to one's political masters as a measure of success during a campaign. Readers interested in the idea of the cumulative effects of operations should read J. C. Wylie, *Military Strategy: A Gen-eral Theory of Power Control* (Annapolis, MD: Naval Institute Press, 2014).

to be a major battle, and it was still unclear whether this must be fought with Wurmser or for a second time with Quosdanovich.

The First Battle of Castiglione on 2 August

This, then, is the situation when Masséna's and Augereau's rear guards are driven back on 2 August. Masséna's, under General Pigeon, is attacked at Peschiera and withdraws in good order to Lonato. However, General La Valette is thrown out of his position at Castiglione in such disorder that he abandons half his troops there and bears the terrible news to Montechiaro. For this, Bonaparte cashiers him on the spot.

General La Valette's defeat is a sign of Wurmser's approach, and from reading Bonaparte's report to the Directory of the battle that took place at Lonato on 3 August, one might suppose that on this day the French army performed an about-face in its strategic deployment and fought with Wurmser's individual divisions. But it is not that simple. On 3 August there were two major battles, at Castiglione and Lonato, and several smaller ones along the line between Brescia and Salò. But until now, they have not been extricated from the wondrous confusion in which the French commander in chief's first battle report left them, because the historical account in the Austrian military journal[24] ends with the retreat into the Tyrol, and nobody has been able to shed light on them from the Austrian official reports. In his history of the revolutionary wars, General Jomini offers an account[25] that contradicts the French official report on this doubtful point, without adequately explaining it. It is thus neither more nor less unclear who Bonaparte was fighting with at Lonato, whether it was a detachment of Quosdanovich's army or of Wurmser's.[26]

24. This is not specified by Clausewitz but is likely Österreichische Militärische Zeitschrift, referenced in chapter 1.

25. Jomini's account does not make it clear where his information comes from; thus, Clausewitz's criticism is reasonable. However, they agree on a key piece of information (much as Clausewitz argues in the first section of the first chapter of this book): Napoleon was facing the forces of Wurmser, which were approaching in two main forces on either side of Lake Garda. See Jomini, *Histoire Critique et Militaire des Guerres de la Révolution*, 8:302.

26. Colin, 134, notes: "Clausewitz knows very well that it is Ocskay's brigade, part of Quosdanovich's division, that is defeated by Masséna at Lonato on the 3rd. He says

We will satisfy ourselves with presenting the matter as it stands at this time, without getting into pointless discussion, since at some point in the future this major confusion will surely be resolved by a couple of reports from the Austrian military archive. As presented by Jomini, events took the following form.

The Second Battle of Lonato and Second Battle of Castiglione on 3 August

On 2 August Bonaparte believes that although Quosdanovich has indeed been repulsed, he must be driven back further into the mountains. Bonaparte assigns some 5,000–6,000 men under General Despinois for that purpose. They are to advance on the 3rd, with Guieu returning to Salò and Despinois himself moving from Brescia to Gavardo, while d'Allemagne maintains communications between them via Pietro, and Adjutant General Herbin threatens the enemy's right flank from Osetto. These are the dispositions against Quosdanovich.

On the other flank, the loss of Castiglione means that position has to be retaken. Augereau, reinforced with Kilmaine's cavalry division, is to attack General Liptay there.

Bonaparte is to remain with Masséna's division in the center at Lonato, to be able to move wherever necessary according to circumstances.

Augereau is successful in his action against Liptay. Even though the latter is supported by some troops from the main army and puts up dogged resistance, Augereau still outnumbers him and forces him to abandon the position, which Augereau then occupies himself.

However, the French advance against Quosdanovich is unsuccessful. On the 3rd this general feels that he must make another attempt to advance toward the Mincio to join up with Wurmser and support him in the event he is already getting to grips with Bonaparte. He therefore advances and meets General Despinois's weak columns with superior numbers. The result is that Despinois is driven back toward Brescia with losses, d'Allemagne escapes with some difficulty to Rezzato on the Lonato-Brescia road, and one of Quosdanovich's columns under Ocskay advances to Lonato. On the other hand, General Guieu does get to the Salò area.

---

so in the account that follows. Ocskay had arrived before Lonato on the evening of the 2nd, moving unnoticed between Guieu and Despinois, and without noticing them."

General Ocskay first catches up with Masséna's advance guard (or, rather, rear guard) under General Pigeon at Lonato, which is driven back with heavy losses, losing three guns and General Pigeon himself being captured. At this moment Bonaparte arrives with Masséna's division from St. Marco. He finds himself in a very constricted and enclosed deployment, with the Austrians trying to outflank him on both sides. He drives through their center, splitting them apart and forcing their left wing to retreat toward Lake Garda. Here, the Austrian left wing would have been almost cut off if the vanguard of the Austrian reserve under Prince Reuss had not freed them again. However, this left wing, driven back in its continued retreat toward Salò and Gavardo, finds the approaches to the mountains occupied by some of Guieu's force, and several battalions are actually cut off. As we shall see below, three of these battalions with three cannon laid down their arms the next day at Lonato.

Quosdanovich concentrated his troops again at Gavardo. Bonaparte remained with Masséna's division at Lonato, reinforced General Guieu with some troops under General St. Hilaire, and ordered General Despinois to advance against Quosdanovich again on the 4th.

This account is not without its unlikelihoods, assumptions, and unknowns.[27]

In his report to the Directory, Bonaparte makes no mention of his dispositions for the 3rd against Quosdanovich, nor of the latter's advance. He presents the action of the 3rd as though his strategic front were toward Wurmser; he refers to Guieu as his left wing, charged with advancing toward Salò (thus in the entirely opposite direction) and stopping Quosdanovich; Augereau as the right wing, to march on Castiglione; and Masséna as the center, to move to Lonato. He does not say a single syllable about which enemy he expected to meet at Lonato, nor which he actually did meet there. Later, in his *Memoirs*, Bonaparte states that the enemy at Lonato comprised two of Wurmser's divisions that had come from Borghetto. But that seems to be completely plucked out of thin air.

Whatever the truth of the events leading up to the affair may be, it is certain that on this day the Austrians were beaten at Castiglione and Lonato and lost a total of 3,000 men and twenty guns.

27. Boycott-Brown, *Road to Rivoli*, 384–400, provides a more detailed account, but even that is relatively sketchy. It seems reasonable to suggest that we know little for certain about this series of actions, and this is unlikely to change.

This so-called battle of Lonato was again not truly decisive in itself; it was obviously still a preparatory action, but it was clearly successful, and this prelude left the outcome of the impending major decision scarcely in any doubt. Cooperation with Quosdanovich was now virtually impossible, Wurmser's own forces were already in contact, and Bonaparte had put himself in a position to confront Wurmser with superior numbers. Since the latter had crossed the Mincio on the 3rd and advanced to Goito, Bonaparte could hope to fight him on the right bank of the river; if Wurmser should refuse battle, he would be driven up into the mountains again, and if relentlessly pursued, many trophies could be expected. Bonaparte therefore decided to march against Wurmser on the 5th. He deferred this march by one day, partly because his troops had fought on the 3rd and may have needed to rest and reorganize, and partly because he intended to cooperate with the two brigades of Sérurier's division that had withdrawn toward the Po, and for that, he needed time.

General Fiorelli, who commanded these brigades ad interim and seems to have assembled most of his force at Marcaria, received orders on the 4th to advance overnight toward Guirdizzolo [Guidizzolo] and be ready to cooperate on the 5th.

The Action at Gavardo on 4 August

Thus, on 4 August Bonaparte was with Masséna's division at Lonato, Augereau and Kilmaine were at Castiglione, and Fiorelli was marching to Guidizzolo. Guieu was attacking Quosdanovich from Salò; the latter, who was somewhat rattled by this and was also being threatened on his right flank from St. Ozetto, decided to continue his retreat toward Riva and withdrew Prince Reuss from Rocco d'Anfo to Lake Idro.[28]

28. Colin, 137, notes: "One may explain Quosdanovich's retreat of the 4th better by noting: 1. That this general had never engaged the whole of his division united, and that Ocskay's brigade had been annihilated on the 3rd. 2. That Bonaparte reinforced Guieu and Despinois with part of Masséna's division. It is this reinforcement that decided the success on the 4th, and on the 5th it returned for the battle of Castiglione, followed by half of Despinois's division. Where would the advantage of a central position be, if one did not move one's forces against each of one's two opponents in turn, and if one split one's army in advance, once and for all, into two parts respectively opposing the two enemy armies?"

Wurmser likewise used the 4th to pull in various detachments. But where he actually was, whether he was still at Goito, and where Liptay was positioned cannot be discovered. The latter had probably stayed at Salferino [Solferino], the next day's battlefield.

On the 4th, while Bonaparte's headquarters was at Lonato, the three isolated Austrian battalions mentioned above appeared there with their three cannon. They had not been able to get through to Gavardo, so they had decided to head for the Mincio in the hope of breaking through to Wurmser, which could have succeeded if they had been lucky enough not to bump into any strong detachments of the enemy. On the 4th they headed for Lonato, probably not expecting to meet the same enemy they had fought the day before. Since they did not meet any troops in the open field (Masséna's division was probably encamped in villages or at some distance from Lonato), they boldly called on the garrison of Lonato to surrender. Given the situation, Bonaparte regarded this demand as an insult, and even though he had only 1,200 men with him, he personally threatened to have all the Austrians shot unless they laid down their arms within the next eight minutes, which they duly did.

40 THE BATTLE OF CASTIGLIONE ON 5 AUGUST

On the morning of the 5th Bonaparte took two more demi-brigades from Despinois's division and advanced to Solferino.

There he found General Wurmser with about 25,000 men in position with his right flank at Solferino and his left on the road from Mantua to Brescia, perpendicular to it. Thus they were perfectly set up to be attacked in the rear most effectively by a corps arriving from Marcaria via Ceresara and Guidizzolo.[29]

At daybreak Fiorelli arrived at Guidizzolo, so Bonaparte's strength can be reckoned at 30,000, if one deducts from his original strength 4,000–5,000 men lost in various actions and 6,000–7,000 detached against Quosdanovich and elsewhere.

29. In Wurmser's defense, this basic disposition makes sense because he was moving from Mantua toward Quosdanovich's supposed location, if the latter's movement south had not met with failure. Wurmser's disposition also served the purpose of blocking Napoleon's line of advance should he attempt to return to Mantua. That Wurmser did little to secure or refuse his left flank is the key problem that Napoleon's forces were able to exploit.

Augereau's division took the right wing, Masséna's the left, Kilmaine was echeloned behind the right wing, and Fiorelli was directed to Cavriana in Wurmser's rear. In order to wait for Fiorelli's intervention, the first attack was just a demonstration with weak forces,[30] while the main bodies remained in column. The Austrians assumed too quickly that victory was in sight and strove to attain the French left flank, hoping thereby to establish communications with Quosdanovich as soon as possible, as they had not yet received the news of his total retreat. This suited Bonaparte's intention even better. The Austrians had strengthened their own left wing with a redoubt, which they established as a secure pivot.[31] Bonaparte had this work intensely bombarded by twelve heavy guns, then assaulted by three grenadier battalions under General Verdier. It was taken after vigorous resistance. Now part of the French cavalry bypassed the left wing and headed for Cavriana, where they soon established communications with Fiorelli. The latter's arrival was such a surprise to the Austrians that Wurmser himself was in danger of falling into the hands of the French cavalry. The Austrians either had no reserve or had already committed it to outflanking the French left wing, so they had to make their second line face about to confront Fiorelli. At this moment, Masséna's and Augereau's divisions struck the front of the Austrian first line with their full force. Wurmser, feeling he was in no position to win the battle, decided it was high time to think about retreating, which he was able to do without great loss, protected by his superior cavalry. Even so, this day cost him 2,000 dead and wounded, 1,000 prisoners, and twenty cannon.

The main body retreated on Valeggio, but the right wing fell back on Peschiera. This shows how far the right wing's original front had changed by its maneuver around the French left.

On the 5th the French pursued only as far as Pazzolengo [Pozzolengo] and Castellaro, 10 to 15 miles from the battlefield.

30. Colin, 139, notes: "This was not a demonstration but a retrograde maneuver. Bonaparte shied away until the moment he heard Sérurier's cannon. At that precise instant, the whole army made an about-turn and went over to the attack."

31. See the discussion on the use of field fortifications in Murray, *Rocky Road to the Great War*, 31–33.

41 WURMSER'S RETREAT TO THE TYROL

This battle may naturally be considered the decisive one. Although Wurmser was not actually defeated, it still sufficed as a decision, as Wurmser could obviously no longer think of defending the Mincio or any other position on the Italian plain. He was too weak to adopt a position anywhere near the French army, and if the Tyrol were no longer open to him, there would be nothing left for him to do but retreat up the valley of the Adige.

However, as often happens in war, in the heat of the moment, Wurmser apparently did not see the necessary consequences of the preceding events, since he now hastily constructed an entrenched camp at Peschiera. Masséna's division stormed this on the 6th and took it from the Austrians, who lost 500 men and ten guns. Wurmser now hurriedly began his retreat to the Tyrol. He garrisoned Mantua anew, raising its strength to 15,000 men, and then withdrew into the valley of the Adige.

At first, the French pursued with all five divisions. However, after using Sérurier's division to persuade the Venetian governor of Verona to open its gates to him again, Bonaparte sent this division to renew the siege of Mantua.

Already on the 7th, Masséna's division had advanced to Rivoli to drive off Wurmser's rear guard and reoccupy its old position.

Wurmser took position at Ala and established communications with Quosdanovich. He had occupied the Corona and other points on Monte Baldo. On the 11th the French took these from him, and he lost seven guns. Likewise, on 12 August the Austrians lost the position of Rocca d'Anfo west of Lake Garda.[32]

Hereupon Wurmser moved back to Trento, leaving his advance guard in Rovereto.

Bonaparte left Masséna's division in the Adige valley and sent Augereau's back to the plain.

Since the siege train had been lost and could not immediately be replaced, Bonaparte could not easily undertake a new formal siege and had to satisfy himself for the time being with a blockade.

So ends the second major act of this remarkable campaign.

---

32. This key position guards the route up the western side of Lake Idro, west of Lake Garda. It was originally constructed by the Venetians in the fifteenth century. See Rocca d'Anfo, accessed 22 May 2017, https://www.roccadanfo.eu/?lang=en.

42 OVERALL STRATEGIC OUTCOME

Before we can deliver a sound verdict on the Austrian attack and its structure, we must be clear about what this attack did and did not achieve; that means we must establish the full strategic impact of this action, which we cannot do without considering its relationship to the war as a whole.[33]

In July Mantua was in danger of falling to siege; that would have meant the loss of a great fortress and its 14,000-man garrison, which together were capable of pinning down the French army in Italy—that is, of preventing any successful powerful offensive through the mountains against the Austrian states. This was the fortress's importance to the Austrians as defenders, but the other half of its importance concerned the Austrians as attackers. If the French ever became the masters of Mantua, there would be little prospect of retaking Lombardy from them with a successful strike, because then everything would turn initially on the successful conquest of Mantua; but if Mantua did not fall, a successful battle would take the Austrians at least as far as the Ticino, thus leading to the reoccupation of Milan.[34]

Now, when the Austrian cabinet made the decision to send reinforcements to Italy from Germany, since the German theater of operations was in a state of equilibrium, that decision was utterly motivated by the importance of Mantua.

Indisputably, the Austrian cabinet thought that if the relief of Mantua succeeded, the reconquest of the province of Milan must follow. This was indeed very probable, and it was bound up with many other matters of the highest importance concerning political relations with the Italian states. This consideration must have placed additional weight on the Italian operation.

What, then, was the outcome? One that scarcely anyone could have foreseen: the siege of Mantua was lifted, so the fortress was out of danger; thus the first part of the aim was indeed achieved, but the second part failed. That first part must obviously be considered the primary objective, and the Austrians had hardly paid too dearly for it—just fifty or sixty guns and some 10,000

---

33. This brings us back to one of the key points Clausewitz makes about war writ large: it must be connected to the political objectives of the government, or else it is just meaningless violence. In particular, see book 1, chaps. 1–2, of Clausewitz, *On War*, 75–99. Clausewitz repeats the idea that the political object is the aim of war in book 4, chap. 3 (227).

34. See the use of fortifications as a base of operations in Murray, *Rocky Road to the Great War*, 33–39.

men—especially when one deducts from that what it cost their opponent. Besides, at the close of this act in Italy, the Austrians were back in their previous position.

Thus, while the Austrians had lost the offensive value of Mantua for the time being, it retained its defensive significance, and this was by far the main thing, given the general state of affairs.

In Germany, the situation was now quite different. Although a true decision had not yet been reached anywhere, the balance was tipping very much against Austria. At this time, the French armies had penetrated into Franconia and Swabia as far as the Regensburg heights; all the clashes that took place along the way had gone against the Austrians. Archduke Charles intended to take advantage of his opponent's divided advance to the middle Danube and turn on Jourdan with a superior force; but there can be little certainty that such an action will lead to a major decision, and the Austrian government could have little certainty that this decision would be favorable. Even the person of the commander himself was but a weak guarantee, since this was his first campaign in command. Thus, if we paint a vivid picture of the state of affairs in Germany in mid-August, the Austrian government actually had little hope of the French advance coming to an end anytime soon; rather, it was much more likely that in the absence of any major decision, the French would simply march on and, within a few weeks, threaten Vienna and the heart of the Austrian empire. If the Austrian government did not wish to be forced to sue for peace by this threat, a major battle was the only way to oppose it, and if that were lost, the peace terms would be very different.

This was a clear and present danger, and next to it, the situation in the Italian theater of operations must have lost most of its importance.

It is, of course, somewhat difficult to imagine the danger on the Danube being so great, because we know that soon thereafter this tension was gloriously resolved; but our verdict can take that into consideration only if it could have been anticipated beforehand, and we claim that there was little or no reason to do so. Archduke Charles was no stronger than his two opponents; on the contrary, he had 20,000 men fewer. All attempts at resistance had so far been in vain, and he could not voluntarily retreat into the heart of the nation, even though this could have significantly increased the power of the defense; at that time, this was not a familiar method.[35] The fact that the Swabian and

---

35. Here, we point the reader to several key parts of *On War*. Book 7, chap. 4 (527),

Saxon governments dropped out of the alliance at this point is sufficient to demonstrate how little hope there was.

Meanwhile, if there was no need to worry about Mantua for the time being, and if the Italian theater had temporarily lost any other significance, nothing would have been more natural than for the Austrian government not only to send all available reserves to the army in Germany but also to have half of Wurmser's 40,000-strong army march to Germany against Moreau's rear. In this way, by the end of August or early September, a decisive blow could have been struck against this general, and its success would hardly be in doubt. If the danger to the heart of the Austrian monarchy could have been deflected like that, and if both the French armies in Germany could have been driven back across the Rhine, that would have been the time to relieve Mantua.[36]

We claim this would have been the natural and correct strategy for the Austrian government. If it took a different path and decided on an immediate reinforcement of the army in Italy, the reason may lie in the fact that the men who direct these matters seldom achieve complete clarity of view. When an individual acts, he usually exercises valuable discretion in making his decision, which is guided by the difficulty of its implementation and his responsibility for it. This discretion is an intuition of the truth. But when a council of war makes a decision, objective reasons have to be asserted, and at the time in question, strategy was far from being able to provide fixed points for the

---

explains how the attack diminishes in strength the further one advances into enemy territory; this occurs because the attacker loses combat power through a "need to occupy the area in their rear so as to secure their lines of communication . . . by losses incurred in action and through sickness . . . by the distance from the source of replacements . . . [and] by sieges and investments of fortresses." In book 6, chap. 1 (358), Clausewitz notes that "*the defensive form of warfare is intrinsically stronger than the offensive*" (emphasis in original). The action he recommends (retreat for the archduke) fits his logic in book 8, chap. 8 (613), where he notes that "the defender is at a *disadvantage*" (emphasis in original). In this case, Clausewitz is pointing out that, all things being equal, a passive defender will simply be worn down, and an attacker eventually "will succeed."

36. In other words, Clausewitz is arguing that the Austrians should have prioritized their strategy based on what they wanted from the conflict and the degree to which the various campaigns facilitated the achievement of their goals. In this case, the siege of Mantua was not that important in the overall scheme of things, and logically, it should have been allowed to continue without further Austrian intervention until the main campaign was decided.

objective reasons from which any reasoning must proceed. The Tyrol must be protected, what was lost in Germany must be won back in Italy, Carinthia must be covered, Hungary cannot be abandoned: in such a council of war, each of these reasons counts as much as any other, even if they are clearly just small fragments of conclusions whose relation to what is actually needed is anything but obvious. Besides, in war as in everything, it seems most natural to combat evil in the place where it shows itself, without asking whether the true remedy is not to be found elsewhere.

Be that as it may, we have looked at the actual conditions at the relevant point in time not to extract criticisms of the Austrian government but rather to show that if the Austrians' attempt at a second relief of Mantua makes the first one appear to be a completely defective operation, this actually casts it in a false light, because the Austrians attached a false value to Italy at this time.[37]

The main thing was that Mantua still stood, and it prevented the French army in Italy from cooperating to achieve a decision in Germany, whereas the Austrian army under Wurmser was indeed in a position to do so.

If this is certain, then it is also certain that the main result of this act was favorable to the Austrians. For Bonaparte to be completely victorious, he would have had to cover the siege of Mantua, or at least rescue the siege train or recoup its loss through a victory that would have allowed him to immediately pursue the Austrian army through the Tyrol into Germany. Since none of

---

37. Clausewitz makes this point in *On War*. In book 1, chap. 2 (92), he discusses the value of the object to be attained in war and the degree of effort one must expend to achieve it. This is worth quoting at length: "Of even greater influence on the decision to make peace is the consciousness of all of the effort that has already been made and of the efforts yet to come. Since war is not an act of senseless passion but is controlled by its political object, the value of the object must determine the sacrifices to be made for it in *magnitude* and also in *duration*. Once the expenditure of effort exceeds the value of the political object, the object must be renounced and peace must follow." Clausewitz argues that Germany was the main theater, where the broader war was likely to be decided; therefore, it follows that the Austrians should have placed a higher value on that campaign than the one in Italy. As such, it follows that by misvaluing Mantua and allocating resources to its relief, the Austrians did not use the resources at their disposal effectively and increased the risk of losing the war and thus failing to obtain their political objective. Thus, the "false value" placed on Italy was worse for the war effort in general but increased the Austrians' chances of success in a theater that Clausewitz argues was less valuable. They increased their chances of success in one place of little consequence at the risk of losing the broader war.

these aims was achieved, between 19 July and 11 August, the situation of the French army in Italy was obviously not improved but made worse.

43 REFLECTIONS ON WURMSER'S ATTACK AND BONAPARTE'S DEFENSE

The admiration this second act of the campaign aroused in the world both at the time and in posterity allowed Bonaparte's mastery to be considered as indubitable as the Austrian commander's blunders. Nevertheless, it is the latter, defeated everywhere, who achieved his central aim [the relief of Mantua]. Even if this was overlooked at first glance, it now stands out as a clear result. There is apparently a major contradiction here, which we must resolve before anything else.

It is a fact that Wurmser was beaten at every point; from that it follows that he must have made some serious mistakes. We will address these mistakes anon. The contradiction must rest either in the French commander's supposed mastery or in the impossibility of Bonaparte's mission. And in fact, after closer examination, it is this mastery that we must deny [as Bonaparte's mission was possible].

Bonaparte's method was new, startling, one of great decisiveness and unprecedented activity; one could call it brilliant. But it was not correct, and it could not possibly resolve the entire problem posed to him.

We have seen that the Austrians' aim was twofold: the relief of Mantua, and a victory over the French army that would give them possession of the province of Milan.

Thus Bonaparte's mission was also twofold: to hold the line of the Mincio, and to cover the siege.[38]

With some 44,000 men, to isolate and besiege a fortress whose garrison is 12,000 strong; to cover that siege against an army numbering 50,000; and to do so in a very disadvantageous theater of operations—namely, one surrounded by alpine mountains that are occupied by the enemy and threaten the strategic flank and line of communications—against an enemy whose heart is set on relieving the siege, this is a mission of infinite difficulty and one that, if

---

38. Clausewitz's assertion makes sense, as the key to France's securing the eastern part of the Po valley was control over the Austrian Quadrilateral.

attempted by means of an army of observation, borders on impossible. Admittedly, the Austrians were not so superior that they could decide the matter through sheer weight of numbers while magnifying their success by outflanking, as seems to have been their intention, but if they had remained concentrated and not made any attempt to outflank the theater of operations, they would have so outnumbered Bonaparte's available forces that he could hardly have expected to win. If, on the other hand, the Austrians had tried to outflank him, it would have been impossible for Bonaparte to prevent the relief of Mantua. Obviously, it was the column advancing to the Chiese that obliged Bonaparte to abandon the siege and relocate his battlefield on the right bank of the Mincio.

There was just one method available to the French commander that would have encompassed the whole mission, namely, to entrench himself in a line of circumvallation.[39] Discredited and out of fashion though this method may have been, still, thoughtful reflection must lead back to it and prompt an examination of the circumstances to see how far they would favor it.

We will defer further development of this idea to the end of the campaign, because it is borne there by the total strategic importance of its aim, and then the reader can clearly see that it is the aim that determines the means, not a preference for this or that method of operation.[40]

---

39. This is a set of fortifications facing both toward the place being besieged and outward so the besiegers can fend off attempts by a relief force to break the siege and relieve the besieged garrison. The most famous example is probably Gaius Julius Caesar's successful siege of Alesia in 52 BCE during the Gallic Wars. Closer to Clausewitz's time, the siege of Breda in 1624–1625 and the siege of Lille in 1708 are good examples.

40. Colin, 149–150, notes: "Clausewitz earned this praise from General Pierron: 'In the first place he has shown us that a plan of operations must make the enemy army its primary objective, and must aim to strike the enemy's organized forces harder and harder until they are destroyed, for then everything else will fall: positions, fortresses, etc.; whereas if the plan seeks some other aim, it will be dissonant and complex, inasmuch as the most thoughtful and skilful maneuvers are no more than a promise, while a victory over the enemy's main army is a result that dominates everything, and compensates for everything.' Here, Clausewitz reneges on his own doctrine: to avoid raising the siege of Mantua, he would expose his line of communications and risk his army's salvation. And after all, why was the fact of raising the siege so serious in itself? If it had such fateful and long-lasting consequences, that was because it had not been prepared long before, and Bonaparte did not manage to evacuate the siege train. When Wurmser approached, if instead of redoubling the bombardment the guns had es-

It was the lack of a comprehensive view of the whole campaign that meant that Bonaparte did not attach enough value to the second part of his mission, and it was his predilection for the positive, the glamorous, and the violent that swept him along a path that could never include this second part. Reviewing the whole campaign and the chain of events has led us to this view, or in other words: we have allowed ourselves to learn from history. If previous criticism has failed to do this, this proves how much it stems from preconceived ideas and how little it has to do with history. A young commander like Bonaparte may be excused if, in his position, he unknowingly overlooked what we now see as fact, but because of this, the accolade of mastery must yet be denied him.

Thus, in resolution of the apparent contradiction we are discussing here, we may say: either Bonaparte's mission was one that bordered on the impossible, and then it is no surprise that he could not achieve it, despite his opponent's errors and despite his victories; or this mission became impossible only because of the method the French commander adopted, because however glorious his feats of arms, he committed an error, and this error was the root cause of the unfavorable result.

As we have stated, this is now our complete conviction, and we pronounce it all the more emphatically since here we see a case that, in our view, is exceptionally rare in war: namely, one where glorious victories failed to achieve an aim that could have been attained by a simple method with much less fuss.[41]

If we turn now to the Austrian plan of attack, as we have said, they had a choice of two very different approaches. Either they could advance against the French strategic front and flank simultaneously, to force the French to abandon the siege simply through strategic maneuver and perhaps even induce

---

caped, the siege could have been resumed on 8 August and Bonaparte would have been master of Mantua before the end of the month." Colin seemingly missed Clausewitz's point, which is that the aim of the operation overall should dictate what Napoleon does. Clausewitz disagrees with Napoleon's choice to abandon the siege of Mantua because Clausewitz thought continuing the siege was the better course of action for the campaign overall. The bigger point is that the strategic objective should drive the operation, rather than vice versa.

41. This returns us to one of Clausewitz's key arguments in *On War*, namely, that any action a commander undertakes should be done with the overarching purpose in mind. Mere tactical success, however fantastic, is not sufficient to win wars unless it is clearly tied to the overarching purpose—that is, strategy tied to the political goals of the government.

them to retreat further; or they could advance down the Adige valley with their force united to deliver a decisive battle on the left bank of the Mincio, where, because of their great numerical superiority (50,000 against 35,000), they could be almost certain of victory, in which case Mantua would be relieved and most likely the whole of Milan conquered.[42]

If the Austrians chose the first option, then, as part of it, they should avoid any decisive battle with the enemy's main body and satisfy themselves with relief of the fortress, whether by Quosdanovich or by Wurmser, giving way before Bonaparte whenever he advanced. This was not a difficult task, and if we just follow the course of events, we can see clearly that, after Quosdanovich learned of Bonaparte's presence through the far-from-decisive action at Lonato on 31 August, he was able to retreat to Gavardo and then needed to do no more than renew his advance very cautiously; Wurmser likewise could have avoided the real battle at Castiglione on the 5th with the greatest of ease. There are very few instances in military history as indisputable as this, where the aim could have been achieved simply through strategic maneuver. But the Austrians, who were actually seeking a major decision, mixed up the two approaches through an all too common confusion of ideas—they wanted to fight to win and, at the same time, to maneuver. We call this a confusion of ideas because if strategic maneuver is to mean anything specific at all, other than merely a more complex plan of attack, its concept lies precisely in seeking to achieve success without a major decision, without a battle or victory in the field.[43]

The Austrians wanted a major decision. In this case, the simplest thing would have been for them to advance down the Adige valley with their entire force; then they would have been certain not to be deprived of the advantage

42. This has much to do with the likely crushing blow such a superior force could deliver. This also fits with Clausewitz's arguments about the use of the engagement, discussed in book 4 of *On War* (225–272). He argues that such a crushing blow could, and should, facilitate the accomplishment of the strategic goals.

43. It is important to note that here Clausewitz accepts the role of maneuver without heavy fighting to achieve the desired result: "*War is thus an act of force to compel our enemy to do our will*" (Clausewitz, *On War*, 75, emphasis in original). In Italy, it is the threat of that force, placed in an advantageous position through effective maneuver, that enhances the likelihood of compelling the enemy to do one's will. This is not contradictory to the idea of the use of force, as Clausewitz makes clear if one reads the whole of book 1, chap. 1, of *On War*.

of their absolute superiority. The simplest plan must always be the first one arrived at, and from which one deviates only if circumstances dictate. Why did the Austrians not follow this simple plan? Probably we have already given the reasons in section 34.

First, they did not want to advance with such a large force along a single road.[44]

Of course, it is nicer to have two major roads in one's rear when traversing a mountainous area, but it is not an absolute necessity; and besides, we are not talking about a single road here, since the Austrians advanced down the so-called Adige Road in four or five columns. Where they advanced with 32,000 men, they could have advanced just as easily with 50,000. They did not depend on it as an actual strategic base, since they had enough lines of retreat to the Brenta and Friuli. In the circumstances, to interpose an obstacle like Lake Garda between the two columns just for the sake of greater breadth of front would be completely unpardonable.

The second reason—to oblige the enemy to divide his forces—actually means nothing, since if I divide the enemy's forces at the cost of dividing my own, that does not help me at all. We would not even list it, except that we know from experience a thousand times over that the fog of this half-baked idea drifts into most strategic plans.

The third reason—to threaten the enemy's retreat—relates to the intention to succeed through maneuver, and it could be effected just by having a small corps advance into the Chiese valley, so small that it would not be missed at the point of decision and would not harm that decision. But as we have said, if the main forces are to strike, they cannot maneuver.

Finally, the fourth reason—to enhance success in the event of a victory in battle—can be justified only with substantial physical or moral superiority. The size of the risk grows in proportion to the size of the aim; this is a quite general principle but one that, despite its great simplicity, is little noticed or heeded. If the risk of failure is very slight in itself, then one may raise one's sights, but the probability of success is still the first principle. The extent to which one is prepared to reduce this probability—that is, how much one is willing to risk—depends on the commander, but in each case, the commander's daring will depend on his appreciation of his own strength. If Wurmser

---

44. This would be extremely difficult to support logistically, given the infrastructure available to armies of the time.

had been a young hero, proud of his genius and grasping at glory, then even if it went wrong, one must not say he made a mistake but rather that he over-reached himself. But the Austrian plan of attack was a completely objective sorry effort, not arising from the commander's spirit but drafted by the chief of the general staff; thus, it may be judged only by its objective dimensions, and we may speak only of wisdom and calculation, not of daring.

If the Austrian army had been 20,000 men stronger, an advance on both sides of Lake Garda could be considered valid; then 55,000 could have come down the Adige valley and offered Bonaparte a battle he could not win, while 15,000 seized the Milan highway and magnified the success of a victory in bat-tle. But since the superiority of numbers the Austrians could attain by the maximum concentration of their forces, 50 to 35, was just barely enough to give them a reasonable probability of success, the division of their forces in such a way that made it almost impossible to reunite them in advance of the decision is quite definitely a major error. Weakened by this separation, yet still pushing for a major decision, Wurmser met Bonaparte's 30,000 men on 5 Au-gust with just 25,000. We ask, given the state of morale of the two armies, was there any prospect of an Austrian victory? If Wurmser had advanced with his whole army along a single road, on the day of decision he could have opposed that same French force with double its numbers.

Having acknowledged that a column advancing down the western shore of Lake Garda could have some value, we do not hesitate to deem the Austrian plan one of those strategic concepts whereby the fallacious science of the gen-eral staff demands complex forms and methods, without understanding why. A colonel of the general staff recoils from the idea of simply advancing against the enemy along a single road because it could raise suspicions of naturalism.[45]

45. Clausewitz uses the word *Naturalismus*, which was closely associated with the early Romantic movement in Germany. It is not clear exactly what he means, but it seems reasonable that, given early Romantic ideas about simplicity and the question-ing of authority, he is getting at officers' reliance on complex prescriptive methods that had little to do with solving the problem at hand; these methods were used merely because they were the tools provided by someone in authority, so their utilization was not to be questioned. This is also part of his broader criticism of the more prescrip-tive nature and complexity of the military writings of his predecessors. For an excel-lent discussion of this topic, see Azar Gat, *A History of Military Thought: From the Enlightenment to the Cold War* (Oxford: Oxford University Press, 2001); Peter Paret, ed., *Makers of Modern Strategy: From Machiavelli to the Nuclear Age* (Princeton, NJ:

In war, as we have said, the first resort should always be the simplest option, and each step away from that must have a clear and specific reason. But to the strategists of this time, this sequence of ideas is something quite foreign. They always start with the most complex, and thus all their reasoning is likewise so complex that one can find in it neither beginning nor end.

44 BONAPARTE'S DEFENSE

Given how matters stood on 29 July, Bonaparte's defense was indisputably one of the most beautiful examples in the history of warfare.

Since it was impossible for him to cover the siege, on the 30th (or the 31st, it remains unclear which)[46] he decided not only to abandon it but also not to bother about the entire siege train. This had the great merit of avoiding half measures, something that was very much to be feared in this situation. His second decision, to cross the Mincio and use his whole force to attack the column threatening his rear, was the simplest and the best; this decision offered the prospect that the second Austrian column would follow him across the Mincio, thereby giving him the opportunity to attack it with the same force that had just beaten the first. It is impossible to conceive of anything better: on the one hand, it led to a decision that, if favorable, would secure the French possession of Lombardy; on the other, it did not involve any particular danger or great daring, being as prudent as a quest for victory ever could be.

If the execution of these combinations does not manifest itself as neatly and tidily as the academic mind would like to see, then as we have said, this should not be treated as a reason to give Bonaparte less credit; even if his decision could have been reached sooner and prepared better, we must remind

---

Princeton University Press, 1986). In large part, direct instructions or formulas do not require the degree of abstract analysis called for by writers such as Clausewitz. Indeed, this problem still confronts militaries today, and one can see examples of this thinking in the metrics used to measure success in Vietnam or, more recently, in Iraq and Afghanistan, such as body count.

46. According to Napoleon's correspondence, the decision was made on 30 July, although the order may not have arrived until early the next morning; hence the confusion over the date. Napoleon ordered General Sérurier to support General Augereau and to abandon the siege guns in the lake in front of Mantua, if necessary. Napoléon I, *Correspondance de Napoléon Ier*, 1:507.

ourselves that he was not yet fully graduated from the school of major war and had not yet established his own doctrine for every type of situation; rather, it was as if he lived from hand to mouth on his own talented intuitions. But the critic is at least justified in taking the matter so seriously in this case where information about it is so extremely sparse.

However, one might say, not without justification, that Bonaparte showed no great skill in initiating the three main battles of 31 July and 3 and 5 August, nor in turning them into completely decisive victories; none of the three was decisive, however much Bonaparte and his generals bragged about them. His reports are full of the ludicrous exaggerations he was prone to subsequently and indeed for the rest of his life. This braggadocio, this complete disregard for the truth, either was rooted in his character or was something he decided on very early as a principle of policy.[47]

If the Wurmserian [*wurmsersche* in the original] army had suffered a genuine defeat, Bonaparte would have pursued it right through the Tyrol;[48] instead, thanks to immediate reinforcements from the interior, fourteen days later we see this same army return to Lombardy just 5,000–6,000 men weaker.

To achieve a more decisive success against Quosdanovich right at the beginning, Bonaparte should have attacked him not on 31 July but on 1 August. Then he probably would have found Quosdanovich more concentrated and further forward, but Bonaparte himself would have concentrated his own forces [given the extra time]. As it was, what happened on 31 July was a kind of *echauffouré* [brawl] with Sauret's and Despinois's divisions, since neither Augereau nor Masséna seems to have been present.[49]

But a vigorous pursuit through Peschiera probably would have made the battle of 5 August much more consequential.

We say this not so much to be directly critical of the French commander but rather to show more clearly what the story was and what it was not.

47. It seems reasonable to believe that Napoleon felt a need to please the Directory in Paris; as such, it is perhaps understandable that he exaggerated his claims for political purposes. He would not be the first commander to do so, nor the last.

48. As he did after the more complete victory at the battle of Rivoli in January 1797.

49. Clausewitz cites "Letter of 1 July 1796 from General Despinois to Bonaparte." *Correspondance inédite, officielle et confidentielle, de Napoléon Bonaparte*, 1:419–420. Division general Hyacinthe Despinois was in in his early 30s at the beginning of the campaign.

7. The Changing Strategic Situation

45 BONAPARTE WAITS THREE WEEKS ON THE ADIGE

In section 42 we have already shown that at the close of this second act it was strategically necessary for the French army to attack the Austrians.

While two armies were striding toward a supremely decisive offensive, for the third to sit idle for any length of time would be a major error, since the first principle of any strategic offensive is simultaneous effort by all available forces.

Before Wurmser descended to the Lombard plain for his first offensive, the Directory in Paris regarded the advance of its army in Italy against Trient and Botzen [Bolzano] as just a necessary strategic alignment with Moreau's army, whose right wing was to be at Inspruck [Innsbruck]. But such an alignment can only mean a simultaneous and consistent effort by these forces. When Wurmser was beaten and driven back into the Tyrol, in its flush of victory, all the Directory could see was his pursuit yielding a bountiful harvest and hastening the great result [victory in Germany and Italy]. But in mid-August, when some apprehensions arose over the outcome of events in Germany, the French arrived at the true strategic node:

"It is now urgent," they say in a letter that is undated but is from between 15 and 23 August, "that you attack the enemy and pursue him before you. The army of Archduke Charles, increased by some reinforcements from Galicia and inner Austria, grew sufficiently imposing to attack that [French army] commanded by Chief General Moreau, and to give him battle between Neresheim and Donauwerth, a battle that was in doubt for a time but was decided in our favor. If General Wurmser should get a moment's respite, he may detach some troops that, combined with Archduke Charles's[1] forces, could

---

1. Archduke Charles was one of Austria's most effective commanders during the entire series of wars. He was heavily criticized by Clausewitz in the latter's campaign history of 1799–1800, although in *On War*, Clausewitz praises Charles. This leads us to wonder whether revisions of *On War* would have been more consistently critical of

oppose the endeavors of the Army of the Rhine and could perhaps fight it at advantage."[2]

With this view, the Directory now steadily urges Bonaparte to advance into the Tyrol as far as the Inn [almost certainly Innsbruck], following hard on the heels of Wurmser's army to pound it to pieces.

Bonaparte, for his part, had a different project. He wanted to march on Trieste to destroy the city and its harbor, and from there threaten the heart of the Austrian empire.

This somewhat Hunnish [*Humische* in the original] project evidently arose from a great impetuosity and from his feeling that he no longer had anything to fear from any Austrian army. Any French army that marches to Trieste leaving an opponent in Trient [on his left flank], along with unreliable Venice on his right, must get a thrill from getting itself into trouble, must actually want to hurl itself into a desperate situation. While our modern Attila headed for Trieste, the Austrian army could advance through the Brenta valley and, unless Bonaparte were willing to relinquish his prize, could cut him off from his theater of operations and oblige him to change front entirely and give battle against its superior forces. But we assert that the Austrian army could have done something even better: march against Moreau and combine with the archduke to wreck Moreau's army.

Nonetheless, that is far from saying that Bonaparte's plan could not have resulted in a very great success. Governments rarely recognize when it is the right time to make sacrifices and to avoid a great evil by incurring a lesser

---

Archduke Charles, given what Clausewitz wrote in his campaign analyses. See Clausewitz, *On War*, 159–160, 246, 423. Also see Paret, *Clausewitz and the State*, 335–340.

2. Clausewitz provides this quote in the original French: "*Il devient même instant que vous attaquiez l'ennemi et que vous le chassiez devant vous. L'armée de l'archiduc Charles, grossie de quelques renforts, venue de la Gallicie et de l'intérieur de l'Autriche, s'est cru assez imposante pour attaquer celle que commande le Général en Chef Moreau, et pour lui livrer entre Neresheim et Donauwerth une bataille dont le succes, qui paroit avoir été un moment douteux, s'est décidé en notre faveur. Si le Général Wurmser obtenoit un instant de repos, il pourroit détacher quelques troupes, qui jointes aux forces de l'archiduc Charles, s'opposeroient aux entreprises de l'armée du Rhin et la combattroient peut-être avec avantage.*" It is also worth noting the interconnectedness of the campaigns and the likelihood that Napoleon was competing for resources with his compatriots fighting in Germany. As such, his exaggerations, mentioned in the previous section, are understandable.

one.[3] Maybe the Austrians would have mobilized everything to protect Trieste and, instead of thinking of a counteroperation, would have marched everything available thither, only in the end to arrive too late and be defeated in detail. But if they did not consider any retaliation from the Tyrol against Bonaparte's rear, he would be free to take up a position on the Laibach [Ljubljana] road that would threaten Vienna. Bonaparte probably preferred to act in this direction for the sake of remaining his own master.

The Directory repeatedly rejected this plan, albeit with great circumspection.

Meanwhile, nothing happened until the beginning of September. Bonaparte wanted to wait for the 20,000 reinforcements he had been promised from the forces on the coast and from the Army of the Alps.[4] He reported that his army on the Adige had 15,000 sick. In addition, as emerges from individual letters from the division commanders, the French troops were suffering from the most painful lack of equipment of every kind, especially clothing, and it is easy to understand why the French army did not immediately embark on further operations. On the other hand, it cannot be denied that the three weeks lost cost the French army a really favorable opportunity and that 25,000 men hard on the heels of Wurmser could perhaps have taken the whole of the Tyrol and struck fear into Germany. We say perhaps, since such success was in no way guaranteed, as it presupposes that the Austrian troops were very demoralized if a region like the Tyrol—which could muster 7,000–8,000 militia of its own—could not be held with 40,000 men against just 25,000. But in any case, this attempt would have kept the Austrian forces there occupied and prevented them from supporting the archduke.[5]

3. This brings us back to Clausewitz's discussion of the value of the object to be attained. See book 1, chap. 2, of *On War* (90–99).

4. This ties in with the note in section 44 regarding Clausewitz's criticism of Napoleon's exaggeration of his successes in his correspondence with the Directory in Paris. This does not justify his behavior, but it underpins the logic of his actions.

5. This would have fit the broader strategy guiding both theaters of war, rather than just that in Italy. Colin, 159–160, notes: "Overall, Clausewitz's critique is perfectly fair. The execution of this maneuver would have caused some difficulty for Wurmser, since on 15 August Moreau had entered Bavaria; it could not be assumed that he would continue to move as slowly as he had been; he could have arrived in Innsbruck in a few days, and Bonaparte would just have asked to combine with him there. If Wurmser returned up the Adige, he might run into Moreau with Bonaparte on his heels. He would have been captured or wiped out in the gorges of the Tyrol, after which the two French

During these three weeks from 7 August until the first few days of September, Bonaparte himself was in the center, with the main body under Masséna at Rivoli; the right wing under Augereau was at Verona; the left wing, Sauret's division, now commanded by General Vaubois, was on the western shore of Lake Garda. Sérurier's division, now under General Sahuguet, was investing Mantua, and the reserve was provided by Kilmaine between the Mincio and the Adige.

At the end of August, the French army's strength reports were as follows:

Division Vaubois:	11,000 men
Division Masséna:	13,000
Division Augereau:	9,000
Division Sahuguet:	10,000
Kilmaine's cavalry:	2,000
Total:	45,000

46 THE AUSTRIANS' NEW PLAN OF ATTACK

While Bonaparte was still waiting for reinforcements and unable to agree with his government what to do next, the Austrian government had likewise sent everything from the interior to reinforce Wurmser's army again. By the end of August, it had been brought back up to 45,000 men. But the Austrian government was not satisfied with simply protecting the Tyrol, which now lay on the right flank and rear of Moreau's army, which had advanced into Swabia; instead, it wanted to continue the offensive in Italy. Wurmser was to descend once more onto the Italian plain to relieve Mantua.

This time, it was not the general staff but the engineer corps that shone its light on the transparency[6] of the strategic plan, which of course simply meant leaping out of the frying pan into the fire. In place of Colonel Weirotter, old

---

armies would have been masters of Germany. The Aulic Council's plan of carrying the war into Friuli seems absolutely sensible. It was the execution that was defective, for which Wurmser was responsible."

6. This was typically a vellum sheet used to provide a trace map that was translucent, light, and fairly durable. As such, it could be placed over an actual map so that plans could be drawn. These remained in use well into the twentieth century.

Wurmser was given Engineer-General Lauer as his chief of staff, who brought a new plan of attack with him.

Wurmser's army was to split up again. While Davidowitsch[7] held the Tyrol with 20,000 men, Wurmser and the other 26,000 were to descend through the Brenta valley down to the plain; if the French army turned against him, a suitable force from the troops left in the Tyrol should descend into the valley of the Adige and advance against the French rear, either to maneuver them out of the region between the Adige and the Mincio or to give battle, or at least to shackle them to the Italian plan and prevent their advance into the Tyrol.

47 OBSERVATIONS

We shall see later on how this very inferior Austrian plan caused a very inferior outcome, but we cannot restrain ourselves from asking the questions it raises right now.

Was the relief of Mantua an urgent objective? Clearly not,[8] since it was not under any pressure and could have held out for months before there was any question of its falling. What does relieving Mantua mean? It means breaking the blockade by driving the French army from the left bank of the Mincio, which, against a general like Bonaparte, could be achieved only by a major battle. Were the Austrians in a better position to do this than they had been four weeks earlier? No, because they were weaker. Were they making better moves this time? No, even less so, since again they were dividing their forces and getting mixed up in the same confusion between maneuver and battle as the first time.

Was it absolutely necessary to attack the enemy's army in Italy? It was doing nothing, which was unarguably the best thing that could happen to the Austrians.

But the French army could not be expected to sit idle for long, so the Aus-

---

7. Paul von Davidowitsch was a 58-year-old Austrian general who would play a prominent role in the rest of the campaign.

8. Colin, 162, notes: "Clausewitz himself has just said, seven lines earlier, that the aim of Wurmser's offensive (which in any case has not been declared) was to keep Bonaparte in Italy, not to relieve Mantua." Again, Colin seems to have missed the point, which was that the plan to keep the French in Italy to fulfill a broader strategic purpose narrowed into one focused on the relief of Mantua.

trians preferred to attack preemptively and fight it on the Italian plain, rather than wait for it on the defensive in the mountains of the Tyrol.

Here arises that common error, that gross violation of common sense: the assumption that attack offers more prospect of victory than defense.[9] Twice in this campaign the defeated Austrian army had fled to the Tyrol, both times finding protection in its mountains and gorges, since both times the French—who, in the plain, would never have let go of the Austrians' heels—stopped short at the foot of the Tyrolese Alps as if spellbound. The Austrians had observed this phenomenon; they were not surprised by it, indeed, they found it quite natural, but they watched it happen as if in a dream, without realizing what caused it, and without asking themselves why. If a beaten army on the run could find shelter in these mountains, then one that was prepared and reinforced and otherwise in the same position would be that much less likely to be attacked. But they could not reach this simple conclusion.

We should like to find the source of this error that operates so powerfully that it prevents not only the Austrian government but also probably nine-tenths of everyone else who expatiates on it from believing that two times two is four.

We are more convinced than any other theoretician or practitioner that mountains disadvantage the defender in a decisive battle. We also want to acknowledge that when a decision cannot be avoided, there are many cases in which the offensive battle is preferable to the defensive. But it does not necessarily follow from these two sentences that the Austrians should have come down out of the Tyrol to make a strategic attack on the Italian plain.

Having put the Austrian commanders Beaulieu and Wurmser to flight, if

9. Clausewitz makes it clear throughout *On War* that defense is the stronger form of war. In particular, he argues in book 1, chap. 1, that it is necessary to calculate "whether the advantage of *postponing a decision* is as great for one side as the advantage of *defense* is for the other. Whenever it is not, it cannot balance the advantage of defense and in this way influence the progress of the war. . . . Consequently, if the side favored by the present conditions is not sufficiently strong to do without the added advantages of the defense, it will have to accept the prospect of acting under unfavorable conditions in the future." Clausewitz, *On War*, 84 (emphasis in original). Throw in Clausewitz's argument about the role of chance and probability, and the risk increases. Thus, acting on the defensive would have bought time for events in Germany to potentially work in the Austrians' favor, and it would have consumed French resources in a siege against a well-prepared fortress, thereby weakening French forces in Italy for a better-prepared Austrian blow.

Bonaparte had had the opportunity to attack them again in the plain, he would have greatly welcomed it, and the more decisive a new battle was, the happier he would have been to see it. In the mountains, this decisive battle would have been even easier to obtain, by our own thesis and certainly in Napoleon's view, but its impact in the mountains would have been quite different.

What was Bonaparte supposed to do with a victory in the Tyrol? He would have to conquer the whole region, since a mountainous region whose inhabitants are taking part in its defense belongs to us only when we have taken and occupied every position, not like the plain, where it can be done with just a triumphal procession by the main body. Even if he could conquer and hold the Tyrol in this way, would he have enough forces left to invade Swabia? We can see that when Bonaparte was considering these questions in mid-June and mid-August, he told himself that he was not strong enough, that it would embroil him in a situation his forces could not handle. What forced him to linger on the Italian plain both times was not the difficulty of beating the Austrians in the Tyrol but the difficulty of achieving a sufficient strategic result through such a victory, the difficulty of continuing his strategic offensive across a region like the Tyrol. One must therefore not confuse the total strategic value of a mountainous region with its value as a battlefield. If the Italian plain had been larger by the 112.5 miles from Rivoli to Innsbruck, Bonaparte would not have hesitated to pursue the Austrians there; thus, it was only the barrier of the Alps that stopped him. So much for the consequences and impact of victory. But there is also a major difference in the way a decisive battle is obtained in the mountains versus one on the plain. On the plain, if the defender wants to avoid a decisive battle and simply retreats, this does not cause the attacker significant cost in terms of forces expended, nor does it entangle him [and restrict his ability to maneuver]. The attacker is a couple of days further forward, and in the worst case, he can just retrace his steps. In the mountains, it is not like that: victory consists not of one simple major battle but of a host of smaller ones, and to become the victor, one must win most or all of these. One is therefore virtually obliged to begin each battle without knowing whether the foe will stand to accept it. If, at every point, the defender offers only as much resistance as he can without risk, and retreats in good time so as not to suffer any significant losses, then in the end, one will have pushed him back everywhere, but without winning an actual victory; one will have occupied a mountainous region without gaining the moral superiority that would enable that occupation to be imposed. In short, one would have spent a portion of one's force and got embroiled in a situation one did not really want. These notions largely account for the caution that halts the attacker at the foot of mountains.[10]

Thus, given that the French commander had twice come to a stop at the foot of the Alps[11] in mid-June and mid-August for good reasons—reasons that appear much clearer in the original circumstances than here in their theoretical dissection—what made the Austrian government think these reasons would no longer apply at the end of August? Yes, Bonaparte had been reinforced, so the probability of his renewed activity had increased somewhat, but were a couple of thousand men really worth as much as the Tyrolese Alps? If any possibility of being attacked were enough to make the defender give up his defense and go on the offensive, then the majority of successful defenses would have been lost, since the main effect of all defense lies in the great advantage of waiting.

Thus, we claim that the Austrian government—which, in its moment of need, had so clearly felt the advantage of its Tyrolese Alps and, in many other respects, perhaps attached an exaggerated value to them—at this moment seriously underestimated that advantage and let itself be misled by egomaniacal plans[12] into a strategic offensive that was not at all in its interest.

We have just one more reason to dispose of. The offensive into the Italian plain may have been undertaken to bolster Rome and Naples, since neither had yet concluded their peace treaties with France. Indeed, in August the latter had moved a corps to its border with the Papal States.

If the Austrians had been prepared to operate in concert with these two states, that could have justified an offensive in Italy, but there was simply no such intention. They wanted to bolster these states, but bolstering requires a victorious outcome; thus, this political consideration could be the reason for the offensive only if they were sure it would be successful. But as soon as they let themselves get entangled in adverse circumstances, they obviously shot themselves in the foot.

---

10. It might have behooved NATO to read this paragraph when formulating plans for the war in Afghanistan.

11. Colin, 165, notes: "It was not so much the mountainous terrain that halted Bonaparte as the bifurcation of the two routes via Tarvisio and Innsbruck. He could not advance along one of them without being attacked from behind via the other."

12. This idea fits well with Clausewitz's trinity (book 1, chap. 1), in that the play of chance and blind natural force have to be taken into account. Clausewitz, *On War*, 89.

So much for the Austrian plan, insofar as it seems to us to be totally point-less and completely at odds with the reality of the situation. To add a positive result to this negative one, we must return to the fact that the best use of the Austrians' combat forces in the second half of August would have been to give all the forces they sent to the Tyrol to the archduke instead, and to have Wurmser march against Moreau with 20,000 men and attack him in combi-nation with the archduke. This approach would have been as decisive as it was infallible. The battles of Amberg and Würzburg had proved that Jourdan's[13] operation across the Danube was far too overextended, so he would have been unable to compensate for what the French lost in Swabia, and later on, his long retreat would have become very hazardous if he did not commence it in good time. If Bonaparte had really been convinced by reports that Wurmser was leaving the Tyrol, he would have arrived too late, and in any case, with only 20,000 men, he could not have made up for what had been decided be-tween 70,000. If the difference in size is significant, large forces inevitably drag small ones along with them in the same direction.

13. General Jean-Baptiste Jourdan was in his mid-30s and commanded a wing of the French army advancing into Bavaria. He was soundly beaten by Archduke Charles later that summer, and the Directory in Paris removed him from command for his failings.

8. The Second Campaign for Mantua

48 BONAPARTE ATTACKS DAVIDOWITSCH

The Austrian corps under Davidowitsch, which was supposed to remain in the Tyrol, was defending this region against attack from three possible directions. A corps of 3,500 men under General Grösser was facing Swabia and covering Vorarlberg; a second under General Laudon, 3,000 strong, held the passes to the Veltlin [the Valtellina]; the other 14,000 were facing the French army around Trient. This main body had one division of 5,000–6,000 men under Prince Reuss on the right bank of the Adige at Mori, between Rovereto and Lake Garda. Its advance guard was on the Sarca. Another division under Wukassowitsch was at St. Marco, as far up the Adige valley as Mori; its advance guard was at Serravalle. The reserve was in the very strong position at Calliano, behind Rovereto. Davidowitsch's headquarters was at Rovereto.

Wurmser himself had begun his march down the valley of the Brenta toward Bassano on 2 September with three divisions under Quosdanovich, Sebottendorf, and Mészáros,[1] 26,000 men in all.

Bonaparte recognized Wurmser's plan of attack. He decided to leave General Kilmaine with 2,500–3,000 men on the lower Adige to cover the blockade of Mantua, but to move up the Adige valley with Vaubois's,[2] Masséna's, and Augereau's divisions to beat Davidowitsch, then follow behind Wurmser down the Brenta valley and give battle wherever he might find him. The move against Davidowitsch resulted in the battle of Rovereto; that against Wurmser

---

1. Peter Quosdanovich and Johann Mészáros were both in their mid-50s and had equally undistinguished careers. It is worth noting that Quosdanovich was Hungarian and Mészáros was a Croat. Ethnic diversity was quite typical of the Austrian army.

2. This is Claude-Henri Vaubois, who was later relieved of command after his poor performance in the campaign. In his memoirs, Napoleon described the performance of Vaubois's division as "a succession of embarrassments." Montholon, *Mémoires pour servir à l'Histoire de France sous Napoléon*, 4:267. This is worth pointing out, as it clearly indicates incompetence on the French side too. However, Napoleon seems to have done a much better job dealing with it than the Austrians did.

gave rise to a series of actions from Bassano to the walls of Mantua that are known collectively as the first battle of Bassano.

Since Davidowitsch's position was north of Lake Garda, Bonaparte felt he could risk having Vaubois's division advance up the western shore of the lake with Mori as its objective. On 3 September Vaubois attacked and took the bridge over the Sarca and advanced to Mori. On the same day, Masséna drove the enemy outposts out of Ala and Serravalle and advanced to St. Marco. Augereau followed in grand echelon over Monte Molare, both to cover the right flank and to act as the reserve.

The Battle of Rovereto on 4 September

On 4 September Vaubois and Masséna attacked the positions at Mori and St. Marco; ejected the Austrians from both; drove them back through Rovereto, apparently with considerable loss; and arrived that afternoon before the Calliano position. Here, Davidowitsch and his corps stood in one of those valley positions, encountered so often in mountainous regions, that look very strong because of their narrowness and steep sides yet are usually swiftly overcome from the flank. This was the case here as well. Well before dusk, the French were masters of the position, and the Austrians were retreating through Trient, having lost 3,000 men. On the morning of 5 September Masséna entered Trient.

On this day, Augereau advanced to the heights of the Arsa,[3] east of Rovereto.

If we reckon Vaubois's and Masséna's divisions at just 20,000 men, after allowing for detachments, and Davidowitsch's at 10,000, for he certainly could not have called in all his detached posts, we see that, thanks to the French commander's strategic combinations, he met the Austrians at the decisive point with double their numbers.

The Action on the Lavis on 5 September

Davidowitsch had taken position behind the Lavis, which flows into the Adige 7 miles north of Trient. Since this point was too close to the entrance to the Brenta

---

3. This is the Val Arsa, which runs along modern-day route SS46, east and then south from Rovereto and then roughly parallel to the Adige valley to its west.

valley for Bonaparte to leave him there, toward evening on the 5th Bonaparte attacked him again in this position and obliged him to retreat to Neumarkt.

49 BONAPARTE TURNS ON WURMSER

Wurmser, who had begun his march down the Brenta valley at about the same time Bonaparte went over to the offensive in the Adige valley, learned of this advance while on the march to Bassano. He decided not to turn around but to continue his march and, if possible, profit enough by his operation via Bassano and Vicenza against Verona and Mantua to balance the loss at Rovereto and force Bonaparte and his main body to return to the Italian plain, back the way he had come—or so Wurmser thought.

The Action at Primolano on 7 September

Bonaparte had decided otherwise. On the 6th, regarding his operation against Davidowitsch as over and having learned that Wurmser was at Bassano, he left Vaubois's division on the Lavis to observe Davidowitsch and marched down the Brenta valley toward Bassano with both Augereau's and Masséna's divisions (about 20,000 men). He forced this march so hard that early on the morning of the 7th, Augereau's division, which had still been at Lewico in the Brenta valley on the 5th, was already at Primolano, 27 miles from Lewico, where it attacked three Croat battalions Wurmser had left there as a rear guard. These were surrounded and, after brief resistance, were obliged to lay down their arms, whereupon 1,200–1,500 men and five guns fell into the hands of the French.

On the 7th Wurmser remained at Bassano. His advance guard under Mészáros had already reached Vicenza on the 6th and patrolled as far as Montebello. With the main body, Sebottendorf's and Quosdanovich's divisions, he had occupied a position at Bassano right in front of the Brenta on the plateau there. His headquarters was in Bassano, and his trains were on the road to Cittadella. He had sent three battalions up the right bank of the Brenta to Campo Lungo and another three up the left bank to Solagna, to receive the Croats from Primolano and to cover the flank and rear of the army in the direction of the Brenta [pass].

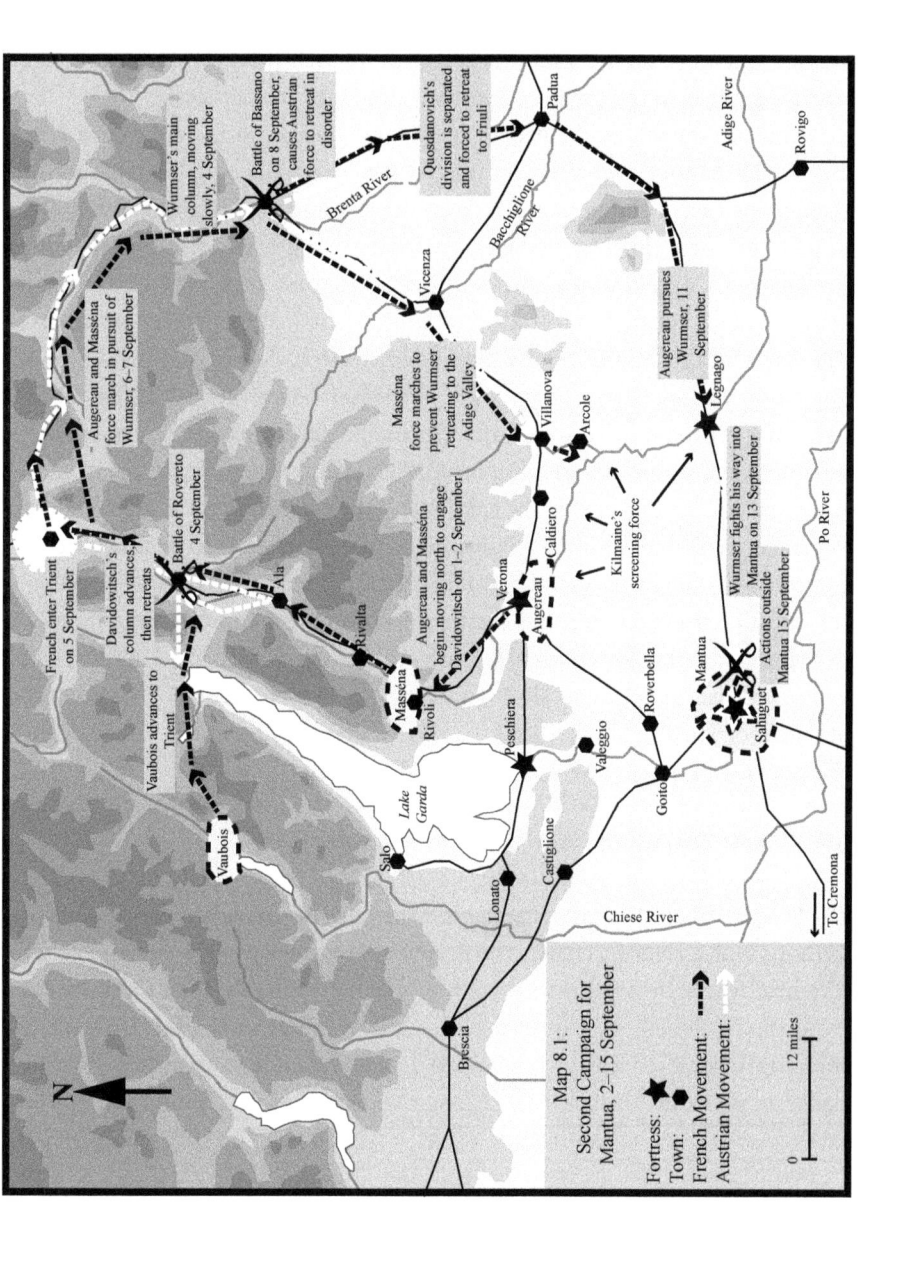

Map 8.1:
Second Campaign for
Mantua, 2–15 September

Fortress: ★
Town: ⬡

French Movement: ⟶ (dashed)
Austrian Movement: ⟶ (white)

0 _____ 12 miles

N

Labels on map:

French enter Trent
on 5 September

Vaubois advances to
Trient

Davidowitsch's
column advances,
then retreats

Battle of Rovereto
4 September

Augereau and Masséna
begin moving north to engage
Davidowitsch on 1–2 September

Augereau and Masséna
force march in pursuit of
Wurmser, 6–7 September

Wurmser's main
column, moving
slowly, 4 September

Battle of Bassano
on 8 September,
causes Austrian
force to retreat in
disorder

Quosdanovich's
division is separated
and forced to retreat
to Friuli

Masséna
force marches to
prevent Wurmser
retreating to the
Adige Valley

Augereau pursues
Wurmser, 11
September

Kilmaine's
screening force

Wurmser fights his way into
Mantua on 13 September

Actions outside
Mantua 15 September

Place names:

Padua, Rovigo, Adige River, Brenta River, Bacchiglione River, Vicenza, Villanova, Arcole, Caldiero, Verona, Augereau, Legnago, Roverbella, Mantua, Valeggio, Goito, Sahuguet, Po River, Ala, Rivalta, Masséna, Rivoli, Peschiera, Castiglione, Lonato, Salo, Lake Garda, Chiese River, Brescia, To Cremona

The Battle of Bassano on 8 September

At 7:00 a.m. on the 8th Bonaparte attacked these outposts; they held out for a while but were then overcome. With the French hard on their heels, they retreated, some to the camp at Bassano, some into the city itself.

What arrangements Wurmser made and how he was deployed are not known. He cannot have been completely surprised, since the six battalions in the outposts were about 4.5 miles from the city and had defended themselves in position for a time. Nonetheless, it seems that great confusion reigned in the Austrians' organization, since the French not only seized Bassano immediately but also captured two pontoon trains and many other transport wagons. The result of this battle about which we know so little was that the Austrians lost 2,000 prisoners and thirty guns. Wurmser had to retreat along the left bank of the Brenta to Fontania, but Quosdanovich's division was completely separated and forced to retreat to Friuli. According to the one source from the Austrian side for this part of the campaign,[4] the Englishman Colonel Graham, Wurmser retreated without a fight; his losses can therefore be attributed to surprise and the unsuccessful rearguard action. Since Graham was in Wurmser's headquarters, his account carries great weight, superficial though it is.

After deducting Mészáros's division and the troops detached in the Brenta valley and elsewhere, General Wurmser was left with some 16,000–18,000 men at Bassano. The French divisions comprised about 20,000 men.

50 WURMSER TAKES REFUGE IN MANTUA

On 8 September Wurmser (perhaps with part of Quosdanovich's division, perhaps with a reserve) crosses the Brenta at Fontania [Fontaniva] and goes to Vicenza, where Sebottendorf joins him, having probably gone there straight from the battlefield. Wurmser decides to take refuge in Mantua with his remaining troops, comprised of 12,000 infantry and 4,000 cavalry. Without pause he sets out to march to Legnago via Montebello [Montebello Vicen-

---

4. Clausewitz cites "*Histoire des Campagnes d'Italie, d'Allemagne et de Suisse en 1796, 97, 98 et 99.*" This four-volume history of the wars is attributed to Colonel J. M. Graham, who served in them. See J. M. Graham, *Histoire des Campagnes d'Italie, d'Allemagne et de Suisse en 1796, 97, 98 et 99* (Paris: Fournier, 1817).

tino], where he meets Mészáros and from which his advance guard leaves at dusk on the 9th. Mészáros has already occupied Legnago with a detachment that is busy hastily fortifying the place.

When Bonaparte realizes which direction Wurmser and his main body are taking, he begins to hope that he might force Wurmser to surrender in the open field. He hopes that crossing the Adige and navigating the terrain between Mantua and Legnago, part of which is crisscrossed by irrigation ditches and a host of small rivers, will delay the Austrians long enough so that Kilmaine can rush up with part of his besieging force and post himself at one of the crossings, while both Masséna's and Augereau's divisions close in on the Austrian flank and rear.

Before anything else, on the 8th Bonaparte has Augereau move to the highway to Padua, making it impossible for Wurmser to retreat to Friuli. But on the same day, Masséna heads for Vicenza, which he probably reaches that night, setting off again on the 9th and marching to Ronco on the Adige, where he collects some ferries and crosses the river on the 10th. Early on the 11th he arrives at Sanguinetto. Thus, in the seventy-two hours from 8 to 11 September, he has fought the battle of Bassano, crossed the river on a few small craft, and put a march of 58 to 63 miles behind him. Such activity is almost unprecedented; it is still more remarkable when one considers that in the immediately preceding seventy-two hours, this division had marched from Trient to Bassano, another 58 to 63 miles.[5]

The Action at Cerea on 11 September

Wurmser arrives at Legnago on 10 September, just as Masséna is crossing the Adige at Ronco [Ronco all'Adige]. He leaves 1,800 men with twenty field guns at Legnago, and on the 11th he continues his march toward Mantua via Sanguinetto. At Cerea, 4.5 miles from Legnago, General Ott, commanding the advance guard, soon bumps into Masséna's advance guard under Murat and Pigeon. The Austrian lead elements defeat Murat, but Pigeon is able to drive them back and take possession of the bridge over the Menago; but General Ott, seeing how weak the French are, and mindful of the danger the Austrian

5. Readers are reminded again that many of the French commanders were significantly younger than their Austrian counterparts, and it is reasonable to suppose that this age difference played a role in the relative dynamism of the French.

army is in, recaptures the bridge from them before Masséna's division can arrive. Thus, at this point, Wurmser manages to get away. Masséna's advance guard is forced to retreat halfway to Ronco and rejoin the division.

The Action at Villa Impenta on 12 September

Wurmser continues his march all night. Arriving at Nogara early on the 12th, he learns that troops from the besieging force under Sahuguet are holding the Molinella [Tartaro River] and the Tion [Tione River][6] at Castellaro [Castel d'Ario]. He leaves General Ott and his advance guard facing them, and he himself turns off to Villa Impenta [Villimpenta], where he finds a weakly held bridge that is seized by the Austrian uhlans. Some reinforcements sent there by Sahuguet are likewise beaten. Wurmser successfully reaches Mantua via Ronco Ferraro, and Ott follows him there without further loss.

On the 12th Masséna sets off in pursuit of the Austrian rear guard but reaches Castellaro after they have all left, and on the 13th he is at Due Castello [Castelbelforte][7] before Mantua.

After forcing the garrison of Legnago to lay down its arms on the 12th, on the 13th Augereau marched to Governolo, in order to close in Mantua from this side.

Sahuguet turned toward the Fort de la Favorite, where he became involved in a fight and got the worst of it.

51 THE ACTION AT ST. GEORGE AND THE FORT DE LA FAVORITE ON 15 SEPTEMBER

Wurmser now found himself at Mantua with a force of 29,000 men, of whom 4,000 were good cavalry. In these circumstances he did not intend to let him-

---

6. In this part of Italy there are numerous small rivers and canals, and the locals often have their own names for them; hence the occasional confusion.

7. Clausewitz likely means Due Castello (two castles): Castel Belforte and Castel Bonafisso appear on old maps. Their position also would fit Masséna's attempt to avoid any Austrian rear guard on the direct road to Mantua. See "Franziszeische Landesaufnahme (1806–1869)," accessed 7 July 2017, http://mapire.eu/de/map/second survey/?layers=osm%2C5%2C42&bbox=1206169.4778398622%2C5649305.394139564% 2C1216201.8378022916%2C5655038.171260951.

self be driven across the lake into the city straightaway, so he set up camp with thirteen battalions and twenty-four squadrons between the Fort de la Favorite and the suburb of St. George. Masséna wanted to exploit this initial moment of uncertainty, and early on the 14th he made a kind of surprise attack on the Austrian camp. At first, alarm and confusion reigned, but after a few infantry units formed themselves up in defense and General Ott's cavalry, which had just returned from foraging, hurled themselves on the French, the attackers were driven back to Castelbelforte and apparently roughly handled.

The successful actions at Cerea on the 11th, Villimpenta on the 12th, and Castelbelforte on 14 September, for which the Austrians could mainly thank their superior numbers of high-quality cavalry, emboldened General Wurmser to seek a general battle with the French on the 15th, combined with a foraging expedition. Thus, on this day he advanced a few thousand paces between the Legnago and Verona highways with some 16,000–18,000 men. As Augereau had left some troops at Governolo, the three French divisions were about 20,000 strong.

Initially, no enemy was visible directly to his front because Masséna was concealed further back, whereas Augereau's division (led by General Bon because Augereau was ill)[8] had pushed forward to the Mincio on the Austrian right flank. Wurmser therefore sent his right wing against Augereau and successfully drove this division back about 3.5 miles from St. George. But now that Wurmser's center was weakened, Masséna's division appeared and was able to push into the area between the citadel and Fort St. George, and Victor[9] pursued the Austrians and seized the fort itself. This naturally obliged the Austrian right wing to retreat, and Wurmser and his force escaped with difficulty across the moat of the citadel and into the fortress, after incurring 2,000 dead and wounded.

The Austrians had now lost every point on the left bank of the Mincio right up to the citadel. However, they remained in possession of the so-called Seraglio, a very fertile strip of land between the Mincio, the Po, and the canal that ran from Mantua to Borgoforte.

In the city there were constant outbreaks of disease, which soon took such a hold that no more than 18,000 men were fit to fight.

---

8. According to Boycott-Brown, *Road to Rivoli*, 435, he "was suffering haemorrhoids and severe rheumatic pains."

9. Claude Victor went on to become a marshal of France. He was 31 at the beginning of the campaign.

Throughout September and October Wurmser made many sorties, but they produced no noteworthy results, either individually or collectively.

The French Directory now decides not to actively besiege Mantua again but instead to wait for it to fall from hunger and sickness.

Bonaparte is deployed as follows:

Kilmaine:	9,000 blockading Mantua
Augereau:	9,000 at Verona
Masséna:	10,000 at Bassano and Treviso
Maquère and Dumas:	4,000 in reserve at Villafranca
Vaubois:	10,000 at Trient
Total:	42,000 men

52 OBSERVATIONS

We have already expressed our opinion of the aim of this second offensive against Bonaparte in section 47. If we accept that the decision to undertake it is irreversible, it still remains to deliver our verdict on its execution.

Let us first ask: what did this second offensive achieve? As we have seen, although Wurmser's first offensive was defeated, it produced an entirely acceptable result: Mantua was relieved and rendered impossible to besiege for the time being.

But this second offensive not only failed to improve the general situation; it quite obviously made it worse. At the end of it, there was a force of 29,000 men, of which 4,000 were cavalry, trapped in Mantua—at least in the strategic meaning of the word—and thus in danger of being lost completely in a short time through hunger. From now on, Bonaparte was spared the effort of initiating any action on that side of the Alps, since the downfall of such a large Austrian army was already well worth Bonaparte's 40,000 men waiting several months for it to occur. We may therefore say that this second Austrian offensive could not have had a worse result.

Let us investigate the causes that led to this result.

The Austrians again advanced with their forces divided, and they divided them in roughly the same way as the first time. If we consider the troops in Vorarlberg and facing the Veltlin as unavailable, even though it is hard to see why the latter had to stay there, that leaves Davidowitsch with 14,000 men and

Wurmser with 26,000. This time, the two columns are separated not by a lake but by a mountain range, with just one road in the Brenta valley for the line of communications between them; if the enemy cuts this road, their separation is as absolute as in the previous case. But it is worse because, this time, the Austrians do not have such a great numerical superiority. Both times, the French had about 30,000 men available, while the Austrians had 50,000 the first time but only 40,000 the second.

Now, if the supposed intention was to defeat Bonaparte in a battle and thereby relieve the siege of Mantua, the lead-up was so obviously unfavorable that it scarcely had any chance of success, and it is pointless to waste any more words on it. But again and again, the published works on this campaign suggest that the Austrians had no intention of fighting a battle; rather, they wanted to achieve their aim by strategic maneuver.[10]

To achieve a positive aim—in this case, driving Bonaparte from the right

10. This is an important point, as Clausewitz focuses on the purpose of the engagement (battle) to further the political aims of the war, whereas eighteenth-century theorists often talked down the importance of the engagement because of its inherent risk. The engagement involves the use of battle to physically break down and destroy the enemy's armed forces so that they are no longer able to attain their political objective, while at the same time allowing one's own forces to achieve their political goals. As one can imagine, and as Clausewitz argues, this is extremely risky. As such, many theorists prior to Clausewitz (and many after him, such as Basil Liddell-Hart, *Strategy* [New York: Praeger, 1967]) have argued for a maneuver (indirect) approach and the avoidance of direct confrontation. For a contemporary example, one of the great eighteenth-century theorists, Maurice de Saxe, does not rule out the use of engagements but argues that they are too risky; he believes they should be avoided and that it is possible to make war "without trusting anything to accident." Maurice Count de Saxe, *Reveries, or, Memoirs Concerning the Art of War* (Edinburgh: Sands, Donaldson, Murray, and Cochran, 1759), 226–227. Saxe's argument—that one can avoid luck and at the same time minimize risk—runs directly counter to Clausewitz's teachings, as luck is a key part of his foundational paradoxical trinity of war. It must be pointed out that prior to the French Revolution, eighteenth-century theorists were writing in an extremely limiting contextual environment; with the preservation of ruling elites being the norm, there was little requirement to focus on anything other than military systems, tactics, and organizations. As such, we must be careful in our criticism. For an excellent analysis of military theory that examines the changes Clausewitz was part of, see Beatrice Heuser, *Strategy before Clausewitz: Linking Warfare and Statecraft, 1400–1830* (Abingdon, UK: Routledge, 2018), 167–202.

[left][11] bank of the Mincio—by means of a strategic maneuver is generally very difficult and assumes that the enemy's position has a weak flank that serves as the actual agent for the maneuver, since without cause, there is no effect. But there was nothing of the kind to be found in Bonaparte's position relative to the two Austrian columns in the Adige and Brenta valleys, and this principle, which had made the column advancing to the Chiese so effective in the first offensive, was entirely absent from the second. Thus, the hope of forcing Bonaparte to retreat across the Mincio through this or that well-designed maneuver was completely plucked out of the air and cannot stand up to criticism. However, one can conceive that it would have been possible through maneuver alone to detain Bonaparte in Italy and prevent him from continuing his offensive through the Tyrol. At the Adige, the axis of Bonaparte's attack turns left almost ninety degrees,[12] and the French base of operations now lies on his left flank, but his right flank is threatened from the whole Austrian border. If an Austrian army now advances down the Brenta valley and does as Wurmser did on 6, 7, and 8 September and deploys at Bassano, there is hardly any doubt that this would neutralize the French offensive in the Adige and Eisach valleys. The French commander would be forced to retreat to the Italian plain, since continuing his blow could not bring about such a change of fortune [in the campaign as a whole] that the Austrian army on the Brenta would be affected by it, and the damage it could inflict on him in his rear by relieving Mantua and cutting his sole line of communications could not be compensated for on his front. The position on the Brenta served here as a flank position, and since its commander could, with some foresight, always retain more than one line of retreat, the risk of being cut off, which flank positions otherwise often run, was not present in this case.

But the critic still has one more very important objection to this use of strategic maneuver. Against a commander who wants and seeks battle, especially decisive battle, maneuver is rarely possible and is therefore out of place. Strategic maneuver is the direct consequence of the interplay of forces and conditions being in such equilibrium that there is no prospect of a major decision because neither of the two commanders wants it. Only then is maneuver natural, protected by general conditions that suit it, and in its element. Deci-

11. He means the left bank, given the flow of the river to the south.

12. Note that the Adige largely flows south and then east, and Clausewitz has Napoleon moving north in this example.

sion by battle is of a higher order to which the lower must yield; it is a sterner element that smites the airy web of maneuver.[13] How can a commander risk dividing his forces and keeping them divided for small successes, for weak and slow effects, when the thunderbolt of devastating battle could strike his main body at any moment?

We have seen this shattering blow strike Wurmser's main body. Wurmser probably thought that if his position at Bassano and his demonstrations against Verona forced his opponent to retreat down the Adige valley, he would have enough warning of any decisive blows to avoid them; but Bonaparte made a mockery of these precautions and caught him from the direction he did not expect. If Wurmser had not been lucky enough to fall back as he did from the battle of Bassano, Bonaparte would not have stopped pursuing him through each successive position until he had driven him into the mountains of Carinthia.

Thus we cannot accept the validity of the entire intention of the maneuver, and we find the Austrian plan of attack to be lacking both a clearly conceived aim and a clearly conceived method; it was a confused mess of half-baked ideas that was doomed to splinter like matchwood before Bonaparte's genius.

Once General Wurmser had set off down the Brenta valley, and once he heard the news of Bonaparte's attack on Davidowitsch, there could be no thought of turning back. This was inherent in the very structure of the operation, so the fact that General Wurmser did not turn back can be considered neither a mistake nor a great virtue. Bonaparte called it the latter in his report to the Directory, for he took a consequence of the system to be a decision of the moment. As a bold stroke at a moment of crisis, Wurmser's move cannot incur the same blame we directed against the plan of attack.

Given the lack of Austrian reports, no judgment can be made on the battle of Bassano. We cannot discover why Wurmser accepted battle there, if indeed that was the case; how he fought it; how Quosdanovich became separated from him; or how he was driven toward Mantua. In short, we lack all the strategic points of reference.

We do have one observation to make in connection with Bonaparte. At this battle he was about 20,000 strong, so against an enemy with overall numerical superiority, he was apparently unable to achieve local superiority at the point of decision. The reason is this: although he left a disproportionately

13. See note 10 on Maurice de Saxe.

large force of 11,000 men under Vaubois to face the beaten Davidowitsch, he secured his passage down the Brenta valley and, with it, two major strategic advantages for his battle—first, to fall on the foe swiftly, astonishingly swiftly; and second, to strike him in his strategic rear. The first factor made his success easier; the second magnified it. Thus, if he was weaker in this battle than he could have been through other strategic combinations, this is not because he let troops sit idle and useless. Trusting his luck, and confident in himself and in his army, he raised the stakes, gambling greater risk for greater gain.

Wurmser's decision to shut himself up in Mantua is seen by some as an act of necessity, by others as a stroke of luck. Whether it was unavoidable after the battle of Bassano, we are not in a position to judge, but a stroke of luck it certainly was not, since nowhere was this army, with its fine cavalry, of less use than in Mantua. We can only consider it the result of complete strategic defeat.[14]

From Wurmser's point of view, it is difficult to understand the point of the battle of the 15th outside the walls of Mantua. It was certainly due mainly to a confused notion that it would be shameful for such an army to hide in the fortress immediately. But in war, that which is of genuine use to the whole war effort never incurs shame, while martial honor is never enhanced by that which is useless and harmful. This sortie was an act of vainglory that was bound to end badly; it would have been much cannier of the Austrians to withdraw to the Seraglio and organize themselves sensibly there.

Bonaparte's conduct against this second Austrian offensive is beyond all praise. He chooses the most decisive course of action because he is certain of his purpose, and he executes it with force and at a ferocious pace that has no equal.

14. If the Austrian plan was to use maneuver to move the French back from the Mincio, it was indeed an enormous failure on Wurmser's part to give up his ability to scout and maneuver in such a fashion.

9. The Campaign and Battle of Arcole

53 THE FRENCH ARMY'S SITUATION

The French army's victory in Italy at Bassano could not launch it on an offensive into the Austrian states because Mantua was now occupied by 29,000
men, of whom 15,000–16,000 still held the Seraglio outside the fortress for the
time being. Investing or observing this mass of troops naturally required a
larger force than it had when the garrison was a third of its present size. How
few men Bonaparte would have been able to lead into the Alps! Besides, as we
have already said, a close investment of the present garrison of Mantua was
a very worthwhile operational aim in itself for the Army of Italy to pursue.
A total blockade must soon lead to the fall of the fortress, since it was not
provisioned to hold so many men. Then, not only Mantua but also a whole
Austrian army would fall into French hands.[1]

Thus, these two considerations soon banished any thought of intervening
beyond the Alps. But there was also a third, namely, the political situation in
Italy.

1. Colin, 183, notes: "Half the garrison of Mantua was in the sick bay. The day after
the battle of St. George, which cost Wurmser serious losses, there were only 14,000
men fit for duty in the fortress, that is to say, about the number that were there in June
and in August. The autumn fevers would again reduce this garrison considerably. It
was therefore not this that held Bonaparte back; but the Directory wanted to make
peace with Austria immediately, and it was important to hold Mantua before opening
negotiations; Clausewitz himself acknowledges this later (page 187 [of Colin; here, the
paragraphs on either side of note 6 in section 53]). Bonaparte, for his part, was thinking ahead to the 1797 campaign, for which he did not have the necessary funds, and
he wanted to go and impose a new contribution on the pope; he could only do that
once the blockading force became available, all his other troops being required in the
front line." Phillip Cuccia provides numbers from the Austrian archives: "By mid-
September the Austrians had 15,746 soldiers in the fortress of whom only 9,004 were
fit for duty." He then points out that after the battle of St. George, these numbers had
risen to "about 30,000 men," of whom "only 18,000 were ready for service." See Cuccia, *Napoleon in Italy*, 56, 64.

The French mistrusted the court of Turin [the government of Sardinia] because they would not commit themselves to offering Sardinia a significant share of their Italian conquests to obtain an offensive alliance, and Turin did not want to get involved for such meager terms and vague promises. The alpine passes on the border between this country and France were seriously troubled by numerous armed bands known as Barbets [*barbetti*]. These bandits were mostly smugglers and men from a disbanded Sardinian regiment of foreign mercenaries, and they may have been abetted or at least left unhindered by Sardinian officials if not by the government itself.[2]

Relations with Genoa were not much better until a peace treaty was concluded with the Republic in October.

The province of Milan itself was peaceful, although behind the Milanese's hugely enthusiastic affection for the French a great ill will toward them was secretly brewing, and it gave cause for concern in the event of a reverse. Even so, the provisional government the French had installed in Milan raised not only national guards but also a corps of 3,000–4,000 troops, which, although they were not yet intended to serve in the line, could still be seen as a provincial garrison.

The French Directory had a great internal need for peace, and this grew as the war in Germany took a turn for the worse for France. Because of this, it could not yet consider republicanizing Lombardy, partly so as not to completely alienate Austria from peace, and partly to be able to offer Austria compensation in Italy for the left bank of the Rhine, possession of which the Directory valued above all else. It was therefore very wary of raising too many hopes among the Milanese and of allowing them too much say in their own government.

The Directory was even more cautious about the occupied provinces on the right bank of the Po belonging to the pope and to the Duke of Modena.[3]

---

2. These have been described as "smuggler-bandits" who fought against external intruders (particularly the French) in the seventeenth and eighteenth centuries. Contrary to Clausewitz's comments, they seem to have been more closely related to local people rather than from a disbanded regiment. See Michael Broers, "Revolt and Repression in Napoleonic Italy 1796–1814," in *War in an Age of Revolution 1775–1815*, ed. Roger Chickering and Stig Förster (New York: Cambridge University Press, 2010), 200.

3. Colin, 185, notes: "This remark by Clausewitz is interesting, even if he does not explain what he is suggesting. It seems that in the summer of 1796 Bonaparte had conceived the project of creating an Italian republic with the Adige as its eastern frontier,

Bologna, Ferrara, and Reggio had likewise set up their own provisional governments, and in the month of October, Bonaparte, who was especially hostile toward the Duke of Modena, decided to break the armistice with Modena on trivial pretexts, depose the regency installed in Modena by the absent duke, and establish a provisional government there on the same basis as the three others. Indeed, he went so far as to give these four provinces a kind of unity in the form of a common Council of Deputies. The Directory was not pleased with these steps taken by Bonaparte, but since everything had been done in such a way that these developments seemed to emerge from the provinces themselves and the French merely tolerated them, the Directory left matters on this footing. Here too, national guards were established, and preparations were made to deploy a corps of 2,000–3,000 men.

If the latitude the French thus allowed their supporters provided them with some degree of internal security and order so long as things went well, it naturally also greatly increased the enmity and hate of the other parties, and the state of affairs became so tense and uncertain that in the event of a general turnaround of circumstances, no good would come of it.[4]

Such a change of fortunes could have been brought about by the king of Naples and the pope. The former was reasonably well armed and was with his troops on the border with Rome. There was a great deal of tension between the pope and the Republic, and a peremptorily dispatched, nonnegotiable peace treaty had given the Holy Father the feeling that if he did not quickly ally himself with his natural friends, Austria and Naples, he would be lost. Thus he rejected all French demands and made preparations to arm. The moment was therefore not far off when Naples and the pope could unleash their forces against Bonaparte together. Even if they mustered an army of only 30,000

---

separating Austria, Piedmont, and the Papal States. The Duchy of Modena, stretching from the Po to the Tyrrhenian Sea, could separate Piedmont from Rome by itself; Bonaparte wanted to incorporate it into the Cisalpine Republic. This is where the hostile attitude Clausewitz detects comes from."

4. Again, this brings us back to Clausewitz's trinity (*On War*, book 1, chap. 1). It is also worth noting that, according to Clausewitz, the tendency of war is to escalate, and he indicates the risks of this here. One can see his logic: if Napoleon was unsuccessful, there was a risk of increased violence between the supporters of the new French order and the supporters of the old one. War, therefore, had unleashed passions simmering below the surface of Austrian-controlled Italy. The same pattern would be repeated across Europe for at least the next quarter century.

men, still, if this coincided with a new Austrian offensive, it could decide the destiny of upper Italy in this campaign. Now it is clear that an advance to the Austrian border, which would involve Bonaparte in operations that would engage all his combat forces, would have emboldened both these powers and thus brought the insecurity of the situation in Lombardy into question again.

All these circumstances completely explain and justify why, after his victory at Bassano, Bonaparte stayed in his previous position for six weeks, that is, until Alvinczy attacked.[5]

Admittedly, immediately after the victory at Bassano, the Directory appears to take something of a fancy to the operation against Trieste that Bonaparte had proposed previously, but this seems to have been more of a courtesy to Bonaparte.[6] In any case, news of the battle of Würzburg (which took place

---

5. General Joseph Alvinczy (age 61) had a long and somewhat mixed career in the Austrian army. He took over command of Austrian forces in Italy after Beaulieu's failure. In 1808 he was promoted to field marshal, presumably as a sinecure, given his lack of success. See Wurzbach, *Biographisches Lexikon des Kaiserthums Oesterreich*, 1:22–23.

6. Clausewitz notes: "The Directory instructed this general to send a courier to Vienna to threaten the emperor. The relevant part of the Directory's letter of 20 September to Bonaparte reads as follows: 'Among the provisions we have adopted to benefit from our advantages and make them decisive in favor of the Republic, whose interests all tend toward peace, the first is to indicate to the emperor that, unless he agrees to send a plenipotentiary to Paris to enter into negotiations, you will destroy his port of Trieste and all his establishments on the Adriatic Sea. As soon as the fate of Wurmser and his division shall be decided, you will send a dispatch to Vienna to notify him of this, and you will march on Trieste, ready to carry out a threat that is justified by the laws of war and by the stubbornness of a proud house that dares everything against the Republic and toys with its good faith.' [*Parmi les dispositions que nous avons adoptées pour tirer parti de nos avantages, et les rendre decisifs en faveur de la république, dont les intérêts tendent tous à la paix, la première est de signifier à l'empereur, que s'il ne consent à envoyer sur le champ un chargé de pouvoir à Paris, pour entrer en negociations, vous allez detruire son port de Trieste et tous ses établissements sur la mer adriatique. Aussitôt que le sort de Wurmser et son division sera décidé, vous dépêcherez à Vienne, pour faire cette notification et vous marcherez sur Trieste, prêt à exécuter une ménace, que légitiment le droit de la guerre et l'opiniatreté d'une orgueilleuse maison qui ose tout contre la republique et se joue de sa loyauté.*] On 2 October, as soon as he received this letter, Bonaparte sent a courier to Vienna with the following letter: 'Sire. Europe desires peace. This disastrous war has lasted too long. I have the honor to tell Your Majesty that if Your Majesty does not send a plenipotentiary to Paris to begin peace negotiations, the Executive Directory orders me to sack the port of Trieste and to destroy all Your Majesty's establishments on the Adriatic. Thus far I have been detained from

on 3 September) and of Jourdan's retreat behind the Rhine made such an impression on the Directory that it (rightly) thought of nothing else but ensuring and expediting the conquest of Mantua.[7]

Wurmser's second defeat and Jourdan's rout, which happened at about the same time, led to the peace with Naples. The Neapolitan court naturally learned of the first development before the second, and thereafter its negotiator in Paris, who had notably fobbed the matter off, now entered into negotiations with great zeal. The Directory, informed of Jourdan's retreat at the end of September, became very worried about affairs in Germany, so on 10 October a peace treaty came into force, the terms of which were, for the moment,

---

carrying out this plan by my hope not to increase the number of innocent victims of this war. I desire Your Majesty to be sensitive to the woes that threaten his subjects, and to make the world restful and tranquil. With respect for Your Majesty, I remain, Bonaparte.' [*Sire. L'Europe veut la paix. Cette guerre désastreuse dure depuis trop long tems. J'ai l'honneur de prévenir Votre Majesté, que si Elle n'envoye pas de Plenipotentière à Paris pour entamer les négociations de paix, le directoire exécutif m'ordonne de combler le Port de Trieste et de ruiner tous les établissements de Votre Majesté sur l'Adriatique. Jusqu'ici j'ai été retenu dans l'éxécution de ce plan par l'espérance de ne pas accroitre le nombre des victimes innocens de cette guerre. Je désire que Votre Majesté soit sensible aux malheurs qui ménacent ses sujets, et rende le repos et tranquillité au monde. Je suis avec respect de Votre Majesté, Bonaparte.*] It is not known whether or not this remarkable courier was turned back by the Austrian outposts, nor what other consequences this indecorous step that was inappropriate in every respect, smacking rather of the sansculottism of the time, might have had." For Napoleon's response and letter to the Austrian emperor, see Napoléon I, *Correspondance de Napoléon Ier*, 2:32–35.

7. That being said, the Directory's letter to Napoleon and his subsequent threat to the Austrian emperor clearly indicate that the limited wars of the seventeenth and eighteenth centuries were very much a thing of the past. Furthermore, this does match Clausewitz's view on the theory of war (*On War*, book 1, chaps. 1–2), which was that its natural tendency is to escalate. Thus, this threat to the Austrians would raise the stakes for them, thereby increasing the cost of their political objective. They would need to decide whether to concede (accepting that the price was too high) or to continue to fight, knowing they had accepted a higher cost for their political object. As such, they would also need to escalate the violence necessary to obtain their policy goals, or they would need to renounce the political object if they thought the cost of achieving it was too high to justify the expense. Given French demands and the nature of the revolutionary state to which Clausewitz alludes above ("sansculottism"), it is logical that the French, in turn, would need to increase the level of violence (military pressure) on the Austrians, and given the increased cost to them, they would again raise the stakes, thus creating an escalating series of demands and reciprocal violence.

in no way onerous for the king of Naples and so appeared very advantageous compared with what one had become accustomed to [from the French]. The king of Naples therefore retreated just when he could have made a major impact. In mid-October the French situation in Germany was irretrievably lost for the rest of the year; if the king's intervention had coincided with Alvinczy's advance, then in all human probability, Bonaparte would have had to evacuate the whole of upper Italy, putting the situation back on much the same footing as at the close of the previous year.[8]

The pope, though deprived of his closest support, saw no alternative but to continue his program of armament and was probably encouraged in this by Austria's promise of a new offensive in Italy.

Meanwhile, Bonaparte let his divisions rest and resupply: Kilmaine outside Mantua, Vaubois at Trient, Masséna at Bassano and Treviso, and Augereau at Verona. Apart from political matters, he himself was very busy dealing with the abuses of military rule and spent most of his time in Milan.

We do not know exactly how things went inside and outside Mantua during this time. Throughout the month of September, Wurmser held his ground in the Seraglio, but by the beginning of October, he seems to have confined himself inside Mantua. Since there were no more than 10,000 French outside Mantua, one can imagine that the investment was not very thorough, and indeed, the place seems to have been constantly resupplied with provisions from the surrounding area.

Bonaparte's method here absolutely cannot be condoned. If, straight after the battle of the Fort de la Favorite on 15 September, he had prevented Wurmser from occupying the Seraglio and had kept him locked up so that he had to live off the garrison's stores, the fortress might have fallen with its entire garrison at the end of October. We can also probably say that, even if Bonaparte was not in a position to follow up his victory beyond his theater of operations, he still neglected to exploit his victory within it—that is, by intensively continuing his attack on Mantua. The only explanation for this is the unhealthy district around Mantua. Bonaparte claims that at the time of the battle of Arcole [Arcola], the Austrian garrison in Mantua had 12,000 sick, and he was afraid that if a large part of his army was encamped outside the place, it would be devastated by disease. Besides, he had braced himself not to expect Mantua

8. Again, it is worth noting the clear link between the success (or not) of the physical engagement of the warring parties and their consequent political actions.

to fall before February, and on 16 October he called on Wurmser to surrender the fortress but offered to allow him and his army to withdraw freely.

When we consider how precarious Bonaparte's situation had become by the time of the battle of Arcole, and how easily a much stronger blow could have been struck against him if the king of Naples had not quit the war or if the Austrians had sent troops to Italy from their army on the Rhine, we must regard this omission of Bonaparte's as a quite eminent strategic error.[9]

Throughout this period, Bonaparte applied constantly to the Directory for reinforcements. Bit by bit, it sent 26,000 men to him, but it is not known how many of them arrived or when.[10] All that seems certain is that at the start of November, his army had the following strengths:

9. Colin, 189, notes: "It is difficult to know whether the blockade was more or less strictly maintained; but the French army there had lost 20,000 men sick or dead of fever, that is to say, more than from a serious defeat. It was important not to keep the troops too long in front of the walls of Mantua." Colin's point about attrition is an important one, as armies of the period typically lost more men from disease and illness than in combat. That being said, Colin's numbers are impossible to verify. If he means the French had permanently lost 20,000 men outside Mantua, he provides no evidence; if he means they had 20,000 sick and dead, this does not tally with Cuccia's figure of 14,000 sick, which he cites from Napoleon's correspondence. See Cuccia, *Napoleon in Italy*, 71. However, reading the letter cited by Cuccia shows that there were 4,000 additional dead too. Thus, the total was 18,000 sick and dead rather than Colin's 20,000 or Cuccia's 14,000 sick. See Napoléon I, *Correspondance de Napoléon Ier*, 2:25 (letter 1055).

10. Clausewitz notes: "How Bonaparte always remains true to his nature at any given point can be seen from the following excerpt from his letter sent to the Directory on 14 November, the day before the battle of Arcole began: 'Not a day passes when [the Austrian army] does not receive 5,000 more men, and for two months it has been obvious that help is needed here, yet all that has reached me is a battalion of the 40th, poor troops, unused to combat. . . .' [*Il n'est pas de jour où il n'arrive (bei der östreichischen Armee) 5000 hommes et depuis deux mois, qu'il est evident qu'il faut des secours ici, il n'est encore arrive qu'un bataillon de la quarantième, mauvaise troupe, non accoutumée au feu" etc. . . .*] But in his *Memoirs* he says on p. 318: 'The Directory promised much but had little. Meanwhile it sent a dozen battalions, taken from the Army of the Vendée, which arrived in Milan in the course of September and October.' [*Le Directoire promettoit beaucoup, mais tenoit peu, il envoya cependant douze bataillons, tires de l'armée de la Vendée qui arrivèrent à Milan dans le courant de Septembre et Octobre.*] What mendacity and what contempt for his government it must have taken for him to allow himself to exaggerate so. We cannot believe that he could have made a mistake in his *Memoirs*, since at the beginning of November his army was 42,000 strong again,

Kilmaine outside Mantua:	9,000
Augereau in Verona:	9,000
Masséna at Bassano and Treviso:	10,000
Vaubois at Trient:	10,000
Reserves under Maquère and	
Dumas at Villa Franca:	4,000
Total:	42,000 men, of which some
	30,000 can be considered available[11]

Bonaparte's mission in the face of a new Austrian offensive was clearly somewhat different this time. The first time, he had abandoned the siege of Mantua because it was impossible for him to cover it; this second time, he had no important reason to prevent the Austrians from reaching Mantua, since nothing could result from it except a reinforcement of the garrison, which seemed of no decisive importance. But this time, Wurmser absolutely had to be prevented from escaping from Mantua and creating a new army by combining the 10,000–12,000 men he could take with him with a substantial Austrian column. It was not just about beating the enemy but also about covering a definite objective.[12]

---

which, as it must certainly have lost 10,000–12,000 men since the start of September, implies considerable reinforcement, even if we assume that Bonaparte called forward some troops from his rear areas." See Montholon, *Mémoires pour servir à l'Histoire de France sous Napoléon*, 3:318–319.

11. Colin, 190, notes: "The total Clausewitz gives is accurate; but the figure for those fit for duty is not. Kilmaine had just 8,000 men rather than 9,000; Masséna, 5,100; Augereau, 5,600; Macquart, 2,600. The 40th and 75th [Demi-brigades] still had not rejoined the army; there were 4,500 men in garrisons and Macquart's division was among them. It was therefore not available for field operations." Boycott-Brown's numbers are closer to Clausewitz's, and Colin's numbers seem too low because, for him to be correct, half of Napoleon's army would need to be sick or wounded. Boycott-Brown, *Road to Rivoli*, 448.

12. Colin, 191, notes: "Clausewitz has recognized perfectly that the operations of November 1796 have a very particular character which distinguishes them from those of August and September and those of January 1797; but he is mistaken about the grounds for Mantua's momentary importance. We know now that Wurmser did not have 10,000 men available for an operation outside the fortress, his total effectives being not more than 10,000 men fit for duty." Boycott-Brown, *Road to Rivoli*, 448, gives the number of Austrian troops fit for duty in Mantua as 12,420.

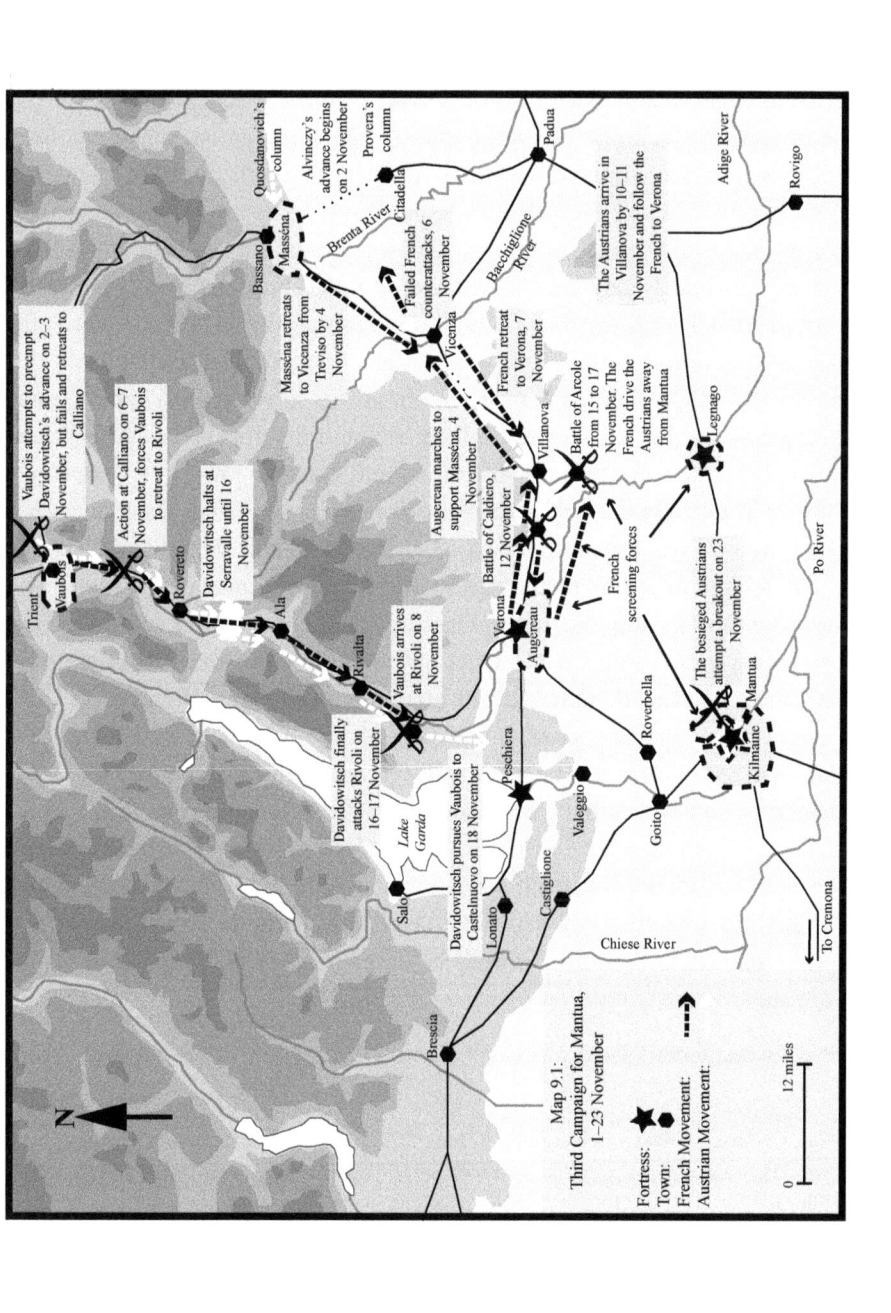

Map 9.1:
Third Campaign for Mantua,
1–23 November

Fortress: ★

Town: ⬢

French Movement: ➔

Austrian Movement: ▬ ▬ ➤

0   12 miles

N

Quosdanovich's column

Alvinczy's advance begins on 2 November

Provera's column

The Austrians arrive in Villanova by 10–11 November and follow the French to Verona

Failed French counterattacks, 6 November

Massena retreats to Vicenza from Treviso by 4 November

French retreat to Verona, 7 November

Augereau marches to support Massena, 4 November

Battle of Arcole from 15 to 17 November. The French drive the Austrians away from Mantua

Battle of Caldiero, 12 November

French screening forces

The besieged Austrians attempt a breakout on 23 November

Vaubois attempts to preempt Davidowitsch's advance on 2–3 November, but fails and retreats to Calliano

Action at Calliano on 6–7 November, forces Vaubois to retreat to Rivoli

Davidowitsch halts at Serravalle until 16 November

Vaubois arrives at Rivoli on 8 November

Davidowitsch finally attacks Rivoli on 16–17 November

Davidowitsch pursues Vaubois to Castelnuovo on 18 November

Padua

Bassano

Citadella

Brenta River

Vicenza

Villanova

Bacchiglione River

Legnago

Adige River

Rovigo

Po River

Massena

Verona

Augereau

Roverbella

Mantua

Kilmaine

Gotto

Valeggio

Peschiera

Rivalta

Ala

Roveredo

Trient

Vaubois

Castiglione

Lonato

Salo

Lake Garda

Chiese River

Brescia

To Cremona

54 THE AUSTRIANS' NEW PLAN OF ATTACK

After the second operation for the liberation of Mantua (as the Austrians re-ferred to it) failed and two-thirds of Wurmser's army practically vanished, for the time being, from the war zone, the Austrian government made the most vigorous efforts to confront the enemy army in Italy with a new one.

The column under Quosdanovich that had retreated to the Piave and the Isonzo comprised some 6,000 men. The Austrian government mobilized ev-erything to quickly reinforce it with newly raised border troops[13] and with some regular battalions that were still in inner Austria. It was sufficiently successful in doing so that, four weeks after Wurmser's defeat, that is, in the second half of October, by very strenuous efforts it was able to deploy some 28,000 men on the Isonzo, the Tagliamento, and the upper Piave at Belluno. Through better concentration of forces, and because Moreau's retreat be-ginning in October made the corps in Vorarlberg available, Davidowitsch's troops in the Tyrol were also increased to 20,000 men in the Adige valley.

Thus, close to 50,000 men could be pitted against Bonaparte. If matters in Germany took a completely favorable turn, then naturally, all available rein-forcements could be directed to Italy, and since there was an entire army to be freed from Mantua, there was clearly an urgent need for an offensive.

In a fairly natural way, given the positions of the forces they now had, the Aus-trians decided to carry this out with two separate columns. Lieutenant General[14] Alvinczy, who was now the commander in chief, was to advance against Verona via Bassano with the 28,000 men from Friuli. Davidowitsch was to attack his op-ponent in the Adige valley, drive down the valley onto the plain, and then, united with Alvinczy or at least acting in concert with him, attack the French army.

The plan of operations for both columns is given in more detail in the Austrian account,[15] in the following words:

That Lieutenant Field Marshal[16] Baron Davidowitsch shall capture Trient

---

13. Croatian *Grenzer*; see chapter 4, note 21.

14. This was *Feldzeugmeister* in the original, which is often translated as general of artillery.

15. Clausewitz notes: "The encounter on the Brenta &c., 1796, in the 'Österreichische Militärische Zeitschrift,' 1828. Vol. 9, p. 222 &c."

16. This is another oddity. Only much later will the Austrians systematize the rank-ings in their army. We have translated this as it was written.

and the position at Calliano and then halt no further forward than the latter, in order to secure the right flank of the Friuli corps and to protect the Tyrol against further French incursions. Lieutenant Field Marshal Baron Quosdanovich shall march across the Piave to Bassano, but as soon as the Tyrol corps shall have taken Trient, he shall advance via Vicenza toward the Adige and give battle to the French army at Verona.

Lieutenant Field Marshal Baron Davidowitsch is generally instructed to employ any suitable opportunity to bring about the union of the Tyrolese and Friulian corps as soon as possible. Either he should establish communications with the Friuli corps by moving his left wing through the Val Fredda or some other suitable route, to reinforce it with his otherwise surplus troops or indeed to join up with it completely—or his corps should descend from Trient down the left bank of the Adige—or finally, if the enemy has neglected to occupy Monte Baldo, he should seize the position at Madonna della Coronna [Santuario Madonna della Corona] and then advance down the right bank of the Adige via Rivoli. Field Marshal Count Wurmser should be asked to sortie from Mantua with all available troops, to drive off the blockading corps, to advance against the rear of the French army and thereby contribute to the successful outcome of the battle to be given at Verona, whereby the liberation of Mantua shall then be brought about.

When Alvinczy took command of the army at the end of October, he ordered more specifically that on 3 November the Friuli corps should attack Bassano and the Tyrol corps should attack Trient.[17] Once the former had taken that city and crossed the Brenta, Alvinczy would wait to hear whether Davidowitsch had taken Trient and cleared the enemy from the Adige valley. Only then would he begin his crossing of the Adige, on whose successful execution the junction of the two imperial corps, the relief of Mantua, and the favorable outcome of the whole campaign depended.

We will make our observations later about the notions on which this plan was founded. Let us now relate the course of events as they came to pass during its execution.

---

17. Clausewitz notes: "Ibid., p. 229." This refers to note 15 above.

55 DAVIDOWITSCH STRIKES AGAINST GENERAL VAUBOIS IN THE ADIGE VALLEY

General Davidowitsch was with his main body at Neumarkt and had a couple of advanced posts at St. Michel and Segonzano, as well as his outposts on the Lavis where it flows into the Adige. Bonaparte was concerned that Davidowitsch might drive General Vaubois back some way and then march through the Brenta valley to join up with Alvinczy.[18] Bonaparte thought that, for the moment, the best way to guard against this was to order General Vaubois to drive away the Austrian outposts from their position on the Lavis in a limited offensive to pin Davidowitsch. However, as was rather in the nature of the beast, it achieved the opposite result. Instead of buying time, it precipitated the Austrian general's advance and indeed most probably made it easier for him.

The Action at St. Michel and Segonzano on 2 and 3 November

On 2 November General Vaubois attacked the Austrian outposts in two columns. At St. Michel, the French under General Guieu seemingly succeeded, but at Segonzano, those under Fiorelli and Vaubois himself were unable to drive off Wukassowitsch. The next day, on the 3rd, Davidowitsch arrived from Neumarkt with the main body, and Vaubois was forced to withdraw through Trient to the Calliano position.

The Action at Calliano on 6 and 7 November

Davidowitsch follows him, but it is not until the 6th, three days later, that he has the resources available to attack Vaubois's position.[19] He cannot break

18. Colin, 195, notes: "This explanation is the opposite of the truth: on the contrary, Bonaparte believed that Vaubois was only facing inferior forces, that he could defeat them and render them *hors de combat*, then send 3,000 men to reinforce Masséna for the operations against Alvinczy. To instruct Vaubois to attack an enemy who one feared would be superior would have been absurd."

19. Colin, 196, notes: "It is customary to criticize Davidowitsch's operations harshly. However, they seem fairly explicable. He did not want to push against Vaubois too

through on the first day, so the action continues on the 7th, with equally little success in the center, but on the right side of the Adige, the outposts at Nomi and Torbole at the northern tip of Lake Garda have already been attacked on the 6th and taken with significant losses to the French; on the 7th General Ocskay[20] manages to eject the French from the position at Mori as well. This obliges Vaubois to begin his retreat to the position at Rivoli and the Corona, which he reaches only with difficulty on the 8th. By their own admission, in these adverse actions the French losses included six guns, so they were not quite as insignificant as one might conclude from the slowness of the Austrian advance.

After this initial success, Davidowitsch halts.[21] He stays put at Serravalle until the 16th. He probably received orders from Alvinczy to halt, but still, this eight-day standstill is inexplicable, and there is no information at all about it.[22]

The Action at Rivoli on 16 and 17 November

Finally, on the 16th Davidowitsch attacks the heights of the Corona in four columns and takes it. On the 17th he attacks the Rivoli position. General Vau-

---

quickly because he was counting on him being driven off by Laudon, debouching from Torbole. This helping hand failed to come off. In Bonaparte's view, who sent Berthier to Vaubois just in time to bring his division back to the right bank of the Adige, the French could have suffered a complete disaster."

20. General Joseph Ocskay was another Austrian army officer in his mid-50s. His performance was mixed, and he retired in 1797.

21. Boycott-Brown, *Road to Rivoli*, 453, writes that Davidowitsch had lost almost a fifth of his force in the actions of 6–7 November and thus was perhaps "not in a great hurry to attack the Rivoli position."

22. Colin, 196–197, notes: "Here again Davidowitsch's immobility seems quite natural: it is the fatal consequence of the combined maneuvers. If Davidowitsch had reached Castelnuovo before Alvinczy was heavily engaged against Bonaparte, the French would have overwhelmed him by the time the Feldzeugmeister had crossed the Adige, then they would have returned against Alvinczy. It was only on the 16th, when Bonaparte was battling against the main Austrian army at Arcole, that Davidowitsch could take the risk. The only person responsible for Davidowitsch's inertia is he who ordered the combined offensive from the Tyrol and from Friuli." No matter who is responsible, Colin's point reinforces Clausewitz's criticism of the Austrians' lack of a clear strategic vision for the campaigns.

bois had been further weakened by the departure of Guieu's brigade, which Bonaparte had called away on the 14th, and he probably had fewer than 6,000 men with which to face the Austrians. Bypassed in several places, he was not only forced to retreat but also lost twelve guns and 1,200 taken prisoner, including Brigadier General Fiorelli. This was therefore a proper defeat that drove General Vaubois to the Castelnuovo area on the 17th, where Davidowitsch followed him on the 18th.

We have presented the events in the Adige valley here in their entirety because none of the to-ing and fro-ing of the French main body happened here, and also because when we look at the operations of the Austrian main army, it is convenient to have an overview of Davidowitsch's operations first.

56 ALVINCZY ADVANCES AGAINST VERONA

On 2 November Alvinczy and his main body crossed the Piave at La Campanna, on the road from Sacile to Bassano. On the 5th they advanced toward the Brenta in two columns, one to Bassano under Quosdanovich, the other to Citadella under Provera.

On 4 November Masséna had retreated to Vicenza as ordered by Bonaparte. Augereau reached Montebello on the 4th. Only rear guards remained on the Brenta. These were driven off by the Austrians on the 4th. Provera sent Liptay across at Fontaniva with the advance guard, while he himself went to Citadella. The right wing moved to Bassano.

The exact French positions on the 5th are not known. Probably Bonaparte advanced with Augereau and the reserve past Masséna through Vicenza against Bassano, while Masséna moved against Fontaniva.

When Bonaparte began his march from the Adige on the 4th, he had already heard the news of Vaubois's reverse of the 2nd and 3rd, and on the 5th he learned of his retreat to Calliano; despite this, he decided to try to attack Alvinczy,[23] since he calculated that Vaubois would not be driven out of the mountains for another three or four days.

23. Colin, 198, notes: "It is precisely *because* [emphasis in original] of Vaubois's failure that Bonaparte attacks Alvinczy. He hopes to attract the Austrian forces in his direction. According to eyewitnesses, the operation against Bassano was a diversion for Vaubois's benefit. [Bonaparte] had left the two entrances to the Brenta corridor

The Austrians kept their right wing at Bassano on the left bank of the Brenta.

When Masséna's advance guard approached, the left wing's advance guard under General Liptay retreated across the old course of the Brenta onto the island formed by it and took up position there, while Provera covered the Brenta above and below the island with the rest of his troops and held his reserve at Citadella.

Now on the 6th Bonaparte advanced to the attack with Augereau's division along the road to Bassano, and Masséna's on the road to Citadella.

Masséna drove back Liptay's outposts that were still on the left bank and then had a protracted fight with Liptay. This took a peculiar form, in that it was Liptay who tried to advance off his island by wading through the old Brenta and was repulsed by Masséna. In the Austrians' rather circumlocutory report,[24] this attack by Liptay is presented as a kind of indirect defense. But the affair is really so bizarre that we cannot blame the French when they present the whole of Masséna's action on the 6th as though he halted Provera's advance guard on the right bank and drove it back on the left. For fear that Liptay might be overwhelmed, Provera took a remarkable measure during the night of 6–7 November when he ordered the destruction of the pontoon bridge connecting the island to the left bank. This showed that the Austrians were not in particularly good shape and that Provera was evidently willing to sacrifice Liptay's whole force.[25]

Augereau had run into Quosdanovich's division of Alvinczy's corps, which was advancing along the Vicenza road and whose advance guard had reached Marostica. They fought over this place for a long time, but in the end, Prince Hohenzollern had to fall back on Quosdanovich, who had taken up an advantageous position between the last spurs of the [mountains northwest of the] Lette Communi[26] and the Brenta. Here, Quosdanovich successfully withstood all further attacks until dusk.

---

in the hands of the Austrians; he had to prevent them using it to concentrate toward Trient or toward Bassano."

24. Clausewitz cites "Ibid." For purposes of clarity, he is referring to "Österreichische Militärische Zeitschrift, 1828. Vol. 9, p. 295."

25. Clausewitz cites "Ibid., p. 302."

26. It is not clear where this is, but the Leva community is just north of Marostica, on the Vicenza road. As such, and being unable to confirm the exact location of the forces at that moment, it seems reasonable to suppose that there was a printing error

Thus Bonaparte saw that on the 6th he had not achieved a single success. The divided state in which his army found itself, and the dangerous threat to his retreat if Provera managed to defeat Masséna's division, did not look very promising to him. On the other end of the front, Vaubois's situation [in the Adige valley near Rivoli] disturbed him greatly. Seeming to regret his previous plan, Bonaparte abandons it and decides to retreat to Verona immediately to draw his forces closer together, so as to be able to pounce on Davidowitsch when the time is right.[27] In fact, Bonaparte—for whom admitting a mistake is almost impossible—claims that what made him change his plan was the news that reached his headquarters at 2:00 a.m. on the 7th that Vaubois had lost Nomi and Torbole, as well as all his outposts on the right bank of the Adige. But this is clearly a complete lie. General Vaubois's letter in which he reports the loss of the positions at Nomi and Torbole is from 6 November, and from the evening at that, because it was written after the action at Calliano; consequently, he could only have started writing it after 12:00 midnight. Now, the road from Calliano to Bassano is 81 miles long, so this report cannot have reached the headquarters at Bassano on the morning of the 7th. Besides, Vaubois states that he had given orders to retake the position; the outpost at Mori on the right bank of the Adige was finally taken by the Austrians on the 7th.[28]

---

in the original and that the line went from the mountains to the northwest of Leva, east toward the Brenta River.

27. Colin, 200, notes: "When he left Verona, Bonaparte was resolved to follow up his advantages in Friuli only if they were decisive; since he did not brush the enemy aside immediately, he had to fall back on Vicenza. If he hoped for a success despite his inferior forces, it was because he knew the Austrian advance guards were a long way from their main body, and that it might happen that he could defeat them in detail. This is what would have happened if he had not met them at precisely the strong position delineated by the Brenta."

28. Clausewitz's criticism of the timeline seems reasonable, as Napoleon castigates Vaubois's troops in a letter of the 7th but does not place Vaubois under Masséna's command until the 8th. This implies that the communication from Vaubois was received later than Napoleon claimed. See Napoléon I, *Correspondance de Napoléon Ier*, 2:103 (letters 1170 and 1171). In addition, Colin, 200, notes: "Dommartin's correspondence confirms that Vaubois's dispatch arrived during the night of the 6th and 7th at Vicenza, where Bonaparte had fallen back to after the indecisive action at Bassano, and where he planned to stay. The dispatch is dated from Rovereto, from whence it could have been sent at 6:00 in the evening. It is 110 km from Rovereto to Vicenza, and Bonaparte had organized courier posts. It is quite natural that its transmission should only have taken 8 or 9 hours. Bonaparte therefore decided to concentrate around Ve-

On the 7th the French divisions broke off and retreated through Vicenza and Montebello to Verona. On the 8th Alvinczy followed to Vicenza, on the 9th to Montebello, on the 10th he rested, and on the 11th he moved to Villanova, where the highway from Verona crosses the Alpon. His advance guard moved toward Verona as far as Caldiero.

Bonaparte and his two divisions had already entered Verona on the 8th. Here he learned that nothing more had been attempted against Vaubois since the action of the 7th, so he let his divisions rest on the 9th and 10th and decided to try to salvage his situation by turning against Alvinczy himself once more on the 11th.

The Action at St. Martin and St. Michel on 11 November

Prince Hohenzollern, commanding the Austrian advance guard, reported to Alvinczy that Davidowitsch's successes against Vaubois had prompted Bonaparte to retreat across the Mincio, just as they had planned. Hohenzollern proposed that he make an immediate attempt to seize Verona. Alvinczy considered this proposal carefully, and although his chief of staff advised against any such attempt, Alvinczy consented to a so-called reconnaissance in force.

To this end, on 11 November Alvinczy's 4,000–5,000-strong advance guard arrived at St. Martin [San Martino Buon Albergo] and St. Michel [San Michele], right under the walls of Verona.

As soon as Bonaparte learned of their approach, he had his divisions advance against the Austrians that afternoon, and Prince Hohenzollern was driven back, with loss, to the vicinity of Caldiero.

The Battle of Caldiero on 12 November

A brigade was posted at Caldiero in support of the advance guard, and the two combined mustered eight battalions and nine squadrons, about 8,000 men. They occupied an exceptionally strong position. Their right flank rested on the village of Colognola [Colognola ai Colli] on the highest point of Monte

---

rona, rather than remain at Vicenza, so as not to let Davidowitsch cut his line of communication."

Oliveto, their left flank on a steep hill behind Caldiero, and their center stood on a gently rising terraced slope. Alvinczy planned to defend this position to the utmost and then, while the French were engaged in attacking it, attack them himself with the rest of his army.

In the gray dawn of the 12th, the French attacked this position. Augereau attacked the Austrian left wing, Masséna the right. After a tough fight, the former took the village of Caldiero. Masséna had outflanked the right wing at Ilassi [Illasi], attacked it, and taken the village of Colognola when Alvinczy's army arrived. One column under Brabeck advanced down the highway against Caldiero, and a second under General Schubirts moved on Colognola; the outflanking Masséna was himself taken in flank in turn, and his left wing was thrown back in some disorder. A third column under Provera moved to Gambion [Gombion] and struck Augereau's right flank. Thus, in this way the battle was renewed and seems to have turned decisively in the Austrians' favor, so Bonaparte abandoned his plan and withdrew to the position on the St. Giacomo[29] he had occupied the previous night. Instead of exploiting the advantage they had gained and going over decisively to the offensive, the Austrians satisfied themselves with some weak efforts that were repulsed and with maintaining their position. Such a victory could not garner any great trophies, just two cannon and 750 prisoners. The total French losses were somewhere in excess of 2,000 men. The morale effect of this victory was naturally even less significant, being so slight that, in his *Memoirs,* Bonaparte says with complete indifference, "The enemy justifiably claimed victory."[30]

Bonaparte says the main reason for giving up on his attack was the rain and hail, which the wind was driving straight into the faces of the French. We could, of course, accept this reason, but we would probably find a better one if we say that he got himself involved in an attack on a position whose true strength he discovered only during the course of the battle, and he preferred to give up on a flawed operation and start again in a better way.

The Austrian account gives Alvinczy's strength as about 20,000 men, albeit

---

29. This is a series of rising hills leading north from a village of that name to the west of Caldiero, on the Verona road.

30. "*L'ennemi s'attribua avec raison la Victoire.*" See Montholon, *Mémoires pour servir à l'Histoire de France sous Napoléon,* 3:325.

contradicting an earlier strength return according to which he had at least 25,000.[31]

On the 13th Bonaparte led his troops back to their camp outside Verona.

57 THE BATTLE OF ARCOLE ON 15, 16, AND 17 NOVEMBER

Bonaparte devised a new plan that consisted of marching his army off to the right, throwing a bridge over the Adige at Ronco [Ronco all'Adige], crossing the river, and striking the Austrians' left flank, whether they held fast in their position at Caldiero, undertook some operation against Verona, or even attempted a crossing of the Adige, in which case it could happen only between Ronco and Verona.

At first glance, this plan appears very promising. If Alvinczy really were trying to effect a crossing of the Adige, then from Ronco, Bonaparte would be closer to Mantua than Alvinczy was. If circumstances changed significantly before the moment he could attack and pin Alvinczy on the left bank of the Adige, he could always turn around and attack him on the right bank. Besides, his whole operation—marching from Verona to Ronco, bridging the Adige, and advancing to Caldiero—would take only about twenty-four hours, and given the Austrians' caution,[32] there was no fear of the situation changing very much in that time. Vaubois at the Corona and Rivoli was still unmolested. It would take at least two days before Davidowitsch could drive him out of this position and force him to retreat to the Verona area. Verona itself was to remain garrisoned by 1,500 men under Kilmaine, in whom Bonaparte had great confidence. So long as Bonaparte and his army were at Verona, there could be no question of the city being attacked; if he began his march at dusk, he could expect that the place still could not be taken the following day. Although the

---

31. Colin, 203, notes: "Here Clausewitz confuses the total effectives for Alvinczy's whole army with the number he could mass for the battle. Of the 25,000 men he had available, Alvinczy had left 7,000 at Vicenza and toward Albaredo. This explains how Bonaparte was able to attack with 14,000–15,000 men without suffering a very decisive defeat."

32. See the earlier comments about the relative ages and dynamism of the leaders of the two sides. It is interesting to ponder what might have happened had the French faced young and dynamic opponents.

garrison was indeed too weak to stand against a serious assault, it would be strong enough against any hasty attack. Bonaparte was in fact counting on the Austrians being busy trying to capture Verona at the very moment he set upon them from behind.

The area between the Alpon [Alpone] and the Adige, opposite Ronco, was a large depression crossed only by causeways.[33] Bonaparte cannot possibly have been ignorant of this; indeed, he himself had passed through the region when Masséna's division crossed at Ronco to cut Wurmser off from the road between Legnago and Mantua. But given that this wetland could in fact be crossed on several causeways, and given that the Austrians guarded the area only with weak outposts, this seemed more like a help than a hindrance for Bonaparte's plan. If he did drive off the Austrian outposts, this would create a kind of bridgehead from which it would be easier to debouch against the Austrian army than from a single bridge.

We do not know whether Bonaparte had already made this decision on the 13th, while he was leading his troops back to their camp outside Verona, as his letters say nothing about it. On the 14th he writes to the Directory, "Today, the troops rest; tomorrow, we act according to the enemy's movements."[34] But the troops had already rested on the 13th, since they had done nothing but retreat another 3.5 miles, and on the evening of the 14th they set off for Ronco. Thus, this part of his letter gives us only a superficial and inadequate explanation of his actual decision. This is an important question for us: why had Bonaparte's army not already started its march on the evening of the 13th? Was he perhaps waiting for more news from Vaubois; was he waiting for the arrival of General Guieu's brigade, which he had summoned from Vaubois as

33. It is worth looking at the area in the Austrian maps from 1818–1829 to gain an idea of the complexity of the terrain. See "Franziszeische Landesaufnahme (1806– 1869)," accessed 17 July 2017, http://mapire.eu/de/map/secondsurvey/?layers=osm%2 C5%2C42&bbox=1243362.9206008196%2C5670136.976708517%2C1261707.807389262 %2C5678487.722048673.

34. "*Aujourd'hui repos aux troupes; demain, selon les mouvemens de l'ennemi, nous agirons.*" Clausewitz has the date wrong (the original states 13 November). See Napoléon I, *Correspondance de Napoléon Ier*, 2:107–110 (letter 1182). This letter goes on to explain that Napoleon was worried about the siege of Mantua and that it might have to be abandoned, forcing the French back behind the line of the Adda River if reinforcements did not arrive. Clausewitz is correct that Napoleon does not clearly explain why he did not act sooner, but the letter discusses the problem of the numerous wounded officers and generals, which is reducing the army's confidence.

a reinforcement; or could the bridge not be completed any sooner? All these matters appear to merit more attention than the mere throwaway comment in his letter about resting the troops. Perhaps a combination of some or all of these things imposed the delay. We search so thoroughly for an explanation because we cannot believe that a general like Bonaparte would have abandoned his attack at Caldiero on the 12th and withdrawn to Verona on the 13th without already having a different plan and without knowing what to do—helpless, as it were. Neither the rest of his letter of the 14th nor his later *Memoirs* gives us any information about this; in both, he bemoans the lack of reinforcements and the danger the enemy's numerical superiority poses to him and to Italy. He claims his two divisions under Masséna and Augereau have only 13,000 men between them, while Alvinczy has 40,000. It is a well-known fact that one should not attach too much value to generals' complaints of this kind, and we need to make allowances for Bonaparte's language here. The enemy's superiority was less (or at best, no more) than in both the previous relief attempts, and the ratio of 13 to 40 at the decisive point is plucked out of thin air. Masséna, Augereau, Guieu, Maquère, and the cavalry must have constituted a force of at least 20,000 men, and the Austrians were perhaps 22,000 strong[35] after Mitrowsky joined them.[36] His two unsuccessful endeavors on the Brenta and at Caldiero may well have left Bonaparte somewhat disgruntled with himself and his situation and less confident of being able to carry out his mission. However, we disagree with the way run-of-the-mill writers depict this commander as being beset on all sides on the 13th and 14th, in a more desperate situation than ever, and as if he could find no way out for a full twenty-four hours, just for the sake of giving his eventual resolution of

35. Colin, 206, notes: "Clausewitz is right not to accept Bonaparte's figure of 13,000 men, but he goes a little too far in estimating the French force at 20,000. It did not exceed 17,000–18,000 men. Alvinczy could have opposed it with very superior force, but on the first day he does not seem to have engaged with any more than his opponent. He concentrated more on the 16th, while Bonaparte received 2,000–3,000 men from Kilmaine, which enabled him to go onto the offensive on the 17th."

36. Napoleon gives a figure of 18,000 for the French. See Napoléon I, *Correspondance de Napoléon Ier*, 2:107–110. There are three Mittrowsky's listed in the main biographical source, but apparently none of them participated in this campaign. We are not certain who this Mitrowsky is, although he seems to have been a brigade-level commander, based on the context. See Wurzbach, *Biographisches Lexikon des Kaiserthums Oesterreich*, 18:392–398.

this enormous task an even more dramatic effect. We disagree, first, because it belies the true situation, and second, because such a helpless state cannot be reconciled with this commander's greatness. One can well imagine that a great commander in a really hard-pressed situation might remain undecided for days or even weeks about how he could possibly find a way out—but not in that moment when it comes to actually doing the deed, when every minute wasted makes his situation worse.

Thus, when we see a period of twenty-four hours elapse during this crisis, without any obvious reason for this hiatus, we would rather believe it is because of external causes than a lack of resolve.[37]

Bonaparte has made his decision to attack Alvinczy's left flank, that is, from the direction he least expects. He begins his march at dusk on the 14th, finds his bridge completed, and crosses the river at dawn.

For his part, on the 13th Alvinczy pushed his advance guard forward to St. Michel, and on the 14th he moved with his army to St. Martin.[38] The Austrian account says General Alvinczy sent Mitrowsky's and Brigido's brigades to the Adige. We subsequently find the latter at Arcole when Bonaparte marches against this village, and since it follows from the preceding events that it did not stay at Ronco and could not have marched there that quickly via Villanova, there is no doubt that Brigido's brigade remained behind the Alpon. Most likely Mitrowsky stayed at Villanova, since on the 15th he is the first to support Brigido. It therefore seems that when Alvinczy advanced

37. On this point, Clausewitz may be on to something, as Napoleon sounds frustrated and lacking in confidence when he writes, in the same letter, "All these new officers are so inept and the soldiers have no confidence in them! The army of Italy, reduced to a handful of men, is exhausted." [*Tout ce qui m'arrive est si inepte et n'a pas la confiance du soldat! L'armée d'Italie, réduite à une poignée de monde, est épuisée.*] See Napoléon I, *Correspondance de Napoléon Ier*, 2:107–110. However, Colin, 207, notes: "Clausewitz does not want to admit that Bonaparte's aim had been to capture Alvinczy's supply trains and to trap him, without supplies, between the Adige and the mountains. If he had accepted this explanation, which all the evidence supports, then he would not be surprised by Bonaparte's inaction on the 13th and 14th. As he himself comments a few lines further on, it was only on the 14th that the Austrians had advanced far enough in the direction of Verona that Bonaparte could try to take Villanova by surprise and to intercept them in the open field."

38. Colin, 207, notes: "It is exactly this maneuver of Alvinczy's that prompts Bonaparte to move on Villanova via Arcole."

against Verona, he left a division of six or eight battalions behind the Alpon.[39]

Alvinczy had effectively reached the natural objective of his route, in the direction he had chosen for it, and it was impossible to state any measure that would have brought him a single step closer to this objective. An assault on Verona was unfeasible so long as the French army was encamped there. Crossing the Adige between Verona and the Alpon was a very risky operation, to say the least, because it would have to be carried out almost in sight of the French army, and the ensuing battle would take place in a very dangerous situation. If he were to wait until Vaubois was beaten by Davidowitsch and driven down onto the Italian plain, he ran the risk of Bonaparte turning against Davidowitsch again and striking him with his entire force, which would mean paying a heavy price for the advantage of Wurmser's liberation, if that were to succeed. But even this success was very unlikely, since Bonaparte might very well return before Alvinczy could cross the Adige and advance to Mantua. In this quandary, as we read in the Austrian account, Alvinczy decided to set twelve battalions across the Adige at Zevio [about 6 miles downstream from Verona], while twelve more were to attack Verona. We do not wish to explore any further what he was thinking in making this plan, nor how he could have believed it was sensible; it seems to us that any such effort would be pointless, and we would rather just say that the reports are too incomplete to allow us to guess at the Austrian commander's true intention. If this really was the plan, then it is extremely fortunate for the Austrians that they took so long to reach their decision, and indeed, it is not surprising that they did, for sound common sense should have recoiled from it a hundredfold. This operation was supposed to be carried out on the night of the 15th and 16th, just twenty-four hours later than Bonaparte acted.

For Bonaparte, the lead-up to his intended strike worked out very well. He found that stretch of river unguarded and completed his bridge unopposed, and just as he had hoped and expected, the Austrian army had meanwhile

39. Colin, 208, notes: "The dispersal of the Austrian army on the 15th is extraordinary. Alvinczy has 3,500 men between Arcole and Albaredo, 3,500 toward Montebello, the bulk of his forces near San Martino, one advance guard under the walls of Verona, and another before Zevio trying to cross the Adige. Bonaparte has moved up to a central position in the middle of all these detachments, with the reasonably justified hope of defeating them one after the other. He had allowed time for the enemy to spread out."

advanced even further toward Verona.[40] It was already 9:00 a.m. when some cannon fire near Ronco attracted Alvinczy's attention; it was not until 10:00 a.m. that he received word of the bridge and of the enemy crossing, and even then, he thought it was just a demonstration to distract him.

But now it became apparent that Bonaparte's operation could not be executed exactly as planned and that, if it could not succeed after all, it would become something quite different, something much more difficult.

The Austrians had only a small force for observation in the area between the Alpon and the Adige; between Arcole and Ronco there was just one battalion and one squadron, and they evidently discharged this duty sufficiently badly that they did not disturb the construction of the bridge in any way and were tardy in reporting it. But at Porcil [Belfiore],[41] where the causeways emerged from the marsh, the Austrians had the Spleni regiment; Colonel Brigido's brigade was holding the bridge over the Alpon at Arcole, and we assume Mitrowsky's brigade was at Villanova. So the area was not as undefended as it appeared.

Furthermore, the terrain seems to have differed from what Bonaparte expected.

From Ronco, two dikes led out through the marshes. One ran alongside the Adige to Porcil, splitting up into several branches before it got there. The other led to the bridge across the Alpon at Arcole; from there, one branch ran through Arcole across the open ground behind the village, while two more clung to the banks on either side of the Alpon as far as Villanova.[42]

---

40. Colin, 209, notes: "After this remark, we do not understand the criticism of Bonaparte expressed earlier, of having waited pointlessly for 48 hours before moving to Ronco. If Davidowitsch had advanced as far as Bossolengo while Alvinczy was still behind Caldiero, Bonaparte would have had a wonderful opportunity to crush the Austrian army of the Tyrol, which was the surest way of finishing off Alvinczy. This was one more reason not to leave Verona until Alvinczy had come close enough."

41. There is no town of that name today, but Belfiore was originally called Belfiore di Porcile and is in the described location. See "Franziszeische Landesaufnahme (1806–1869)," accessed 17 July 2017, http://mapire.eu/de/map/secondsurvey/?layers=o sm%2C5%2C42&bbox=1242474.3401470042%2C5678922.457647044%2C1251646.78354 12256%2C5683097.830317123.

42. The dikes are marked on the survey maps. Ibid.

The Action of 15 November

Essentially, only the first of these dikes, with its various branches leading to Porcil, fully served Bonaparte's purpose. The second was partly on the left bank of the Alpon, where Bonaparte did not want to go. Admittedly, it also had a branch on the right bank, but this quickly diverged from the first dike and ran toward Villanova, so that upon emerging from the marshes, his divisions would have been 4.5 miles apart, with no way of supporting each other. Knowing the circumstances as we do now, we can say that if Bonaparte had taken the first of these two routes with his entire army, he undoubtedly would have achieved his aim completely. He would have reached Porcil without encountering any significant resistance; between here and Caldiero, he most likely would have met part of the Austrian force and defeated it in detail; he then would have attacked the main army while it was retreating from Verona, before it could cover enough of its retreat route to Villanova.[43] Surveying the sequence of events now, all this seems to be beyond argument. But Bonaparte could not have known that he would have such an easy job on one causeway and such a hard time on the other; so naturally, the idea of advancing along a single causeway while leaving the other in enemy hands so close to his bridge at Ronco would not have occurred to him, and it would have been a hugely daring deed. But that reason is nowhere near as compelling as another one: since the enemy only had this area under observation, any serious resistance at the bridge at Arcole seemed very unlikely; and if Bonaparte remembered

43. Colin, 210, notes: "Bonaparte's army was weaker than Alvinczy's, and its recent defeats had damaged its morale; it would have been all the more reckless to seek a decisive battle on the plain after the 15th, when a defeat would have made the French situation almost desperate. By contrast, since Alvinczy had committed the error of advancing on Verona while separated from Davidowitsch, the simple fact of taking up a position between Porcil and Arcole gave Bonaparte the upper hand over him. If Alvinczy concentrated his army west of the marshes, toward Caldiero, he surrendered his line of communications, his depots, and his supply trains; if he concentrated to the east, toward Arcole, he would move further from Verona, consequently retreating and exposing Davidowitsch to being defeated in isolation; finally, if he stayed divided in two by Bonaparte's army, he condemned himself to being crushed in detail and to being unable to obtain a decisive success. The solution Clausewitz proposes would not have gained the French any of these advantages, and it is impossible not to regard Bonaparte's solution as wonderful, as it forced the enemy by necessity to release his grip or be defeated."

the bridge at Lodi, as well as the crossing of the Mincio at Borghetto and of the Brenta at Bassano, it must have seemed impossible that this bridge at Arcole could be a major obstacle to his whole operation. He therefore advanced confidently along both causeways, Masséna's division toward Porcil and Augereau's toward Arcole. Alvinczy threw the Spleni regiment and a battalion of Croats against Masséna. When the two sides ran into each other at Bionde [about halfway between Ronco and Porcil], the Austrians were thrown back and were pursued to Porcil, and after a lively fight, the village was taken. That was Masséna's work done for the day.

Augereau's division, however, during its advance along the causeway to Arcole, encountered a terrain problem that the French commander probably could not have known about. From Ronco, this causeway ran directly to the Alpon and then along the right bank of this river for about 3,000 paces to Arcole. On the far side of the Alpon, another causeway also ran right next to the river, which gave the Austrians the opportunity for an almost impregnable deployment; they posted infantry on the causeway on the left bank and thus raked that on the right with close-range musketry all along its 3,000 paces. The bridge itself was defended by a few guns and by some infantry that established themselves in the nearest houses in front of Arcole and fortified them. In this situation, an attack on this point could not possibly succeed, since before the French column ever reached the well-defended bridge, it received such fearful flanking fire that this alone was enough to drive off the attack. Augereau's advance guard therefore turned back before it reached the bridge. He himself rushed forward, seized a flag, and planted it on the bridge. But in vain. Since the generals could see that they were caught in a predicament they could not fix through tactical deployments, they tried to force a result through gallantry and self-sacrifice, hoping they could still break through and rectify the mistake by the shortest route. All in vain. Four generals are wounded—Lannes, Verdier, Bon, and Verne—and each time the column falls back again. Bonaparte gallops up, leaps off his horse, addresses the troops, reminds them of Lodi, thinks he has swept them along with him, seizes a banner, charges onto the bridge—in vain! The column turns back. The Austrians advance onto the bridge after the routers and drive into their midst, and it is only with some difficulty that Bonaparte's own grenadiers frog-march him away and rescue him from being captured.[44]

44. Colin, 212, notes: "Augereau's division got as far as the bridge at Arcole; there-

Thus, this example shows like none other in the world that there are some tactical deployments against which no amount of courage, decisiveness, self-sacrifice, and motivation can achieve anything.[45]

Bonaparte now realized it was pointless to make any more attempts here. Earlier on, he had charged General Guieu with crossing the Adige by ferry at Albaredo with 2,000 men to take the Arcole position in the rear. Guieu finally arrived at dusk, at which point this position, which had been fought over so fiercely, was vacated by the Austrians with almost no resistance.

While the French were dissipating their forces in vain and then, by day's end, just managing to claim the objective of their sanguinary exertions, Alvinczy was changing his position. In front of Verona he left only Prince Hohenzollern and his advance guard, strengthened by four battalions. Alvinczy himself hurried up with the rest of his troops to face front against Bonaparte. Provera was between Caldiero and Porcil, with six battalions; Mitrowsky, with fourteen battalions, had his right wing resting on St. Bonifacio and his left toward St. Steffano [Santo Stefano di Zimella].

Clearly, Bonaparte had now gained something he had not originally sought, a mere sideshow he had not meant to get involved in: the breakthrough at Arcole. On the other hand, Alvinczy's retreat across the Alpon had defeated Bonaparte's purpose for marching into this patch, and he himself admits how painful it was for him to watch from the tower in Ronco and realize the Austrians were retreating. In this situation, the crossing captured at Arcole became something it had not been earlier: his shortest path to reach Alvinczy. Of course, even if successful, this attack on Alvinczy offered no special advantage, and Bonaparte's situation on the evening of the 15th could not be considered a good prelude to the battle. With one division in Porcil, the other 7 miles away in Arcole, and an extensive marsh between them, these were not

---

fore it was not the flanking fire that stopped it. The head of the column cannot have been mown down by volleys of fire when it reached the bridge, since most of the officers who tried to lead it across were unharmed. In particular, Bonaparte remained at the end of the bridge for some time and must have been a target for enemy fire. It therefore seems that the reverse suffered at the bridge at Arcole was due simply to the troops' reluctance, and besides, this was the impression of all the eyewitnesses, Bonaparte, Marmont, etc. This was not one of those situations where it was an impossible task."

45. Understanding this would have benefited many a decision to attack during subsequent conflicts.

promising conditions for victory.[46] If anything was to come of continuing the attack, Masséna's division would have to be brought back, a defensive position would have to be set up at a suitable distance along the causeway from Porcil to Ronco, and the Austrian left wing would have to be outflanked via Albaredo or even Legnago.

Bonaparte feels he cannot stay all night in the bad position he finds himself in on the evening of the 15th. He fears the Austrians could attack his divisions with superior force, drive them into the marshes, and cut some of them off from the bridge at Ronco; in addition, General Vaubois has now been attacked by Davidowitsch, and Bonaparte needs to turn against the latter. He therefore decides to give up everything he has gained and pull his army back to the right bank of the Adige again. Just two demi-brigades remain in front of the bridge at Ronco to protect it. After this decision, one might think that Bonaparte had given up on the idea of attacking Alvinczy. Not a bit of it! He decides to renew the attack on the following day, provided Vaubois's situation does not oblige him to choose otherwise.[47] Given this decision, it is inexcusable that he does not continue to hold the Porcil causeway somewhere near Bionde to protect the bridge at Ronco and the village of Arcole to secure his debouchment from there, and that he makes no arrangements during the night for an outflanking move through Legnago, especially with his cavalry.

This total retreat over the Adige could be excused only if he had given up his attack in this area, while continuing the attack the next day could be excused only if he had held on to Arcole. The fact that he did neither is quite incomprehensible, and it is impossible to say on what basis he expected a better result on the day after his attack on the bridge at Arcole. Even the outflanking move through Albaredo, which is what finally enabled him to take Arcole, did

46. Colin, 214, notes: "The difficulties Clausewitz refers to affected Alvinczy far more than Bonaparte; it was Alvinczy whose two wings were divided by the marshes, and by the enemy, whereas Masséna and Augereau were in contact with each other and with the detachment left at Ronco." This really depends on which phase of the battle one is looking at. Early on, this is probably true, as the Austrian force is split between the two sides of the marsh. Once the French cross the marsh to the bridges in and south of Arcole, the opposite is true.

47. Colin, 214, notes: "Clausewitz absolutely wants Bonaparte to seek a decisive battle by attacking. But the French only needed to wait for the Austrian attack, and that is what they did. Alvinczy was forced to go on the offensive, given the objective he was pursuing."

not feature in the second day's attack, and General Guieu is not mentioned in any report.

We must confess that it has been impossible for us to discover a central thread of coherence; this second day of the battle remains completely unintelligible to us, as does the third day in many respects. Sometimes we cannot find reasons for actions, sometimes we lack causes for effects. Neither Bonaparte's first report nor Berthier's, despite being drafted on the day after the battle and therefore providing quite an animated view, allows us to guess at the successive notions that laid the foundations for the commander's decisions.[48]

The Action of 16 November

The simple fact is that at dawn on the 16th, Bonaparte advances again with both his divisions, in the same way as on the previous day.[49] But Alvinczy has likewise decided to attack, and his left wing has already pushed through Arcole and across the bridge. The French and the Austrians now clash on both causeways. On both, the latter are thrown back. Masséna again advances triumphantly to Porcil, Augereau to the bridge at Arcole. But again, all the efforts of the bravest of troops, led by the bravest of generals, shatter on this famous bridge.

Two endeavors distinguish this day from the day before. On the French side, Bonaparte tries in vain to cross the Alpon near its mouth without a bridge, using just fascines, but the current carries the fascines away. A demi-brigade

48. Colin, 215, notes: "Bonaparte's report and Berthier's letter, written the day after the events, show the French general's aim very clearly; but Clausewitz clings to the idea that Bonaparte wanted to deliver a decisive attack, and he rejects anything that does not fit with his theory." Bonaparte's report, which Colin and Clausewitz both mention, begins by explaining that it is impossible for Napoleon to describe all the maneuvers prior to the battle of Arcole, a battle "which has just decided the fate of Italy." Napoleon explains that he planned to cross the river at night and "hoped to arrive at Villanova in the morning and by this means to destroy the enemy's artillery parks, his baggage, and attack the enemy army's flank and rear." Napoléon I, *Correspondance de Napoléon Ier*, 2:116. This description of Napoleon's initial plan better fits with Clausewitz's argument.

49. Colin, 215, notes: "Not at all in the same way as on the previous day, but only so as to take up a position on the dikes in front of the bridge. That is where Alvinczy was going to attack."

under Adjutant General Vial wades into the water up to the men's shoulders but is forced to turn back by the Austrians' fire.

On the Austrian side, Alvinczy has the idea of having a detachment of infantry move from St. Bonifacio down both causeways on either side of the Alpon. But a single infantry company with two cannon puts an end to these troops' advance before they get close to Arcole. Thus, neither of these attempts has any influence on the day's outcome, and at nightfall both sides' positions are roughly the same as the day before, except that this time the French have not taken the bridge at Arcole. Bonaparte is obliged to pull his forces back across the Adige yet again, for the same reasons as before, leaving just one of Augereau's demi-brigades holding the bridge at Ronco.

This second day changed the two opponents' situations very little; yet we must not overlook a couple of nuances that probably begin to tip the scales toward Bonaparte. One is that on this day, it was the Austrians who attacked and were repulsed; the second is that Provera's division suffered a genuine defeat at the hands of Masséna, losing 700–800 prisoners and six guns.

Since General Vaubois was still in his position at Rivoli and the Corona, the latter only being lost on the 16th (which Bonaparte could not yet have known),[50] Bonaparte decided to attempt yet another attack on Alvinczy. Although the two previous days had not produced the results he had hoped for, they had not generated any real disadvantage for him either. The loss of time had not yet done him any harm, and the casualties on the Austrian side had been greater than his own.[51] He thought these two bloody days would have left the Austrians very fragile and that a new attack, especially with somewhat different dispositions, would probably end in their retreat. In this, as his success proves, he certainly gauged his opponent well. We ask ourselves: why did Bonaparte assume this, when Alvinczy's tactical position was just as advantageous on the 17th as on the two previous days?[52] We have to say that, of

50. Colin, 216, notes: "Here Clausewitz commits the same error as he did concerning the actions at Roveredo on 6 November: it would have taken no more than 4 hours for a dispatch to come from Rivoli to Ronco."

51. Colin, 217, notes: "In addition, Bonaparte had received 2,000 to 3,000 reinforcements."

52. Colin, 217, notes: "We do not know how Clausewitz can describe an army's situation as favorable when it is cut into two sections and can no longer have any thought other than a fighting withdrawal, even though its mission is to attack." This is not what Clausewitz said. He said the situation was no less favorable than it had been previously.

course, at this remove in time and space, it is exactly this kind of thing that is hardest to understand. Assessing the state of an enemy army depends on picking up on the smallest features or nuances—in a word, on perception. Bonaparte is like a fencer divining his opponent's intention from the flicker of his eye. How can we possibly analyze that?[53]

The main changes in the plan of attack were as follows: not all of Masséna's division should advance toward Porcil again, but only one demi-brigade, so far as was necessary to protect the attack against the left wing of the Austrian army; Masséna should lead the rest of his troops against Arcole; Augereau's division should cross the Alpon between Arcole and its mouth by means of a trestle bridge; and, finally, the two battalions and four guns garrisoning Legnago should mount a diversion against the Austrian flank and rear. The reserve cavalry was to follow and support Augereau. Again, the report makes no mention of Guieu.

Alvinczy, who (according to Bonaparte's *Memoirs*) had been falsely informed by a spy that the French were retreating to Mantua, intended to pursue the French on the 17th just as he had on the 16th, for at dawn his columns' advance guards pushed down the causeways from Porcil and Arcole toward Ronco. Right at the moment the French wanted to move against them, the bridge at Ronco was damaged. Augereau's two battalions that had been left on the far side would have been lost, and the crossing could have been seriously impeded, if not for the fact that both causeways ran close to the Adige for a while before reaching Ronco, one following it downstream, the other up. In this situation, the French artillery on the right bank of the Adige was able to

---

53. This brings us to another of Clausewitz's key ideas: genius in war and the coup d'oeil. This attribute allows a genius to see through the friction and fog of conflict, both real and metaphorical, to make a decision. For example, a commander can hear and see things, but because of the size and nature of a battlefield, it is unlikely that any commander can see everything that is happening at any one time. Thus, a commander has to be able to make decisions in an environment where uncertainty and a lack of information are the norm. With that in mind, a genius (in Clausewitz's concept of the term) is someone who can make good decisions despite a lack of information because he can visualize—in his mind's eye—what is occurring even when he is unable to actually see and hear for himself. In essence, Clausewitz's argument is that because only a few people can do this, armies cannot expect this to be the norm. Therefore, they must prepare all leaders to be comfortable in such an environment, so they do not become dependent on a genius emerging from their ranks. See Clausewitz, *On War*, 101–112, 577–578 (book 1, chap. 3, and book 8, chap. 1).

halt both Austrian columns on its own, gaining enough time to repair the bridge. As soon as this was done, two of Masséna's demi-brigades crossed, each consisting of three battalions; the one led by Masséna himself advanced along the Porcil causeway, and the other under General Robert moved on Arcole. Both drove back the Austrian advance guards. Now the divisions' main bodies crossed. Augereau, still fourteen battalions strong after leaving two at the bridge, turned right off the Arcole causeway toward the lower Alpon and crossed it on a trestle bridge that had apparently been constructed overnight, intending to attack the Austrians in the position they had chosen somewhat further back. For the time being, the remaining twelve battalions of Masséna's eighteen-battalion division remained near the junction of the two causeways.

Meanwhile, the demi-brigades advancing along the two causeways ran into the Austrian columns proper. Heavy fighting ensued, and both demi-brigades were overwhelmed by superior numbers and violently repulsed. Masséna committed a brigade of his division to support the one on the Porcil causeway and was able to drive the Austrians back far enough so that they were no longer a threat to the bridge at Ronco or to the security of the French left wing.

In this situation, there were still six of Masséna's battalions at the bridge at Ronco, as well as the two from Augereau's division that had been guarding the bridge earlier. Bonaparte made three of those battalions—the 32nd Demi-brigade—lie down in the cover of the brush to the right of the Arcole causeway and posted the others partly on the Arcole causeway and partly on the one to Porcil, so that the Austrians advancing from Arcole could be taken in flank.

Overwhelmed by superior numbers of Austrians around Arcole, General Robert fell back on Augereau's division with some of his troops, while the rest were driven toward the bridge at Ronco. But here the Austrians now fell into the hands of the reserves Bonaparte had deployed. The 32nd Demi-brigade burst out of its cover into the left flank of the Austrian column, while the battalions posted on the Porcil causeway attacked its right. Attacked on all sides, this column, which was probably a couple of thousand strong (Bonaparte says it was a column of 3,000 Croats), succumbed to superior numbers and superior dispositions and withdrew to Arcole half wiped out, or at least with heavy losses.

During these events on the two causeways, Augereau attacked the Austrian left wing, which had adopted a fairly advantageous position about 1,000 paces behind the Alpon. The right wing rested on Arcole, the left on a marsh, and the center was covered both by the Alpon and by broken ground that was marshy in places. According to the Austrian account, Alvinczy was more or less surprised by Augereau's crossing and had already decided to retreat, but he ordered his left wing forward to buy time for the troops still in front of Verona to withdraw to Villanova. Be that as it may, the Austrian position was so strong that for a long time, Augereau could achieve nothing against it. Between the marsh covering their left flank and the Adige, there was a path around the marsh, but it was too risky to send a column along this dangerous route. Bonaparte had the idea of sending an officer and twenty-five Guides [Napoleon's personal escort unit] to sneak along it, with orders to make several trumpet calls when they reached the Austrian left flank, as if a significant column of cavalry was on its way. Bonaparte claims this scared the Austrians and made them retreat, but such ruses look better in books than on the battlefield, and particularly when large bodies of troops are involved, they just seem like gimmicks. More likely, the reason for the Austrians' retreat was their general situation and the news that a column was approaching from Legnago.

Thus, at around 2:00 p.m., once both his columns on the causeways have been beaten, Augereau is across the Alpon, and troops from Legnago are advancing against the Austrian left flank, the Austrian commander decides to commence his retreat to Villanova. Masséna, meanwhile, has returned to Arcole, breaks through at this village, pursues the Austrians toward Villanova, and links up with Augereau. The French take position with their left on Arcole and their right on St. Steffano, and the Austrians at Villanova.

The French give the Austrian losses in this three-day battle as 7,000–8,000 men dead, wounded, and prisoners, which is a couple of thousand too high. The French losses cannot have been many fewer.

58 REFLECTIONS ON THE BATTLE OF ARCOLE

Throughout this clear narrative of the battle, we have included only what appears in the accounts by Jomini and General Neiperg or in Bonaparte's and Berthier's original reports; we have presented these available data to give the whole thing some comprehensible coherence. We are very far from thinking that our representation must necessarily be accurate, for when the data are so few and so confusingly told, even the most meticulous collation cannot safeguard against errors, nor is a much keener mind than ours any guarantee against getting the wrong picture entirely. Still less do we believe that the course of events in these actions appears entirely natural and understandable from our account. We ourselves find this so far from being the case that, on the contrary, we find a whole host of things inexplicable, such as committing entire brigades and divisions along these mere causeways. Most likely the ground off the causeways was not actually impassable everywhere, as in the Dutch inundations of 1672 and 1787, but did in fact provide firm going in particular places. Only a very accurate map or a personal inspection of the area could shed light on this. The map offered by General Jomini, which we used as the basis of our description, is extremely poor and better suited to making the matter incomprehensible than explicable. However, if the fighting generally happened in the way the various reports say it did, we can reassure ourselves that the characteristics of the terrain must have made it possible.

The decisions of the two commanders are quite another matter. Admittedly, here and there these may have been qualified somewhat by minor individual circumstances that have long been forgotten, but their main thrust can only have been derived from their general situations, and our mind naturally wants to make some intelligible connection between these decisions and those situations.[54]

We have already remarked during the narrative that Bonaparte's plan of the 15th can be seen as quite natural, on the assumption that there was no reason to fear any obstruction of his debouchment from the wetland. It may look risky, but the risk is not an unreasonable one.

In the situation he found himself in, the fact that Bonaparte did not gamble on just advancing along the Porcil causeway or even up the right bank of the Alpon, if need be, without possessing Arcole is likewise understandable; it explains the heavy fighting for Arcole, for even if he had recognized the importance of this point earlier and seen that outflanking it via Albaredo would have been better, at that moment, there was no time to do so. Even his retreat on the evening of the 15th would be understandable enough in itself if it were not that the decision to attack again in the same way on the 16th imposed on Bonaparte the necessity of holding the places he had already taken.

But as for attacking on the 16th in exactly the same way as on the 15th— why should this have produced any better result than the first time?[55] And if

---

54. Paret addresses these issues in *Clausewitz and the State*, 335–337.

55. Colin, 222, notes: "There was no French attack on the 16th. They moved to face the enemy when he attacked their outposts. Clausewitz's criticism is therefore without

the result were the same, it would leave Bonaparte in the same position again. Or if, indeed, the French commander did not think this position was so bad—why did he abandon it the evening before? Did he think spending the night in this position was especially dangerous, and did he expect to take Arcole more quickly on the 16th? There is as little reason for the one as for the other.

The simplest and most natural explanation for this second attack could be that Bonaparte thought the Austrians would be retreating. But there is nothing to that effect in any report, and it is also contradicted by his apprehensiveness about what might happen overnight. Thus, this attack of the 16th remains completely unexplained.

The retreat on the evening of the 16th is more powerfully motivated than that on the evening of the 15th, since this time, Bonaparte had not even taken Arcole.[56] By the same token, the attack of the 17th is much more understandable than that of the 16th for the single reason that it has a different configuration whose feasibility Bonaparte had recognized on the 16th and on which he could base new hope. It is quite acceptable that a commander should not give up on a battle that has already cost him many men but has cost the enemy more, so long as a chance of victory remains; if he were to retreat, the enemy would claim an undeserved victory and also enjoy some of its benefits, whereas if the attack were continued, the results of the preceding efforts could be considered half the job already accomplished. So long as Davidowitsch did not push any further forward, so long as each individual fight cost the Austrians more than the French, so long as any prospect of overall success remained, and so long as such an impassable area prevented the Austrians from inflicting a real defeat on their opponent even if they got the upper hand,[57] Bonaparte could continue his attacks, for these depended primarily on courage and endurance, in both of which the French could hardly be surpassed. But of course,

---

foundation." Napoleon's letter to the Directory is not completely clear on the timeline, but it implies there was a French attack, thus contradicting Colin. Napoléon I, *Correspondance de Napoléon Ier*, 2:116–118.

56. Colin, 223, notes: "When Bonaparte fell back to the bridge at Ronco on the evening of the 15th, he was no longer master of Arcole, where Guieu arrived only as night was falling. Arcole had such little value in itself that the Austrians and the French ignored it at the end of the battle."

57. Colin, 223, notes: "Therefore it was not so inept of Bonaparte to establish himself in this marshy region, rather than attacking a superior enemy in the open field who had already beaten him twice."

some chance of overall victory had to be present; Bonaparte thought he had it on the 15th because he did not know the true situation, and again on the 17th because he had made new dispositions, but on the 16th he had no reason at all.

If we can find that it was justified and necessary to attack on the 17th and that his dispositions were at least understandable, this is still very far from calling them commendable. Since the Austrians had already retreated behind the Alpon on the 15th, and thus the value Bonaparte had attached to advancing between the two rivers no longer existed, it is unforgivable that he stubbornly persisted with his original plan. Throwing a bridge across at Albaredo and sending a sizable column to Legnago, just 9 miles away, are such obvious measures that we cannot understand why Bonaparte did not choose them sooner. After he had seen on the 15th how difficult it would be to debouch from his chosen ground and that there was no longer any need to worry about Verona, crossing at Albaredo and Legnago would have achieved Bonaparte's entire aim of meeting his opponent at an advantage, and there is probably no doubt that the French would have won the resulting battle. The Austrians apparently did not outnumber the French either in cavalry or overall, and they [the Austrians] found their left flank under attack and their line of retreat threatened; all these circumstances promised victory to the French.

The most natural place to look for information about these matters would be Bonaparte's *Memoirs*, but all we find there is an obvious fable that tries to conceal his own mistakes, of which he is well aware.

The reasons he adduces to justify his advance between the Alpon and the Adige against the criticisms ringing in his ears are verbatim as follows:

The bridge at Ronco was thrown across [the Adige] onto the right [bank] of the Alpon, roughly a mile from its mouth, which has been an object of criticism from poorly educated soldiers. In fact, if the bridge had been built on the left side [of the Alpon] toward Albaredo: 1. the army would have found itself debouching onto a vast plain, which its general wanted to avoid; 2. Alvinczy, who was occupying the heights of Caldiero, would have been able to cover the march of the column that he would have directed against Verona by guarding the left side of the Alpon; he would have forced his way into this weakly guarded city and effected his junction with the army of the Tyrol; the division at Rivoli, caught between two fires, would have been forced to retreat to Peschiera; the entire army would have been bizarrely compromised; instead of which, by throwing the bridge across on the right side of the Alpon, we obtained the incalculable advantage 1. of luring the enemy onto three causeways,[58] across a vast marsh; 2. of reestablishing communication with Verona via the dike that runs back up along the Adige River and leads to the villages of Porcil and Jambione, where Alvinczy had his headquarters, without the enemy having any position available to occupy, nor any natural obstacle to cover the movement of the troops he might have set in march to attack Verona. This attack was no longer possible, since all the French army had seized [the Austrian army] by the tail, while the walls of the city would have stopped its head, etc.[59]

Both the advantages he cites for his chosen dispositions are clearly just the inverse of the two disadvantages associated with advancing on the right bank of the Alpon.

We will allow the second reason to stand, but of course, only on the 15th, and absolutely not on the next two days. But Bonaparte seems to attach special value to the first reason, because earlier he says this about the march from Verona to Ronco:

So the officers and soldiers who had crossed this area when they pursued Wurmser began to guess their general's intention: that he wants to turn

---

58. Clausewitz notes: "Bonaparte always likes to talk about three causeways, in which he includes the one running from Ronco to Albaredo along the right bank of the Adige. But this one obviously has no connection with the purported aim."

59. "*Le pont de Ronco fut jeté sur la droite de l'Alpon, à peu près à un quart de lieue de son embouchure, ce qui a été un objet de critique pour les militaires mal instruits. En effet si le pont eut été place sur la rive gauche vis à vis Albaredo: 1. l'armée se fut trouvée deboucher sur un vaste plaine et ce que son general voulut éviter; 2. Alvinzi, qui occupait les hauteurs de Caldiero, eut, en garnissant la rive gauche de l'Alpon, couvert la marche de la colonne, qu'il aurait dirigé sur Verone; il eut force cette ville faiblement gardée, et eut opéré sa junction avec l'armée du Tyrol; la division de Rivoli, prise entre deux feux, eut été obligée de se rétirer sur Peschiera; l'armée toute entière en eut été etrangement compromise; au lieu qu'en jettant le pont sur la droite de l'Alpon on obtenoit l'avantage inappreciable 1. d'attirer l'ennemi sur trois chaussées,* traversant un vaste marais; 2. de se trouver en communication avec Verone par la digue qui remonte l'Adige et passe au village de Porcil et de Jambione, où Alvinzi avoit son quartier general, sans que l'ennemi eut aucune position à prendre, ni peut couvrir d'aucun obstacle naturel le movement des troupes qu'il auroit fait marcher pour attaquer Verone. Cette attaque n'étoit plus possible, puisque toute l'armée française l'eut prise en queue, pendant que les murailles de la ville en auroient arrêté la tête etc.*" See Montholon, *Mémoires pour servir à l'Histoire de France sous Napoléon*, 3:329–330.

Caldiero, as he could not carry it frontally; that being unable to fight 40,000 men in the open with 13,000, he moves his battlefield onto some causeways surrounded by a vast swamp, where mere numbers can achieve nothing, but where everything is decided by the courage of those at the head of the column, etc.[60]

The reader can see what we are supposed to make of this strategic monologue of his army. It is a fable, just like the reasoning that he has invented this public voice of his army to support. Bonaparte knew the Austrian army was at Caldiero and was seeking it there, not in the marshes; he was the attacker, so if he wanted his attack to happen, he would have to leave the marshes behind and fight the Austrians on the plain. The fact that things turned out quite differently and the Austrians were so kind as to go on the offensive against him along the causeways was never part of the calculation.[61] But this reason offered by the historian of St. Helena is not only at odds with the aim he describes, without any connection to probability; it is also contradicted by the business itself. What was the purpose of these bloody attacks of the 15th against the bridge at Arcole, which was the exit from the causeway, if Bonaparte wanted to avoid the plain?[62] Why not instead entice the Austrians onto the causeway, as actually happened on the 17th?[63] It is quite obvious that he has just lifted this reason from the course of events, particularly those of the 17th, even though things turned out quite differently from what Bonaparte intended or expected.

60. "*Alors les officiers et soldats qui, du tems qu'ils poursuivoient Wurmser, avoient traversés ces lieux, commencèrent à diviner l'intention de leur general, il veut tourner Caldiero, qu'il n'a pu enléver de front; avec 13,000 hommes ne pouvant lutter en plaine contre 40,000; il porte son champ de bataille sur des chaussées entourées de vastes marais, où le nombre ne pourra rien, mais où le courage des têtes de colonne décidera de tout.*" Ibid.

61. Colin, 226, notes: "On the contrary, it seems as though he could have every confidence of it. As has already been noted on page 176 [of Colin], Alvinczy had either to attack, or to carry out a fighting withdrawal, or to abandon his trains; and, so as not to sacrifice Davidowitsch, he had to attack. War offers no better example of an enemy being placed in check as perfectly as Bonaparte did to Alvinczy."

62. Colin, 226, notes: "He did want to move onto the plain, but at Villanova, where the enemy's siege parks and supply convoys were."

63. Colin, 226, notes: "It was certainly more attractive to seize the line of operations of the entire enemy army than to try to lure 2,000 Croats onto a dike, even assuming they were willing to play along."

Thus, from the battle of Arcole we can permit the French commander to boast only of great boldness and tenacity. These qualities are indeed not unworthy of the victory they won for him, but we must consider the first day's dispositions as thoroughly misguided, and those of the two other days as being the result of obstinacy and contrary to the most basic tactical principles.

Woe to any less distinguished general[64] who dared to attempt such an operation and failed!

The actions of the Austrian commander are also highly reprehensible.[65]

On a causeway, the defender necessarily has a great advantage; unless it is done very badly or the troops are really poor, a proper defense in the middle of a causeway, even where the defender cannot get any more troops into the fight than the attacker can, offers a very high probability of success. But the defender has an even bigger advantage at the end of a causeway, because there he can bring more forces into action than his opponent can. Thus it was natural for the Austrians to establish themselves in Arcole and Porcil at the causeway exits and wait for the French to advance. If Porcil was not so suitable for this because the causeway split up into several branches before it, then a position had to be chosen at the junction or some other suitable spot. In this situation, the Austrians could render all French efforts futile with very small forces and thus retain a significant reserve against any outflanking maneuver. Of course, this would not lead to a victory of the kind they needed, but neither would advancing along the causeways, and anyway, in their strategic situation—which we will discuss later—this victory was almost impossible. In these conditions, the French attack turning in this direction was nearly the most favorable thing that could happen to them. But now the Austrians gave up all these advantages to march down the causeways against the French and engage them on equal terms [*al pari*]. This would seem almost incomprehensible, were it not for the

64. Colin, 227, notes: "But if he only adopted bad dispositions, how come Bonaparte was not mediocre? If his only remaining virtue is relentlessness, a courageous nobody could have done just as much. It is easy for Clausewitz to criticize; but we can tell that there is something special about these days at Arcole that impresses him." Again, Colin seems to have missed Clausewitz's point. Clausewitz is getting at the idea that Napoleon made mistakes that would have ended the careers of other officers, but his fame and prestige allowed his mistakes to be more easily ignored.

65. Colin, 227, notes: "More so than Clausewitz thinks, since he does not question the astonishing dispersal of Alvinczy's troops, which contributed a great deal to the outcome and to Bonaparte's success."

fact that on the 15th the Austrians initially believed the force that had crossed at Ronco was just a small detachment they could easily drive back, so they advanced along the Porcil causeway; while on the 16th and 17th they believed Bonaparte was in the process of retreating, so it was just a matter of pursuing. But even under these assumptions, Alvinczy cannot be excused, at least not for the 16th and 17th. A small advance guard would have convinced him of his error, without getting him into circumstances that would cost him significant losses like those suffered by his two columns advancing down the causeways.

We will leave open the question of whether Augereau's crossing of the Alpon on the 17th was supposed to be left undisturbed, or whether the reason for this was negligence.

So what was it that obliged Alvinczy to retreat on the 17th, to lower his flag and give up the fight? After three days of mishandled fighting, Alvinczy's combat forces were already significantly reduced, as was his army's morale and his own; his previous tactical advantage was nullified somewhat by Augereau crossing the Alpon and by the news of a French advance through Legnago. After such an adverse lead-up, without outnumbering the French, his hastily cobbled together, poorly trained army could not risk a decisive battle on the plain on the 18th, a battle Bonaparte would have forced on him without fail, and whereby a total defeat could transform a mere failed Austrian operation into a complete disaster. This reasoning should not surprise us, as it is in the nature of all generals who find themselves in a tight spot and are not distinguished by great strength of character.

So what enabled Bonaparte to end up as the victor in such a poorly conceived battle? Better conduct of the individual actions, braver troops, more determined persistence, more audacious daring.[66]

59 BONAPARTE TURNS AGAINST DAVIDOWITSCH

On the 17th, the day Alvinczy decided he had been beaten and began his retreat, Davidowitsch achieved his victory over Vaubois's division, driving it out

---

66. Again, Clausewitz returns to this theme, and it fits with his thoughts on genius. One can also see the later imprint on German military decision making and operations orders that became the norm from the middle of the nineteenth century onward: rapid decision-making, decentralized control, and daring.

of the Rivoli position with considerable loss and back toward Castelnuovo, as we related above (see section 55). Naturally, a victory won by 6,000 men could not compensate for the damage done by a battle lost by 22,000. Davidowitsch pursued General Vaubois and deployed at Castelnuovo on the 18th, while Vaubois fell back across the Mincio.

When he learned of Vaubois's defeat, Bonaparte immediately decided to turn against Davidowitsch. On the 18th he pursued Alvinczy with the reserve cavalry. He directed Masséna's division to Villafranca, where Vaubois was to retreat via Borghetto, and he assigned Augereau's division to move through Verona and over the Molare heights, descend into the Adige valley at Dolce, and thus cut General Davidowitsch's line of retreat.

But the latter recognized how dangerous his situation was in good time; on the 19th he retreated into the valley of the Adige toward Ala, before the planned moves against him could be completed. Nonetheless, his rear guard suffered heavily at Campara, an entire battalion being cut off.

Upon hearing of the danger Davidowitsch was getting into, Alvinczy, who was at Montebello [Montebello Vicentino] on the 19th, sent some battalions into the Molare mountains to threaten Augereau's left [right] flank;[67] to support this demonstration, on the 20th he himself advanced on Villanova again. But when Bonaparte got word of this, he immediately turned back toward Verona, whereupon Alvinczy found it advisable to retreat behind the Brenta.

On 23 November Wurmser finally made a sally from Mantua, which naturally could not succeed, since the columns coming to his rescue had long since retreated, and the besieging French forces weakened during the crisis had already been reinforced again.

Herewith the third relief attempt ended. The crisis was past, and for the time being, both sides rested. The Austrians deployed in winter quarters behind the Brenta, with their left wing in Padua and their right in Trient.

Bonaparte resumed his former position on the Adige.

67. This must be an error, as it would have been Augereau's right flank as he moved north into the southern mountains with Alvinczy to his east (right).

60 REFLECTIONS

We now wish to offer our observations on strategy concerning this fourth act of the campaign.

We said earlier that the situation made this third Austrian attack imperative (see section 54). Wurmser had shut himself up in Mantua with 16,000 men; even if only 12,000 of them could be regarded as superfluous for the defense of the fortress and brought out again if it was relieved, that was no mean object in terms both of the value of these combat forces in themselves and of military honor and glory. Since matters in Germany had already been decided, the most urgent demand was to send all available reinforcements to Italy to relieve Wurmser's corps in Mantua, which was already suffering from a severe shortage of supplies. This was the sole objective of the Austrian offensive, but it was very natural that they did not stop there. Rather, they sought to obtain a decisive victory over Bonaparte and, by that victory, not only to relieve Mantua for this campaign but also to win back all of upper Italy. The quest for such a victory was all the more important because the pope was continuing to arm himself, probably relying on Austrian assistance, and could not be left in the lurch. As we have seen, the forces the Austrians could muster for this new attack on Bonaparte came to some 48,000 men. Given the manner in which the French had invested Mantua and Wurmser's inactivity, the French always had some 30,000 men available for field operations, so the Austrians had an estimated four-to-three numerical superiority. If the relative morale of the commanders and their armies had been in complete equilibrium, this ratio would have been a fairly strong guarantee of victory; but given the very marked French moral superiority, it actually gave the Austrians only a very slim chance of winning. When we consider that enemy strength is generally reported to be greater than it really is,[68] we have to wonder at the Austrian government promising itself that this third offensive would bring gloriously decisive success. Governments often make such mistakes because they never attach enough weight to these mundane factors; they always let themselves be hoodwinked by the generals and by other commentators who attribute the bad outcome to a single error that easily could have been avoided or to an unfortunate accident that will not happen again. Thus, instead of thinking be-

68. General George C. McClellan of American Civil War fame is perhaps the most famous example of someone who routinely overestimated the strength of his enemy.

forehand how to improve the situation, and treating the matter not as a mere attempt but as a well-calculated action, they summon renewed hope where there is basically none to summon and tentatively go to work a second time.[69] If a new commander takes over, this is seized on as a source of great optimism, without anyone asking whether the new man is very different from the previous one. He would have to be if there is any hope of decisive good fortune after such decisive misfortune the first time, because a minor difference of personality means little. But Beaulieu, Wurmser, and Alvinczy were evidently all the same kind of man, and none of them could reasonably be expected to add any significant new weight to the scales.

At this point, we should say that the Austrians had no great aspirations for a decisive victory or for the reconquest of Lombardy. But strategically, this is a very important point; after all, strategic questions always increase in importance the greater their ambition. If on this point the Austrian government had held on to a very clear and simple reasoning, such as we demand here, perhaps it would have gone to more trouble to provide favorable conditions for success, such as by moving 10,000–15,000 men from Germany to Italy. But strategists and cabinet committees are always so engrossed in the myriad details of implementation that it seems incomprehensible to them when someone merely wants to satisfy the simple principle of sufficient reason.[70]

Let us accept that at the beginning of November the Austrians wanted to launch a new offensive against the French in Italy with 48,000 men and that

---

69. This ties in with Clausewitz's arguments in the first two chapters of book 1 of *On War*, where he discusses what war is, as well as the purpose and means required for success in war. See Clausewitz, *On War*, 75–99.

70. In essence, Clausewitz is arguing for the Austrians to place a specific value on the object of the conflict, as well as on the respective theaters of war in relation to the overarching goals. Once they have made these decisions, they need to commit the resources required to achieve a decision in at least one of the theaters: ideally, prioritizing the most important one. By not doing this and, effectively, hedging their bets, they reduced their chances of success in both theaters and in the overall war. By not clearly prioritizing the theaters in terms of importance to their policy goals, they increased the chance of not gaining their overarching objective, for which they were at war in the first place. See Clausewitz, *On War*, 90–99, 582–610 (book 1, chap. 2, and book 8, chaps. 3–6). For an explanation of the philosophical principle of sufficient reason, see Yitzhak Y. Melamed and Martin Lin, "Principle of Sufficient Reason," in *The Stanford Encyclopedia of Philosophy*, ed. Edward N. Zalta (Spring 2017), accessed 21 August 2017, https://plato.stanford.edu/archives/spr2017/entries/sufficient-reason/.

this offensive had twin aims: first, to rescue Wurmser from Mantua, and then, to win a victory over Bonaparte. The question then arises, what was the best form this offensive could have taken?

Both the previous offensives had begun with the Austrian forces united, and they had intentionally divided them. Now, with Alvinczy's army newly formed on the Isonzo and Davidowitsch's corps still in the Tyrol, this force was, by its nature, divided by a large and partly mountainous stretch of country. Whereas previously we first and foremost demanded to know a good reason for the Austrians dividing their forces, this time, the initial deployment of their troops provided an important reason for separate operations, and a better question would be: why should they unite? The same two common reasons that are always cited on such occasions were given in favor of bringing together the whole force on the Italian plain: that the Austrians were thereby sure of bringing their absolute four-to-three numerical superiority onto the battlefield; and that unity could not be left out of the plan. This union was possible at least insofar as the corps that was to be left in the Tyrol could be made very weak. Although the Tyrolese passes no longer had their earlier importance for the German theater of operations, since Moreau had retreated back over the Rhine, perhaps the Austrian government did not want to denude the region of troops entirely. This would have made a bad impression on the locals, who had mobilized a militia of 7,000–8,000 men and would have felt abandoned to the revenge of the French if the whole Austrian army had been withdrawn from their area. But if the Austrians had left, say, 5,000 men in the Tyrol under a famous general, these could have formed a corps with the Tyrolese militia, which the French would have to oppose with something, and whose strength they would have been unable to estimate very accurately. If the Austrians had now spread the rumor that 10,000 men were on their way to the Tyrol from the Rhine army, the local inhabitants would have been reassured, and the French would not have been able to assess the situation clearly. Thus, a corps of 15,000 of Davidowitsch's 20,000 men could have marched down onto the Italian plain, and a total force of about 43,000 could have been deployed there. Having this union happen via the Brenta valley was an unnecessary and awkward business because Bonaparte could interpose himself between the two columns. A couple more days' delay really would not have mattered.

So much for combining the forces.

However, it could be said that in the present case Bonaparte had just one definite objective to protect—namely, Mantua—and this is always easier to do if the attacker advances with his force united because then the defender can just place himself between the attacker and the objective. But if the attacker divides his forces, the defender must do likewise, which means there will now be several points of decision; the defender is thereby at a disadvantage, in that he has to be victorious at every point to achieve overall success, whereas the attacker needs to succeed in only one place, which gives him a much greater chance of success.

According to this view, in the present case anyway, attacking in several columns could have somewhat increased the intrinsically small chance of success. But the situation and the strength of the French theater of operations were a powerful obstacle to exploiting this advantage.

Two basic principles are the ultimate arbiters for divided strategic attacks in most cases. The first: that each column should be given an independent mission; that is, each should deliver its own decision, and the plan should make no provision for combining before the decision, nor should each step taken by one column depend on each step taken by another. The second: that the columns' routes of advance should be as far apart as their bases and their objectives allow.

The first principle is the salvation of all divided attacks, for if the situation makes communication between separate columns very difficult—indeed, often impossible—and they constantly have to pay attention to each other's actions in carrying out their own, this is highly unnatural and usually has the most dire consequences. Their unity of action must be found in their common goal. Each must pursue this goal in its own way, not crazily, blindly, and thoughtlessly—for one should absolutely never do that in war—but with the indefatigable effort necessitated by a business over which we no longer have control once it is begun.[71]

---

71. This brings us to two of Clausewitz's key ideas: genius and friction. Once the fighting starts, a commander often has a limited ability to control events; therefore, it is critical that all the goals of the campaign line up with the political objectives, maximizing the likelihood of the desired outcome. That being said, if one accepts Clausewitz's logic regarding his trinity (*On War,* book 1, chap. 1), then even if everything is done correctly, there is no guarantee of success, only an increased likelihood of it. This in turn relates to the role of genius in war (*On War,* book 1, chap. 3) and the need for well-educated and well-trained officers. The latter are required, especially if no genius happens to be available, because they must decide how and when to implement the necessary tactical and strategic decisions connected to the government's policy goals. Much of Clausewitz's argument boils down to this: keep it simple, clear, and straight-

Thus, even if each commander does everything he possibly can in his situation, then of course, just because of the characteristics of a divided attack, he could easily be in danger of being soundly beaten, but the collective action of the whole will not turn out so poorly, and what is lost at one point will most probably be made up for at another. We say most probably because we have assumed that the task is indeed a suitable one for a divided attack.

To satisfy this first principle more easily, our second principle demands that the columns be as far apart as possible, since it is clear that the further each of them and their enemy are from the other, the more independent they become. In particular, the defender is in a position to take advantage of his interior lines by unexpectedly hurling his main body against first one column, then another, only if their separation is not too great.

If we now apply these principles to the attack against Bonaparte on the Adige, we find that the specific circumstances defy them both.

In the first place, the French theater of operations is unusually strong. If we ignore the road down the western shore of Lake Garda for now, it is not enveloped at all by the attacker's base; from Peschiera through Verona to Legnago, it is just 40 miles in extent, which is very narrow. An attack below Legnago is not feasible because it gets tangled up in the difficulties of countless water-

---

forward, and think through what one wants and what one is willing to sacrifice to attain it—and even that provides no guarantee of success. This is important, because based on Clausewitz's definition, genius is rare. Indeed, he agrees with Napoleon's comments about war's problems being so difficult that they are "worthy of the gifts of a *Newton* or an *Euler*." Clausewitz, *On War*, 100–112. In addition to being incredibly complex, war makes it extremely difficult to do anything. "Everything in war is very simple, but the simplest thing is difficult." Ibid., 119. This is Clausewitz's concept of friction, and he means that even the smallest thing can be extremely difficult to accomplish successfully: the horse carrying a commander might stumble, killing its rider; a rainstorm might intervene; fog might obscure the battlefield; a snowstorm might block a mountain pass; a soldier might panic and flee, precipitating a rout. Any one of these small things can ruin an entire enterprise, and even a small problem can be extremely difficult to solve. For an excellent example of something that seems simple but is, in reality, exceedingly difficult, see Ernest Swinton, *The Defence of Duffer's Drift* (Washington, DC: US Infantry Association, 1916), accessed 1 September 2017, https://books.google.com/books?id=dKhJAAAAIAAJ&pg=PA21#v=onepage&q&f=false. It is worth noting that this classic of military education is still widely used, and it takes the main character six attempts to solve a relatively simple problem. A campaign consists of thousands of similar small, simple problems that must be solved.

courses and leaves the line of retreat to Friuli very exposed. But on this short front there are the fortified towns of Verona and Legnago, which cannot be attacked as long as there is an enemy force behind them. Some of the approaches to the Adige, like that on the right of the Alpon, are very restricted by marshes; the river itself cannot be crossed without pontoon bridges. Between the Adige and the Mincio there are another five or six smaller rivers parallel with them, such as the Tartaro, the Thione, and the Molinella, whose banks are marshy in places and thus easily defended. The route out of the Tyrol down the Adige is blocked on one side by the Chiusa, on the other by the position at Rivoli; even if these places are overcome by superior force, the route remains a defile that can easily be seized from Verona if the attacker leaves it behind, in which case his line of retreat is as good as totally lost.

Thus we see that an Austrian column that overwhelms the Rivoli position cannot easily advance into the area of Castelnuovo so long as it is in danger of running into a superior enemy; for if the enemy beats it during its continued advance toward Mantua, he also will have closed the Adige valley to it from Verona. Since in some places Monte Baldo cannot be crossed by artillery, and in other places it even obliges infantry to detour down into the valley, a corps that has lost the use of the highway in the valley can easily be forced to lay down its arms. Thus, if an Austrian column advances energetically against Mantua for as long as its luck holds, in conformity with our first principle, it runs a very serious risk.

Furthermore, we see that the second principle cannot be employed either, since the crossing of the Adige probably cannot happen anywhere other than above Legnago; and if the left wing of the French army has retreated to Castelnuovo or Villafranca, it will be so close that if the French commander heads there with his main body, it is very doubtful that the column advancing on Legnago will have enough time to cross the Adige, force its way across all the other rivers, get to Mantua, and defeat the besieging force before the enemy's main body can get back.

One could conceive of having the Tyrol column advance down the western shore of Lake Garda rather than down the valley of the Adige, but if one does not also hold the Adige valley, thus keeping a portion of the forces for the offensive idle, the retreat of such a column is again endangered [by a French move north up the Adige or Brenta valleys where they conjoin], and the separation is increased by the Mincio in a way that only favors the defender.

These considerations must lead away again from the idea of attacking in separate columns and back toward uniting the force as much as possible, and this is all the more so, the more weight one attaches to the second aim of the offensive: a decisive battle. If we now take into consideration the characteristics of both armies and their commanders, the great skill and decisiveness of the French commander, the lightning speed of his maneuvers, the incredible endurance of his army, the habit of victory, and his confidence in both himself and his good fortune, then we must emphasize again that, for the Austrians, the simplest plans are the best,[72] for with these, in the end, the main determinant is the result of the decisive battle. It is clear that if there was any way the Austrian troops could restore the balance against the various advantages the French had over them through advantages of their own, it would have to be in a great massed battle.

Thus, we believe that if the author of the Austrian plan of operations had taken all these considerations into account, if he had not expected the sheer structure and complexity of his plan to increase his combat power—which it can never do by itself, but only when it is generated by appropriate conditions—his plan would have entailed massing a force of 40,000 on the Italian plain to move against Bonaparte and force a decision in one simple, hard-fought battle to the last man. We say one simple battle because we consider this stipulation to be a crucial strategic one. By that, we mean a battle that aims for nothing more than victory plain and simple and whose plan includes no attempt to enhance success through powerful outflanking maneuvers and the like, for such enhancements of success always come at some cost to the certainty of success, which was already none too great. A simple victory would be entirely sufficient for all their purposes, since once Bonaparte was beaten, and given a suitably energetic pursuit, the relief of Mantua and the reconquest of the province of Milan could not fail. We are not saying that the battle had to be a linear frontal attack, which, according to our tactical views, we certainly do not think is the form that gives the best chance of success. If we were to explain ourselves further on this point, we would lose ourselves in debates about tac-

---

72. Simple plans also reduce the degree of friction experienced by armies. Each complication in a plan increases the likelihood that the plan will fail, and every added complexity represents an extra point of potential failure. Given the role of chance and probability, the more complex something is, the more individual points of potential failure exist. See Clausewitz, *On War*, 119–121 (book 1, chap. 7).

tics, which is not our intention; so we will satisfy ourselves with that remark, which we have made only so the reader does not get the wrong impression.

Given that in this case the Austrians did decide on a two-pronged advance from the Tyrol onto the plain, let us compare the way they implemented it with the way our principles say they should have.

They quite evidently acted against these principles.

Alvinczy tries to get close to Davidowitsch as quickly as possible, and then as soon as he gets close, he is at his wit's end.[73] The two of them are separated by Verona, the Adige, and the French army; each of them is waiting for the other, and not a soul can say how they are supposed to help each other. From the very beginning, in their uncertainty Davidowitsch and Alvinczy are each like a nervous little beetle that runs quickly for a couple of inches and then stops motionless for a few minutes, without its feeble little mind being able to give a clear reason for either the one or the other. Finally, Alvinczy and his attack are left hanging in the air, from which nothing good can possibly result. He is thrown back on the defensive, and like a guilty man who knows the avenging sword will unerringly strike him, he stands there helplessly and lets his opponent probe around him until he eventually finds a weakness.

According to our principles, Alvinczy should have advanced on Legnago via Padua, and at about the time he reached Legnago, Davidowitsch should have taken the position at Rivoli. Both should have directed their operations on Mantua and advanced with the utmost energy so long as they saw any hope of victory. This simple instruction was the only practical one, and if it involved some danger, at least this danger was balanced by some possibility of success, whereas any other plan lacked this possibility.[74]

73. Clausewitz uses the phrase "*hat sein Latein ein Ende.*"

74. This would have allowed them to concentrate their forces in time; although the Austrian forces are separated, their effort could be concentrated by their simultaneous action, which would compel Napoleon to choose which force to engage as they approached Mantua, thereby allowing the other to relieve Mantua and accomplishing the goal of the operation. Or, had Napoleon chosen simply to guard Mantua, he would have had to allow them to concentrate against him, which would have led to a worse outcome for him. As Clausewitz points out, such a plan and its execution at least would have stood a chance of success, whereas separate forces operating independently of each other in space and time provided Napoleon with the best opportunity to counter them. Note that this is different from concentrating a force in space, where, using the above example, two forces would be trying to move so that they end up in the same space at the same time, thereby maximizing their physical force at one place.

If we first make the basic assumption that Bonaparte's main body would be victorious every time, that could yield the following cases:

1. That both columns are beaten one after the other by the French main body.

In this case, naturally the operation is a failure. But whether Alvinczy or Davidowitsch is beaten first makes a significant difference. If it is the former, and Alvinczy is not in a position to assist General Davidowitsch's retreat, then, as we have shown, Davidowitsch is in a very nasty situation and could be obliged to lay down his arms. If Davidowitsch is beaten first, Alvinczy's intact state is enough to ensure Davidowitsch's safe retreat, because Bonaparte has no time to lose in turning his main body against Alvinczy.

2. That only one of the two generals is beaten, and the other relieves Mantua.

Here again, there is a very significant difference. If Alvinczy is beaten and Davidowitsch breaks through, then after he and Wurmser have combined their 30,000 men, there is nothing else he can do but retreat through Governolo via Castel Baldo to join Alvinczy or, in the worst case, head for Ferrara, as General Wurmser was later enjoined to do by the emperor himself. But if Davidowitsch is beaten, then Alvinczy and Wurmser combined can pursue the French main body facing Davidowitsch and deliver a second battle under favorable conditions between the Adige and the Mincio.

Thus we see that in both cases it was always more advantageous for the Austrians if Bonaparte's main body turned first against Davidowitsch, who would act in a sense as a diversion; but this should not tempt them into giving him too much of a head start over Alvinczy or reducing Alvinczy's activity too much, since constant common action is always the main issue with separate columns.[75] So we can see that with our plan, out of the two main cases we adduce, in the first the Austrians fail to achieve their aim, but in the second they

---

Either way, Clausewitz is getting at the idea that the Austrians should have coordinated their efforts with a clear plan of action.

75. Colin, 241, notes: "It is rather difficult to reconcile this with the fundamental principle expressed earlier, that the various columns must act in an entirely independent manner, without paying any attention to each other." Colin is being somewhat disingenuous, as Clausewitz argued for concentration in time as well as space, and to achieve that, the columns would have to work independently, to a degree. He was not arguing for all the columns to do their own thing.

at least manage to free Wurmser, and even if the French main body is victorious, the Austrians still have a chance of achieving their aim.[76]

If our first assumption above does not apply, there are three other possible cases: first, that one of the columns manages to join up with Wurmser, while the other is agile and lucky enough to avoid battle; second, that battle is offered and the French main body loses; third, that Bonaparte manages to prevent either column from joining Wurmser but cannot prevent them from combining before giving battle.

The first of these is an enhancement of success. The first part of the aim is achieved without any loss, and one then has the means and the prospect of obtaining the second part, a victory over Bonaparte.

The second case is another enhancement, since both aims are as good as achieved.

The third case may be considered at least a good preparation for complete success because it assumes that the Austrians will give battle against Bonaparte under the walls of Mantua with the whole of their force.

We admit these last three cases had only a small probability. However, we cannot leave them out of our calculations entirely.

We believe we have hereby shown that if the Austrians had carried out their advance with their columns separated throughout, then a plan developed according to our principles would have had some prospect of success, more or less, whereas the plan the Austrians actually followed was totally pointless.

In these reflections we have assumed that Bonaparte would stay within his theater of operations between the Adige and the Mincio, because we think that is most sensible. But if Bonaparte made the mistake he actually made, of going to meet the Austrians as far away as the Brenta, then there was no reason for Alvinczy to press him hard. On the contrary, it was in his interest to stay away from Mantua for as long as possible, because then Davidowitsch could relieve it without any danger to himself. After that, even if Alvinczy lost a battle against Bonaparte, it would not prevent Davidowitsch from retreating to the Tyrol after freeing Wurmser. Bonaparte actually moved against the Austrians at Bassano on the 5th, but he realized his mistake and quickly turned back toward Verona on the 6th.

The direction of the Austrian general's march on Verona seems to have

---

76. With Wurmser free, Austrian forces would have gained strength and probably morale too.

been based on the confident assumption that Bonaparte would either retreat outright or turn his force against Davidowitsch. In the first event, Alvinczy wanted to combine with Davidowitsch as soon as possible, which in that case, would be no great matter; in the second, he wanted to threaten Bonaparte's line of retreat by retaking Verona or crossing the Adige nearby. What a fatuous assumption! In this war the Austrians kept making the same mistake of being more concerned with the fruits of victory than with earning them, of gearing their plans toward what they wanted victory to lead to rather than victory itself. Complete encirclement means a general's downfall if he is defeated; but so long as he is not defeated, it usually means nothing or is even to his advantage, unless his army has a very weak moral constitution and is already panic-stricken for some reason. The fact that the Austrians did not understand this distinction and did not recognize the influence of this moral weight meant that they always clumsily overreached their aim.

Instead of marching from Villanova to Verona, how much more natural it would have been for Alvinczy to turn left through Albaredo and suddenly cross the Adige there. Once he gained the right bank of the Adige, it would have been much more difficult for Bonaparte to get away from him. Davidowitsch could have advanced into the vicinity of Villafranca, where combining the two columns before the decision would have been much easier to imagine than it would have been outside Verona.

Bonaparte's conduct in this fourth act of the campaign seems to us to be much less praiseworthy than in the previous three.

The march to Bassano was a total blunder, the attack of the 6th a half measure, and that of the 12th at Caldiero not much better, since it is highly unlikely that the Austrian position could not be attacked in the flank on both sides, as it should have been. The march to Ronco should have been something quite sublime, but it degenerated into the most dire situation. The battle of Arcole itself has already been discussed.

If he finally emerged from this battle as the victor, he owes it as much to the Austrians' totally confused plans and actions as to his own courage and persistence, but not by any means to his cleverness. This victory was also a rather negative one that brought him few trophies; the Austrians had to give up on their aim, but they took up a position behind the Brenta.

10. The Crushing of Austria in Italy

The battle of Arcole ended on 17 November; the victory at Rivoli entailing the decisive action of the fifth act took place on 14 January. Between the two, there was a period of about two months during which peace reigned in the Italian theater of operations.

On Bonaparte's side, this lull is easily explained. The reasons preventing him from doing anything other than besiege Mantua are the same as after the battle of Bassano. The Austrians needed this interlude to reinforce their army yet again. It was only after this period that their formations were ready and their army was back up to the strength it had for Alvinczy's previous attack, some 40,000 men. The reinforcements were therefore no more than he had lost, about 8,000–10,000 men.

While the lull at the front allowed him time to do so, Bonaparte occupied himself with Italy's political affairs again.

In general, the Directory greatly desired peace because that is what the people wanted, and the government felt the need to strengthen its position at home. So far as the Italian provinces were concerned, the Directory was very wary of embarking on anything relating to their independence because it wanted to give them back to Austria in exchange for Belgium. It was not possible to use part of them to expand Sardinia and to pay for an auxiliary corps from that state; nor could Parma be used to reach an offensive alliance with Spain.[1]

---

1. Ferdinand, the Duke of Parma, was a member of the Spanish branch of the House of Bourbon that was then ruling Spain. As such, Parma might have been used as a bargaining chip with Spain. However, the French had already agreed to a deal with Parma (see section 25), one that had been negotiated through the Spanish minister resident in Parma. This would have made any renegotiation problematic, especially given that France was not in an overall position of strength at this time and that it needed Spain's help, not vice versa. For details of the treaty, see Pommereul, *Campaign of General Buonaparte in Italy*, 30–31n.

Bonaparte viewed all these things rather more audaciously. He did not consider peace to be so necessary; he relished the possibility of adding 10,000 Piedmontese and 10,000 Spaniards to the French combat forces, and he thought a force of 10,000 Albanians[2] raised by Venice would not go amiss either. That way, he reckoned, France could demand much more favorable peace terms from Austria. Incidentally, he did not want to buy alliances with these two kingdoms by ceding territory; he thought that merely guaranteeing the continued existence of the governments of Turin and Parma if they allied with France, and suspending the revolutionary intrigue in Piedmont and Spain, would be an adequate price. But to those who wanted to republicanize all of Italy and who saw an alliance with a monarchy as a retrograde step, he replied that Sardinia would not be able to last for long surrounded by the Ligurian, Cispadane, Lombard, and French republics,[3] and its consequent fall would just be in the nature of things, not due to any political action by France.

"The alliance between France and Sardinia," he said, "is like a giant embracing a pygmy; if he suffocates him, he does not mean to, it is just the effect of their extreme difference in size."[4]

The way he fostered the creation of the Cispadane Republic was in exactly the same spirit of large-scale continuation of the war, and he gladly would have fostered a republic in Lombardy as well, if the Directory had not been opposed to him on this last point.

2. Venice was busy trying to raise forces to defend itself against the French and looked to its holdings on the Adriatic coast. Ultimately, however, this was irrelevant, as the doge in Venice did not have the political support to secure his position, and French-inspired risings on the mainland facilitated his removal and the destruction of the Venetian empire following the Treaty of Campo Formio. See Michael Hochedlinger, *Austria's Wars of Emergence, 1683–1797* (New York: Routledge, 2013), 428–437; William H. McNeill, *Venice, the Hinge of Europe 1081–1797* (Chicago: University of Chicago Press, 1986), 229–230.

3. These were the republics France established in the wake of Napoleon's successes in Italy in 1796. As such, it would be reasonable to assume that the revolutionary republican fervor there might spread into Piedmont, bringing down its monarchy. In 1797 these republics would be merged along with other territories into the Cisalpine Republic.

4. Clausewitz notes: "*L'alliance de la France avec la Sardaigne, c'est un géant, qui embrasse un pygmée; s'il l'étouffe, c'est contre sa volonté, et par le seul effet de la différence extrême de leurs organs.*" Montholon, *Mémoires pour servir à l'histoire de France sous Napoléon,* 3:348.

Victor (reserve) at Goito:	2,000
Cavalry reserve:	700
Lannes in Bologna:	2,000
Total:	46,700 men

The Austrians had brought their strength up to 45,000 men again, but because of the way they were distributed, only 42,000 were available. Perhaps 3,000 men were allocated to some or other defensive role and thus taken out of the attack.

The plan of operations they followed this time was a kind of inversion of the previous one.

Once again, they wanted to advance in two separate columns through the Adige valley and on the plain. But this time, the main army under the command of General Alvinczy was to attack the French positions at the Corona and Rivoli and then advance down the Adige toward Mantua while a weaker corps of 14,000 men advanced across the plain. This latter corps itself was split into two columns—one of 5,000 under General Bayalitsch[13] moving on Verona, and the other of 9,000 under Provera from Padua against Legnago.

The column advancing on the plain was mainly supposed to attract the enemy's attention and, if possible, pin his main body on the lower Adige, while the Austrian main body attacked and wore down the French division in the Alps. But both these two large columns, acting otherwise independently of each other, were to advance constantly on Mantua to join up with General Wurmser there. A dispatch was sent to this general (and captured by the French) containing the emperor's order that in the worst case, Wurmser should head for Ferrara and the Papal States, where he would be well received.

As usual, we will offer our reflections on this plan of operations at the end of the episode [see section 66]. For now, we will just note that the Austrians reckoned on a portion of the French combat forces being diverted by the papal troops, who had been sent some Austrian generals and officers. The papal formations supposedly amounted to some 15,000 men, and even if they diverted only 5,000–6,000 French from the Adige theater, that would still have had some impact—except that Bonaparte, with the utmost disdain for this whole panoply, left just 1,000 men to face it, apart from 4,000 Italians he sent from

---

13. Adam Bayalitsch (Bajalics) was a Croat in Austrian service and was in his early 60s at the start of the campaign.

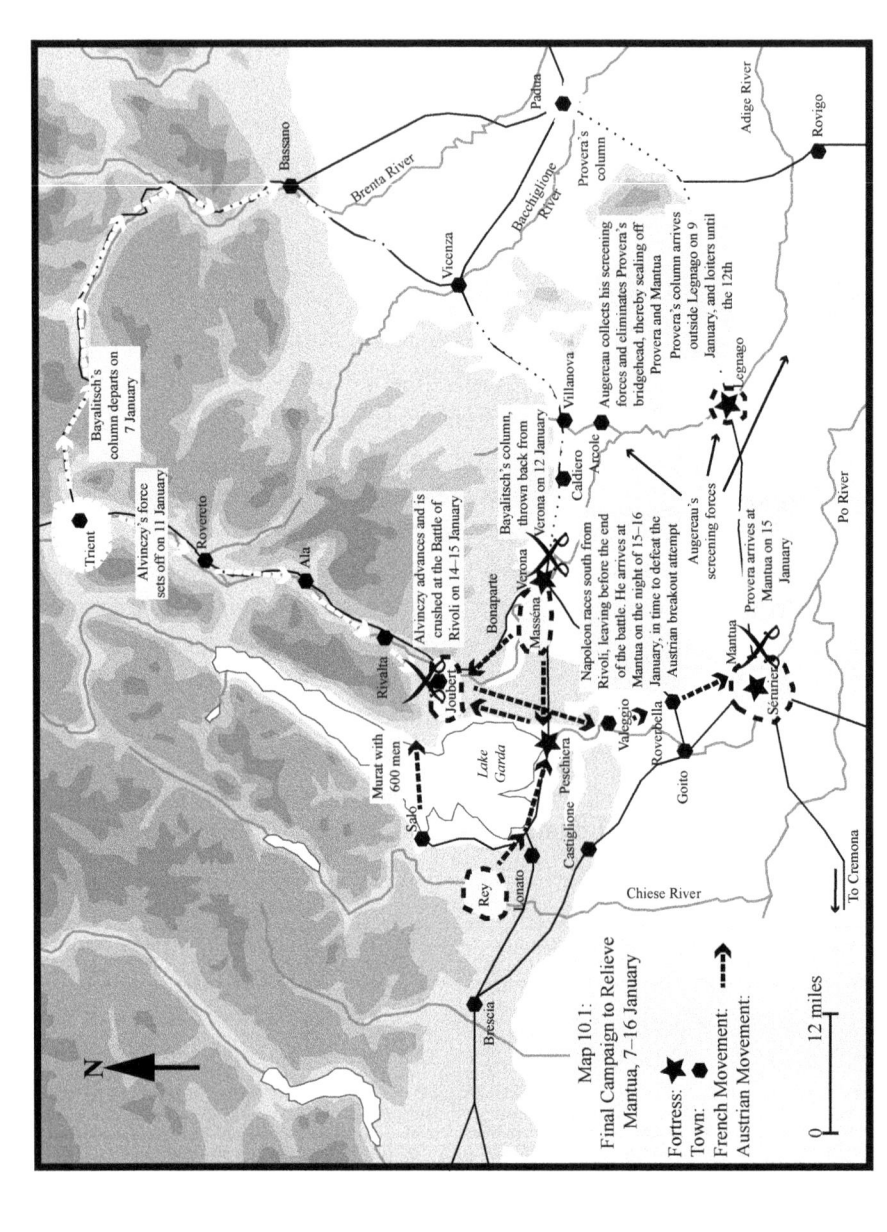

N

Map 10.1:
Final Campaign to Relieve
Mantua, 7–16 January

Fortress: ★
Town: ⬢
French Movement: 🠒
Austrian Movement: ┅🠒

0   12 miles

Bassano

Brenta River

Vicenza

Bacchiglione River

Padua

Adige River

Rovigo

Provera's
column

Bayalitsch's column departs on
7 January

Trient

Alvinczy's force
sets off on 11 January

Rovereto

Ala

Rivalta

Alvinczy advances and is
crushed at the Battle of
Rivoli on 14–15 January

Bonaparte

Joubert

Murat with
600 men

Saló

Lake
Garda

Rey

Lonato

Peschiera

Castiglione

Valeggio

Roverbella

Goito

To Cremona

Chiese River

Brescia

Masséna

Verona

Bayalitsch's column,
thrown back from
Verona on 12 January

Napoleon races south from
Rivoli, leaving before the end
of the battle. He arrives at
Mantua on the night of 15–16
January, in time to defeat the
Austrian breakout attempt

Caldiero

Arcole

Villanova

Augereau collects his screening
forces and eliminates Provera's
bridgehead, thereby sealing off
Provera and Mantua

Provera's column arrives
outside Legnago on 9
January, and loiters until
the 12th

Legnago

Augereau's
screening forces

Provera arrives at
Mantua on 15
January

Mantua

Serrarero

Po River

Milan to Bologna. Nobody understood better than he how to ignore secondary matters in order to unite as much of his force as possible at the crucial point.[14]

63 THE BATTLE OF RIVOLI ON 14–15 JANUARY

The Austrians configured their maneuvers so that Provera's column turned up in front of Legnago on the 9th, after his advance guard under General Hohenzollern had fought a fairly vigorous action with Augereau's advance guard at Bevilacqua on the 7th and 8th, whereas Bayalitsch's column only arrived outside Verona on the 12th. The attack on Joubert's position was likewise supposed to happen on the 12th. This early move by the left wing was probably supposed to make it even more effective as a diversion, but naturally it had the opposite effect, since the longer Provera spent in proximity to Augereau, the better the latter would know his true strength and intentions.

The main blow was supposed to strike Joubert's position at the Corona[15] and Rivoli.

As we have already said, the Corona position can be considered a natural outpost of the Rivoli position.

The Rivoli position is part of Monte Magnone, which can be considered a terrace of Monte Baldo down toward the Adige. The position at the Corona is on the steep incision made by a stream that runs from Monte Baldo past Ferrara [Ferrara di Monte Baldo] and into the Adige at Brentino. The right side of this stream is very high and steep, and between Ferrara and Brentino, the only ways to ascend it are a few rocky staircases.

As described earlier, the Rivoli position itself is a plateau separated from Monte Baldo by the Caprino valley, which is about 2,000 paces wide, but connected with the crest of Monte Magnone along the Adige. The point of connection is San Marco;[16] from this point to the Osteria Pass,[17] the continuation of this crest constitutes the rear of the position, but at the Osteria, it runs right

14. This relates back to Clausewitz's previous point in section 60 about clearly identifying the purpose of an action and committing to it.

15. This is probably Monte Della Corone, which is located by the sanctuary Madonna Della Corona outside Spiazzi.

16. There is an early-twentieth-century Forte San Marco on the site.

17. The monument to Napoleon in Rivoli Veronese is just south of this location.

next to the Adige. From there, the road on the right bank of the Adige is no longer down in the valley, as it climbs up at the Osteria, so from that point, it is the Adige that protects the rear of the position.

The position itself comprises a double semicircle of not especially high hills. The outer semicircle starts at San Marco, which is therefore the right wing of the position, and meets the Adige below Rivoli at Monte Pipolo.

The perimeter of this semicircle was 10.5 miles long, and it was 3.5 miles in diameter; the village of Rivoli lies almost at the center of this half disc.

A second range of hills, separated from the first by a narrow depression, constitutes another semicircle whose right wing connects to Monte Magnone[18] between San Marco and the Osteria, while its left runs toward Rivoli. Its circumference is about 3.5 miles.

Both ranges of hills are anything but regular, being interrupted and in some places even split into several parts. They generally have low ridges, and the slopes on the inside of the position are steeper than those facing the enemy; in this respect, as well as several others, they resemble the Landshut[19] position. The segment of the outer ring of heights between San Marco and the village of Trombalore,[20] a good 1.5 miles or so across, should be considered the actual front, because this sector includes the majority of the minor roads and footpaths leading from the Corona and Monte Baldo. Essentially, San Marco is its right wing, but the Osteria is an important point to its rear. By contrast, the other parts of the outer ring from the village of Trombalore to Monte Pipolo should be considered reserve terrain, if we may use that term, on which troops would be posted if the enemy sought to outflank the position proper as described above. The inner semicircle could also be considered reserve terrain, but because it is overlooked by the outer one, which is only about 1,000 paces away, it does not seem to provide a good defensive position.

The defender's approaches to this position come from the area of Ve-

18. Clausewitz incorrectly (or at least imprecisely) identifies this as Monte Baldo, which is to the northwest. Monte Magnone is the long southeasternmost spur of Monte Baldo.

19. The 1809 battle of Landshut, in Bavaria, took place in a mountain valley with short but fairly steep hills, similar to those described by Clausewitz. The 1760 battle of Landeshut, which took place in Silesia, also involved hills, but maps show them to be less similar than those in Bavaria. As such, it seems reasonable to suppose that Clausewitz was referring to the 1809 battle.

20. Today, this is near the site of the Via Trombasore, south of Caprino Veronese.

rona and Castelnuovo via Orza and Colombaro and go past the left of Monte Pipolo to Rivoli.

On the left bank of the Adige, directly opposite Monte Pipolo, is the Chiusa, which, as we have already said, hermetically seals the highway running down the left bank.

The main strengths of this position at Rivoli were the fact that the defender can enter it via Orza and Colombaro with all three arms[21] and that all three arms can be used within it, whereas the attacker cannot cross the four or five paths over the Corona and Monte Baldo with conventional artillery, so he must equip himself with special mountain artillery, which limits him to very few pieces of small caliber; that the attacker cannot bring many cavalry with him; that both these arms can use only the road in the valley of the Adige; and that it is almost impossible to force the Osteria Pass where the road climbs up through it.

Thus the battle must be fought almost exclusively with infantry, which therefore has to be very superior to the enemy's if a good result is to be expected.

Joubert, 10,000 strong, had previously occupied the Corona with only a couple of thousand men, quartering the rest in the villages in the Caprino valley. Although General Jomini describes the battle for the Corona as though Joubert held it with only his advance guard, it emerges from the original reports that when the Austrians advanced, he initially mustered his whole division in the Corona position, with the intention of defending this first and then fighting a second time at Rivoli; however, the powerful Austrian outflanking maneuver had already obliged him to send part of his division back to Rivoli on the 12th to cover this position.

Alvinczy knew that Bonaparte was busy in Bologna with the business of the Cispadane Republic. Besides that, he thought the columns advancing across

---

21. This is a significant point, as these wars, as well as the Napoleonic and subsequent wars, demonstrated the immense importance of combined arms (artillery, cavalry, and infantry) to military success. Using each of the main arms in coordination exponentially increased the combat power available; thus the position chosen by Napoleon facilitated an increase in French combat power (in terms of the size of their force) while degrading that of the Austrians. The use of combined arms remains incredibly important to contemporary fighting forces. For an example, see US Army, *Unified Land Operations*, Army Doctrine Publication No. 3.0 (Washington, DC: Headquarters, Department of the Army, 2011).

the plain would attract Bonaparte's attention and cause him to mistake the true point of attack. In this situation, Alvinczy hoped he would have time not only to overwhelm General Joubert in his positions on the Corona and at Rivoli but also to encircle him and force him to lay down his arms. The dispositions adopted for the attack were designed toward this end.

Alvinczy split his 28,000 men into six columns. The first, 5,000 strong under Colonel Lusignan,[22] was to leave from the western slope of Monte Baldo via Lumini and then Pezzena, so as to take not only the Corona but also the Rivoli position in the rear.

The second column of 4,700 men under General Liptay and the third of 4,000 under General Köblös were to ascend the mountainside via the valleys from Belluno [Belluno Veronese] and Avio and attack the Corona partly from the front and partly on its left flank from Ferrara.

The fourth column, 3,400 men under General Ocskay, was to follow the fifth in the valley of the Adige, in effect, acting as a reserve to support either this column or the previous two.

The fifth column under General Quosdanovich was to move down the right bank of the Adige and attack the Rivoli position through the Osteria Pass, through which the road climbed up to the Rivoli plateau.

The sixth column under General Wukassowitsch was to move down the highway on the left bank of the Adige against the Chiusa,[23] partly to take that position, and partly to bombard the Rivoli position with artillery from behind.

The two last columns had a combined strength of 10,000 men. Because the sixth column probably comprised only a few thousand, Quosdanovich would have been 7,000–8,000 strong.

In the way of artillery and cavalry, the first three columns had only a couple of mountain guns and a couple of hundred horse because they were advancing along mere forest trails and footpaths, which at this time of year were still largely snow covered. The majority of the artillery and of the 1,700 cavalry were therefore with the fifth and sixth columns in the valley of the Adige.

The columns set off on 11 January to attack the Corona position on the 12th.

The attack happened early on the 12th. The second and third columns found themselves facing the French in the vicinity of Ferrara; General Köblös

22. Franz Joseph Lusignan was 42 and a regimental commander.
23. This is Forte Della Chiusa, on the east bank of the Adige River south of Ceraino.

attacked them, but General Liptay did not support him because he wanted to wait to coordinate with the first column, exactly as scheduled. But because of the very deep snow on the paths, the first column had not advanced as far as hoped, so its participation failed to materialize on the 12th. Furthermore, General Joubert was able to hold on all day in the Corona position, and he was preparing to continue to resist on the 13th when he was told during the night that the first column was moving around his left flank, which convinced him to retreat to Rivoli at 4:00 a.m. on the 13th. He carried out this retreat without significant loss.

At Rivoli, he deployed again. Because the Austrians pursued very slowly and did not really attack him on this day, he stayed in position all day awaiting Bonaparte's orders.

Alvinczy felt somewhat cheated of the result he had expected from his plan for the 12th, so he used the whole of the 13th to organize his troops for an attack on the Rivoli position on the 14th. Thus the second and third columns advanced only to the foot of Monte Baldo at the villages of Caprino and San Martino. The first column had reached Lumini. The records do not say exactly where the three columns advancing down the Adige valley had got to.

Joubert had received neither orders nor reinforcements on the 13th, and when night fell, he saw the heights around him lit up by the Austrians' camp-fires. Fearing that the next day he would be crushed by their superior force and perhaps cut off completely, he decided to begin his retreat via Campara to Villanova at 10:00 that night. Just as he was doing this, he received word that Bonaparte would arrive imminently and that he was to hold in front of Rivoli. He immediately turned around and adopted a temporary deployment concentrated right in front of Rivoli, while occupying the inner ring of hills around the plateau with his light infantry.

The Austrians had pushed their advance guards as far as the outer ring of hills, where they plinked away all night.

On the 10th Bonaparte was still in Bologna when he learned of the Austrian advance. He hurries to Roverbello, issues orders there for how the besieging troops should act if the Austrians manage to approach the fortress, and then goes to Verona, arriving before midday on the 12th. Here he finds that the out-posts of Masséna's division are already skirmishing with Bayalitsch's Austrian division. He makes the whole division advance against the Austrian general, throwing him back with considerable loss, and easily confirms that he is not facing the Austrian main body here. However, he knows that Augereau is also under attack, and it is not until ten in the evening that a report from Joubert convinces him that the enemy's main body is advancing in the mountains. He orders General Augereau not to get involved in any decisive battle, moves General Victor's reserve to Villafranca, and sets off for Rivoli with Masséna's division on the evening of the 13th.

Masséna's division comprises five demi-brigades, of which only three come with him (the 18th,[24] 32nd, and 75th). The 25th remains facing Bayalitsch; the assignment of the 18th Light is not mentioned, but it probably also stays to face Bayalitsch. On the 12th Bonaparte has already ordered General Rey's reserve at Desenzano to move to Castelnuovo and, from there, follow Masséna's division. General Murat is to set out across Lake Garda from Salò with a demi-brigade of 600 men, land at Torre, and move against the Austrian rear.

While Bonaparte approaches with some 12,000 reinforcements on the night of 13–14 January, by his own account, bringing the French combat forces up to 22,000 men and sixty guns, Alvinczy conceives his new plan of attack for the 14th.

Lusignan is to continue his outflanking maneuver via Pezzena on the right bank of the Tasso, which flows through the Caprino valley toward Affi; he will bypass the Rivoli plateau on the west and approach the road on which the reinforcements from Verona and Castelnuovo could arrive. From there, he could also attack the plateau itself on its southern slope, that is, in its rear in relation to the main position.

The second and third columns are to advance against the northern side of the plateau: Liptay via Caprino against the Trombalore height, the left wing of the main position; Köblös against its right wing, mainly against San Marco. This position looks down into the Adige valley and half opens the Osteria Pass.

The fourth column is to go back up the Adige valley to Belluno, ascend the heights just as the second and third columns did, and reinforce them.

The fifth column under Quosdanovich is to attack the Osteria Pass, and the sixth is to march on the Chiusa.[25]

Bonaparte has raced ahead of the troops he was leading and meets Joubert at 2:00 a.m. He orders him to attack the Austrians at dawn with his whole

24. Colin, 258, notes that this is the 18th Line, not the 18th Light, which was also in Masséna's division and is mentioned later in the same sentence.

25. At this point, it is worth reminding readers of Clausewitz's discussion of friction and simplicity (see section 60).

division, even before Masséna arrives, leaving only the 39th Demi-brigade to hold the Osteria Pass.

Since only the Austrians' advance guards occupied the heights that constitute the actual position, Joubert quickly recaptures these and also the important position of San Marco without great difficulty; he even advances into the Caprino valley against the Austrians' main formations. These move to the attack, and fierce fighting develops between the Austrian second, third, and fourth columns—about 12,000 men altogether, led by Alvinczy himself—and Joubert's division of perhaps 8,000 men. This battle may have taken some hours before it turned against the French. Joubert's right wing could not break through; on the contrary, San Marco seemed in danger of falling again at any moment. But the left wing, which had advanced as far as the foot of Monte Baldo, was mostly put to flight by Liptay, and only one battalion holed up in the village of San Giovanni could not immediately be overwhelmed.

At this point, around 10:00 a.m., Masséna arrives. He has sent the 18th Demi-brigade toward Garda to cover his left flank; the 32nd Demi-brigade is on point. Bonaparte hastens to the aid of Joubert's left wing with these 2,000 men of the 32nd, while the 75th Demi-brigade, 3,000 strong, stays in reserve at Rivoli.

With these reinforcements, Bonaparte was able to renew the battle on Joubert's left wing and drive General Liptay back to the foot of Monte Baldo again.

During this time, the Austrian columns that are bypassing the French commander more circuitously make progress and reach the battlefield. On their right wing, Lusignan advances against Affi. Bonaparte has had two battalions brought up from the demi-brigade Masséna sent to Garda, which oppose Colonel Lusignan at Costerman [Costermano] and slow his advance on Affi but do not stop him. But on the Austrian left wing, Wukassowitsch has reached the area of Somano[26] on the left bank of the Adige; he sets up his cannon here and bombards the 39th Demi-brigade, which is deployed in defense of the Osteria. Quosdanovich himself has advanced there, and groups of his skirmishers scale the steep mountainside just as Joubert's hard-pressed right wing is forced to give up the San Marco position. In this situation, the 39th Demi-brigade has to abandon the Osteria position, and one battalion and a squadron from Quosdanovich's column get a foothold on the Rivoli plateau itself, while the rest of the host presses down the highway behind them in column. Thus,

---

26. This is the flat area directly across the river from the monument to Napoleon in Rivoli Veronese.

Joubert's right wing is beaten, the Osteria Pass has seemingly been taken, and it is only with difficulty that Masséna's left wing is still holding up General Liptay at Trombalore in the position proper.

This moment in the battle is identified in the French accounts as a moment of extreme emergency, as a true crisis when Bonaparte has to hold out with no more than 15,000 men against some 20,000 who surround him, when the key points of the Osteria and San Marco have already fallen, when Lusignan threatens the line of retreat, when all that is left in reserve is a single demi-brigade of 3,000 men and perhaps 600 cavalry. But this moment, we say, was in fact not at all as desperate as it is portrayed for dramatic effect.

What Bonaparte really faced was the 12,000 men of the second, third, and fourth Austrian columns. During the battle, these columns had become greatly disordered, and their men were so spent and exhausted by their preceding efforts that they dragged themselves slowly and painfully forward in great skirmish lines scattered across the snowy fields; they did not have the guts for a decisive, powerful blow. It was Quosdanovich's column that found itself in a moment of maximum crisis. It was still stuck in the defile of the highway, climbing steeply up the heights, and it had only a very weak vanguard on the plateau, which, thanks to the unfavorable turn of the battle on Joubert's right flank, found itself very close to the French main strength. We shall soon see how far Quosdanovich's column was from being in a combat-capable state. Lusignan was more than 2.25 miles away[27] from what was, for now, the decisive point—namely, the right wing of the Rivoli position—and General Rey was expected at any moment with the 3,000 men of the reserve. Thus, even if Lusignan did manage to cut Bonaparte's line of retreat, he himself would be taken in the rear by Rey. In the midst of the mayhem and the din of battle, Bonaparte saw the positive side of his situation, and his calm certainty made him seem like a demigod to his generals and soldiers. As we know, the 75th Demi-brigade was behind Rivoli, too far away to help the right wing with its crisis. Bonaparte orders the 75th to occupy the Tifaro [Tiffaro] heights on the western front of the plateau, to incorporate the two battalions of the 18th Demi-brigade, and to hold off Lusignan. But then and there, he personally throws part of Joubert's division, the 600 reserve cavalry,

---

27. Clausewitz used 2,000 *toises* as his measurement. A *toise* is an old French unit of measurement that was used by the Prussians. One old *Pariser toise* is equal to 1.94 meters.

and the 39th Demi-brigade in a concentric attack against the head of Quosdanovich's column; this is easily tumbled back down off the plateau onto the dense masses of infantry, cavalry, and artillery columns jammed together on the highway. A lively artillery fire is opened up on these columns, and they are forced to turn back. To top it all, a couple of ammunition wagons blow up, causing such confusion and dismay that General Quosdanovich suffers utter defeat from this single blow.

Meanwhile, Masséna had held the Trombalore heights with his 32nd Demi-brigade and Joubert's left wing. As soon as Quosdanovich had been decisively dealt with, Joubert turned on Ocskay and Köblös again with his right wing and the cavalry. These had advanced just far enough for their right flank to be exposed to Masséna holding fast; now, when they saw the masses of the French right wing with its cavalry and artillery coming at them again, in their disorganized state and lacking these two arms themselves, they were thrown into a kind of fearful panic. All Alvinczy's efforts to rally them were in vain, and it became easy for the French to drive them back to the foot of Monte Baldo with the loss of about 1,000 prisoners. General Liptay felt that in this situation he could not continue his action against Masséna either, and he too fell back on Caprino.

Thus, Alvinczy's left wing and center were completely beaten before the right wing under Lusignan could exert a decisive influence on the battle. But from this point on, that wing was itself threatened with total destruction. As is the nature of the affair in such cases, Lusignan had advanced deeper and deeper into the French rear, in accordance with his mission, and therefore did not learn of Alvinczy's defeat in time. As a result, Colonel Lusignan unwittingly threw himself into the abyss. He had gradually driven back the five battalions facing him and had taken Monte Pipolo when Bonaparte turned on him in person. Bonaparte reinforced the troops against Lusignan with just a single battery[28] of 12-pounders, but this reinforcement was a telling one against a corps without any artillery at all.

Colonel Lusignan saw the other columns' fire receding, indicating that they had been beaten, leaving him utterly abandoned and threatened by an enemy column advancing against his rear. This corps belonged to General Rey, who was moving through Orza with his 3,000 men. In this situation, any

---

28. Clausewitz notes: "According to Bonaparte's *Memoirs* it had fifteen guns, which, however, is unlikely, as the other reports talk of it having just a few pieces." Montholon, *Mémoires pour servir à l'histoire de France sous Napoléon*, 3:378.

pressure on Colonel Lusignan's corps would have been enough to make it yield. His attempt at further resistance only led to worse disorder; his whole force was scattered, some slaughtered, others captured. The core of this corps, about 1,200 men and their leader, tried to escape to Garda, where they were confronted by some companies of the French battalion left there. In the broken terrain, the fugitives could not gauge the strength of the enemy, and as so often happens, they thought they were surrounded everywhere by overwhelming numbers, and at the first call to surrender, they laid down their arms in the field. Thus, of these 5,000 men, only their commander and a few other individuals escaped, fleeing across Lake Garda.

This was the fate of the right wing. Let us now return to the other columns.

On the 14th Quosdanovich had retreated up the Adige valley as far as Rivalta, 10 miles away, so he had no further influence on the fate of the center. Alvinczy had rallied the three beaten corps of the center at the foot of Monte Baldo; thus he found himself forsaken by both his wings, exposed to attack by the combined enemy might, and in a position from which the only retreat was along snow-covered footpaths down steep mountainsides. But at that moment, just as Bonaparte prepared to use the last glimmer of daylight to attack Alvinczy again, he receives the news that Provera has crossed the Adige at Anghiari and advanced against Mantua. He entrusts further operations against Alvinczy to Joubert, reinforces him with Rey, and returns as fast as possible to the Italian plain with Masséna's division, with which he had hastened to the battlefield the night before. Joubert now postpones any further attack until the next day. Thus, Alvinczy could have begun his retreat that night and gained the lead time he needed to descend the rocky staircases of the Corona into the Brentino valley without danger. But he had no definite word about the fate of his right wing and was naturally extremely concerned about it. He thought he could not leave the foot of Monte Baldo until he had bought enough time for this column (which had already ceased to exist twelve hours ago) to get the necessary head start on its very circuitous line of retreat. It also seemed essential to remain near the French main body on the 15th to help Provera's operation against Mantua by preventing the French from marching away too soon. Alvinczy therefore reinforced himself during the night with another two battalions and two squadrons from Quosdanovich and decided to attempt one more attack against the French front on the morning of the 15th. Perhaps he thought this would be a better way to protect himself from being outflanked than a defensive deployment.

For his part, General Joubert naturally likewise decided to attack, and in such a configuration as to entirely cut off the enemy's retreat if possible. His right-wing column under Vial[29] bypassed the Austrian left wing by crossing Monte Magnone, another under Veaux[30] advanced on the left [eastern] slope of Monte Baldo, and a third still further left marched over Monte Baldo itself; thus, both these latter columns moved around the Austrian right flank. The last of these columns made contact with Murat, who had landed at Torre on the 14th and was on his way to Ferrara. While these flanking columns were tasked with cutting off the Austrians' retreat, in the center, Baraguay d'Hilliers attacked their front at St. Martin [San Martino-Platano]. Alvinczy soon realized that his attack had no chance of success, as his troops displayed little energy or spirit; the battle had lasted less than an hour when he began his retreat. This soon degenerated into great disorder. When the Austrians learned that French columns were racing around their left and right to the Corona Pass, they were overcome by the fear of being cut off and raced for that footpath in wild flight. There, they all piled up, pushing and shoving, and before this panicked mass of routers could make any headway along the steep and narrow path, the indefatigable French arrived. As a result, a large proportion was cut off, and at this point alone, another 5,000 were taken prisoner.

So ended the battle of Rivoli as an utter defeat for the Austrians. Out of 28,000 men, about 14,000 were lost, of which 10,000–12,000 were captured.[31]

64 THE BATTLE OF THE FORT DE LA FAVORITE OUTSIDE MANTUA ON 16 JANUARY[32]

As we have seen, on the 8th and 9th General Provera fought an action with

---

29. This is brigade commander Honoré Vial. He was 30 years old during the campaign in Italy and went on to become a division general before dying of wounds following the battle of Leipzig in 1813.

30. This is brigade commander Antoine Veaux, who was 32 at the time. He went on to command a division.

31. The effective use of pursuit was one of Napoleon's hallmarks, and he would use it successfully at Austerlitz in 1805 and after Jena in 1806. Of course, he himself was subjected to an extremely effective allied pursuit after Waterloo in 1815.

32. Jomini gives the date as 15 January. See Jomini, *Histoire Critique et Militaire des Guerres de la Révolution*, 9:299.

Augereau's advance guard at Bevilacqua. On the 9th this brought him before Legnago, where he remained inactive on the 10th, 11th, and 12th. The reasons for this hesitation are not given in any account, but it can quite naturally be attributed to Provera's concerns about arriving too early and being caught by the French main body without actually creating an effective diversion for Alvinczy. If he had thrown his bridge across on the 10th, a decisive battle against him would have been possible on the 11th. But on the 11th Alvinczy had only just set his force in motion, and it was clear that he would need at least two days, maybe three, for his operation against Joubert, by which time the French main body could have turned away from Provera and against Alvinczy again. Even by simple calculation, then, Provera had arrived at the Adige a couple of days too early, but actually, it was more than this. The decision at Rivoli, which might have been reached on the 12th and surely by the 13th at the latest, in fact happened only on the 14th, so there were four days between the two columns' blows. Given the rapidity of the French maneuvers, this was too long for one column to act as an effective diversion for the other, even though the battlefields were 40.5 miles apart.

Nonetheless, Provera's early arrival was hardly an accident or at all unintentional. It seems the Austrian commander planned this to attract more attention in that direction, to ensure he would not have to contend with the French main body in the mountains. But he entirely failed in this aim,[33] because now Provera's protracted sojourn under the eyes of the French right wing made it easy for them to discover his secondary strength and role.

But in hesitating for three days, Provera allowed too much time to elapse. If he had crossed on the 12th, he could have appeared before Mantua on the 13th; then Bonaparte would have either marched against him and been unable to rush to Joubert's aid or gone to Rivoli and been unable to move against Provera on the 13th and 14th. Whether the latter would have been able to draw Wurmser to him may yet be doubted, but at least this was the only possible way he might do so.

From this, we can see how difficult it is for a separated column to strike at exactly the right time, as it must when it is dealing with an adversary like Bonaparte. Besides, it is possible that other circumstances prevented Provera from crossing sooner.

33. Colin, 267, notes: "Bonaparte, however, claims that he remained uncertain until the last moment as to how the Austrian forces were distributed."

Let us return to the events.

Augereau stood on the Adige with the 9,000 men of his division and General Dugua's 700 reserve cavalry, defending the river from Verona to below Legnago. Since an enemy intent on Mantua cannot cross far below Legnago, this stretch was about 27 miles in extent. In a letter to Bonaparte on 9 January, Augereau says that he has concentrated a large part of his division at Zevio, Ronco, and Legnago. However, in a letter of the 26th, he says, in apparent self-justification: "When a division of 10,000 men is scattered across an extent of more than 100 miles it takes more than a quarter of an hour to reassemble it."[34] This turn of phrase makes no sense, unless it relates to General Lannes, whom Bonaparte had sent from Bologna to reinforce Augereau. However, it can be assumed that Augereau's division was extended significantly beyond Legnago, since he mentions a bridgehead at Castagnara [Castagnaro, south of Legnago] (where the Castagnara flows into the Adige), and besides, Augereau was mainly worried that the Austrians intended to move on Ferrara.[35]

On the evening of the 13th Provera moved up to the river opposite Anghiari, about 3.5 miles above Legnago, while demonstrating against several other points at the same time. He managed to build a bridge before General Guieu, commanding Augereau's left wing, could hurry there with 1,200–1,500 men. Guieu opposed the crossing on the 14th but had to give way to superior numbers. Provera left 1,500 men with fourteen guns to guard the bridge, and with his other 7,000 men he continued toward Mantua via Cerea and Sanguinetto to Nogara, where he spent the night.

It is quite incomprehensible that the Austrians at Anghiari were confronted first by Augereau's left wing under General Guieu when Augereau himself was

---

34. Clausewitz quotes this as: "*Quand une division de 10,000 hommes est disséminée sur une etendue de plus de trente lieues, il faut plus d'un quart d'heure pour la rassembler.*" *Correspondance inédite, officielle et confidentielle de Napoléon Bonaparte (Italie)*, 2:389, accessed 23 August 2017, http://gallica.bnf.fr/ark:/12148/bpt6k1073398s/f1.image. One can read a great deal of sarcasm into the original, which might explain why it makes no sense to Clausewitz.

35. Colin, 268, notes: "Bonaparte was seriously worried that, after making a demonstration before Legnago, Provera might move via Ferrara in the Romagna. He [Bonaparte] had massed 6,000 men at Badia and Castagnaro, of which about 3,000 were from Augereau's division. The latter was therefore indeed extended from Zevio to Badia."

just 3.5 miles away in Legnago with the right wing.[36] Augereau surely must have had more than a couple of thousand men with him there, however far to the right he may have been extended. It seems Augereau thought it would be better not to let himself be defeated in detail; that it did not matter whether he attacked the enemy a couple of hours sooner or later, since they were already across the river; and that it would be more advisable to concentrate the majority of his right wing first. Perhaps he was also somewhat misled by his own preconceived idea expressed in his letter of the 9th: that Provera would probably head for Ferrara.

General Guieu retreated toward Ronco, and the result of Provera's break-through was that Augereau was separated from Guieu and 4,000 men of his division. On the 14th Augereau moved against Anghiari with the other 5,000 and with General Lannes, who had joined him, making 7,000 in total. But Augereau did not meet General Provera, who had already moved on; he encountered only the 1,500 men Provera had left behind. They had apparently not had enough time to fortify their position and so decided to follow Provera. However, their route along a causeway was barred by one of Augereau's columns; they saw they were surrounded by the enemy and, after a brief resistance, laid down their arms. Augereau burned the bridge and prepared to meet Provera when he returned from Mantua and, in the other direction, prepared to offer resistance to whatever force might come from Padua. According to a letter he wrote to Bonaparte on the 15th from Legnago, he was busy with this all day. The remaining Austrian detachments on the left bank of the Adige, which could not have been very strong, managed to virtually keep him in check for some time. These are the reasons why Augereau did not arrive before Mantua until the 16th, and even then, not until after the actual battle.

At midday on the 15th Provera arrived outside the suburb of St. George [San Giorgio di Mantova], which was held by General Miollis[37] with 1,200 men. It was fortified on all sides. Provera called on Miollis to surrender but received a dismissive reply. After a few futile cannon shots, he decided to march off to the right and approach the citadel [Citadel of Porto]. The citadel and St. George are Mantua's two bridgeheads; they are separated from each other by an impassable marsh. The first approaches to the citadel that Provera came to, coming

36. Colin, 268, notes: "Augereau's right wing was at Badia; Legnago was only held by the minimum garrison necessary."
37. This is Sextius Miollis.

from St. George, were those of Montado [just south of Montata Carra] and the Fort de la Favorite. He approached both these places on the night of the 15th and 16th and awaited the sally he had agreed on with Wurmser.

During the night of the 14th and 15th Bonaparte had arrived at Castel-nuovo, where he received news from Sérurier that Provera was on the march toward Mantua. He ordered General Sérurier to defend St. George to the ut-most and to post himself at the Favorite. Since Bonaparte had heard nothing from Augereau, he concluded that the general was on Provera's left flank and might yet find the opportunity to confront him while crossing the Molinella at Castellaro. He spent the 15th gathering Masséna's division, Victor's brigade, and Dugua's cavalry reserve at Roverbello, where he went himself. Guieu was ordered to move to Castelbelforte; Augereau was told that if he could not in-tercept the enemy, he should follow hard on his heels.

From this exposition, it follows that the only force Provera faced outside Mantua on the 15th was that part of Sérurier's division on the left bank of the Mincio. This may have been about 7,000 men, of whom 1,200 were holding St. George, so no more than 5,000–6,000 men could have opposed him on the ap-proaches to the citadel on the 15th. This was approximately the same strength as his own. Now if Wurmser had sallied on the 15th with 8,000–10,000 men, it is hard to see how General Sérurier could have withstood this combined at-tack. With one confident action by both Austrian generals, Sérurier could have been totally defeated, their union accomplished, and the march to Governolo and Ferrara begun. But as always happens in such cases, various *faux-fraix* [incidental expenses] arose that cost time.[38] The understanding with Wurmser had not been reached quickly enough for him to think that he could carry out his sortie the same day, so it was postponed until the next morning. This was incontrovertibly a major error. Even if the Austrian generals did not fear that Bonaparte could arrive early on the 16th from Rivoli—where he had struck on the 14th and from where they might still have heard cannon fire on the 15th, because Rivoli is 36 miles from Mantua—they must have been concerned that Augereau was probably following after Provera, that other reserve troops from

---

38. This brings us back to the role of chance in Clausewitz's trinity, as well as to his concept of friction, in that many small things occur in war that are not always predictable and can have an unanticipated effect on plans and operations. As such, it is important to consider the problems that might be caused by friction and chance, even though one cannot know what form they will take and what effect they will have.

the area might arrive, and that what was easy to accomplish on the evening of the 15th might be impossible or at least highly doubtful by early on the 16th. As soon as the French combat forces became as numerous as the Austrians, there was much less chance of success. In these circumstances, the Austrian generals should not have balked at a night operation.

But it all turned out differently from what should have been expected. As we have said, Wurmser postponed his attack until the next morning. Augereau lost time with useless preparations and was not there for the actual decision. But early on the 16th, Bonaparte—who the Austrian generals thought was still at Rivoli or still marching back from there—was already in position at the Favorite. He and his troops had arrived on the night of 15–16 January. Since the French forces can be estimated at 8,000 men, it follows that the Austrians now had to deal with a combat force the same size as their own.

The French had deployed mainly at Montada, the Favorite, and St. Antonio on the road from Verona. Thus they stood between Provera and the citadel.

At 6:00 a.m. Wurmser sortied and attacked the French troops at the Favorite and St. Antonio. He actually captured this latter position but had to relinquish it when Bonaparte sent some battalions of reinforcements there.

The accounts are silent concerning Provera's part in the action. It is likely that he moved at the same time against Montada and the Favorite but was halted by Masséna's and Victor's troops so far back that he had no influence on the outcome of Wurmser's attack.

After some hours of battle, the Austrian generals became convinced that they could not break through. Wurmser either went back into the fortress or at least became passive. Augereau's troops were getting closer along the roads from Ronco and Legnago; the French numerical superiority against Provera on his own grew to at least three- or fourfold; Wurmser's road to the Adige was lost, and given the many rivers he would have to cross, there was no prospect of breaking through to it. Whether the possibility of a retreat to Governolo still existed is not clear; Augereau's position is not given precisely, so we do not know whether he had already advanced along the road from Legnago beyond Stradella and was in a position to link up with St. George. But of course, even if a small gap was still open, a retreat in the face of such a superior enemy and in broad daylight was an almost impossible business. General Provera saw it that way too, and at 10:00 a.m. he and his 6,700 men laid down their arms.[39]

39. Clausewitz notes: "It is quite extraordinary that in a letter to Bonaparte on 29

65 RESULT OF THE FIFTH ACT

Thus Bonaparte had thwarted the fourth relief of Mantua or, rather, the second attempt at freeing Wurmser. He had achieved the hitherto unprecedented result of taking 20,000 prisoners and putting perhaps 5,000–6,000 men out of action from an army of 42,000, in just three days. This success, achieved with a smaller army and with the insignificant loss of a few thousand men, is one of the most glorious that military history can offer, and we may say that Bonaparte surpassed even himself.

This huge success in the destruction of enemy combat forces also assured the French commander that no new attempt would be made anytime soon, and it entitled him to expect that the fall of Mantua was now inevitable. It was hard to say exactly how long the fortress could hold out, but it could be anticipated that it would surrender in the first half of February.

A strategic offensive against Austria's German borders would have to be deferred until then, in any case, since it is clear that such an attack could not be begun with the 20,000 or so men the French commander still had available.

Likewise, relations with Rome needed to be put on a firmer footing. The fearful blow suffered by the Austrian army was very good preparation, and waiting for Mantua to fall allowed the leisure to accomplish it.

Finally, two divisions were marching from the Rhine to reinforce the Army of Italy; operations against Austria had to be put off until they arrived.

But if it seems that, for the moment, this glorious victory was more of a negative success for the French than a positive one, this does not mean it had

---

January (*Corrésp. Inédite, Italie*, vol. 2, p. 466), Brigadier-General Miollis, who commanded at St. George, claimed the honor of this day for himself, adducing in support of his claim the fact that General Provera turned to him first, sending him his proposed terms written in pencil on a piece of paper, that he [Miollis] had made some amendments on it, and thus he had edited the terms of the surrender. From the very fact that he submitted this claim it follows that the army did not see it that way, but still it is odd that Provera addressed himself to this general, who, according to Jomini's account, had only 1,200 men, with which he had to hold the suburb of St. George and thus could only have delivered a very weak attack against Provera. General Miollis's report is suitably ingenuous, making it sound as though he alone had trapped Provera and forced him to capitulate." *Correspondance inédite, officielle et confidentielle de Napoleon Bonaparte (Italie)*, 2:466, accessed 23 August 2017, http://gallica.bnf.fr/ark:/12148/bpt6k1073398s/f1.image.

no influence on the outcome of the 1797 campaign, which began in March on the Italian front. The Austrian losses could not be replaced so quickly, and the moral impact [of the victory at Rivoli] reached far beyond the initial events of the 1797 campaign, right up to the peace negotiations at Leoben and Campo Formio.

For the moment, Bonaparte contented himself with pushing his three divisions forward far enough to make him master of the Brenta.

Alvinczy had retreated to Trient, where he wanted to concentrate his troops and then lead them through the valley of the Brenta to the Piave. General Laudon had deployed 8,000 men, mostly militia, at Rovereto to cover the Tyrol, and Bayalitsch, reinforced from the main army, was at Bassano. But neither could hold his position.

On 24 January Joubert advanced against Laudon, obliged him to abandon his position, pursued him to the Lavis, and, on 26 January,[40] forced him to give up this point as well, whereby the entrance to the Brenta valley fell entirely into French hands.

Masséna advanced on Bassano, driving the Austrians out on 24 January. Bayalitsch retreated to Conegliano. The French now cleared the Brenta valley and thereby established communications between Joubert's and Masséna's divisions.

Augereau advanced via Padua against Treviso, which was occupied by his advance guard.

In this situation, Alvinczy was obliged to take the troops intended to protect Carinthia and march them through the Drau [Drava] valley to Villach, from where they advanced on the Tagliamento.

66 REFLECTIONS

We have the following remarks to make about the battle of Rivoli, which is certainly one of the most remarkable in the annals of war, as much for its uniqueness as for its result.

---

40. The original said February, but this must be an error because Napoleon's correspondence has Joubert in Trient on 12 February 1797. *Corréspondance inédite, officielle et confidentielle de Napoleon Bonaparte (Italie)*, 2:474, accessed 23 August 2017, http://gallica.bnf.fr/ark:/12148/bpt6k1073398s/f1.image.

1. The position at Rivoli is one of those rare mountain positions where the defender enjoys, on the one hand, the advantage of strong and in some places insurmountable terrain obstacles and, on the other hand, the use of all arms and a completely united force. In effect, it is like a position on a flat mountain plateau whose steep edges the enemy has to struggle up, while on top we can move freely with all arms, which is pretty much the strongest position imaginable. Admittedly, Monte Baldo and Monte Magnone, which run around the outside of the Rivoli position and constitute the obstacles to its approaches, are much higher than the position itself and are not actually its slopes. But that does not really matter, since they are too far away to dominate it and are so inaccessible that they permit the attacker to advance only with infantry (at least, that is their effect in the month of January), which is a decisive advantage if the enemy must do without artillery, which is, of course, the most powerful arm in terms of the principle of destruction.[41] The entire rear of this position, along the Adige, is invulnerable, because the only pass, the Osteria, can easily be held. In this situation, it matters less that the rings of heights constituting the position proper are not especially strong and do not present any great obstacle to the attack. And now consider the strategic strength of this position: For a stretch of 54 miles from Lake Garda to Bassano, the valley of the Adige is the only route that artillery and columns of any significant size can take through the foothills of the Alps; the position rests on this valley. Although the position is very elevated, nonetheless, it seals the valley, since the road on the right bank of the Adige climbs up into it through the Osteria; that on the left bank is barred first by the Chiusa and then by Verona when it emerges onto the plain. Furthermore, the Rivoli po-

41. This principle is one of the key ideas running through *On War*. Probably the clearest example Clausewitz provides is: "The fighting forces must be *destroyed*: that is, they must be *put in such a condition that they can no longer carry on the fight*. Whenever we use the phrase 'destruction of the enemy's forces' this alone is what we mean." Clausewitz, *On War*, 90 (book 1, chap. 2); see also 90–99 (book 1, chap. 2), 226–229 (book 4, chap. 3), 529 (book 7, chap. 6), 595–600 (book 8, chap. 4). It is important to point out that destruction in this context is applied in its theoretical construct and might not necessarily apply in real war. That being said, unless both sides agree on any constraints, annihilation or complete destruction should be the goal, as any miscalculation or misunderstanding will result in one's arms getting cut off by an adversary who does not play by the same rules. Ibid., 260 (book 4, chap. 11). For readers interested in this whole line of argument and its underlying logic, it is worth reading books 4 and 7 in full.

sition lies between the Adige and Lake Garda. But the Adige provides a very strong line of defense; thus for the Rivoli position, all that really matters is that the area between the Adige and Lake Garda should be covered, which is just 9 miles across. All these circumstances mean the defender is not obliged to disperse his forces at all, and after he has put a couple of hundred men in the Chiusa, all the rest can be kept within the position right in front of his eyes. Finally, this position does not suffer the same inconvenience as most mountain positions, where one is surrounded by forests and mountains and cannot assess the enemy's dispositions. The attacker's approach is, of course, concealed, but only as far as the Caprino valley. This valley is 3,000 paces wide and consequently allows observation of the enemy's attack, with enough time to take any necessary countermeasures.

An attack on such a position is justifiable only if one has significant superiority, since with that, all difficulties can ultimately be overcome. Masséna and Vaubois were driven out of it by an enemy twice or thrice their strength, in the season when the mountains were most accessible. Thus, if the Austrian main army was to be led against this position, and if its capture was to be the major blow of the operation, this could happen only so long as it was a question of defeating Joubert's division alone. Since Bonaparte was in Bologna, 90 miles from the battlefield, the columns advancing on the plain had to keep him guessing for a while, and then the hope of striking a decisive blow against Joubert's division before he could come to its aid would not be without foundation; but it is clear that the most essential factor was suitably rapid execution. If Alvinczy had moved vigorously against Joubert on the 12th or at least on the 13th, he would have driven him to Castelnuovo before Bonaparte could arrive, and he certainly would have gained much by doing so.

Alvinczy wanted not just to beat Joubert but to take much of his force prisoner. There is no blame attached to this; it was quite justified, as he was by far the stronger. But this attempt at capture should not have become the main aim, and the arrangements for it should not have entailed much delay, since much more depended on haste. But because of his dispositions and the lack of decisiveness and urgency on his part, Alvinczy lost two days, and therein lies the major error of his battle.

2. There was no good reason for the strength of the columns down in the Adige valley. At best, their only purpose was to attack the Chiusa—which, being completely unfeasible, had to be considered merely a demonstration—and to protect the cavalry and artillery left in the valley. For these purposes,

4,000–5,000 men would have been entirely sufficient; but on the 12th and 13th, General Alvinczy had 14,000 men in the valley of the Adige, and on the 14th, 10,000. If he had sent 24,000 men against Joubert on the first two days instead of just 14,000, he probably would have driven him out completely and perhaps half destroyed him.

3. The fact that on the 12th Alvinczy took his column on a long detour around the left flank of the position on the Corona may be attributable to the terrain, which was not depicted in enough detail on the available maps to evaluate it; but his plan for an envelopment on the 13th and 14th was a wholly unnecessary complication that cost him everything.[42] If he had arrived in the Caprino valley on the 13th with his entire force at the villages of Caprino and San Martino and found himself sufficiently superior in numbers to destroy the enemy by means of an enveloping attack, there would have been time to do that, since the envelopment would have been derived from his superiority, not from surprise. He certainly could not have relied on achieving an envelopment, since the nature of the area is not suited to it. But he could have sent a detachment to his right, in full view of Joubert, and thereby obliged his opponent to either stretch his line to an extremely dangerous extent or else withdraw. If, however, he found himself facing not Joubert with 10,000 men but Bonaparte with 20,000, it would be high time to give up his idea of an envelopment.

This obsession with envelopment is a strange idiosyncrasy of the Austrians that stems entirely from their general staff and nowhere else. They always want to reap before they have sown, or rather they cannot tell the difference between the two.[43]

42. Despite his criticism of the use of envelopment, Clausewitz does not dismiss the value of a flanking attack. This, he argues, is easier and aids in the development of the pursuit, which is a key part of the battle in terms of destruction of the enemy. Clausewitz, *On War*, 530–531 (book 7, chap. 7).

43. Book 7, chap. 7, of *On War* contains a pointed criticism of the use of envelopment at the strategic level, and it might have behooved Alfred von Schlieffen and Helmuth von Moltke to read it thoroughly. It is also worth noting that Napoleon successfully used a similar style of movement—*Manoeuvre de Derrière*—that differed from envelopment in key ways. An envelopment quite literally seeks to envelop the enemy force and place pressure on its flanks to reduce the amount of room available to move in, thus reducing the enemy's ability to fight effectively. The space an enveloped army requires to fight at its full effectiveness is compressed, so it is unable to bring its maximum combat power to bear. In addition, the enveloped force's flanks are either overwhelmed by the enemy or pushed back so that the force as a whole cannot fight effectively. Such

4. The attack of the 15th was the act of a drowning man clutching at a red-hot horseshoe. If he wanted to give Colonel Lusignan time to retrace his roundabout path, all he had to do was hold on as long as possible at Caprino and San Martino, after moving 4,000–5,000 men from Quosdanovich's column up onto the Corona to hold the approaches to the defiles there and secure the retreat.

As far as the defender is concerned, one might say that his conduct was beyond all praise. We should like to make one observation: that, in its character, the battle belongs among those in which offensive defense is combined with the benefit of an excellent position. We should like to remind anyone who sees this battle as just an offensive one, and who attributes its success primarily to the French commander's decisiveness, that the success at the Osteria, the strength of the post at St. Marcus [San Marco], the not entirely negligible advantage of the Trombalore heights that helped Masséna fend off superior numbers, Lusignan's slow advance over the heights in his way, the Austrians constantly having to attack without cavalry or artillery, and, finally, the great danger during their retreat—all these are causes and effects of a defensive nature that made it possible for Bonaparte's attacks on the enemy center to take the form they did and to have the effect they had.

Another observation concerns the arrival of General Rey's reserve from Desenzano. We are absolutely of the opinion that in modern defensive battles, reserves that are held a long way back and thrown into action very late, so that they are like corps that arrive only toward the end of a battle—or indeed,

---

a maneuver allows the enveloper to maintain its combat power while decreasing the combat power of the enveloped force. As such, an envelopment can lead to spectacular results: think Cannae (216 BC) or Tannenberg (1914). However, it is extremely difficult to pull off such a maneuver in the face of the enemy, as Clausewitz notes, and it is also extremely risky because the enveloper often needs to greatly weaken its center in order to develop sufficient combat power on its flanks, thus leaving the center exposed to an aggressive counterattack. Napoleon's *Manoeuvre de Derrière* was different, in that he maneuvered into the rear of an opponent and onto its lines of communication, thus placing his army in a position where he could choose the location and the terms under which his army accepted battle. A successful move of this type allowed Napoleon to gain a tactical or operational advantage over his opponents, as they were forced to conform to his will and were often at a disadvantage when responding. This too was risky, but Napoleon understood that his opponents were unable to counter his maneuver because their armies were often too slow and cumbersome to do so. This situation changed only when Napoleon's enemies fundamentally reformed their armies following the disasters of Austerlitz in 1805, Jena-Auerstedt in 1806, and Friedland in 1807.

such corps themselves—are splendidly effective. The further back the reserves are held, the harder it is for enemy outflanking columns to envelop them; but there are very few battles in which the attack entirely refrains from any out-flanking maneuver, and the columns outflanking the defender are then in turn outflanked by a simple advance by such reserves. Furthermore, battles now-adays rarely have an actual critical moment, or if they do have one, it comes only after the two combatants have wrestled each other to the ground; conse-quently, one can always use a reserve or a newly arrived corps to continue the battle, so long as one has not quit the battlefield.

Both the characteristics we attribute to reserves here are demonstrated by the reserve led by General Rey. It arrived in the rear of Colonel Lusignan, who had himself outflanked Bonaparte, and it apparently arrived just as the deci-sion was being delivered against Lusignan, that is, at midday, six to eight hours after the battle began. As we have seen, the arrival of the Austrian right wing at the battle of Caldiero offers a similar example.

We have less to say about the strategic plan for this fourth attack because our criticism of it is partly contained in the development of our view offered in section 60 concerning the third attack.

According to this view, we would have found a united advance onto the plain a better option in this case too. The divided dispositions accord with our principles somewhat, insofar as one of the main columns advanced via Padua on Legnago and seems to have been ordered to break through to Man-tua come what may, without regard for events in the upper Adige valley. This column even succeeded in breaking through; if it then not only failed in its aim but also ended up in the catastrophe of capitulation, that was due partly to Wurmser's very feeble sortie, partly to loss of time, and finally to the fact that it was too weak and was further weakened by a pointless detachment at the bridge at Anghiari. As far as the latter is concerned, if the Austrians were generally victorious against Bonaparte, then the bridge at Anghiari was irrel-evant, whereas if they only barely made it to Mantua (as Provera actually did), then there was no question of retreating over that bridge.

The major error in the dispositions for this divided attack lay in having the main force advance down the valley of the Adige. How perverse to have the main body advance where it could use neither its cavalry nor its artillery. And above all, what a miscalculation to strike the main blow there, where the defender is aided by incredibly strong terrain.

If the main body had advanced via Legnago, either it would have reached

Mantua and relieved Wurmser or it would have been attacked by the French main body. In the latter case, if the column from the Tyrol had meanwhile managed to reach Mantua, it could have been in danger of losing its line of retreat, as we have shown in section 60; but even if the main body had lost a battle, it still would have been able to assist with and protect the retreat of this column, at least infinitely more than Alvinczy helped Provera after Rivoli.

Finally, the division into three columns must be regarded as another major mistake. General Bayalitsch's column had no purpose other than as a demonstration, and to use 5,000 men for that, just to pin half their number, is very poor economy of force.

Incidentally, we should beware of overstating such things. The strategic dispositions of one kind or another alluded to here have their value, but it is by no means these alone that determine the outcome of the affair; in the end, the outcome mostly comes down to execution, and it is quite certain that taking 20,000 prisoners in three days owes more to execution than to planning.[44]

67 END OF THE CAMPAIGN, MANTUA FALLS, AND THE PEACE OF TOLENTINO IS IMPOSED ON THE POPE

Soon after the battle of the Favorite, Bonaparte set Generals Victor and Lannes in motion against the Papal States with 5,000 men. On 2 February Victor entered Immola [Imola].

---

44. This is interesting, as it ignores the obvious retort that if the plan were so bad that it placed all the forces too far away to affect a given campaign, no amount of outstanding execution would be sufficient for success. That might be reasonable, but it is not really what Clausewitz means. He is getting at a couple of ideas. The first involves the energy and dynamism of the respective commanders, and we have already discussed this at length in earlier sections of the book; the second relates to war planning. Indeed, he devotes an entire book of *On War* (book 8) to the subject of planning for war, and it is clear that he believes it is critical to get this right. In fact, thinking through exactly what one wants from conflict is one of his two main principles for strategic planning (book 8, chap. 9), but he also argues that dynamism of execution is vital for success. With this in mind, he argues that the initial dispositions of forces are not necessarily as important as time. Taking too long to put together the perfect dispositions is worse than acting speedily and without full concentration. Thus, if we take this into account, Clausewitz's comments make sense.

On this day, some fourteen days after the battle of the Favorite, Wurmser surrendered Mantua. As a mark of personal respect, he was given free passage for himself with 500 men and six guns; the garrison had to lay down its arms. This was estimated at 15,000 men, plus another 6,000 sick in its hospitals.[45] Thus, of the 28,000 men the fortress had absorbed after Wurmser's second invasion, 7,000 were dead or missing.

The defense of the fortress had lasted eight months altogether, and this garrison had resisted for more than six months.

Now Bonaparte could devote himself entirely to the matter of Rome.

Although he assigned only a few thousand men to this operation, he actually expected to reach the point where he would have to advance on Rome itself; indeed, in a letter to the Directory on 1 February, he speaks of not only combining Ferrara and the Romagna with Modena into the Cispadane Republic but also giving the Holy See's other possessions to Spain in exchange for Parma, which he wanted to offer to Austria to achieve peace sooner.[46] In its reply of 12 February, the Directory also seems to show some interest in this idea. Thus, when Bonaparte began his operation against Rome, he did so with the intention of embarking on a major political upheaval.[47] The forces he allocated to it comprised 5,000 men under Victor and Lannes; a mobile column setting off from Siena under Marmont, which apparently was not from the active Army of Italy and probably had no more than 1,000 men; and perhaps a few thousand men from the newly established Cispadane Republic. Altogether, then, it totaled about 8,000–9,000 men, which indicates the contempt Bonaparte felt not just for the papal troops but for the Romans in general. The Directory expresses some faint misgivings about this. Even if this meager force, protected by the aura of the recent French victories over the Austrians, were sufficient to impose such radical political change, the 6,000 men it would divert could not easily be spared from an attack aimed at the heart of the Austrian state. Finally, such a revolution in Italy would undoubtedly make peace with Austria more difficult and more remote. From this, it seems to us that this plan for revolution had not been fully thought through, a claim that seems

---

45. Clausewitz notes: "According to General Sérurier's report to Bonaparte dated 3 February." *Corréspondance inédite, officielle et confidentielle de Napoleon Bonaparte (Italie)*, 2:471, accessed 23 August 2017, http://gallica.bnf.fr/ark:/12148/bpt6k1073398s /f1.image.

46. Napoléon I, *Correspondance de Napoléon Ier*, 2:291 (letter 1435).

47. See *On War*, book 1, chap. 2: "Purpose and Means in War."

all the more reasonable as Bonaparte himself suddenly abandoned this idea without any external cause, since it was only fourteen days between his letter to the Directory and the peace of Tolentino.

In the last days of January Bonaparte traveled to Bologna.

In the first days of February Lannes encounters 3,000–4,000 papal troops deployed behind the Sennio [Senio]; these are immediately driven back, and fourteen guns taken. The French move to Faenza.

On 9 February Victor beats 1,200 men who were in position at Ancona and takes the town. On the 12th he enters Marcerata [Macerata] and directs his march via Camerino to Foligno, where he is supposed to join up with the small column from Siena.

But already on the 12th Pius VI writes a letter to Bonaparte asking for a peace treaty, which is duly signed eight days later in Tolentino.[48] The pope cedes Avignon, Venessin [Comtat Venaissin], Bologna, Ferrara, and the Romagna; the French are authorized to occupy Ancona until there is a state of general peace. The pope will pay a war levy of 15 million francs more than he was obliged to pay under the terms of the armistice, and he will hand over a number of works of art.

This is effectively the end of the 1796 campaign.[49] However, one should not underestimate the fact that it not only secured the French occupation of Italy but also left them with a definite moral ascendancy with which they could begin some new task, solve some new problem (if it were not too difficult). But this ascendancy would be lost if there was an interlude of any significant duration. In fact, the part of the campaign that carried the Army of Italy to the initial peace talks at Leoben in 1797 is purely the product of this magnified force. While each campaign has a causal relationship with the next, because it essentially lays its foundations, the campaign of the Army of Italy in 1797 behaves rather differently.

If the three French armies had advanced at the same time, delivering a major battle somewhere and, with it, a major decision, this would have been a new campaign in which the direct influences of the previous campaign would

48. Napoléon I, *Correspondance de Napoléon Ier*, 2:344–347 (letter 1511).

49. Colin, 284, notes: "Bonaparte did not see it that way. For him, Italy did not count, because it did not have an army. The aim of the expedition to Tolentino was to obtain the necessary funds to finish the war with Austria, and it was not by any means dedicated to the conquest of Italy. He knew that not one of the Italian powers had any intention of meeting any of their treaty obligations while the French were not there."

have trailed away as mere modifications of the new one. But this campaign is not like that; instead, the Army of Italy and its audacious commander rush on six weeks ahead of the others because they cannot wait to exercise their victory rights. It is, of course, the moral momentum they acquired that both compelled and enabled them to go off course in this way. Since the aim was achieved by this single thrust while the major forces still had not come to blows and reached a new decision, this campaign of 1797 should be considered merely a part of the previous one, as its sixth act.

Any reader who thinks we have expended so many words here just to excuse ourselves for treating the campaign of 1797 as an annex to the 1796 campaign in our account would misunderstand us, as it needs no excuse. Likewise, any reader who thinks we attach a pedantic value to the distinction between this and what could be called a new campaign would be mistaken; of course, this rule of distinction would not stand up throughout the whole of military history, but what we find characteristic about the 1797 campaign is that it is nothing more than a movement that was already happening, one that propagates itself virtually involuntarily until it is exhausted by friction and enemy resistance; and it can be fully understood only by seeing it in this light, as we will show more precisely when we present our reflections on it.[50]

Before we proceed to this next episode, let us cast one more critical glance over the 1796 campaign as a whole.

68 REFLECTIONS ON THE CAMPAIGN AS A WHOLE

The French offensive carried them as far as the Austrian state's alpine borders. Given the separation of the Sardinians from Austria, Bonaparte's dynamism, and the moral superiority of his army, this was fairly natural and

---

50. Colin, 285, notes: "These observations are absolutely without foundation. The campaign of 1797 is characterized by the fact that Bonaparte had received enough forces to protect the Innsbruck road while marching on Vienna. There is no 'acquired momentum' that would have allowed 30,000 men to march on Vienna, and whenever two campaigns succeed one another without being separated by a period of peace, the second is the natural sequel to the first." Colin seems to have misunderstood Clausewitz's point, which is that the continued French campaign into the Alps and into Austria was a natural continuation of the fighting against Austria in Italy and Germany. Thus, they both appear to be arguing the same point.

needs no special epiphany to explain it. On his way to the Austrian frontier, the victorious commander was brought to a standstill when he came to the large and strongly held fortress of Mantua. This fortress and the nature of the alpine border prevented him from linking up with the two armies advancing in Germany. His four successive series of multiple victories had yielded only negative results; but one single victory on the part of his opponent would cost him the whole of Lombardy and probably hurl him back to the Maritime Alps. Does this apparent magic ratio perhaps emerge from the use of some particularly effective strategic variable? Is it down to certain lines and angles, or is it the influence of individual points, the power of individual positions that generates these effects?[51] We pose these questions because ever since strategy has aspired to become a science, it is reluctant to satisfy itself with seeking the causes of remarkable successes in the most simple and obvious factors; instead, it feels the need to detect secret powers in inconspicuous things that escape the unblessed eye. But in any case, it is important to be clear about the total outcome of a campaign, since this total outcome is not just the mere accidental conjunction of all the individual causes that generated the individual effects of which it consists; rather, a general look at those individual causes will always reveal one or more persistent ones that the others group themselves around. If we educe these causes clearly, we will find that if we just examine the major factors closely, everything else will follow quite easily.

The reason Bonaparte could not cross the Alps before Mantua had fallen was his numerical weakness. It takes at least 20,000 men to besiege 12,000; though in fact he decided to do it with just 10,000, that was possible only if the rest stayed nearby.[52] If he had been 20,000 stronger, nothing would have

---

51. This is a direct criticism of eighteenth-century theorists such as Heinrich von Bülow, who argued that mathematics and geometry were an important means of understanding and conducting strategy using precise calculation. For an example of this thinking, see Heinrich von Bülow, *Geist des Neuern Kriegssystems* (Hamburg: August Campe, 1835), 183–197, accessed 1 August 2017, https://books.google.com/books?id=Rh xOAAAAcAAJ&pg=PA122&dq=Geist+des+neuen+Kriegssystems&hl=en&sa=X&ve d=0ahUKEwjb-aTqnKzVAhWENT4KHUz3DZYQ6AEISzAF#v=onepage&q&f=false.

52. Colin, 287, notes: "We cannot see how the presence of 20,000 men at Verona or Legnago diminished the power of resistance of the Mantua garrison. Clausewitz is forced to seek obscure explanations to give Mantua overwhelming importance, and at the very moment where he is mocking secret powers, he invents a totally mysterious

held him back—not any of the other strategic conditions in question—from crossing the Alps and probably the Noric Alps as well, on the direct road to Vienna. Since at this time the Army of the Rhine was already past the Tyrol, the Austrians probably would have withdrawn the majority of their combat forces from there, partly to rush to the aid of the capital, and partly to avoid them being completely lost.

Thus Mantua, the Alps, and the projecting position of the Tyrol were weights that burdened the French operations, but they were not any kind of magical strategic crisis. It would be ridiculous to draw the invariable conclusion from this one example that unless the French hold Mantua, they cannot advance into Germany, or unless they hold the Tyrolese Alps, they cannot cross the Noric Alps.[53]

Let us turn now to the apparent disparity that exists between the strategic outcomes for the two sides.

So long as Mantua had not fallen, Bonaparte was actively continuing his offensive, but of course only weakly. The tension and the critical situation that attend every operation until it is completed did not let up during this whole time. All the victories he won could move him forward only insofar as their moral weight influenced Mantua to fall sooner, which conveniently could have been the case and probably would have been if Wurmser had not replaced the garrison once and later shut himself up in there as well. But the moral weight of these victories was their only direct result; because Bonaparte could not pursue his defeated opponent and thus had to allow him time to rally and recover, all their direct consequences failed to materialize, and the cumulative effect of all the losses suffered by the Austrians only appeared

---

effect by presence." What Colin ignores is that Bonaparte would have had to protect his lines of supply and that a large surplus of troops would have been required to shield against any Austrian countermove out of Mantua or to control the passes in the Tyrol or Noric Alps. After all, a fortress or a fortified position can also be used as a base of operations for area denial, not simply for refuge. See Murray, *Rocky Road to the Great War*, 1–44.

53. Colin, 287–288, notes: "It must, however, be maintained that a French army cannot march on Vienna via Friuli without occupying the Tyrol if an Austrian army is operating in Bavaria and could descend on Verona via Innsbruck. This is the true reason that held Bonaparte on the Adige, and which he invokes in his correspondence of 1796 and 1797." Here, Colin has effectively ignored his own logic in criticizing Clausewitz in his previous note.

later,[54] when Bonaparte was in a position to advance further. Thus, it would have been a higher art if Bonaparte had been able to achieve his aim, the conquest of Mantua, without having to win all these victories.[55] By contrast, a battle lost would have had much greater consequences, and in that respect, this case has much in common with all those in which an operation has to be abandoned before it has been completed: it is like snapping an overtensioned bow. But in this instance, the impact would have been unusually large because in Italy there were so many political factions tensely poised against one another, just waiting for the military decision. It is mainly this last factor that would have obliged the French army to retreat to the Maritime Alps.

But while this situation of such unequal outcomes follows quite naturally from the conditions, it always remained an unfavorable one. If it were not unavoidable, one might well say this implies an error in the higher-level strategic plan: to be in this same situation for six months and to be subjected to the uncertain fate of decisive battle four times, with the success of the entire campaign at stake each time.

But this situation was not unavoidable, either for the French government or for its commander.

The former could have relieved Bonaparte of his long quarantine in Italy if it had reinforced the Army of Italy with 20,000–30,000 men right after his first victory. Nobody can claim that such a reinforcement would not have been possible, since there was a host of troops in the interior. In particular, there was an entire army on the Atlantic coast: just refraining from the intended expedition to Ireland would have enabled the use of this force as sufficient re-

54. The cumulative effects of actions are extremely well explained by Wylie, *Military Strategy*.

55. Colin, 288, notes: "Let us imagine Bonaparte master of Mantua, still having 30,000 to 40,000 men against the 80,000 men that have had to be sent to Wurmser and Alvinczy because of his victories. Could he have marched on Vienna? He himself says to the Directory that the impossibility of protecting both the roads to Innsbruck and through Friuli at the same time obliged him to 'limit himself to the Adige.'" If the Austrians had indeed sent 80,000 men, then of course the situation would have been different. If we follow this line of reasoning, perhaps we should give Napoleon 100,000 for good measure and then analyze the outcome. Colin completely misses Clausewitz's point, which is that the Austrian hold on Mantua restricted Napoleon's options to the extent that he could not easily inflict a decisive blow until the fortress had fallen. Clausewitz's position on the matter is quite logical. Once Mantua had fallen, Napoleon was in a much better position to inflict a decisive result on the Austrians.

inforcement. But at that time, the French Directory did not appreciate the full value of an advance over the Alps, and it did not understand what Bonaparte understood later: how to trace the solution of a very complex question back to a single point, to seek the center of gravity[56] of all the enemy's resistance and to aim his blow there. The most certain way to defeat the Austrian protagonists was in inner Austria, as Bonaparte pointed out to the Directory many times.

Yet another way to curtail this long crisis in Italy would have been for the French commander to act differently.

A commander from the time of Louis XIV would have besieged Mantua and covered the siege with lines of circumvallation.[57]

In recent times, such lines have become officially abominated, and commanders everywhere have preferred to confront a relieving army in the open field with a force half as strong. Far be it from us to raise doubts about this principle, but we must still insist on the condition that this measure should have at least some possibility of fulfilling its purpose. But in the present case, that possibility did not exist. Because the Austrians were able to advance down both sides of Lake Garda at the same time, and subsequently on both sides of the Mincio, Bonaparte would have had to deploy two armies of observation, which of course, was impossible. Thus, his only remaining options were to abandon the siege, as he did, or to fight from within lines of circumvallation.[58]

Nobody who bases their opinions on military history, rather than on contemporary prejudices or superficial appearances, could think that a successful resistance within such a line was highly unlikely. Of all the innumerable sieges during Louis XIV's reign that were protected by lines of circumvallation, we

56. Again, the translation of *Schwerpunkt* as center of gravity (see the discussion in the notes in chapter 2) makes sense in the context of what is being discussed by Clausewitz.

57. Colin, 289, notes: "Provided his communication with his supply depots was not threatened. The appearance of the enemy in his rear would have made him evacuate his lines. Bonaparte tried to cover the siege of Mantua using the natural circumvallation formed by the Mincio and the Molinella, up until the moment when he knew that Quasdanowitsch [Quosdanovich] had an army corps capable of cutting off his retreat."

58. The problem with the latter option, which would influence the thinking about field fortifications for the next century on (see Murray, *Rocky Road to the Great War*), is that it would essentially fix Napoleon in place and allow his opponents time and space to maneuver potentially superior numbers into a confrontation to their advantage.

know of only three cases in which these lines were taken by relieving armies: at Arras in 1654 (Turenne against Condé), at Valenciennes in 1656 (Condé against Turenne), and at Denain in 1712 (Villars against Eugene). But we can gauge how weakly these lines were held when we know how many infantry the defender had at Arras and Valenciennes—just 12,000—and that the circumference of the line at Valenciennes was 9 miles and that at Arras 20 miles. It follows from this that there were a great many cases of similar lines that the most enterprising commanders—such as Turenne, Condé, Villars, Vendome, and Eugene—considered unassailable.[59]

If Bonaparte had wanted to employ this measure at Mantua, he would have had to fortify a perimeter of only 6 to 7 miles and deploy 40,000 of his best infantry inside it. At Bunzelwitz,[60] Frederick the Great had a perimeter of 9 miles and about 50,000 infantry. The force with which the enemy could have attacked Bonaparte in his line comprised 45,000 men; that which confronted Frederick the Great at Bunzelwitz had 160,000. We think it highly unlikely that Wurmser or Alvinczy or anyone else would have attempted to storm the French lines.

Now of course, it may be claimed that the Austrians would have dominated the surrounding countryside and cut off the French supplies. But this would have been for a period of a few weeks at most, since General Chasseloup had declared to Bonaparte that the fortress could be taken in fourteen days. Furthermore, it could be anticipated that most of this time would have passed before the relief force approached, since according to Bonaparte's own report on Wurmser's first attack, only a few more days would have been needed to effect the fall of the fortress. Thus, if Bonaparte could have supplied himself

---

59. Colin, 290, notes: "Turenne considers that it is almost impossible to prevent an attacker from breaching lines. Bonaparte has discussed this question at length, and he completely recognizes the value of lines of circumvallation; he considers it a mistake not to establish them; but, in 1796, he could not wait in place and surrender his line of retreat to a superior enemy. Clausewitz's thesis is not even superficially plausible." Again, Colin seems to have missed the point. Clausewitz is arguing that Napoleon would have done better to keep his force concentrated and in defensive positions, rather than splitting it up to watch the various approaches to Mantua and risk being defeated in detail.

60. This was a temporary fortified camp built by Frederick in Silesia in 1761 to protect his army against a greatly superior enemy force. So well known was the reference that Clausewitz used it six times in *On War* (171, 381, 389, 411, 497, 615).

in his camp with provisions for four weeks, of which there is really no doubt, he could have let the Austrians wander across the open country as far as they liked.

In this way, Bonaparte would not have been under the obligation imposed by his chosen method of response, of always having to bring about a decisive battle himself, and one that otherwise, in all probability, would not have happened.

But Bonaparte did not want to get involved in the difficult problem of maintaining a siege while covering it at the same time; it seemed much easier to strike at the Austrians without this handicap. We do not wish to examine further whether he considered the consequences properly or whether there was not a hint of youthful recklessness here. The whole world has praised him highly for his conduct, but nobody has considered that precisely because of that conduct the fall of Mantua was delayed for five months and he failed to coordinate with the advance of the army in Germany. If we bear this differential in mind, then however much we may love glorious victories, we are forcefully brought back to the question of whether what Turenne or Eugene would have done might not have been better.[61]

In any case, we can see that this loss of time, this sacrifice of the siege is what bought Bonaparte the possibility of winning such a succession of glorious victories. In reality, he was not battling the pressure of unprecedented circumstances with his glittering talent; rather, it was just a choice between two paths, and whatever else it may have been, the one he chose was not the shortest. Although his succession of fine victories redounds greatly to his credit, in evaluating their strategic worth, we should not forget to take into account the sacrifice that made them possible.[62]

---

61. Colin, 292, notes: "Eugene evacuated the lines at Landrecies because the victory at Denain threatened his communication with his supply depots." Colin ignores the fact that the main allies in this campaign (in 1712 in Flanders during the war of Spanish succession) had stopped cooperating after the British defection and that part of Eugene's force had just been isolated, attacked, and destroyed by the French under Villars. These details emphasize Clausewitz's earlier point about the importance of concentration, and they undermine Colin's point, as he is clearly being disingenuous. See John A. Lynn, *The Wars of Louis XIV 1667–1714* (New York: Routledge, 2013), 352–354.

62. This is an important point, in that Napoleon gained a number of tactical victories, but they did not gain him a truly strategic success until the defeat of the Austrians at Rivoli and after Mantua had fallen to his troops. It should be pointed out, however,

Finally, we have one more remark to make concerning the Austrians that we consider very important. They made four successive attempts to relieve Mantua.

The first was at the beginning of August. It lasted until mid-August.

The second was at the beginning of September. It lasted until mid-September.

The third was at the beginning of November. It lasted until mid-November.

The fourth was in mid-January.

The strength of their army was always approximately the same, at about 45,000 men.

In the first three attempts combined, the Austrians lost about 20,000 men. Wurmser had shut himself up in Mantua with 16,000, so that made 36,000 who had to be replaced bit by bit, up until the fourth attempt, to bring the army back up to its original strength at the time of the first one. Now it is only natural to ask: what would the outcome have been if the Austrians had been able to wait long enough to commit these 36,000 men at the same time—for events show that it was possible to raise them—and thus to make their first attack with some 80,000 men? There is no doubt that this superior force would have sufficed to reconquer Lombardy.

Now of course, this first attempt was extremely urgent, because Mantua was besieged at the time and might fall any day. Thus it was quite correct to make the first attempt with whatever was available at that moment; but the second and third attempts were no longer so urgent and could justifiably have been postponed to gain the advantage of being 20,000 men stronger. Of course, people will say that in September (the time of the second attempt) it was not possible to know for certain that Mantua could hold out until January (the time of the fourth attempt). But for one thing, there was no reason at all to fear that it might fall sooner, and for another, there is no doubt that

---

that there was constant pressure from the Directory in Paris for victories, as Clausewitz himself attests. Thus, it is reasonable to say that the tactical victories Napoleon gained served a political purpose, which in turn allowed his strategic plan to come to fruition. Clausewitz argues for this very point throughout *On War* and includes the idea that the parts of his trinity are not separable; therefore it seems unfair to criticize Napoleon for focusing on these tactical successes when they were so valuable politically. Napoleon was surely getting the strategic benefit too, no matter how indirect the connection.

those reinforcement formations created in mid-November, after the third attempt, could have been mobilized three months earlier if the decision to do so had been made three months earlier.[63] In a word: if the Austrian monarchy was in a position to send 26,000 reinforcements to its army in Italy between mid-August (when the first attempt ended, after costing about 10,000 men) and mid-January, then it could have done so by mid-October if the government had been convinced of the need for such a strenuous effort early enough.

The error the Austrian government committed here contravenes one of the fundamental principles of strategy: namely, that all available forces should be used simultaneously. Committing forces in a sustained succession of repeated blows, which is of infinite importance in tactics, is entirely contrary to the nature of strategy. It would take too long to expound this principle in full, but it takes only objective reflection to discover its essential importance. Strategy brings all available combat forces into action simultaneously or, in the event all forces are not required, as many as are necessary to ensure success. Only whatever absolutely cannot be provided at the moment the business begins may be employed as the reserve and for long-term use.

Now nobody will claim that the Austrians properly secured the success of their attack, since they advanced with an army that was roughly the same numerical strength as the enemy's, and preceding events must have persuaded them of the French moral superiority, whether one attributes that to the French army or to its commander. But to ensure success, if one is not aware of any moral superiority of one's own, a significant numerical superiority is always required, and if one is forced to acknowledge the moral superiority of the enemy, one must outnumber him twofold. Furthermore, as we have al-

---

63. Colin, 293, notes: "What Clausewitz calls the second attempt, namely Wurmser's maneuver on Bassano, was intended above all to keep Bonaparte in Italy at the moment when Moreau reached the Inn. This objective, of rather more importance than the preservation of Mantua, was achieved. It prevented the French from crushing the archduke and marching on Vienna with 100,000 men." If we accept what Colin says, it still leaves the question of why send Wurmser at all if the siege of Mantua is holding Napoleon in Italy without the commitment of extra troops to that theater? Surely, this would have allowed the Austrians to send that force to Germany to achieve a decision over Moreau. As such, Clausewitz's point about the concentration of force is valid: choose something and concentrate on that. This is one of his biggest criticisms of the Austrian strategy, in that they never seem to focus on and commit to one clear objective.

ready said, there is no reason to believe the Austrians could not have deployed the combat forces they massed in five months in three months instead, if they had tried a bit harder. Since there was now no time pressure, we are justified in saying that the Austrians were at fault, in that those combat forces required for success and that could have been brought to bear were committed to action in succession rather than simultaneously.

The human reason for this mistake is not hard to discover. In anything that demands an effort, one is willing to do only as much as necessary; thus, great efforts need very strong motives that push people hard. For the Austrians, these situations occurred each time one of their commanders in Italy suffered a defeat; then fear and dismay arose, and new forces were mobilized. But so long as there was no defeat and no strong pressure of circumstances, these efforts were lacking. In this sense, of course, we might say that the forces needed to concentrate at this time were not available simultaneously because there was not enough energy to procure them. But are we then to condone deriving this energy only from fear and trepidation? Surely in war, and especially in strategy, it should be the work of calm and intelligent calculation.

But it was exactly this clear insight that was lacking. The Austrian government did not say definitely enough that if it wanted to restore its position in Italy, it must start with superiority; and it did not perceive clearly enough that simultaneous effort by all forces has deep foundations in the nature of strategy.[64]

64. Here, it is worth looking at what Clausewitz says in *On War*, book 1, chaps. 1–2. Had the Austrians honestly answered the questions Clausewitz posed there, they would have at least been aware of the problems with their chosen course of action, as well as its likely outcome: failure.

11. The 1797 Campaign in the Alps

The absence of any Austrian account of this campaign prohibits any tolerably adequate overview of it. Thus we can only offer the main themes of events up to the preliminary peace of Leoben,[1] but we are not in a position to present the essential situation exhaustively, even at the key moments. However, even if we do not know the archduke's[2] strength in actual numbers, but only that he was very much weaker than his opponent, that at least suffices to understand it as a whole, and the position this whole assumes in strategy is more important than the course of the individual events, since these are basically just stages of a somewhat forced retreat.

However, this is not to say that it would not be of great interest if the Austrians were to give us the precise details of their strengths and positions necessary for a meaningful representation of the events of this retreat, which is very interesting because of the nature of the predominantly mountainous region.

Four weeks elapsed between the peace of Tolentino and the beginning of the 1797 campaign, because Bonaparte wanted to wait for the arrival of Delmas's and Bernadotte's[3] divisions from the Armies of the Rhine and of the Sambre and Meuse. Both were on the march over Mont Cenis and were expected at the end of February. It is not easy to pin down what reinforcements

---

1. This was the preliminary peace agreement signed between the French Republic and Austria on 18 April 1797. See "*Traité préliminaire de paix conclu à Leoben le 18 avril 1797 contre la France et l'Autriche*," accessed 23 August 2017, http://gallica.bnf.fr/ark:/12148/bpt6k95781s/f337.image. The formal treaty ending the war, Campo Formio, was signed 18 October 1797.

2. This is Archduke Charles of Austria, who was to become one of Austria's best generals. He had been sent to defend the Austrian border against Napoleon's invasion from Italy.

3. Antoine-Guillaume Delmas was 30 and Jean-Baptiste Bernadotte was 32 at the beginning of the campaign. The latter became a marshal of France and later king of Sweden.

they brought to his army, since Bonaparte puts them at 18,000 men, but the Directory and General Kellermann, in command in the Alps, say 30,000. They probably came to 20,000 or so; in any case, they brought the strength of Bonaparte's army close to 80,000 men.

On 10 March, at the commencement of the campaign, this army was assembled as follows:

1. The main army under Bonaparte (44,000)
   Masséna's division: 11,500
   Guieu's division: 10,500
   Sérurier's division: 10,500
   Bernadotte's division: 10,500
   Dugua's cavalry reserve division: 1,100
2. Joubert's corps in the Tyrol (19,500)
   Joubert's division: 7,500
   Baraguay d'Hilliers's division: 6,500
   Delmas's division: 5,500

Victor en route from Ancona to Ferrara: 6,500
   Garrisons in Lombardy: 9,000 (total of garrisons and Victor, 15,500)
   Grand total: 79,000 men

At the end of February the positions of these forces were:

Masséna at Bassano.
Sérurier at Castelfranco.
Guieu (formerly Augereau) at Treviso.
Bernadotte at Padua.
Joubert, Baraguay d'Hilliers, and Delmas in the Tyrol around Trient.

There are no detailed reports on the strengths and positions of the Austrians. We only know the following in general terms. Generals Laudon and Kerpen were in command in the Tyrol. The former had taken a position behind the Lavis, the latter behind the Nos [Noce]; both seem to have been characteristic cordon deployments. The whole of the Tyrolese *Landsturm* [militia] was mobilized and incorporated into these formations, whereby these intrinsically weak corps must have accrued very significant reinforcements. Alvinczy had led the remnants of his army to the Tagliamento, where the new main army was to muster. Lusignan held an intermediate position at Feltre with one brigade; Hohenzollern was acting as advance guard on the lower Piave. Two divisions under Mercantin and Kaim were on the march from the Rhine to reinforce the army in Italy, but when Bonaparte began the campaign, they were still on the far side of the Alps, and the archduke could combine with them only by retreating into the Drava valley.

The archduke had arrived in Innsbruck on 7 February, where he had taken over command of the army in Italy and made arrangements with Count Lehrbach for the mobilization of the Tyrol militia. Finding his army still in such a state as to be scarcely worthy of the name, he traveled back to Vienna to arrange for the necessary reinforcements and apparently returned to Friuli only shortly before the campaign began. One can easily calculate that whatever may have been decided in Vienna at that time, that is, fourteen days before the campaign began, none of it can have been accomplished. To get a reasonable idea of how weak the archduke was, we need only consider that in January Alvinczy's army had only 20,000 men left, and the reinforcements from the Rhine had not yet arrived; even if there were other ways to provide reinforcements, these could hardly have totaled more than 10,000–15,000 men. Now if we find Generals Laudon and Kerpen in the Tyrol and Lusignan at Feltre, that leaves at most only about 20,000 men for the archduke's main body, but of these, the archduke had detached Ocskay and Köblös to hold the two routes into the Julian Alps created by the Fella and the Isonzo toward the Tarvis [Tarvisio] Pass; the former was at the Veneta Gorge and Ponteba [Pontebba], the latter at the Plez Gorge [Bovec].[4] From this, it can be assumed that the army the archduke concentrated on the Tagliamento had at most 15,000–20,000 men.

70 OPERATIONAL PLANS

There is nothing satisfactory about the French Directory's operational plan. But this only makes it more important to know what was in the mind of this government as Bonaparte begins his campaign on 10 March, while Hoche's

---

4. To get an idea of the extremely rugged terrain involved, it is worth looking at photographs of the fortress at this location. See "Trdnjava Predel," accessed 23 August 2017, http://www.kluze.net/trdnjava-predel.

Army of the Sambre and the Meuse crosses the Rhine only on 18 April, and Moreau's Army of the Rhine on the 21st. This is an interval of almost six weeks, during which Bonaparte obviously closed half the distance to the heart of the enemy's power. Everything we know about this matter is contained in a letter from the Directory to Bonaparte on 12 February 1797:

> "We hope," it says, "that the twelve demi-brigades and three regiments of horse that are joining the army of Italy as reinforcements will put you in a position after the expedition to Rome to debouch from the Tyrol with superior numbers, and at that time we will order General Moreau to cross the Rhine and to coordinate his movements with yours. General Hoche, at the head of the Army of the Sambre and the Meuse, will detain part of the enemy forces in the direction of Franconia and will blockade the Rhine fortresses."[5]

This does not tally at all with the actual course of events, and it is most likely that there was no previously planned unity to the operations in these three theaters of war; rather, each of the three generals began their operations as soon as their preparations were complete.

Bonaparte, whose reinforcements arrived at the end of February and who knew how weak his opponent was just then, did not want to lose any time in exploiting his superiority. He calculated that whatever reinforcements the Austrians might have sent from their Rhine army to Italy would still be en route; in the end, he would still have to deal with just as many enemies as if he had waited for the French Army of the Rhine to move, but at first, he would have the priceless advantage of attacking the archduke before his reinforcements had arrived, thus neutralizing that portion [the reinforcements] of the Austrian force, for any troops that are obliged to be on the march while the moment of decision is being reached may be considered neutralized. Thus, Bonaparte hoped to obtain decisive superiority right away in the initial phase; then he would just trust his luck as to what objective and what kind of resolution of the

---

5. Clausewitz notes: "*Nous esperons que le renfort des douze demi-brigades et trois regimens de troupes à cheval, qui se rendent à l'armée d'Italie, vous mettra en état, après l'expédition de Rome, de déboucher du Tyrol, avec supériorité, et nous ordonnerons à cette époque au Général Moreau de passer le Rhin et de combiner ses mouvemens avec les vôtres. Le Général Hoche, à la tête de l'armée de Sambre et Meuse, occupera vers la Franconie une partie des ennemis et bloquera les places du Rhin.*" *Corréspondance inédite, officielle et confidentielle de Napoléon Bonaparte (Italie)*, 2:458–460.

whole matter this might lead him to. The validity of this calculation is undeniable, and Bonaparte, convinced of the truth of it, probably did not seek any further instructions from his government but just made his own rules.[6] His long series of victories had made the Directory not just malleable but almost submissive toward him,[7] so it was hard to imagine there would be any objection. Let us save further consideration of this topic for the conclusion.

The section of the Directory's letter quoted above talks about Bonaparte attacking out of the Tyrol, thus into Swabia; however, we should note that an earlier letter also mentions occupying the Friulian alpine passes, as well as dividing the army into two corps, one for the Tyrol and one for Carinthia. Nonetheless, the view of the Directory does seem to have been that Bonaparte should smash through the Tyrol with his main body.[8]

By contrast, in mid-February Bonaparte still thought there was a chance the archduke might combine some reinforcements with his troops in the Tyrol and break out from there onto the Italian plain. In this case, he intended for Joubert to hold for about ten days between Trient and Mori, giving himself enough time to come through the Brenta valley against the Austrians' left flank, as proved by the instructions he gave to Joubert.

But after the Austrian troops were drawn mainly to Friuli, Bonaparte saw that he need no longer fear an attack from the Tyrol. Accustomed to always striking the center of gravity of the enemy force, and convinced that any advance on the direct route to Vienna must be more decisive than an operation from the Tyrol directed against Swabia, he never doubted for a moment that he and his main body should find the archduke's army in Friuli, defeat it, and then advance as far along the road to Vienna as the situation allowed. In mak-

6. If said forces are not in a position to intercede in a fight, they are essentially useless. In that respect, Napoleon's boldness makes sense and contrasts well with his opponent's frequent caution. It is also significant that Clausewitz repeatedly highlights examples of boldness, and the concept features prominently in *On War*; see book 3, chap. 6 (190–193).

7. This brings us back to Clausewitz's trinity. Even though Napoleon's successes in these campaigns were often only tactical, they provided him with the scope for greater strategic victories.

8. Colin, 300, notes: "This is a fair and important comment. There was every reason to think that the bulk of the Austrian forces was massed in the Tyrol and that an attack would happen on this flank. One army corps was to be directed upon the Trieste road to cover Bonaparte's line of operations against that side. This initial plan was reversed at the last moment as a consequence of the way the enemy forces were apportioned."

ing that decision, he was certainly not without the proud hope that he might be the first of the French commanders to fly his flag before the gates of Vienna.

In these circumstances, Joubert greatly outnumbered the Austrian troops in the Tyrol, at least initially, until the militia mobilization became fully effective. This superiority had to be used to drive Austrian generals Laudon and Kerpen back as far as the foot of the Brenner Pass, if possible, so that Joubert would have the valley of the Rienz behind him. If Bonaparte needed him in Carinthia, or if his own situation in the Tyrol became too worrying, he could join Bonaparte via the so-called Puster valley.

This is all we have to say about Bonaparte's plans. Let us now turn to the archduke.

It is well known that there are only two main ways across the mountain ranges of Carinthia and Carniola, the so-called Julian Alps. The one that is the road to Austria crosses the watershed via the Tarvis Pass [at Tarvisio] to Villach in the Drava valley; the other is actually the road from Hungary through Laibach [Ljubljana] in the Sau [Sava] valley, which angles right via the Loibel [Loibl] Pass into the Drava valley and then to Klagenfurt. There is also a third route, a longer detour through the Mur valley to Bruck [Bruck an der Mur]. The first two routes meet at Klagenfurt, which, from the Tagliamento, is a good one-third longer by the second route than by the first.

From Valvassone [Valvasone] on the Tagliamento, the Tarvis Pass can be reached by two routes. The shortest is the main road, which runs along the Tagliamento and the Fella through the passes of the Veneta Gorge and Pontebba. The other runs via Udine, Cividale [del Friuli], and Canale [Kanal, in Slovenia] to the Isonzo, and up this river through the pass of the Plez Gorge [Plezzut].

The archduke had decided to concentrate his army behind the Tagliamento near Valvasone, making the river his front. This placed him squarely across the road to Laibach, while also putting the road through the Isonzo valley to Tarvisio behind him and keeping the other road to it through the Fella valley right in front of him on the other side of the Tagliamento. Thus, all three were covered, since the enemy obviously could not follow this last route without having driven off the archduke. However, the archduke effectively had to give up any idea of retreating to Tarvisio. Because he only indirectly covered the shortest route there, having it in front of him rather than behind him, he could not use it; nor was it practical for him to use the other longer route through the Isonzo valley. Thus, his true line of retreat was to Laibach, and hence the

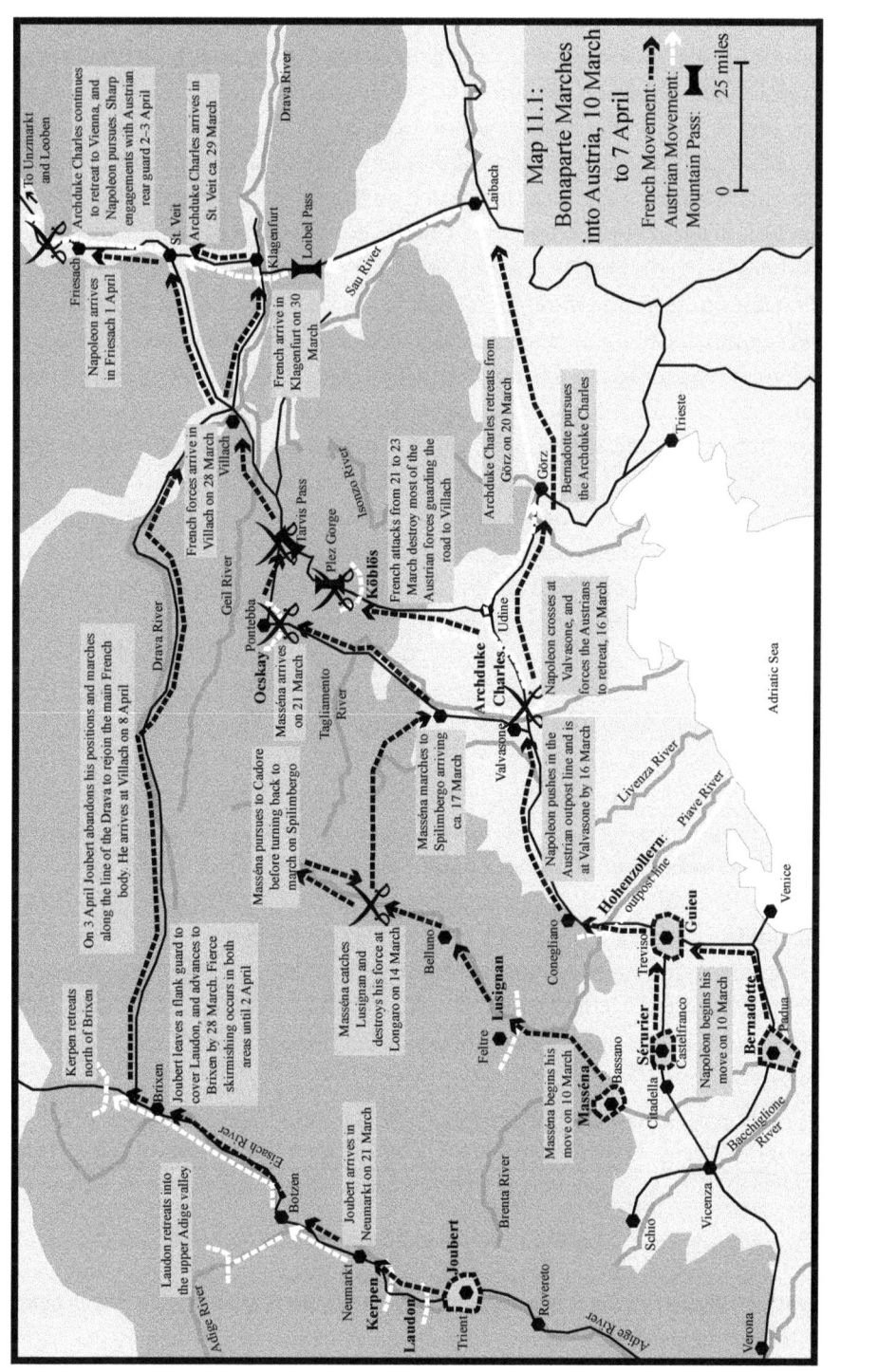

Map 11.1:
Bonaparte Marches
into Austria, 10 March
to 7 April

French Movement: ▪▪▪▶
Austrian Movement: ▬▬▶
Mountain Pass:)(

0   25 miles

To Unzmarkt
and Leoben

Archduke Charles continues
to retreat to Vienna, and
Napoleon pursues. Sharp
engagements with Austrian
rear guard 2–3 April

Napoleon arrives
in Friesach 1 April

Friesach

St. Veit

Archduke Charles arrives in
St. Veit ca 29 March

Archduke Charles arrives in
St. Veit ca 29 March

Drava River

Klagenfurt

Loibol Pass

French arrive in
Klagenfurt on 30
March

Sau River

Laibach

French arrive in
Klagenfurt on 30
March

French forces arrive in
Villach on 28 March

Villach

Isonzo River

Drava River

Tarvis Pass

Plez Gorge

Köblös

French attacks from 21 to 23
March destroy most of the
Austrian forces guarding the
road to Villach

Geil River

Pontebba

Oeskay

Masséna arrives
on 21 March

Tagliamento
River

Archduke Charles retreats from
Görz on 20 March

Bernadotte pursues
the Archduke Charles

Görz

Trieste

Kerpen retreats
north of Brixen

On 3 April Joubert abandons his positions and marches
along the line of the Drava to rejoin the main French
body. He arrives at Villach on 8 April

Eisach River

Brixen

Joubert leaves a flank guard to
cover Laudon, and advances to
Brixen by 28 March. Fierce
skirmishing occurs in both
areas until 2 April

Laudon retreats into
the upper Adige valley

Masséna pursues to Cadore
before turning back to
march on Spilimbergo

Masséna marches to
Spilimbergo arriving
ca. 17 March

Udine

Napoleon crosses at
Valvasone, and
forces the Austrians
to retreat, 16 March

Archduke Charles

Valvasone

Napoleon pushes in the
Austrian outpost line and is
at Valvasone by 16 March

Livenza River

Piave River

Adriatic Sea

Masséna catches
Lusignan and
destroys his force at
Longaro on 14 March

Belluno

Lusignan

Feltre

Conegliano

Hohenzollern:
outpost line

Treviso

Guieu

Venice

Botzen

Joubert arrives in
Neumarkt on 21 March

Masséna begins his
move on 10 March

Bassano

Sérurier

Castelfranco

Bernadotte

Padua

Napoleon begins his
move on 10 March

Neumarkt

Kerpen

Laudon

Joubert

Trient

Rovereto

Brenta River

Adige River

Citadella

Bacchiglione
River

Schio

Vicenza

Verona

position at Valvasone was really a flank position. Since the archduke had Generals Ocskay and Köblös holding the two approaches to the Tarvis Pass, and the divisions coming from the Rhine were expected in the Drava valley and could advance through the Tarvis if they arrived in time, he probably expected to achieve more by this flank position than by any direct frontal deployment. Indeed, this last would have had the major disadvantage of dividing his force and deploying on both roads leading to the Tarvis, since, given the enemy's superior numbers and the alpine region to his rear, he could not afford to risk being outflanked; furthermore, by taking up such a position, he would leave the road to Gradisca, and from there to Triest and Laibach, completely open, and that was probably where the majority of his supply depots were. Finally, the archduke could still hope to use the road from Valvasone through the Isonzo valley to Tarvisio, since it was not especially indirect and, as we have seen, the direct route was already held by Ocskay and Köblös. Of course, it was possible that the enemy might detach a corps to the Fella valley ahead of the decision to be delivered on the Tagliamento; however, given Bonaparte's preferred method, there was not much fear of that.

71 BONAPARTE CROSSES THE JULIAN ALPS

The French divisions left their winter quarters on 10 March. Bonaparte advanced with three of them (Sérurier, Guieu, and Bernadotte) and the cavalry reserve in two columns via Sacile and Porto Bufole [Portobuffolè] to Valvasone, where these 35,000 men assembled on 16 March, after driving back the archduke's advance guard under General Hohenzollern.

But Masséna had been given an instruction that is not expressed clearly anywhere, nor is it satisfactorily revealed by his movements. He likewise left on the 10th to attack Lusignan and was at Feltre on the 11th;[9] he followed the

---

9. Napoleon sent a cryptic letter to Masséna on 10 March 1797: "General, adopt what you proposed yesterday evening." But the letter refers to the town of Feltre, some 45 miles west of the area Masséna ended up operating in. Furthermore, a letter of 12 March refers to Bellune (Bellano), which is in the same valley as Feltre. In addition, the letters are sent to Masséna's location in Bassano and Ciano, respectively—both of which are in close proximity to Feltre. By 21 March, Masséna is in Görz. As such, his exact whereabouts cannot be known with certainty. See Napoléon I, *Correspondance de Napoléon Ier*, 2:371–408.

retreating Lusignan into the Piave valley to Belluno on the 13th and then to Longaro [Longarone] on the 14th, where he caught up with Lusignan's rear guard, surrounded it, and captured 500 men, including General Lusignan himself. Masséna pressed on as far as Piave di Cadore [Pieve di Cadore], then turned around and marched across the mountain range dividing the Piave from the Tagliamento and down the valley of the Celline until he reached the Tagliamento. Supposedly on the 14th he was already at Spilimbergo, two hours upriver from Valvasone, where he crossed the Tagliamento, and by the 15th he was at Gemona and 20 miles from Valvasone on the road to Tarvisio. This would have put him two hard marches closer to Tarvisio than the archduke, if the latter were heading there via the Isonzo valley. Except that Masséna's maneuvers must have turned out differently from how they are presented in the accounts by Bacler d'Albe and Jomini. First, the distance from Longaro to Spilimibergo via Pieve di Cadore is 54 miles across a high mountain range, which Masséna could not have covered in a day; second, the archduke would not have allowed this general to cross the Tagliamento alone, 4.5 miles from his own position, two days before the battle of the Tagliamento; third, Masséna did not attack General Ocskay's position at Casa Sola [Casasola] until the 20th, but if he was already at Gemona on the 15th, just 15 miles away, he must have sat entirely inactive for five days. Most likely, Masséna got to Spilimbergo only after the battle, on the 17th at the earliest, then reached St. Daniele [San Daniele del Friuli] on the 18th and Gemona on the 19th; then on the 20th he took the Veneta Gorge [Chiusaforte] and drove General Ocskay out of his position at Casa Sola south of Pontebba.[10]

There is no account or report that tells us what strategic significance this maneuver of Masséna's into the Piave valley was supposed to have. It has been described as an outflanking maneuver around the enemy's right wing, but it became that only after it reached Spilimbergo, and its very elliptical route into the Piave valley and back was not appropriate for that. It seems much more likely that Masséna was originally ordered to advance through the Piave valley into the valley of the Drava, since from Pieve di Cadore, he turned off toward Toblach [Dobbiaco]. Now this could indeed be considered a wide outflanking

---

10. Colin, 305, notes: "This calculation of Clausewitz's is accurate. Having pursued Lusignan as far as Cadore, Masséna retraced his steps to rejoin via Serravalle. The mountains were impassable because of snow, and even the road from Longarone to Serravalle was very difficult."

of the right wing of the enemy positions on the Fella and the Isonzo, or even a move to maintain communications between the main army and Joubert, but it has no logical connection at all with what Masséna did next. Either of these putative missions undoubtedly would have been a bad idea, smacking more of an Austrian strategy than a Bonapartean one. Now Masséna's return to the Tagliamento through the Zellino [Celline] valley is a genuine immediate U-turn, which indicates a changed or canceled plan. From this, it seems likely that Bonaparte was initially tempted by an idea that he soon realized was defective, and he then ordered General Masséna to march to the Tagliamento by the most direct route so as to act in closer cooperation with the main army.[11]

The Encounter of 16 March on the Tagliamento

As we have seen, the archduke had deployed his army of no more than 15,000–20,000 men behind the Tagliamento opposite Valvasone, with the intention of accepting battle if offered, but not holding his ground too stubbornly, so as not to expose himself to any risk of serious defeat. The infantry were mostly occupying the villages, with the cavalry behind them ready to be used offensively. If the outcome did not look promising, he wanted to conduct a fighting withdrawal of the kind that would force the enemy to fight for every inch of ground, as they say. The Tagliamento was very low, and the French crossed the riverbed easily above and below Valvasone virtually in battle formation. It was probably already after midday, and the Austrian resistance lasted for only a few hours until nightfall, whereupon the archduke began his retreat, having lost about 500 men and six guns.

The archduke decided not to retreat to Laibach with his whole force. Instead, his right wing under Bayalitsch and Contreuil took a divergent route via Udine, Cividale, and Caporetto [Kobarid, Slovenia], through the valley of the Isonzo to Tarvisio, while the archduke himself with Hohenzollern and Reuss took the road through Gradisca and Görz [Gorizia] for Laibach. He was in-

11. Colin, 306, notes: "The truth is much simpler than all these speculations. Masséna was charged with destroying Lusignan's corps, so as to prevent the two enemy forces from communicating other than via Toblach. This done, he rejoins the army, where he forms the second line in place of Bernadotte, who is pushed into the first line. Bonaparte had hoped that Masséna would arrive on the Tagliamento with the other divisions of the army, but the poor state of the roads prevented it."

duced to make this risky maneuver because he thought the forces holding the road to Villach were too weak,[12] and the divisions coming from the Rhine were still too far off to be able to resist the French. He therefore ran the risk of the troops moving through the Puster valley being cut off from their rendezvous at Villach and of seeing the French reach Klagenfurt before his retreating left wing could get there on its big detour through Laibach and Krainburg [Kranj]. Being cut off from Klagenfurt like that would have forced him to take his left wing through the valley of the Mur via Graz, in which case he would not have reached the great Vienna highway and united his force until he got to Bruck, 110 miles further to the rear.

We cannot gauge how risky this retreat of the right wing appeared at the time, because we do not know what news the archduke had of Masséna's advance. According to our conjecture above, this general reached the Tagliamento only on the 17th, so it would have been quite natural for the archduke to have no great concerns about Ocskay on the 16th. It is 70 miles from Valvasone to Tarvisio via Udine and the Isonzo valley. The right wing certainly could have covered this distance in four days, since half of it was on the flat, and it could have reached Tarvisio on the 20th, ahead of Masséna, who did not get there until the 21st.

Bonaparte and his three divisions pursued along the Gradisca road. Palma Nuova [Palmanova] had been abandoned by the Austrians, but Gradisca was held by 2,000 men with ten guns, and some preparations had been made for the defense of the Isonzo. But this fortress and its garrison soon fell into the hands of Bernadotte's and Sérurier's divisions on the 19th, and the archduke had to withdraw to Görz.

While Bernadotte and Sérurier were busy capturing Gradisca, Guieu arrived in Cormons and was directed by Bonaparte to pursue the Austrian right wing toward Caporetto via Cividale. Bernadotte was to pursue the archduke toward Laibach, but Bonaparte himself and Sérurier moved through Canale on the 22nd, heading for Caporetto to support Guieu, if necessary.

As we have already mentioned, on the 20th Masséna attacked General Ocskay at the bridge at Casa Sola and drove him back; on the 21st he attacked him

---

12. Unless he was willing to detach troops to defend the Tarvis Pass, which would have prevented such a French maneuver. Had he done that, however, he would have reduced his smaller force, with no guarantee that any force so placed would actually be of use.

again at Pontebba and threw him back through Tarvisio into the Sava valley toward Wurzen [Podkoren, Slovenia], with the loss of 600 men.

On this day—the 21st—the main body of the Austrian right wing, which could have been at Tarvisio by then, was still 27 miles away at Caporetto, after its rear guard had been pressed by Guieu at Buffero [Pulfero]. On the 21st, when Masséna becomes master of the Tarvis Pass, as we have seen above, Contreuil, who probably forms the advance guard, arrives at Oberpret [Oberbreth = Strmec na Predelu, Slovenia], 7 miles from Tarvisio. At Tarvisio, he finds only finds Masséna's advance guard deployed, so it seems that the main body of Masséna's division had not yet reached Tarvisio. Contreuil attacks and throws it back on the rest of the division at Safnitz [Saifnitz = Camporosso in Valcanale]. But early on the 22nd he himself is attacked by Masséna's division and driven out of Tarvisio and along the road to Villach, with significant loss. Thus, Contreuil had made it through the pass, albeit with difficulty and loss. Now Masséna turned toward Raibl [Cave del Predil] against Bayalitsch. On the 22nd Bayalitsch was on the march to Oberpret through the Plez Gorge, which was still being held by Köblös, so he ran into Masséna. Bayalitsch had scarcely put the Plez Gorge behind him when Köblös was attacked by Guieu.[13] This place was not strong enough to resist superior numbers for long; the French battalions scaled the steep slopes that surround and overlook the position, and after a brief resistance, General Köblös laid down his arms. Now Bayalitsch was completely trapped. Masséna was coming at him from one end of the narrow valley, from which there was no other exit, while Guieu and Sérurier pursued him from the other end. So on the 23rd Bayalitsch too surrendered, along with his 3,000–4,000 men, 25 guns, and 500 wagons.

The reports again leave us in ignorance as to the exact details of subsequent operations. To our astonishment, we learn that Bonaparte and his three divisions—Masséna, Sérurier, and Guieu—arrive in Villach only on the 28th, even though he easily could have been there on the 25th. Since it was crucial to drive the archduke away from Klagenfurt and the direct route to Vienna, this should have been sufficient reason for haste. Admittedly, the Austrian commander, who could have set off from Görz around the 20th, could have reached Klagenfurt comfortably on the 25th via Laibach and Krainburg, since it was only 108 miles. Therefore, because of the delays caused by the conquest of Gra-

---

13. Guieu had been ordered to work in conjunction with Masséna. See Napoléon I, *Correspondance de Napoléon Ier*, 2:412.

disca, Köblös's and Bayalitsch's surrender, and the difficult terrain, Bonaparte would have arrived too late—except that this could not be foreseen, and the archduke might have arrived in Klagenfurt a few days later. Since Bonaparte easily could have arrived there on the 25th himself, the prospect of cutting off his opponent was not so remote and seems well worth attempting. There is therefore a gap in the strategic logic here, which can only provisionally be explained by the fact that the French divisions had a lot of stragglers they wanted to collect, and foraging for supplies caused a delay.[14]

There is still less information available about the archduke's march.[15] All we know is that, as Bonaparte is setting out for Klagenfurt on the 29th, the archduke leaves Mercantin's newly arrived division from the Rhine there and goes to St. Veit [Sankt Veit an der Glan] with the rest of his army. The archduke's army can now be assumed to have about 30,000 men.

On the 30th, after driving Mercantin out of Klagenfurt, Bonaparte goes to St. Veit. He sends one small corps down the Drava valley toward Marburg, and another under Zayontscheck[16] up the Drava to establish communications with Joubert. This latter is apparently not just repulsed but largely wiped out by the Tyrolese *Landsturm*.

Bernadotte's division has left an infantry detachment with the cavalry reserve to occupy Trieste and is on the march to Krainburg.

Before we describe the conclusion of the campaign, we must turn to the Tyrol, to learn about events there and to get an overview of the general situation.

14. Colin, 309, notes: "In divining Bonaparte's intentions, Clausewitz never takes account of the line of operations, which plays an essential role. Here, Bonaparte pursues the archduke toward the Isonzo with all his forces, but he had his line of operations protected by Masséna initially, and then, once he has passed the Caporetto road, by Guieu; then he halts on the Isonzo until he is informed of the archduke's movements; he does not want to engage in Carinthia while leaving the Carniola road open to the enemy."

15. Even Archduke Charles of Austria's own account does not contain a great deal of information. See Karl von Österreich, Erzherzog, *Grundsätze der Strategie erläutert durch die Darstellung des Feldzugs von 1796 in Deutschland*, 4 vols. (Vienna: Anton Strauss, 1814).

16. A Polish officer who had recently entered French Service (Józef Zajączek).

72 JOUBERT'S OPERATIONS IN THE TYROL

While Bonaparte was crossing the Julian Alpine chain, Joubert had advanced to the foot of the Brenner Pass.

Joubert waited until Bonaparte had crossed the Tagliamento, probably because it was only then that he knew for certain that the enemy's main body was in Friuli.[17] With his whole force, Joubert attacked General Kerpen, who was deployed in a cordon defense behind the Lavis; threw him back toward St. Michel [San Michele all'Adige], with the loss of 1,000 men and several guns; and then drove him out of there toward Botzen [Bozen/Bolzano].

On 21 March Joubert was in Neumarkt [Egna, Italy] with all three of his divisions. On that day the Austrian general Laudon, who had been posted in the Noce valley, advanced toward Egna with the aim of taking it, but he ran into too much opposition. He therefore stayed on the right bank of the Adige and retreated up the valley to Meran [Merano]. On the same day, Joubert entered Bolzano.

Here, the road to Innsbruck enters the Eisach valley, but Laudon had retreated into the valley of the Adige, where the majority of the Tyrol *Landsturm* were, so Joubert's situation was becoming precarious. Nonetheless, he decided to keep advancing but left Delmas in Bolzano with 5,000 men.

On the 22nd he advanced with the rest of his troops to Klausen [Chiusa, South Tyrol], where General Kerpen held a strong position. Joubert attacked; for a long time, the fighting was inconclusive, until finally the French got onto the heights that outflanked the position and forced General Kerpen to retreat.

Kerpen then took a position at Mittenwalde [Mezzaselva/Mittewald, Italy] in the Eisach valley, 6 to 10 miles above Brixen [Bressanone], leaving the entrance to the Puster valley open.

Joubert attacked him in this position on 28 March, throwing him back yet again, this time beyond Sterzing [Vipiteno]. This place is just 56 miles from Innsbruck, but of course, to get there, the road has to cross the Brenner Pass.

---

17. Colin, 311, notes: "Joubert's mission consisted of covering the army's line of operations while being as far away from it as possible. Since the supply depots were in Verona and the army was in Venetia, it was sufficient for Joubert to hold Trient and the exits from the Pergine [Pergine Valsugana] valley. When Bonaparte moved his center of operations to Palmanova or Osoppo, he called Joubert to the mouth of the Ampezzo Pass, etc. When he reached Klagenfurt, he ordered Joubert to rejoin him there."

Joubert, not knowing what was happening with Bonaparte's army at the time, still uncertain as to whether the Army of the Rhine was ready to enter the lists,[18] and surrounded by a warlike people in full revolt,[19] did not dare advance any further. He decided for the time being to hold with both his divisions at Bressanone, so he returned there.

Now the Austrian generals went over to a kind of raiding war. On 31 March and 2 April there was heavy fighting with the outpost at Unteraue [slightly upstream from Fortezza/Franzensfeste, northwest of Bressanone]. On the latter occasion Laudon also appeared before Bolzano, engaged the French there, and sent a detachment to block the road from Egna. Bolzano itself was under serious threat, since Laudon's force had grown to 12,000 men.

Within a few days, this situation surely would have led to General Joubert's complete downfall. However, on 3 April he had the incredible luck to learn for certain, from a colonel (Eberle by name, so probably a Tyroler) who had managed to get into the Drava valley disguised a peasant, that Bonaparte had successfully crossed the Alps. Joubert instantly decided to march through the Puster valley to join him, thus moving his line of retreat to that region, where at least there were no enemy regular troops, and, at the same time, combining with the main army in the critical situation it must be in, to be of decisive use to it.[20] On the 4th Delmas vacated Bolzano. On the 5th the whole corps combined marched from Bressanone to Brünnecken [Brunico/Bruneck, Italy], destroying the bridges above Bressanone behind it. This last measure and the effective action of his rear guard against Laudon gained Joubert enough time to escape both Austrian generals. Now Joubert continued his march without pause, crossing the Toblach [Dobbiaco] Pass, through Lienz to Villach. On his 108-mile trek, he only once had to fight the *Landsturm*, at Spital [Spittal an der Drau], 25 miles from Villach, where he took some more prisoners. It seems that he arrived in Villach on the 8th,[21] immediately after the armistice was signed at Leoben.

18. This means joining a contest, such as a medieval tournament.

19. Clausewitz pays special attention to the unique nature of mountain warfare and to "The People in Arms" in *On War*, book 6, chaps. 15–17 (417–432) and chap. 26 (470–483), respectively.

20. This was a bold and risky move. If Eberle's information had been inaccurate, Joubert would have essentially cut off his own retreat. This is another example of a bold move paying off.

21. Montholon, *Mémoires pour servir à l'Histoire de France sous Napoléon*, 4:85–86.

It is not known how many men Joubert lost on the way. In his *Memoirs*, Bonaparte says that Joubert joined him with 12,000 men,[22] so it follows that he must have lost 6,000–8,000, if he deliberately left 1,200 men on the Adige, as Bonaparte claims. Probably these 1,200 were a detachment that got cut off.

73 THE END OF THE CAMPAIGN

When he arrived in St. Veit on the 30th, Bonaparte was informed by the Directory that the Rhine armies were still not ready to commence their campaign and he could not count on their cooperation. He still had no news from General Joubert, but he knew the Tyrolese were in a general state of insurrection; he could expect similar insurgencies in Hungary and Croatia, and his appeasing and exhortatory proclamation to the inhabitants of Carinthia and Carniola shows that he feared the same from them. Venice's equivocal position and its armament became ever more threatening. In these circumstances, if we consider that the line of operations from Mantua to Klagenfurt was 225 miles long and ran through hostile territory throughout, and that the French army's combat strength had been reduced by one-third by detachments, stragglers, and other losses, we can see that when Bonaparte reached Klagenfurt, he was in a tense and critical situation. If Joubert joined him there, the Tyrol would be lost, and the Austrians would be free to descend to the Lombardy plain, link up with the Venetians, and completely cut off the French army's communications in the event it had to retreat. If Joubert stayed in the Tyrol, those three divisions would probably be abandoned to their doom, and Bonaparte himself would have no more than 30,000 men to continue his advance. Admittedly, Victor's and Lannes's detachments were on their way from the Papal States, but their 7,000–8,000 men could not compensate for all these difficulties. The archduke's combat forces now almost equalled his own; the reinforcements that might join him on the far side of the Styrian Alps that still lay ahead of Bonaparte could not yet be calculated. If Bonaparte were to lose a battle in Styria or even beyond Simmering [just south of Vienna], it would be difficult to bring back any substantial part of his army, and the reversal of fortunes would be so violent that all of Italy could be lost with this one blow,

22. Ibid., 4:74.

and the French flung back 450 miles. Bonaparte felt the inordinate tension of a situation that could not endure and must end in either an almost unprecedentedly glorious victory or his downfall. To turn back was morally impossible; he might save his army, but all the blame for a strategic defeat would have landed on him. The campaign of all three armies would have been ruined, his reputation destroyed, and everything he had gained so far would have been lost; his political career would have been annihilated, and he himself abandoned to factional revenge. How could a man of Bonaparte's character have made this decision? But if he just sat tight and waited for the other armies, that would have invited the Austrians to bring all the forces surrounding him to bear at once. Then he would have been unable to cope with all the threats unleashed on him, and the result would have been little different from that of a lost battle.

If he were to continue his advance, its happy resolution could be a glittering victory won by Bonaparte before the gates of Vienna; its moral impact could paralyze the forces raised in local defense in all the provinces beside and behind him, coinciding with the breakout of the Army of the Rhine. But such an outcome could not be relied on; it mostly had to be left to blind guesswork. As bold and audacious as Bonaparte had constantly shown himself to be, he felt the odds against him in this particular game were too high not to take the middle way out through a political solution, which he either knew or assumed he was empowered by his government to implement, and to satisfy himself with the advantages this could bring. He knew how desperately the French government wanted peace, and he knew what he could offer the Austrians. Heralded by alarm and consternation on his way to Vienna, he hoped to find a receptive ear.[23]

Thus, on the 31st he wrote to the archduke from St. Veit and made initial overtures. The Austrian commander replied evasively, as he always did, but said he would report to Vienna. To maintain the balance of this first stage of the negotiation, it had to be accompanied by a fearless, uninterrupted advance. Bonaparte therefore moved to Friesach on 1 April. Just behind this place is the Dirnstein [Dürnstein] Pass, where the road climbs up the main ridge of the

---

23. This relates to the value of the object to be gained, which must be weighed against the resources expended to achieve said object. The resources expended to achieve the goal should not exceed the value of that goal. See Clausewitz, *On War*, book 1, chap. 2 (90–99).

Styrian Alps, then descends to Hundsmarkt [Unzmarkt][24] in the Mur. This was where the archduke had deployed.[25]

On his march to Friesach, Bonaparte received a proposal for a four-hour truce. The short duration led him to infer an ulterior motive, and he guessed that reinforcements were on the march in the Mur valley, which the archduke was keen to have join him. Bonaparte decided to reject the proposal.

On the 2nd he attacked the archduke's rear guard at Dürnstein and drove it back, whereupon the archduke moved to Unzmarkt.

On the 3rd Bonaparte pursued him there, and another stubborn rearguard action ensued.

At Scheiflingen [Scheifling], where the road from Villach first reaches the Mur, Bonaparte learned that Spörken's Austrian division was now in the Mur valley. He immediately sent General Guieu against it, but without success, because it had gone back along the Salzburg road to join the archduke.

On the 5th Bonaparte advances to Judenburg, where he wants to concentrate his forces. He knows that Bernadotte will join him in a few days, but he still has no news of Joubert, who is nevertheless in the vicinity, just a few marches away. In the middle of his worry and anxiety about this, Generals Bellegarde and Meerfeldt arrive in Judenburg on 7 April to negotiate an armistice, which takes effect immediately and is followed just ten days later, on 17 April, by the preliminary peace of Leoben.

24. This is a typographical error. Clausewitz is almost certainly referring to Unzmarkt, a town in the Mur valley and on the way to Leoben. Furthermore, Napoleon wrote a letter to Masséna on 1 April 1797 in which he tells him to take a route through that town on the road to Vienna. Napoléon I, *Correspondance de Napoléon Ier*, 2:444–445 (letter 1671).

25. There were Austrians in the area around Neumarkt in der Steiermark as well as Unzmarkt, and there was fighting in both places.

12. Conclusions

74 REFLECTIONS

The Army of Italy's rapid advance to within 80 miles of Vienna, while the Austrian commander had no combat force to oppose it that was still fit to give battle before the gates of the capital, brought about the armistice of Leoben and the peace of Campo Formio [Campoformido]. Both appear to have been induced by the armed threat, which naturally draws our eye to the military factors prevailing at the time. In examining these factors, however, we must not only look at the Army of Italy but also consider the Rhine armies.

But before we busy ourselves with that, let us cast our critical gaze over the operations of the Army of Italy itself.

We have already said what motivated Bonaparte to open the campaign on his front at the beginning of March. According to his *Memoirs*, he believed he could join hands with the Army of the Rhine on the Enns.[1] He imagined that this army, 120,000 strong, would cross the Rhine at Strasbourg under the command of a single general and advance inexorably through Bavaria. He thought they would then march on Vienna together with 200,000 men and lay down the law to the emperor.

We doubt this is an entirely true representation of his actual view at the time. It is inconceivable that he thought the French combat forces on the Rhine could unite 120,000 men to cross at Strasbourg at the end of February, when six weeks later they were still in two separate armies 180 miles apart.[2]

That fierce desire to be the first at the gates of Vienna, to raise his name

1. In his memoirs, Napoleon references the "Ens" River. The Ens is a small river in Germany that is not close to the Danube. The Enns River in Austria more closely matches the location and likely line of advance to which Clausewitz is referring. See Montholon, *Mémoires pour servir à l'Histoire de France sous Napoléon*, 4:57.

2. Colin, 319, notes: "The Army of the Rhine and Moselle moved off on 19 April, exasperated by its commander's tardiness. Its situation had not changed significantly for a month. It could have crossed the Rhine toward the end of March if Moreau had understood the importance of a rapid offensive in Bavaria."

high above his rivals while he dictated peace to the emperor with no one else involved, that sense of his personal power, that trust in his luck: that is what swept Bonaparte onto the victory path that opened up before him, with little calculation or weighing of risk. He dared to take a huge gamble because it was in his character and in his personal interest.[3]

But he certainly did not expect that, a few weeks after the campaign began, the situation would become so dangerous. Although he surely must have known that the Army of the Rhine could not arrive at Vienna at the same time he did because of the difference in distance, he could not have expected that, by the time he was able to descend from Simmering, it would not have moved at all. He did not think Joubert would encounter such difficulties in the Tyrol, nor that insurrection would stir in Carinthia and Carniola. As these things gradually developed, it almost became harder to hold back than to go on.

While we can understand how an audacious commander like Bonaparte would stride down this murky path, contemptuous of the enemy as ever and borne along by the prospect of glittering success, and while we have no right to drag him into the dock in the court of criticism for this, we must wonder at the recklessness of a government that embarks on a campaign as aimlessly as the Directory did.[4] How was it possible to let the Army of Italy march on Vienna alone, and with only two-thirds of its strength, while the other armies rested on the Rhine for another six weeks? If Archduke Charles could have found a reserve of just 20,000 men behind the Styrian Alps, the Army of Italy most likely would have been beaten and then half wiped out on its long retreat through the high mountains held by the insurrection, and the campaign would have been ruined from the outset. Nevertheless, not once does the Directory betray any great embarrassment about this, so evidently, it never

3. Again, Clausewitz references the elements of his trinity. By repeatedly drawing attention to its parts, he drives home the role played by chance, passion, and reason in war. In addition, this serves as a constant reminder of his criticism of eighteenth-century theorists' belief that war could be waged using reason alone and that chance could be removed almost entirely (see the comments on Maurice de Saxe in chapter 8, section 51). Clausewitz is directly attacking the thinking of the Enlightenment: that is, reason alone cannot explain war, so when thinking about war, one must not assume that these elements (the parts of his trinity) can be separated from one another and that war can be predicted or controlled.

4. This too is important, as Clausewitz devotes much of books 1 and 8 of *On War* to understanding what the purpose of war is and how to determine the means to success.

realized the overwhelming importance of simultaneous action by all its forces in harmony.[5]

There is no real contradiction in excusing the commander but not the government. Its point of view was different from his; he did not have such a clear picture of the Army of the Rhine's situation, he was not in a position to do anything about it, and, finally, his personal ambition prevailed, which a commander must always be permitted up to a point, because in war nothing is achieved without this powerful driving force.[6]

However, even if we regard the isolated advance of the Army of Italy as being crowned with happy success by the peace of Campo Formio, that still does not justify it, since this success would have been achieved with much more certainty by the simultaneous advance of all the armies. The one reason that prompted Bonaparte to move first, the fact that Mercantin's and Kaim's divisions had not yet reached the archduke, could not have carried such weight in a broader view of the situation.

The French commander can, however, be criticized for sending 20,000 men up the valley of the Adige while he took 44,000 men on the route over the Julian Alps. Such a force [the 20,000] was hardly sufficient to conquer the Tyrol, that is, to drive out the regular troops and disarm the militia; and if this force was not enough, then it was bound to get into a difficult situation. If he had simply left 10,000 men on the plain at Verona instead, these would have been in a much better position to secure his line of communications, intimidate the Venetians, and protect themselves against any mishaps, and it would have made the main army 10,000 men stronger.[7]

Even if this advance into the Tyrol relied on a simultaneous advance into Swabia by the Army of the Rhine, it deserves criticism. In this case, Joubert's

---

5. Clausewitz omits another reasonable explanation: it would not behoove a revolutionary government to admit to major errors in such a successful campaign. Doing so surely would have enhanced Napoleon's prestige while undermining the government's, with possibly fatal political consequences.

6. Here, it is worth noting Clausewitz's comments in *On War* on the military commander and his genius (book 1, chap. 3), as well as the role played by moral factors in war (book 3, chaps. 1–7).

7. Clausewitz is pointing out the problem of dividing a force. He is not saying it should never be done but that the size of the forces should be matched to the task to give them a realistic chance of success. If this is not possible, he suggests finding an alternative means of achieving the same aim or not dividing the force.

corps would have been merely maintaining communications, and so long as the main bodies are set on striking major, decisive blows, such corps are not really necessary and are therefore a pernicious dissipation of effort. General Joubert got into a most adverse situation and was lucky to join Bonaparte four weeks later with his army reduced by a third. This adequately demonstrates that he belonged there, not in the Tyrol.

In his *Memoirs*, Bonaparte presents the episode as though this had been Joubert's mission from the beginning; but he is doing the same as he does with the instruction he gave to Ney after the battle of Ligny, when he subsequently tries to distort it from being a divergent maneuver to a convergent one. What a strange idea it would have been to direct this general to the foot of the Brenner to start with and thereby march to Villach by a detour of more than 135 miles! This notion does not appear at all in the contemporary documents, and in his history of the campaign, General Jomini presents General Joubert's decamping through the Puster valley as simply an escape route the general took on his own initiative.[8]

With regard to the Austrians, we must resolve one very important question of strategy, concerning a major topic that recurs frequently.

If the Austrians had concentrated Archduke Charles's army in the Tyrol rather than in Friuli, leaving Carinthia and Carniola open, they easily could have had an army of 40,000 there before Bonaparte began his campaign, since the divisions from the Rhine army could have joined it much sooner. These 40,000 men, supported by the Tyrolese militia, would have constituted an armed host very different from the corps the archduke mustered on the Tagliamento.[9]

Let us consider the advantages and disadvantages of this measure.

Such a deployment in the Tyrol would have been a flank position in relation to the road to Vienna through Friuli and Carinthia, and as such, it was unarguably very strong in many respects:

8. Colin, 321, notes: "Joubert did indeed have to undertake this march on his own initiative, since he had received no orders from Bonaparte; but his instructions said to stay at Trient until the army had crossed the Tagliamento, then to move to Toblach, and finally to Klagenfurt when this city became Bonaparte's center of operations."

9. In his memoirs, Napoleon explicitly references the support of the people of the Tyrol for the Austrians, implying its obvious importance. See Montholon, *Mémoires pour servir à l'Histoire de France sous Napoléon*, 4:282–283.

1. This position's lines of communication with its depots and with the actual theater of operations, and via these with the rest of the empire, could not easily be taken or even threatened;
2. Whereas if the enemy wanted to march past this position and take the Friuli road, his line of communications would have been threatened in a most effective way, so that even Bonaparte would not have risked taking the road to Vienna that had been left uncovered;
3. Vienna, which may be regarded as the principal object of the enemy's operation, was so far away that it could be considered completely protected by such a flank position.

Because of all these circumstances, it is beyond doubt that if the archduke had stayed in the Tyrol, the French would have been able to advance only through the Tyrol.

However, even if the archduke had been 40,000 strong in the Tyrol, and even if the assistance of the militia increased his power of resistance by a not insignificant amount, we must not forget:

1. That in this situation, Bonaparte certainly would not have divided his force, but would have invaded the Tyrol with close to 70,000 men;
2. That a mountain region is advantageous for the defense only where a small force needs to put up a comparatively long resistance,[10] but in an outright decision between both sides' main bodies, it is always unfavorable for the defender because, in the mountains, the defender loses the advantage that, in contemporary warfare, he normally derives from being able to respond to the enemy's actions with concealed reserves.[11]

10. Clausewitz argues that, by the end of the Napoleonic Wars, the defensive in mountain warfare had evolved greatly, and although the benefits of mountainous terrain appear to favor the defender, this is not always the case. If a defender is too passive and has created a cordon of small, strong positions—typical in mountainous terrain—an attacker can more easily concentrate on one of these. Now the defender is in the position of trying to reinforce a threatened point in the mountains, with all the physical difficulties this entails. Thus, the attacker has the advantage in this case. See Clausewitz, *On War*, book 6, chaps. 15–17 (417–432).

11. Clausewitz actually refers to the defender losing the *Vortheil der Hinterhand*. The *Hinterhand* is a term from card games, especially Skat, which was popular in Germany in the nineteenth century. The player who plays last, after all the other players'

Now, the fact that Bonaparte was more than a third stronger, and that the decisive action must take place in an extended position in the mountains, leaves scarcely any doubt that Bonaparte would have beaten the archduke and driven him out of the Tyrol with manifold losses. But this likely event was further bedeviled by the fact that the major highway to Vienna makes a bend through the Tyrol, so there was a high risk that the archduke's army would be driven away from Vienna and the lower Danube and would then be caught in a most disadvantageous situation for its retreat.

If, in addition, we consider that the archduke could no longer believe the Austrian army could put up a successful resistance on the Rhine, and that he could not know when or how quickly the French army would advance toward the Danube, then in these circumstances, the idea of deploying the main army for the defense of the Austrian empire in the Tyrol becomes very risky, and it is understandable that neither the Austrian government nor the archduke had the courage to do so. It could well have been called staking a briefly increased power of resistance against the risk of a major catastrophe.

This method would have been quite suitable if the Austrians' forces had been physically and morally equal to their opponent's and could aspire to secure their border against any invasion; however, when that balance of power has already been lost, this method is exactly the one that will produce an enemy invasion or, more precisely, one's own retreat into the interior of the country.

In his *Memoirs*, Bonaparte reproaches the archduke for not preferring the position in the Tyrol, but at the same time, he says elsewhere that he would have waited until he saw the archduke appear in the Tyrol and then would have pounced on him.[12]

---

cards are on the table, has the advantage of the *Hinterhand*. This is also interesting because Clausewitz states, "In the whole range of human activities, war most closely resembles a game of cards." *On War*, book 1, chap. 1, pt. 21 (86). Thus, one wonders whether he is referencing the popular game of Skat, and if so, what this means for his concept of chance.

12. We are not certain which section of the memoirs Clausewitz is referring to. However, for an analysis of the situation the archduke was dealing with that will help the reader understand Napoleon's argument, see Montholon, *Mémoires pour servir à l'Histoire de France sous Napoléon*, 4:282–283.

Let us turn now to the conditions that brought about the armistice of Leoben and the peace of Campo Formio.

This decision was obviously imposed on the Austrians primarily by Bonaparte's army and its menacing march on Vienna.

At the same time, this army seemed to be in a perilous situation itself. The Austrian state's forces were still intact; Bonaparte's army had just blazed a small trail into them and therefore looked like a weak vanguard. Consequently, it is commonly thought that Bonaparte was saved from the very brink of disaster by the weakness and hastiness of the Austrian government. Insofar as we regard Bonaparte's choice of a political solution as a prudent means of getting himself out of a dangerous situation, we depict his opponents as if they did not know how to appreciate these dangers. But it is really not like that. Bonaparte's situation was desperate if continuing his advance on Vienna would result in him clashing with superior forces that would make him pay for his impudence and against which victory would be very doubtful or even impossible; but in the absence of such a host, his situation ceased to be dangerous to that degree. It was only because he could not be certain about that, and because he knew nothing of Joubert's march through the Puster valley, that he thought his situation was worse than it actually was and worse than it could appear to the enemy. But here we are compelled to embark on a special digression to justify the way we have presented this situation.

In his *Memoirs*, Bonaparte specifically claims that his situation prior to the Leoben armistice did not seem at all dangerous to him and that, in concluding the armistice, he was not motivated by anything other than the Directory's assertion that he could not rely on any cooperation from the Army of the Rhine.

Sadly, we must not give full weight to a commander's assessment of his own actions; indeed, anyone who seeks the truth will come to the same conviction, and if he finds that the truth lies more in the circumstances than in the commander's testimony, he cannot sacrifice it to mere authority.

Bonaparte wrote his *Memoirs* fifteen to twenty years after these events, and with the intention of rebutting criticisms that had come to his attention concerning the individual deeds of his campaigns. In the circumstances, he is no longer unbiased, and even less so because he cannot tolerate any kind of blame, and it is quite impossible for him to acknowledge a single mistake, as the other great commanders so frequently do. This means that in using his *Memoirs*, we must be on our guard and must necessarily give more credence to contemporary reports and to conclusions that follow from the circumstances and from the course of events.[13]

We therefore have to ignore Bonaparte's claim that his situation in April 1797 did not seem at all dangerous to him and must hold to the view that emerges from every other known account. After all, what could have made this proud commander accept an armistice and thereby the start of peace negotiations? The Directory's news that he could not rely on any cooperation from the Army of the Rhine could not be interpreted in any other way than that the two Rhine armies would enter the field too late to render the Army of Italy any assistance with its impending decision. But even if this news arrived so dramatically that it pierced his wisdom like a bolt from the blue, it did not mean, as Bonaparte claims, that the other armies absolutely could not help him; the offensive on the Rhine had been decided on, and the force ratio left no doubt about its outcome.[14] Thus, he was motivated to open negotiations simply because he was worried that, in his situation, he could not wait for this cooperation. To make his claim seem more plausible, he also gives the number of troops available to him in Carinthia and Carniola as 60,000, when in fact he had only 45,000.

These are the reasons that have led us to stand by the view that Bonaparte offered the archduke an armistice to escape from a situation that was becoming more worrisome with every step. We do this only because we wish to be as truthful as possible, since the worry we attribute to the French commander makes no further contribution to the rest of our reasoning.

Having made this important disclosure, we return to our topic.

After Kaim's and Mercantin's divisions had joined him in the Julian Alps, increasing his strength by little more than what he had lost in the preceding two weeks, the archduke found no other troops on any of the other roads to Vienna, except for Spörcken's division, likewise newly arrived from the Rhine.

---

13. See *On War*, book 2, chaps. 4–6, for Clausewitz's take on critical analysis and the use of historical examples. Clausewitz is very clear on the need for facts, and they are pivotal in the first of his three intellectual activities required for critical analysis and understanding. The three are: "the discovery and interpretation of equivocal facts. . . . The tracing of events back to their causes. . . . The investigation and evaluation of the means employed. This last is criticism proper, involving praise and censure. Here theory serves history, or rather the lessons to be drawn from history." Clausewitz, *On War*, 156.

14. See Clausewitz's own explanation later in this text.

Thus, he was still so weak that Bonaparte could bring superior forces against him beneath the walls of the capital to give battle, which there was no doubt Bonaparte would have won. Since at this time the Rhine armies were still on the Rhine, 360–540 miles from Vienna, there could be no thought of quickly bringing up enough forces to overcome Bonaparte.

Thus, despite his very fraught situation, Bonaparte was still in a position to threaten Vienna.[15]

If the Austrians had been able to take advantage of the French commander's precarious position, to pounce on and overwhelm him with superior forces, to smash this isolated army, they would have had so much credit in the profit column that they could have settled the account for the rest of the campaign. If the means to do that had been available, then of course, there would have been no excuse for making peace.

However, since the Austrians lacked the means for a vigorous response against Bonaparte, all they could do was continue to retreat and defer the day of decision. This could have been done by the archduke defending Vienna and withdrawing into it, without a battle; by giving up Vienna and continuing his retreat toward Moravia; or by retreating from Bruck toward Hungary rather than Vienna, thereby taking the capital out of the game.[16]

Each of these three paths leads to Bonaparte cooperating with the other French armies. What matters, then, is not the balance between the Austrian

15. Here, it is worth reminding readers about the concept of the center of gravity. Often, the term refers to the center of mass or the main effort of an opposing force. However, in this case, those forces were miles away, and the key here was the threat to the Austrian capital: Vienna. Napoleon's direct threat to it had become the key to winning the campaign. It also shows that, in his arguments about the use of mass against the enemy's main force, Clausewitz was discussing circumstances in which that main force was the center of gravity, not that it was always the center of gravity. Given the presence of the Austrian government and the royal family's palaces in Vienna, all such courses of action would have carried serious negative practical and political consequences for the Austrians. With that in mind, it is reasonable to assume that in this case, the capital (Vienna) was the center of gravity at that time.

16. Unless, of course, the capital (object) was worth more to the Austrians than the ignominy of its abandonment to the French. In this case, either the Austrians overvalued their capital and caved in to Napoleon's threat to the city, or they were correct and gave in as soon as the cost of the conflict was greater than the potential gain to be obtained by holding out longer. See Clausewitz, *On War*, book 1, chap. 1 (75–99), book 8, chap. 4 (595–600).

state and Bonaparte's army but the balance between it and all three French armies, upon which collectively we must therefore turn our gaze.

The Army of the Rhine under Moreau was 70,000 strong, and the Army of the Meuse and Sambre under Hoche was 60,000, giving 130,000 French combined. The former faced Latour's 50,000 and the latter Werneck's 30,000, making 80,000 Austrians in total. This force ratio left no doubt that the two enemy armies could advance from the Rhine without any substantial delay and establish communications with the Army of Italy. Thus, there was no prospect of the Austrians recovering on this front what they had lost on the Italian one; they were at as much of a disadvantage here as there. If they lacked the means to destroy the Army of Italy while it was alone in its perilous position, the decision would have to be postponed and would have to rely in part on the combat forces currently on the Rhine; thus, the loss of the Tyrol, Austria, Styria, Carinthia, and Carniola was inevitable, and the loss of Vienna itself highly probable.

But still, this would not have meant the defeat of the Austrian empire; Bohemia, Moravia, and Hungary, with 120,000 men under arms, provided enough of a core of resistance to keep the final decision in doubt. If territorial conquests were to lead to the Austrian empire's defeat, allowing the imposition of whatever peace terms might be desired, there were only two ways to do so: to keep advancing with the intention of further destruction of enemy combat forces, pursuing them to the furthest frontiers of the empire and forcing them to lay down their arms there, as was done to the Prussians in 1806;[17] or, if this did not seem possible, to halt on some given line, establish oneself suitably in occupation of that stretch of country and hold on to what had been conquered, continue the war, and wait for the enemy's increasing weakness to bring about his surrender.[18]

As far as the first way is concerned, we must consider the Austrians' lines of retreat through Bohemia and Moravia to Hungary; that a mass of Austrian provinces would have been left to the flanks and rear of the advancing French

17. This was followed by the Treaty of Tilsit in July 1807, which imposed exceptionally hard terms on Prussia. Of course, as Clausewitz himself argues, the results of a conflict are never final. That is, the circumstances ending a war, and the means by which peace are maintained, are critical to the stability and duration of the outcome of a conflict. See Clausewitz, *On War*, book 1, chap. 1 (80).

18. This again returns us to Clausewitz's discussion of a culminating point. Ibid., book 8, chap. 22 (566–573).

armies, provinces that were partly armed already or could yet arm themselves; and that, although the three French armies were 200,000 strong initially, they would have to besiege Mainz, Mannheim, and Ehrenbreitstein and leave a force facing the Tyrol, and, as a result of the usual losses and inevitable weakening during the course of continuous advances across extensive stretches of territory, they would have been very much reduced. Taking all these things into consideration, we can hardly regard such an uninterrupted pursuit as anything more than a fiction, at most a remote possibility that is listed here purely for intellectual satisfaction. To march from one end to the other through an empire of 25 million people, while guarding a line of communications 600 miles long, requires an army of more than just 150,000 men. The flanking positions in Hungary and the Tyrol, not to mention Bohemia and the extensive alpine mountain ranges that would come into play, are very problematic factors. Such an operation requires large masses of troops, reserves following on (which the French entirely lacked), a firm and consistent government (which the French one was not), and good, secure, and reliable administrative organs (which France did not have). Hence we do not believe the French would have embarked on an invasion on this scale, and we are convinced that if they had, sooner or later they would have had to yield to circumstances and retreat, even without being forced to do so by a battle. This retreat would have involved heavy losses and would have carried the war back to the Rhine and the Mincio again. Thus, if its interests had urgently required it to act differently, the Austrian government could have carried on to the bitter end.[19]

The second way was, of course, much more feasible for the French—except that however much the French commanders concentrated their forces on whatever line they adopted, in the long run, the combat forces they brought with them would never be sufficient to maintain themselves in such an advanced position; so here too, significant reserves would be necessary. But the difference here was that the reserves would not be needed so quickly because matters would not be brought to a decision so soon. Significant resources could be mustered by autumn or winter, which was when the French might be

---

19. Clearly, in the Austrians' assessment, the value of the object was not sufficiently high in relation to the cost of continuing the conflict. Clausewitz is hammering home this point, presumably because of his own experience, along with Prussia's, following the latter's miscalculation in starting the disastrous war with France that culminated in the Prussian defeat at Jena-Auerstädt on 14 October 1806.

in danger of being overwhelmed. Furthermore, in the first case, the Austrians really just needed perseverance, because the turn in fortunes would have come about by itself, whereas in the second case, the Austrians would have to undertake more active efforts, and they would have to conduct them well.

If we therefore find that the only path the victorious enemy could take was not without hazard for him, and if we hold that, given appropriate effort and endurance on the part of the defeated party, the final outcome would probably be more against the victor than in his favor, then the reader must wonder what causes the disappearance of a factor that was very much present, and he may justifiably demand that the critic demonstrate what happened to it. The French advance victoriously and in superior numbers, yet they end up at the same unfavorable result they started with. This seems to entail a contradiction.

The solution to this riddle lies in the weakening that any strategic offensive suffers during its progress *eo ipso* and increases until the opponent is rendered defenseless, that is, until his combat forces are destroyed. Thus, the victor's superiority must be in proportion to the size of the enemy state if the latter is not to attain parity and later superiority on the decisive battlefield. But here, this was not the case; against an empire like Austria, an advantage of 50,000– 60,000 men in the field must soon be exhausted.

Thus, we believe that in 1797, despite their great moral advantage and whichever path they took, the French would not have been in a position to render the Austrian monarchy defenseless and thereby force it to accept whatever terms they wished. From this, it follows that the Austrian government needed only persistence, energy, and wisdom to come through this crisis and return to a state closer to parity with France.[20]

Does it follow from this that the Austrians agreed too hastily to the Treaty

---

20. Here, Clausewitz's point is that, if the enemy has not lost the ability to resist, imposing one's will on him is more difficult, especially if the enemy chooses a negative aim. That is, the enemy continues the fight but seeks merely to avoid total defeat, thus prolonging the conflict. See *On War*, book 1, chaps. 1 and 2, for his discussion of "What Is War" and "Purpose and Means in War." Clearly, for whatever reason, the Austrians had lost the will to resist the French, based on what they expected to gain from the conflict. When they discovered that the French Revolution had moved the goalposts, they were unwilling to accept the revised outcome and thus more willing to renew the conflict, as the benefits again outweighed the likely costs. This cycle was the norm for the next twenty years, until Napoleon and France were crushed after Waterloo and an acceptable peace was made after 1815.

of Leoben? We think not. The question arises: was the sacrifice entailed in riding out the whole crisis, and the possible danger associated with doing so, worth the aim that could be achieved? If, by their efforts and endurance, the Austrians became the strategic victors and the French had to withdraw from their German lands, the war would have been carried back to the Rhine and the Mincio; the rebound could not have reached any further.

This is not to contradict what we said earlier, that a reversal of fortunes could have thrown Bonaparte's army back to the Maritime Alps, since this applied only if that one army could be overwhelmed and crushed before the others arrived. The same consequences would not ensue if all three armies had linked up and then made a concerted withdrawal.

If we now cast an eye over the peace terms of Leoben, we find that the Austrians only gave up what they could hardly have recovered anyway—the Low Countries, the province of Milan as far as the Oglio—or they relinquished what was of no great value to them, such as Nice, Savoy, and Modena. At that time, the French did not demand the right bank of the Rhine. Those same concessions still would have been appropriate even if the Austrians had been standing on the Rhine and the Mincio, since they were occupied by the French, and the Austrians did not have the means to drive them out.[21]

Thus, it is natural that at the moment the Austrians were seriously threatened by the impending blows, facing the prospect of a series of unfavorable passages of arms and of their moral strength taking another battering, the peace terms they were offered—which could not have been much better even if they did come through the crisis well—seemed very appealing.

This was the motivation for the Austrian decision of April 1797, insofar as it arose directly from the military situation. What the Austrian government agreed to later that year, the much greater concessions they made to the French system (the left bank of the Rhine and the right bank of the Adige),[22]

---

21. Here, Clausewitz makes another important point about matching strategy to policy ends. In this case, it was not possible to hold on to those possessions militarily, so why not make the best of the situation and use them as a bargaining chip to get something more useful? In other words, alter the ends of strategy to match the means available to achieve them. This advice would be applicable to our political leaders of the last decade or so.

22. The Treaty of Campo Formio, 27 October 1797, moved the French frontier to the Rhine and French influence via the Cisalpine Republic to the Adige. The Austrian concessions to the French in the Treaty of Campo Formio were substantially greater

was no longer a consequence of desperate straits in military terms. It was a purely political transaction, since in exchange, they received compensation at the expense of Venice and Germany. The Austrian government, deserted by all its allies on the Continent, and with no prospect of finding new ones, decided to seek its salvation in a shortsighted and selfish policy; as such, this was no longer a product of need, a direct consequence of their military situation, so it is of no further interest to us.[23]

We concede that it would have been more heroic and magnificent to continue the fight right to the edge of the abyss and then, through perseverance and energy, return to military parity; that favorable new political combinations might become not only possible but even probable; that to act thus would be not only a fine thing but also a wise one, since the loss of political parity with France made it quite foreseeable that sooner or later it must engage in a fight to the death with that power. But what policy heads for the most extreme horizon? And there is a big difference between a government that refrains from raising the stakes to include absolutely everything, and one that commits a sheer blunder, a folly of hasty weakness.

Besides, we must not forget that the strategic reasoning we can and should wield now did not come so naturally then. The growing power of resistance carried to its utmost limits by great states, and the difficulty of maintaining the occupation of extensive captured territories, had not yet shown such vivid examples as those we have seen since, when Bonaparte's immense power carried him more than once to those limits, where it was not so much his opponent that defeated him as the nature of things.[24]

---

than they had been in the preliminary Treaty of Leoben on 18 April 1797. Had these revised costs been clear to the Austrians, it is possible they would not have agreed to the peace at Leoben, given that their preliminary agreement was based on a calculation of the costs and benefits at that time. See Clausewitz, *On War*, book 1, chap. 2 (90–99).

23. Again, Clausewitz is referring to the value of the object to be attained, its likely cost, and his argument that the result of war is never final.

24. Here, in particular, Clausewitz is referring to the war in Spain from 1808 to 1814, the French invasion of Russia in 1812, and, to a lesser extent, the war of liberation in Germany in 1813. In each of these conflicts, the value of the object to some (if not many) of the participants was so great that they were prepared to escalate the violence to attain their ends. In these three wars, within the longer series of wars, frightful massacres and depredations were commonplace, and the scale of destruction increased immensely.

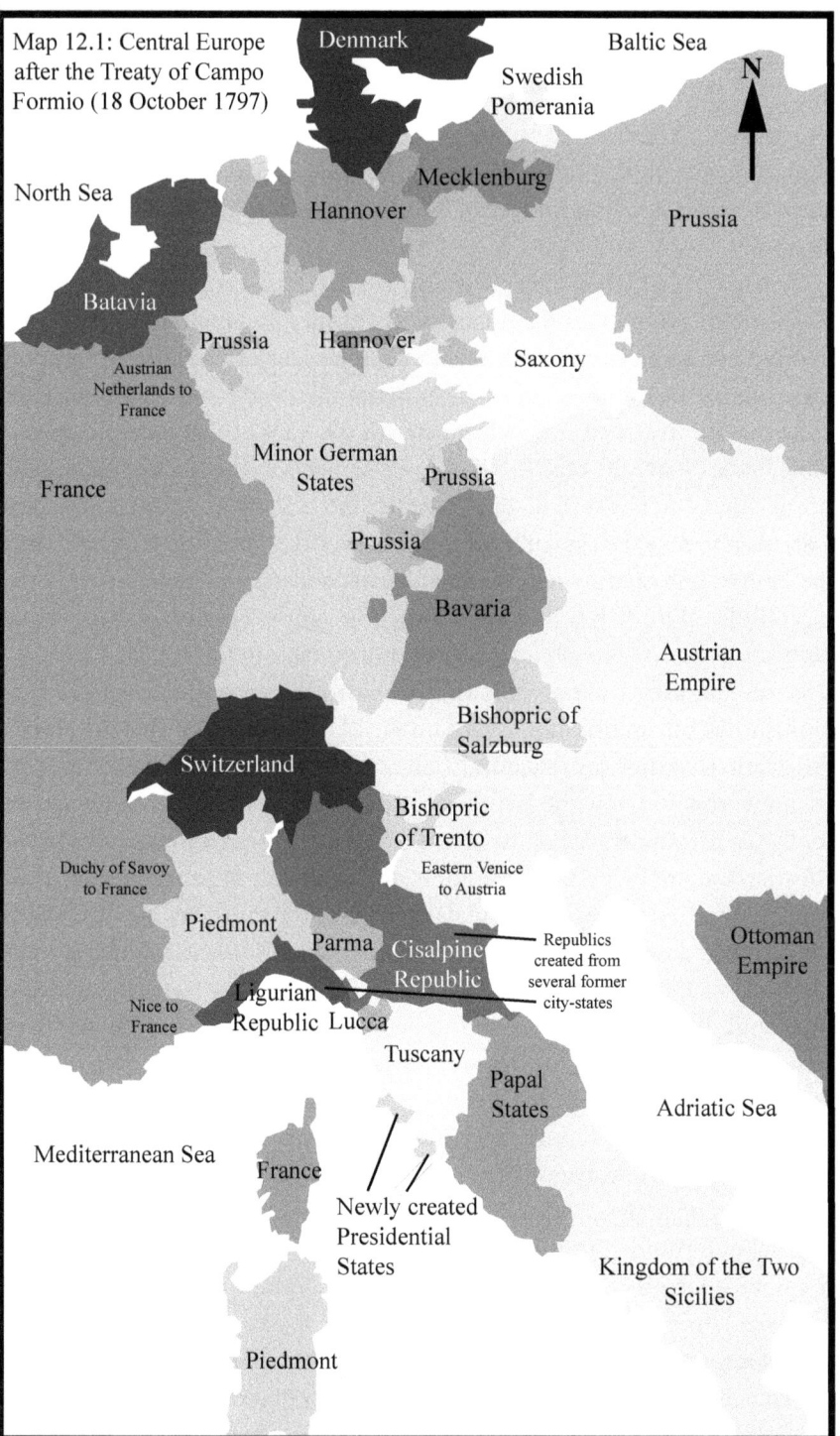

Map 12.1: Central Europe after the Treaty of Campo Formio (18 October 1797)

CLOSING REMARKS

Our reflections on the 1797 campaign and on how its lines finished at the conclusion of the whole lead us to emphasize how differently the verdict on a given strategic situation turns out, based on how we shift our standpoint or viewpoint.

Bonaparte's situation after crossing the Julian Alps seems highly dangerous if we have to assume that the Austrians are mustering superior forces beyond the Styrian Alps to overwhelm him; but if our horizon extends so that we know these masses are not there, this danger disappears, and now it is the Austrian army that is threatened with defeat beneath the walls of Vienna if it risks one more battle to save the capital. The Franco-Italian army seems like a gathering storm cloud. But if we extend our gaze once more, if the Austrians do not seek a decision to save the capital but defer it to save the whole, then straightaway the Franco-Italian army appears inadequate, and seen in isolation, it could be considered to be heading for destruction simply because of the delayed decision. Thus, the probable outcome is unfavorable to the French. However, if we do not restrict ourselves to this one army but expand our field of view over the two other armies appearing on the Rhine, this reveals that the French force ratio is so superior that it must carry the war from the Rhine to the Austrian interior, and now the insufficiency of the Army of Italy is compensated for by the preponderance of the others. Now an invasion into the heart of the Austrian empire by all three armies is no longer out of proportion to their strength, and this invasion is the danger that now threatens Austria. While the Austrian government sees this invasion as an evil in itself, which it must seek to avert through a speedy peace, to the French, it just seems like a means to an end. If we consider this end to be the total overthrow of the Austrian state, that is, continuing the invasion to its furthest frontier to destroy its last combat forces there, then the result, the likely final outcome, changes again. According to all our recent experience, if the Austrian people did not lack loyalty to their ruling dynasty, the French combat forces would be insufficient for such an operation, and the continued invasion itself would bring about a reversal of fortunes. But if we do not limit our gaze to this possibility and let it embrace the other, that the French do not continue their invasion to the opposite border but stop on a given line, then the hope of a spontaneously arising reversal of fortunes in favor of the Austrians disappears again, because the French have time to make good the deficiency in their forces. Now even in this situation, the final outcome probably remains in favor of the Austrians, but this probability is much less, and it will require great sacrifice, great effort, and appropriate action.

Among these various standpoints, the one from which the strategic situation should be judged is determined by the nature of things, either because one's gaze cannot penetrate beyond a certain line—as in the case of Bonaparte when he crossed the Julian Alps—or because the object on which one's gaze is fixed and to which all one's lines of perspective lead is overwhelmingly important, as retaining Vienna and preventing an enemy invasion were for the Austrians. In 1814 and 1815 the capture of Paris was of such primary importance that it necessarily dictated the perspective of all lines of strategy.

If this importance is so great that no price is too high for the peace terms that will avert the evil, then this simple corollary must result in peace.

The verdict on this last calculation, which has profound strategic implications, must come out differently according to whether this importance has been recognized or misjudged. It is in the nature of things that, even here at the highest level and in a simple act of deliberation, character and attitude, which play such a large part in war, still have a major influence on the verdict. This is why the steadfast and courageous commander will see his situation differently from the fainthearted. This is especially the case during the actual business. But when we are merely evaluating—especially in the world of writers, where everyone is steadfast and courageous—differences of view arise mostly from misjudging the prevailing conditions. This often occurs through lack of data, but more often through lack of a true spirit of critical inquiry.

Appendix
Select Orders of Battle

The following orders of battle are meant to provide a guide to the makeup of the armies involved in the campaign and should not be considered definitive.[1] This is because the number of soldiers fit for duty changed daily due to injury, death, sickness, detachments, reinforcements, and so forth. That being said, we believe this information will give readers a better idea of what an army looked like in terms of the men, horses, and equipment involved. This information also helps explain Clausewitz's concept of friction (*On War*, book 1, chap. 7) and the corresponding need for genius in war (book 1, chap. 3). Each piece listed below is made up of hundreds if not thousands of individual parts, any one of which might fail at an inopportune moment, bringing disaster.

AUSTRIAN ARMY, APRIL 1796

Commander in chief: Feldzeugmeister Freiherr Beaulieu de Marconnay.

Infantry—36 battalions (bns) (strengths per returns of 10 April)

Carlstädter Grenz-Regiment (Regt) (2 bns—2,208)
Szluiner Grenz-Regt (1 bn—928)
Nadasdy Regt (2 bns—1,518)
Archduke Anton Regt (2 bns—1,156)
Alvinzi Regt (2 bns—1,643)
Reisky Regt (3 bns—1,788)
Terzy Regt (3 bns—1,848)
Brechainville Regt (1 bn—607)

---

1. Orders of battle from Hermann Joseph von Kuhl, *Bonapartes erster Feldzug 1796: der Ausgangspunkt moderner Kriegführung* (Berlin: R. Eisenschmidt, 1902), 322–335. This is a secondary source and should be treated as such, although even primary sources for this sort of material are good only for the day of the record itself, assuming it was recorded accurately in the first place.

Lattermann Regt (2 bns—1,200)
Strassoldo Regt (2 bns—1,199)
Schröder Regt (1 bn—570)
Thurn Regt (3 bns—2,233)
Colloredo Regt (2 bns—1,497)
Huff Regt (2 bns—1,561)
Pellegrini Regt (1 bn—806)
Deutschmeister Regt (1 bn—822)
Preiss Regt (1 bn—811)
Stain Regt (1 bn—869)
Grand Duke of Tuscany Regt (1 bn—755)

Arrived in Pavia mid-April:

Wallis Regt (1 bn)
Warasdiner Banal Grenz-Regiment (1 bn)

Garrison duty in Milan—unfit for field service: Jordis Regt (1 bn).
Average strength of the line battalions, 685 men fit for duty; of the *Grenzer* battalions, about 1,000 men

Cavalry

Meszaros Uhlan Regt (8 squadrons [sqns])
Erdödy Hussar Regt (2 sqns)
Archduke Joseph Hussar Regt (10 sqns)

Total strength: 3,139 men fit for duty; average strength, 157 men per squadron.[2]

Artillery (approximately 150 pieces)

76 3-pounder (pdr) battalion guns (2 per infantry bn)[3]

2. If one includes spare horses, the number of horses for the cavalry alone would be around 3,200. This is approximate and is mentioned merely to help the reader gauge the size of the forces involved.

3. For artillery, a quick method to assess the number of horses is roughly 1 horse per pound of shot for horse artillery and about half that for foot artillery, along with another 4–6 horses for the ammunition caissons. A single 6-pounder cannon would

69 guns in the Reserve Artillery:

26 6-pdr cannon

20 12-pdr cannon

14 7-pdr howitzers

3 1-pdr mountain guns

4 6-pdr horse artillery cannon

2 7-pdr horse artillery howitzers

(Per 21 April; therefore, possibly excluding some guns lost on 13–15 April.)

Neapolitan Auxiliary Cavalry

This force was in Lombardy at the start of operations in April 1796. Its strength was estimated at about 600 men per regiment:

Commander: Prince Cuto

King's Regt (4 sqns)

Queen's Regt (4 sqns)

Crown Prince's Regt (4 sqns)

Arrived in Lombardy in second half of April: (unnamed) cavalry regt.

Austrian Auxiliary Corps

This force operated with the Sardinian forces under Colli's command:

Belgioioso Infantry Regt (2 bns)

Strassoldo Infantry Regt (2 grenadier companies)

2nd Garrison Regt (1 bn)

Gyulay Freikorps (3 bns)

Staff Dragoons (4 sqns)

---

need 3–4 horses to move it, along with a similar number of horses to move its ammunition. However, gun teams were pulled by pairs of horses, so that must be taken into account. A six-gun 6-pounder foot battery with ammunition wagons would need roughly 48 horses and 100 men. Furthermore, larger guns would require a corresponding increase in the size of the crew. For a more detailed examination of the topic, see George Nafziger, *Imperial Bayonets: Tactics of the Napoleonic Battery, Battalion and Brigade as Found in Contemporary Regulations* (London: Greenhill Press, 1996).

Artillery reserve—stationed in Turin throughout: 1st Garrison Regt (1 bn)

Strength return for 25 April 1796 lists total strength as 2,919, of which 2,477 fit for duty. Allowing for serious losses from the Belgioioso regiment at Cosseria, and for 7½ companies of the Gyulay Freikorps that surrendered with Provera on 14 April, the total fit for duty at the start of operations was estimated at 3,500.

SARDINIAN ARMY, 1796

Sardinian Infantry Regiments

> Guard Regt (2 bns)
> Savoy Regt (2 bns)
> Montferrat Regt (2 bns)
> Piedmont Regt (2 bns)
> Saluzzo Regt (2 bns)
> Aosta Regt (2 bns)
> La Marina Regt (2 bns)
> Chablais Regt (2 bns)
> Queen's Regt (2 bns)
> Sardinia Regt (2 bns)
> Lombardy Regt (2 bns)

> Newly raised since 1792: Oneglia Regt (2 bns).

Foreign Mercenary Infantry Regiments

> Royal German Regt (2 bns)
> Valais (Swiss) Regt (2 bns)
> Bern (Swiss) Regt (2 bns)
> Graubünden (Swiss) Regt (2 bns)

> Newly raised since 1792:

> Schmid (Swiss) Regt (2 bns)
> Zimmermann (Swiss) Regt (2 bns)

Bachmann (Swiss) Regt (2 bns)

Peyer-im-Hof (Swiss) Regt (2 bns)

Expanded from the Depot Legion since 1792: King's Grenadier Regt (2 bns).

Created in 1795–1796 from the infantry regiments' grenadier and light companies:

Grenadier Bns 1–11

Light Bns 1 and 2

Provincial Infantry Regiments

Genoa Regt (2 bns)

Maurienne Regt (2 bns)

Ivrea Regt (2 bns)

Turin Regt (2 bns)

Nizza Regt (2 bns)

Mondovi Regt (2 bns)

Vercelli Regt (2 bns)

Asti Regt (2 bns)

Pinerolo Regt (2 bns)

Casale Regt (2 bns)

Novara Regt (2 bns)

Tortona Regt (2 bns)

Susa Regt (2 bns)

Acqui Regt (2 bns)

Other Infantry

Light Legion (4 bns)

Expanded from the Depot Legion since 1792: Pioneer Regt (2 bns).

Cavalry Regiments

King's Dragoon Regt (4 sqns)

Piedmont Dragoon Regt (4 sqns)

Sardinia Dragoon Regt (4 sqns)

Queen's Dragoon Regt (4 sqns)
Chablais Dragoon Regt (4 sqns)
Chevauleger Regt (4 sqns)
Royal Piedmont Regt (4 sqns)
Aosta Regt (4 sqns)
Savoy Regt (4 sqns)

Other

4 artillery bns
1 labor/miner company
Engineers (2 bns)
Freikorps (10 companies)
Nizza Light Infantry (2 bns)
King's Bodyguard (a small body of household troops, both infantry and cavalry)

FRENCH ARMY OF ITALY, 4 APRIL 1796[4]

Commander in chief: Général de division Bonaparte.
  Chief of staff: Général de division Berthier.

Division La Harpe

Brigadiers: Pigeon (absent sick), Ménard, Cervoni.

1st Light Demi-brigade (17th Light)[5]

---

4. The composition of formations changed constantly during the campaign, as demi-brigades were reallocated among brigades and brigades were transferred between divisions. Kuhl, *Bonapartes erster Feldzug 1796*, 324–325.

5. Unit designations in parentheses are those superseded in the *amalgame* (reorganization) of May 1796. The French army was undergoing a process of reorganization, and not all the units had been reformed. Where the order of battle notes "old formation," it indicates that this is an unreformed unit. In the reorganization process, the unit would become a demi-brigade, which was made up of three battalions of roughly 800 men each, and four cannon. This combined-arms formation proved extremely flexible and useful in combat and contrasted well with the more rigid

16th Light Demi-brigade (22nd Light)[6]
21st Line Demi-brigade (32nd)
70th Line Demi-brigade (75th)

Division Meynier

Brigadiers: Dommartin, Joubert.

3rd Light Demi-brigade (11th Light)
84th Line Demi-brigade (25th)
99th Line Demi-brigade (51st)
4th Light Demi-brigade (27th Light)
51st Line Demi-brigade (old formation)
55th Line Demi-brigade (old formation)

Division Augereau

Brigadiers: Beyrand, Victor, Banel, Rusca.

8th Light Demi-brigade (4th Light)
18th Light Demi-brigade (29th Light)
39th Line Demi-brigade (4th)

---

organization of the armies of France's opponents. Furthermore, the demi-brigade used a mix of regular and conscript troops, thus combining the enthusiasm of revolutionary French conscripts with the discipline and knowledge of regular soldiers. This made a potent combination, and it also allowed mass armies to quickly generate combat formations with only a relatively small drop in initial combat power. For analyses of the changes in the French and other armies of the period, as well as the wars more broadly, see Frederick C. Schneid, ed., *European Armies of the French Revolution: 1789–1802* (Norman: University of Oklahoma Press, 2015); Jean Paul Bertaud, *The Army of the French Revolution: From Citizen-Soldiers to Instrument of Power* (Princeton, NJ: Princeton University Press, 1988); Daniel Moran and Arthur Waldron, *The People in Arms: Military Myth and National Mobilization since the French Revolution* (Cambridge: Cambridge University Press, 2003); John A. Lynn, *The Bayonets of the Republic: Motivation and Tactics in the Army of Revolutionary France, 1791–94* (Urbana: University of Illinois, 1984); Charles J. Esdaile, *The Wars of Napoleon* (New York: Routledge, 1995).

6. Kuhl notes: "The 16th did not take part in the initial operations as it was still on the march via Nice." Kuhl, *Bonapartes erster Feldzug 1796*, 322.

69th Line Demi-brigade (18th)
14th Line Demi-brigade (old formation)

Division Sérurier

Brigadiers: Guieu, Pelletier, Fiorella, Miollis.

19th Line Demi-brigade (69th)
46th Line Demi-brigade (39th)
56th Line Demi-brigade (85th)

Division Macquard

100th Line Demi-brigade (45th)
22nd Line Demi-brigade (old formation)

Division Garnier

20th Line Demi-brigade (11th)

Coastal Divisions

1st Coastal Division (Marseille): General Puget
2nd Coastal Division (Toulon): General Mouret
3rd Coastal Division (Nice): General Casabianca
4th Coastal Division (Oneglia): General Casalta

Cavalry

Général de division Stengel.
1st Division: Général de brigade Beaumont.

1st Hussars
10th, 22nd, 25th Chasseurs
5th and 20th Dragoons

2nd Division: Général de division Kilmaine.

7th and 13th Hussars

24th Chasseurs
8th and 15th Dragoons

Artillery

1st, 2nd, 4th, and 5th Artillery Regts (19 companies)
Infantry regimental artillery (42 companies)

Approximately 400 guns (including about 90 mountain guns and 145 siege guns).

Engineers

5th Sapper Bn (6 companies)
6th Sapper Bn (8 companies)
3 sapper companies (auxiliaries)
2 mining companies

FRENCH ARMY OF ITALY, 29 APRIL 1796

Division La Harpe

Brigadiers: Robert, Ménard
Regiments: 15th Light (newly attached, still en route), 70th, 99th, 14th (old formation)

Division Augereau

Brigadiers: Beyrand, Victor, Rusca
Regiments: 4th Light, 18th Light, 39th, 69th

Division Masséna

Brigadiers: Joubert, Dommartin
Regiments: 1st Light, 3rd Light, 8th Light, 21st, 84th, 51st (old formation)

Division Sérurier

Brigadiers: Guieu, Pelletier, Fiorella
Regiments: 16th Light, 19th, 20th, 100th

Cavalry

1st Division: Général de division Kilmaine.

> 1st Hussars
> 22nd and 25th Chasseurs
> 8th and 20th Dragoons

> 2nd Division: Général de brigade Beaumont.

> 7th and 13th Hussars
> 10th and 24th Chasseurs
> 5th and 15th Dragoons

Of the four divisions' original infantry regiments, two of Sérurier's (46th and 56th) were garrisoning Tortona and Cuneo, one of Meynier's (55th) was in Cherasco, and one of Macquard's (22nd) was in Ceva. The 12th Regiment from Casalta's coastal division was in Mondovi.

Artillery

> 1st, 2nd, 4th, and 5th Artillery Regts (19 companies)
> Infantry regimental artillery (42 companies)

Approximately 400 guns (including about 90 mountain guns and 145 siege guns).

Engineers

> 5th Sapper Bn (6 companies)
> 6th Sapper Bn (8 companies)
> 3 sapper companies (auxiliaries)
> 2 mining companies

Kuhl cites Koch, who gives the total strength of the Army of Italy on 4 April 1796 as 63,000 (including 3,604 en route). Of these, the field army, excluding cavalry, was only 31,300; the coastal divisions, 21,500; and Macquard and Garnier, some 6,800. By contrast, Kuhl reckons the coastal divisions had been reduced to 11,900 by Bonaparte, which would increase the field army to some 44,000 men. However, Kuhl thinks this figure is too high.[7]

The four divisions of the field army can be estimated with some certainty at 37,000 men, including infantry, artillery, and engineers. Estimates of the cavalry strength vary from 3,354 to 4,868, of which the lower figure is more likely.[8]

7. Kuhl, *Bonapartes erster Feldzug 1796*, 324, references Koch, "Offiziellen Etats aus dem Kriegsarchiv," which is from Koch, *Mémoires de Masséna*, vol. 2 (Paris: Paulin et Lechevalier, Libraires-Éditeurs, 1848).

8. Kuhl, *Bonapartes erster Feldzug 1796*, 322–335.

Bibliography

BOOKS AND ARTICLES

Adlow, Elijah. *Napoleon in Italy 1796–1797*. Boston: William J. Rochefort, 1948.
Bassford, Christopher. "Clausewitz and His Works." http://www.clausewitz.com /readings/Bassford/Cworks/Works.htm. Accessed 23 February 2017.
———. "Tip-Toe through the Trinity: The Strange Persistence of Trinitarian Warfare." https://www.clausewitz.com/mobile/trinity8.htm. Accessed 14 August 2017.
Bellinger, Vanya Eftimova. *Marie von Clausewitz: The Woman behind the Making of On War*. Oxford: Oxford University Press, 2016.
Bertaud, Jean Paul. *The Army of the French Revolution: From Citizen-Soldiers to Instrument of Power*. Princeton, NJ: Princeton University Press, 1988.
Bouvier, Félix. *Bonaparte en Italie 1796*. Paris: Librairie Léopold Cerf., 1899.
Boycott-Brown, Martin. *The Road to Rivoli: Napoleon's First Campaign*. London: Cassell, 2001.
Brewer, John. *The Sinews of Power: War, Money and the English State 1688–1783*. Cambridge, MA: Harvard University Press, 1990.
Broers, Michael. "Revolt and Repression in Napoleonic Italy 1796–1814." In *War in an Age of Revolution 1775–1815*, ed. Roger Chickering and Stig Förster, 197–218. New York: Cambridge University Press, 2010.
Bülow, Heinrich von. *Geist des Neuern Kriegssystems*. Hamburg: August Campe, 1835.
Carlyle, Thomas. *The French Revolution: A History in Three Volumes*. London: Chapman and Hall, 1896.
Clausewitz, Carl von. *La Campagne de 1796 en Italie*, trans. Captain J. Colin. Paris: Librairie Militaire de L. Baudoin, 1899.
———. *On War*, ed. and trans. Michael Howard and Peter Paret. Princeton, NJ: Princeton University Press, 1989.
———. *On War*, trans. O. J. Matthijs Jolles. New York: Modern Library, 2000.
———. *Vom Kriege*. 3 vols. Berlin: Ferdinand Dümmler, 1832–1834.
Correspondance inédite, officielle et confidentielle, de Napoléon Bonaparte avec les cours étrangères, les princes, les ministres et les généraux français et étrangers en Italie, en Allemagne et en Égypte. 14 vols. Paris: C. L. F. Panckoucke, 1819–1820.
Cuccia, Phillip. *Napoleon in Italy: The Sieges of Mantua 1796–1799*. Norman: University of Oklahoma Press, 2014.
Decker, Karl von. *Der Feldzug in Italien in den Jahren 1796 und 1797*. Berlin: Ernst Siegfried Mittler, 1825.
Douglas, Major-General Sir Howard. *An Essay on the Principles and Construction of Military Bridges, and the Passage of Rivers in Military Operations*. London: Thomas and William Boone, 1832.

Echevarria, Antulio J., II. "War, Politics, and RMA: The Legacy of Clausewitz." *Joint Forces Quarterly* 9 (Winter 1995–1996): 76–80.

Erdmannsdorf, G. A. von. *Der Feldzug von 1796 in Italien.* Magdeburg: Verlag von Fabricus und Schaefer, 1847.

Erzherzog, Karl von Österreich. *Grundsätze der Strategie erläutert durch die Darstellung des Feldzugs von 1796 in Deutschland.* 4 vols. Vienna: Anton Strauss, 1814.

Esdaile, Charles J. *The Wars of Napoleon.* New York: Routledge, 1995.

Forsyth, William. *History of the Captivity of Napoleon at St. Helena; from the Letters and Journals of the Late Lieut.-Gen. Sir Hudson Lowe.* 3 vols. London: John Murray, 1853.

"Franziszeische Landesaufnahme (1806–1869)." http://mapire.eu. Accessed 18 September 2017.

Gahan, Daniel. *The People's Rising: Wexford, 1798.* Dublin: Gill and Macmillan, 1995.

Gat, Azar. *A History of Military Thought: From the Enlightenment to the Cold War.* Oxford: Oxford University Press, 2001.

Graham, J. M. *Histoire des Campagnes d'Italie, d'Allemagne et de Suisse en 1796, 97, 98 et 99.* Paris: Fournier, 1817.

Handel, Michael. *Masters of War: Classical Strategic Thought.* 3rd ed. London: Frank Cass, 2001.

Heuser, Beatrice. *Strategy before Clausewitz: Linking Warfare and Statecraft, 1400–1830.* Abingdon, UK: Routledge, 2018.

Hilgers, Philipp von. *Kriegsspiele eine Geschichte der Ausnahmezustände und Unberechenberkeiten.* Munich: Wilhelm Fink Verlag, 2008.

Hochedlinger, Michael. *Austria's Wars of Emergence, 1683–1797.* New York: Routledge, 2013.

Honig, Jan Willem. "Clausewitz and the Politics of Early Modern Warfare." In *Clausewitz the State and War*, ed. Andreas Herberg-Rothe, Jan Willem Honig, and Daniel Moran, 29–48. Stuttgart: Franz Steiner Verlag, 2011.

Jomini, Lieutenant-Général. *Histoire Critique et Militaire des Guerres de la Révolution.* 15 vols. Paris: Chez Anselin et Pochard, 1819–1824.

Kuhl, Hermann Joseph von. *Bonapartes erster Feldzug 1796: der Ausgangspunkt moderner Kriegführung.* Berlin: R. Eisenschmidt, 1902.

Liddell-Hart, Basil. *Strategy.* New York: Praeger, 1967.

Lynn, John A. *The Bayonets of the Republic: Motivation and Tactics in the Army of Revolutionary France, 1791–94.* Urbana: University of Illinois, 1984.

———. *The Wars of Louis XIV 1667–1714.* New York: Routledge, 2013.

Marchina, C., G. Bianchini, C. Natali, et al. "The Po River Water from the Alps to the Adriatic Sea (Italy): New Insights from Geochemical and Isotopic (δ18O-δD) Data." *Environmental Science and Pollution Research* 22, 7 (April 2015): 5184–5203. http://link.springer.com/article/10.1007%2Fs11356-014-3750-6. Accessed 18 September 2017.

Masson, Frédéric. *Les Diplomates de la Révolution: Hugou de Bassville a Rome, Bernadotte a Vienne.* Paris: Charavay Fréres Editeurs, 1882.

McNeill, William H. *Venice, the Hinge of Europe 1081–1797.* Chicago: University of Chicago Press, 1986.

Melamed, Yitzhak Y., and Martin Lin. "Principle of Sufficient Reason." In *The Stanford Encyclopedia of Philosophy,* ed. Edward N. Zalta (Spring 2017). https://plato.stanford.edu/archives/spr2017/entries/sufficient-reason/. Accessed 21 August 2017.

Montholon, Général, ed. *Mémoires pour servir à l'Histoire de France sous Napoléon.* 8 vols. Paris: F. Didot, Père et Fils; Bossange, Frères, 1823–1825.

Moran, Daniel, and Arthur Waldron. *The People in Arms: Military Myth and National Mobilization since the French Revolution.* Cambridge: Cambridge University Press, 2003.

Murray, Nicholas. *The Rocky Road to the Great War: The Evolution of Trench Warfare to 1914.* Washington, DC: Potomac Books, 2013.

Nafziger, George. *Imperial Bayonets: Tactics of the Napoleonic Battery, Battalion and Brigade as Found in Contemporary Regulations.* London: Greenhill Press, 1996.

Napoléon I. *Correspondance de Napoléon Ier.* 32 vols. Paris: Henri Plon and J. Dumaine, 1858.

Nicolas, Nicholas Harris, ed. *The Letters and Dispatches of Vice Admiral Lord Nelson.* 7 vols. New York: Cambridge University Press, 2011.

Page, Anthony. *Britain and the Seventy Years War, 1744–1815: Enlightenment, Revolution and Empire.* London: Palgrave Macmillan, 2015.

Palmgren, Anders. "Visions of Strategy: Following Clausewitz's Train of Thought." Doctoral diss., National Defence University, Helsinki, 2014.

Paret, Peter. *Clausewitz and the State.* New York: Oxford University Press, 1976.

———, ed. *Makers of Modern Strategy: From Machiavelli to the Nuclear Age.* Princeton, NJ: Princeton University Press, 1986.

Pommereul, François René Jean. *Campaign of General Buonaparte in Italy, in 1796–7,* trans. T. E. Ritchie. Edinburgh: G. Houston, 1799.

"Projekt zur Erschließung historisch wertvoller Altkartenbestände." http://ikar.sbb.spk-berlin.de/werkzeugkasten/sonderregeln/4_3.htm. Accessed 2 February 2017.

Rodger, N. A. M. *The Command of the Ocean: A Naval History of Britain from 1669–1815.* New York: W. W. Norton, 2005.

Saxe, Maurice Count de. *Reveries, or, Memoirs Concerning the Art of War.* Edinburgh: Sands, Donaldson, Murray, and Cochran, 1759.

Schneid, Frederick C. "The Campaign against Piedmont-Sardinia, April 1796." In *Napoleon and the Operational Art of War Essays in Honor of Donald D. Horward,* ed. Michael V. Leggiere, 88–117. Leiden, Netherlands: Brill, 2016.

———, ed. *European Armies of the French Revolution: 1789–1802.* Norman: University of Oklahoma Press, 2015.

Six, Georges. *Dictionnaire Biographique des Généraux & Amiraux de la Révolution et de L'Empire (1792–1814).* 2 vols. Paris: Libraire Historique et Nobiliaire, 1934.

Smith, Digby. *The Greenhill Napoleonic Wars Data Book.* London: Greenhill Books, 1998.

Strachan, Hew. *Clausewitz's* On War: *A Biography.* New York: Atlantic Monthly Press, 2007.

Strachan, Hew, and Andreas Herberg-Rothe, eds. *Clausewitz in the Twenty-First Century.* Oxford: Oxford University Press, 2007.

Swinton, Ernest. *The Defence of Duffer's Drift.* Washington, DC: US Infantry Association, 1916.

US Army. *Unified Land Operations.* Army Doctrine Publication No. 3.0. Washington, DC: Headquarters, Department of the Army, 2011.

Vego, Milan. "Clausewitz's Schwerpunkt: Mistranslated from German, Misunderstood in English." *Military Review* 87, 1 (January–February 2007): 101–109.

Work, Deputy Secretary of Defense Robert. Memorandum for Secretaries of the Military Departments. "Wargaming and Innovation." 9 February 2015.

Wurzbach, Dr. Constant von. *Biographisches Lexikon des Kaiserthums Oesterreich.* 60 vols. Vienna: Universitäts Buchruderei von L. E. Zamarski, 1856–1891.

Wylie, J. C. *Military Strategy: A General Theory of Power Control.* Annapolis, MD: Naval Institute Press, 2014.

Zimmerman, F. G. *Military Vocabulary German-English and English German.* London: Hugh Rees, 1915.

ONLINE RESOURCES

http://gallica.bnf.fr
http://mapire.eu/
http://www.napoleon-series.org/
https://www.bsb-muenchen.de/
www.kluze.net/trdnjava-predel
www.literature.at
www.roccadanfo.eu

Index

Numbers in italics refer to pages with maps.

Lightning Source UK Ltd.
Milton Keynes UK
UKHW022200241120
374031UK00006B/298